HISTORY

OF

THE REFORMATION IN EUROPE

IN THE TIME OF CALVIN.

CALVIN.

HISTORY

OF THE

REFORMATION IN EUROPE

IN THE TIME OF CALVIN.

BY

J. H. MERLE D'AUBIGNE, D.D.,

AUTHOR OF THE 'HISTORY OF THE REFORMATION OF THE SIXTEENTH CENTURY,' ETC.

Les choses de petite durée ont coutume de devenir fanées, quand elles ont passé leur temps.

'Au règne de Christ, il n'y a que le nouvel homme qui soit florissant, qui ait de la vigueur, et dont il faille faire cas.'

CALVIN.

VOL. I.

GENEVA AND FRANCE.

NEW YORK:

ROBERT CARTER & BROTHERS,

No. 530 BROADWAY.

1864.

ELECTROTYPED BY
SMITH & McDOUGAL
82 & 84 Beekman-st.

PRINTED BY
E. O. JENKINS,
20 North William-st.

AMERICAN INTRODUCTION

TO THE

HISTORY OF THE REFORMATION IN THE TIME OF CALVIN.

THIS history, though a separate work, may be considered as a second series of the History of the Reformation in the Sixteenth Century. Two elements are found combined in this narrative, more intimately than in the events detailed in the preceding work. These two elements are political liberty and evangelical liberty.

The author, when writing this work, often thought of the United States of America, in whose existence this two-fold element seemed more particularly embodied. When going over the struggles which were encountered for liberty at Geneva, when tracing the principles which, though so true, were at that period so little understood in Europe, but which were even then loudly proclaimed in this small State; when recounting the instances of unalterable attachment to right, to national institutions and to law, of which the Genevese gave so many proofs, and the heroic devotion with which the citizens made every sacrifice, even that of life itself, for the independence of their country; the author felt that some pious, but unenlightened men, might perhaps say that such subjects ought not to be treated at length in these volumes. But he comforted himself with the thought, that Christian men in different countries, friends of independence and of truth, would understand the intimate union that exists between liberty and the Gospel.

The author asks himself whether this work will be received with any interest in America, or whether the anxieties that now pre-occupy the minds of the citizens, are not too absorbing to leave room for sympathy with the story of the olden times. He, however, hopes that the history of the struggles of a heroic republic in past ages, may prove some relief to the anxieties of the present.

If any thing in the publication of his former work was calculated to rejoice the heart of the author, it is the cordial manner in which its appearance was hailed by the Anglo-Saxon race in general, and especially in the United States. Letters received from the solitary shores of some great inland lake or from some distant region of the great continent of America, have given him the most precious reward that an author can have—the assurance that, by the blessing of God, his writings have not only excited some passing interest in the breasts of his readers, but that they have been the means by which some souls have received the light which lighteneth unto the perfect day.

There is a circumstance connected with the present publication which has also given satisfaction to the author; it is made with his consent and concurrence, and in consequence of an arrangement with the editor. A foreign author can not find in the United States the same advantages that he meets with in England, in France, and in other parts of the Continent, where all literary property is protected by law. It is, nevertheless, only justice to recognize (even where the law does not), that literary works are the property of their authors, acquired by an intellectual labor more toilsome than that of the husbandman. "By the sweat of thy face thou shalt eat bread," is applicable to a writer as well as to the sons of toil. It is a satisfaction for an author to know that his writings will be transmitted to a distant nation by virtue of an honorable commercial arrangement. This the author has found in his dealings with Messrs. Carter & Brothers; and he puts it to the honor of the American nation, that these editions published by the Messrs. Carter, from which alone he derives some advantage, will be purchased by the citizens of the United States, and that they will not countenance the pirated editions that other booksellers may issue, without his consent.

MERLE D'AUBIGNÉ.

PREFACE.

At the conclusion of the preface to the first volume of the *History of the Reformation*, the author wrote, 'This work will consist of four volumes, or at the most five, which will appear successively.' These five volumes have appeared. In them are described the heroic times of Luther, and the effects produced in Germany and other countries by the characteristic doctrine of that reformer—justification by faith. They present a picture of that great epoch which contained in the germ the revival of christianity in the last three centuries. The author has thus completed the task he had assigned himself; but there still remained another.

The times of Luther were followed by those of Calvin. He, like his great predecessor, undertook to search the Scriptures, and in them he found the same truth and the same life; but a different character distinguishes his work.

The renovation of the individual, of the Church, and of the human race, is his theme. If the Holy Ghost kindles the lamp of truth in man, it is (according to Calvin) 'to the end that the entire man should be transformed.'—'In the kingdom of Christ,' he says, 'it is only the new man that flourishes and has any vigor, and whom we ought to take into account.'

This renovation is, at the same time, an enfranchisement; and we might assign, as a motto to the reformation accomplished by Calvin, as well as to apostolical christianity itself, these words of Jesus Christ: *The truth shall make you free.**

When the gods of the nations fell, when the Father which is in heaven manifested Himself to the world in the Gospel, adopting as His children those who received into their hearts the glad tidings of reconciliation with God, all these men became brethren, and this fraternity created liberty. From that time a mighty transformation went on gradually, in individuals, in families, and in society itself. Slavery disappeared, without wars or revolutions.

Unhappily, the sun which had for some time gladdened the eyes of the people, became obscured; the liberty of the children of God was lost; new human ordinances appeared to bind men's consciences and chill their hearts. The reformation of the sixteenth century restored to the human race what the middle ages had stolen from them; it delivered them from the traditions, laws, and despotism of the papacy; it put an end to the minority and tutelage in which Rome claimed to keep mankind for ever; and by calling upon man to establish his faith not on the word of a priest, but on the infallible Word of God, and by announcing to every one free access to the

* John viii. 32.

Father through the new and saving way—Christ Jesus, it proclaimed and brought about the hour of christian manhood.

An explanation is, however, necessary. There are philosophers in our days who regard Christ as simply the apostle of political liberty. These men should learn that, if they desire liberty outwardly, they must first possess it inwardly. To hope to enjoy the first without the second is to run after a chimera.

The greatest and most dangerous of despotisms is that beneath which the depraved inclination of human nature, the deadly influence of the world, namely, sin, miserably subjects the human conscience. There are, no doubt, many countries, especially among those which the sun of christianity has not yet illumined, that are without civil liberty, and that groan under the arbitrary rule of powerful masters. But, in order to become free outwardly, men must first succeed in being free inwardly. In the human heart there is a vast country to be delivered from slavery—abysses which man cannot cross alone, heights he cannot climb unaided, fortresses he cannot take, armies he cannot put to flight. In order to conquer in this moral battle, man must unite with One stronger than himself—with the Son of God.

If there is any one, in the present state of society, who is fatigued with the struggle and grieved at finding himself always overcome by evil, and who desires to breathe the light pure air of the upper regions of liberty—let him come to the Gospel; let him seek for union with the Saviour, and in his Holy Spirit he will find a power by which he will be able to gain the greatest of victories.

We are aware that there are men, and good men too, who are frightened at the word 'liberty;' but these estimable persons are quite wrong. Christ is a deliverer. *The Son*, He said, *shall make you free.* Would they wish to change Him into a tyrant?

There are also, as we well know, some intelligent men, but enemies of the Gospel, who, seeing a long and lamentable procession of despotic acts pass before them in the history of the Church, place them unceremoniously to the account of christianity. Let them undeceive themselves: the oppression that revolts them may be pagan, jewish, papal, or worldly . . . but it is not christian. Whenever christianity reappears in the world, with its spirit, faith, and primitive life, it brings men deliverance and peace.

The liberty which the Truth brings is not for individuals only: it affects the whole of society. Calvin's work of renovation, in particular, which was doubtless first of all an internal work, was afterwards destined to exercise a great influence over nations. Luther transformed princes into heroes of the faith, and we have described with admiration their triumphs at Augsburg and elsewhere. The reformation of Calvin was addressed particularly to the people, among whom it raised up martyrs until the time came when it was to send forth the spiritual conquerors of the world. For three centuries it has been producing, in the social condition of the nations that have received it, transformations unknown to former times. And still at this very day, and now perhaps more than ever, it imparts to the men who accept it a spirit of power which makes them chosen instruments, fitted to propagate truth, morality, and civilisation to the ends of the earth.

The idea of the present work is not a new one: it dates more than forty years back. A writer, from whom the author differs on important points, but whose name is dear to all who know the simple beauty of his character, and have read with care his works on the History of the Church and the History of Dogmas, which have placed him in the foremost rank among the ecclesiastical historians of our day—the learned Neander—speaking with the author at Berlin in 1818, pressed him to undertake a *History of the Reformation of Calvin.* The author answered that he desired first to describe that of Luther; but that he intended to sketch successively two pictures so similar and yet so different.

The *History of the Reformation in Europe in the time of Calvin* naturally begins with Geneva.

The Reformation of Geneva opens with the fall of a bishop-prince. This is its characteristic; and if we passed over in silence the heroic struggles which led to his fall, we should expose ourselves to just reproaches on the part of enlightened men.

It is possible that this event, which we are called

upon to describe (the end of an ecclesiastical state), may give rise to comparisons with the present times; but we have not gone out of our way for them. The great question, which occupies Europe at this moment, also occupied Geneva at the beginning of the sixteenth century. But that portion of our history was written before these late exciting years, during which the important and complex question of the maintenance or the fall of the temporal power of the popes has come before, and is continually coming before, sovereigns and their people. The historian, while relating the facts of the sixteenth century, had no other prepossessions than those which the story itself called up.

These prepossessions were quite natural. Descended from the huguenots of France, whom persecution drove from their country in the sixteenth and seventeenth centuries, the author had become attached to that hospitable city which received his forefathers, and in which they found a new home. The huguenots of Geneva captivated his attention. The decision, the sacrifices, the perseverance, and the heroism, with which the Genevans defended their threatened liberty, moved him profoundly. The independence of a city, acquired by so much courage and by so many privations, perils, and sufferings, is, without doubt, a sacred thing in the eyes of all; and no one should attempt to rob her of it. It may be that this history contains lessons for the people, of which he did not always think as he was writing it. May he be permitted to point out one?

The political emancipation of Geneva differs from many modern revolutions in the fact that we find admirably combined therein the two elements which make the movements of nations salutary; that is to say, order and liberty. Nations have been seen in our days rising in the name of liberty, and entirely forgetting right. It was not so in Geneva. For some time the Genevans persevered in defending the established order of things; and it was only when they had seen, during a long course of years, their prince-bishops leaguing themselves with the enemies of the state, conniving at usurpations, and indulging in acts contrary to the charters of their ancestors, that they accepted the divorce, and substituted a new state of things for the old one, or rather returned to an antecedent state. We find them always quoting the ancient *libertates*, *franchesiæ*, *immunitates*, *usus*, *consuetudines civitatis Gebennensis*, first digested into a code in 1387, while their origin is stated in the document itself to be of much greater antiquity. The author (as will be seen) is a friend of liberty; but justice, morality, and order are, in his opinion, quite as necessary to the prosperity of nations. On that point he agrees with that distinguished writer on modern civilization, M. Guizot, though he may differ from him on others.

In writing this history we have had recourse to the original documents, and in particular to some important manuscripts; the manuscript registers of the Council of Geneva, the manuscript histories of

Syndic Roset and Syndic Gautier, the manuscript of the *Mamelus* (Mamelukes), and many letters and remarkable papers preserved in the Archives of Geneva. We have also studied in the library of Berne some manuscripts of which historians have hitherto made little or no use; a few of these have been indicated in the notes, others will be mentioned hereafter. Besides these original sources, we have profited by writings and documents of great interest belonging to the sixteenth century, and recently published by learned Genevese archæologists, particularly by MM. Galiffe, Grenus, Revillod, E. Mallet, Chaponière, and Fick. We have also made great use of the memoirs of the Society of History and Archæology of Geneva.

With regard to France, the author has consulted various documents of the sixteenth century, little or altogether unknown, especially in what concerns the relations of the French government with the German protestants. He has profited also by several manuscripts, and by their means has been able to learn a few facts connected with the early part of Calvin's life, which have not hitherto been published. These facts are partly derived from the Latin letters of the reformer, which have not yet been printed either in French or Latin, and which are contained in the excellent collection which Dr. Jules Bonnet intends giving to the world, if such a work should receive from the Christian public the encouragement which the labor, disinterestedness, and zeal of its learned editor deserve.

The author having habitual recourse to the French documents of the sixteenth century, has often introduced their most characteristic passages into his text. The work of the historian is neither a work of the imagination, like that of the poet, nor a mere conversation about times gone by, as some writers of our day appear to imagine. History is a faithful description of past events; and when the historian can relate them by making use of the language of those who took part in them, he is more certain of describing them just as they were.

But the reproduction of contemporary documents is not the only business of the historian. He must do more than exhume from the sepulchre in which they are sleeping the relics of men and things of times past, that he may exhibit them in the light of day. We value highly such a work and those who perform it, for it is a necessary one; and yet we do not think it sufficient. Dry bones do not faithfully represent the men of other days. They did not live as skeletons, but as beings full of life and activity. The historian is not simply a resurrectionist: he needs—strange but necessary ambition—a power that can restore the dead to life.

Certain modern historians have successfully accomplished this task. The author, unable to follow them, and compelled to present his readers with a simple and unassuming chronicle, feels bound to express his admiration for those who have thus been able to revive the buried past. He firmly believes that, if a history should have truth, it should also have life. The events of past times did not resemble, in the days when they occurred, those grand museums of Rome, Naples, Paris, and London, in whose galleries we behold long rows of marble statues, mummies, and tombs. There were then living beings who thought, felt, spoke, acted, and struggled. The picture, whatever history may be able to do, will always have less of life than the reality.

When an historian comes across a speech of one of the actors in the great drama of human affairs, he ought to lay hold of it, as if it were a pearl, and weave it into his tapestry, in order to relieve the duller colors and give more solidity and brilliancy. Whether the speech be met with in the letters or writings of the actor himself, or in those of the chroniclers, is a matter of no importance: he should take it wherever he finds it. The history which exhibits men thinking, feeling, and acting as they did in their lifetime, is of far higher value than those purely intellectual compositions in which the actors are deprived of speech and even of life.

The author, having given his opinion in favor of this better and higher historical method, is compelled to express a regret:

> Le *précepte* est aisé, mais l'art est difficile.

And as he looks at his work, he has to repeat with

sorrow the confession of the poet of antiquity: *Deteriora sequor!*

This work is not a biography of Calvin, as some may imagine. The name of that great reformer appears, indeed, on the title-page, and we shall feel a pleasure, whenever the opportunity occurs, in endeavoring to restore the true colors to that figure so strangely misunderstood in our days. We known that, in so doing, we shall shock certain deeply-rooted prejudices, and shall offend those who accept without examination, in this respect, the fables of Romish writers. Tacitus indeed assures us that malignity has a false show of liberty: *Malignitati falsa species libertatis inest;* that history is listened to with more favor when she slanders and disparages: *Obtrectatio et livor pronis auribus accipiuntur.* But what historian could entertain the culpable ambition of pleasing at the expense of truth? Moreover, we believe that, if our age still labors under great errors with respect to many men and things, it is more competent than those which went before, to hear the truth, to examine, appreciate, and accept it.

We repeat, however, that it is not a history of Calvin, but of the reformation in Europe in the time of that reformer, which we desire to narrate. Other volumes are already far advanced, and we hope to publish two more in the ensuing year. But may we be permitted, in conclusion, to transcribe here a passage of Holy Scripture that has often occurred to our mind in executing a new work? It is this:

*Ye know not what shall be on the morrow. For what is your life? It is even a vapor, that appeareth for a little time, and then vanisheth away. For that ye ought to say, If the Lord will, we shall live and do this or that.**

* James iv. 14, 15.

EAUX VIVES, GENEVA.

CONTENTS

OF

THE FIRST VOLUME.

BOOK I.

GENEVA AND THE FIRST HUGUENOTS.

CHAPTER I.

THE REFORMATION AND MODERN LIBERTY.

ANCIENT TIMES.

CHAPTER II.

FIRST USURPATIONS AND FIRST STRUGGLES.

MIDDLE AGES.

CHAPTER V.

BERTHELIER AND THE YOUTH OF GENEVA AROUSED BY THE BISHOP'S VIOLENCE.

(1515–1517.)

CHAPTER VI.

THE OPPOSING PARTIES PREPARE FOR BATTLE.

(1516–1517.)

CHAPTER VII.

ASSEMBLY, AGITATION, AND JOKE OF THE PATRIOTS.

(1516–1517.)

CHAPTER VIII.

PÉCOLAT TORTURED AND BERTHELIER ACCUSED.

(1517.)

CHAPTER IX.

BERTHELIER CALLS THE SWISS TO THE AID OF GENEVA; HUGUENOTS AND MAMELUKES; THE BISHOP'S VIOLENCE.

(1517–1518.)

CHAPTER X.

FRESH TORTURES; PÉCOLAT'S DESPAIR AND STRIKING DELIVERANCE.

(December, 1517, to March, 1518.)

CHAPTER XI.

BERTHELIER TRIED AT GENEVA. BLANCHET AND NAVIS SEIZED AT TURIN. BONIVARD SCANDALISED AT ROME.

(February to September, 1518.)

CHAPTER XII.

BLANCHET AND NAVIS PUT TO DEATH. THEIR LIMBS SUSPENDED TO THE WALNUT-TREE NEAR THE BRIDGE OF ARVE.

(October, 1518.)

CHAPTER XIII.

THE HUGUENOTS PROPOSE AN ALLIANCE WITH THE SWISS, AND THE MAMELUKES AMUSE THEMSELVES AT TURIN.

(October to December, 1518.)

CHAPTER XVII.

THE DUKE AT THE HEAD OF HIS ARMY SURROUNDS GENEVA.

(MARCH AND APRIL, 1519.)

CHAPTER XVIII.

THE ARMY OF SAVOY IN GENEVA.

(APRIL AND MAY, 1519.)

CHAPTER XIX.

ARREST OF BONIVARD AND BERTHELIER.

(APRIL TO SEPTEMBER, 1519.)

CHAPTER XX.

PHILIBERT BERTHELIER THE MARTYR OF LIBERTY. TERROR AND OPPRESSION IN GENEVA.

(August and September, 1519.)

CHAPTER XXI.

STRUGGLES OF LIBERTY. LUTHER. DEATH OF THE BISHOP. HIS SUCCESSOR.

(1520–1523.)

CHAPTER XXII.

CHARLES DESIRES TO SEDUCE THE GENEVANS. THE MYSTERIES OF THE CANONS AND OF THE HUGUENOTS.

(August, 1523.)

CHAPTER XXIII.

AIMÉ LÉVRIER, A MARTYR TO LIBERTY AND RIGHT AT THE CASTLE OF BONNE.

(MARCH, 1524.)

CHAPTER XXIV.

INDIGNATION AGAINST THE MAMELUKES; THE DUKE APPROACHES WITH AN ARMY; FLIGHT OF THE PATRIOTS.

(1524–1525.)

CHAPTER XXVII.

GENEVA AND THE SWISS ALLIED—THE BISHOP, THE DUCALS, AND THE CANONS ESCAPE—JOY OF THE PEOPLE.

(FEBRUARY TO AUGUST, 1526.)

BOOK II.

FRANCE. FAVORABLE TIMES.

CHAPTER I.

A MAN OF THE PEOPLE AND A QUEEN.

(1525–1526.)

CHAPTER II.

MARGARET SAVES THE EVANGELICALS AND THE KING.

(1525–1526.)

CHAPTER III.

WILL THE REFORMATION CROSS THE RHINE?

(1525–1526.)

CHAPTER IV.

DEATH OF THE MARTYRS—RETURN OF THE KING.

(1526.)

CHAPTER V.

DELIVERANCE OF THE CAPTIVES AND RETURN OF THE EXILES.

(1526.)

CHAPTER VI.

WHO WILL BE THE REFORMER OF FRANCE?

(1526.)

CHAPTER VII.

CALVIN'S EARLY STRUGGLES AND EARLY STUDIES.

(1523–1527.)

CHAPTER XI.

FETES AT FONTAINEBLEAU AND THE VIRGIN OF THE RUE DES ROSIERS.

(1528.)

CHAPTER XII.

PRISONERS AND MARTYRS AT PARIS AND IN THE PROVINCES.

(1528.)

HISTORY

OF THE

REFORMATION IN EUROPE

IN THE TIME OF CALVIN.

BOOK I.

GENEVA AND THE FIRST HUGUENOTS.

CHAPTER I.

THE REFORMATION AND MODERN LIBERTY.

FACTS alone do not constitute the whole of history, any more than the members of the body form the complete man. There is a soul in history as well as in the body, and it is this which generates, vivifies, and links the facts together, so that they all combine to the same end.

The instant we begin to treat of Geneva, which, through the ministry of Calvin, was to become the most powerful centre of Reform in the sixteenth century, one question starts up before us.

What was the soul of the Reformation of Geneva? Truly, salvation by faith in Christ, who died to save—truly, the renewal of the heart by the word and the Spirit of God. But side by side with these supreme elements, that are found in all the Reformations, we meet with secondary elements that have existed in one country and not in another. What we discover at Geneva may possibly deserve to fix the attention of men in our own days: the characteristic element of the Genevese Reform is liberty.

Three great movements were carried out in this city during the first half of the sixteenth century. The first was the conquest of independence; the second, the conquest of faith; the third, the renovation and organisation of the Church. Berthelier, Farel, and Calvin are the three heroes of these three epics.

Each of these different movements was necessary. The bishop of Geneva was a temporal prince like the bishop of Rome; it was difficult to deprive the bishop of his pastoral staff unless he were first deprived of his sword. The necessity of liberty for the Gospel and of the Gospel for liberty is now acknowledged by all thoughtful men; but it was proclaimed by the history of Geneva three centuries ago.

But it may be said, a history of the Reformation has no concern with the secular, political, and social element. I have been reproached with not putting this sufficiently forward in the history of the Reformation of Germany, where it had relatively but little importance. I may perhaps be reproached with dwelling on it too much in the Reformation of Geneva, where it holds a prominent place. It is a hard matter to please all tastes: the safest course is to be guided by the truth of principles, and not by the exigencies of individuals. Is it my fault if an epoch possesses its characteristic features? if it is impossible to keep back the secular, without wronging the spiritual, element? To cut history in two is to distort it. In the Reform of Geneva, and especially in the constitution of its church, the element of liberty predominates more than in the Reforms of other countries. We can not know the reason of this unless we study the movement which gave birth to that Reform. The history of the political emancipation of Geneva is interesting of itself; liberty, it has been said,* has never been common in the world; it has not flourished in all countries or in all climates, and the periods when a people struggles *justly* for liberty are the privileged epochs of history. One such epoch occurred at the commencement of modern times; but strange to say, it is almost in Geneva alone that the struggles for liberty make the earlier decades of the sixteenth century a privileged time.

* M. de Remusat.

It is in this small republic that we find men remarkable for their devotion to liberty, for their attachment to law, for the boldness of their thoughts, the firmness of their character, and the strength of their energy. In the sixteenth century, after a repose of some hundreds of years, humanity having recovered its powers, like a field that had long lain fallow, displayed almost everywhere the marvels of the most luxuriant vegetation. Geneva is indeed the smallest theatre of this extraordinary fermentation; but it was not the least in heroism and grandeur, and on that ground alone it deserves attention.

There are, however, other reasons to induce us to this study. The struggle for liberty in Geneva was one of the agents of its religious transformation; that we may know one, we must study the other. Again, Calvin is the great man of this epoch; it is needful, therefore, to study the country where he appeared. A knowledge of the history of Geneva before Calvin can alone enable us to understand the life of this great reformer. But there remains a third and more important reason. I am about to narrate the history of the Reformation of the sixteenth century in the time of Calvin. Now, what chiefly distinguishes the Reformation of Calvin from that of Luther is, that wherever it was established, it brought with it not only truth but liberty, and all the great developments which these two fertile principles carry with them. Political liberty, as we shall see, settled upon those hills at the southern extremity of the Leman lake where stands the city of Calvin, and has never deserted them since. And more than this: earthly liberty, the faithful companion of divine truth, appeared at the same time with her in the Low Countries, in England, in Scotland, and subsequently in North America and other places besides, everywhere creating powerful nations. The Reformation of Calvin is that of modern times; it is the religion destined for the whole world. Being profoundly spiritual, it subserves also in an admirable manner all the temporal interests of man. It has the *promise of the life that now is, and of that which is to come.*

The free institutions of Protestant countries are not due

solely to the Reformation of Calvin: they spring from various sources, and are not of foreign importation. The elements of liberty were in the blood of these nations, and remarkable men exerted a civilizing influence over them. Magna Charta is older than the Genevese Reform; but we believe (though we may be mistaken) that this Reformation has had some small share in the introduction of those constitutional principles, without which nations can never attain their majority. Whence did this influence proceed?

The people of Geneva and their great doctor have each left their stamp on the Reformation which issued from their walls: Calvin's was truth, the people's, liberty. This last consideration compels us to narrate the struggles of which Geneva was the theatre, and which, though almost unknown up to the present hour, have aided, like a slender brook, to swell the great stream of modern civilization. But there was a second and more potent cause. Supreme among the great principles that Calvin has diffused is the sovereignty of God. He has enjoined us to *render unto Cæsar the things that are Cæsar's;* but he has added, "God must always retain the sovereign empire, and all that may belong to man remains subordinate. Obedience towards princes accords with God's service; but if princes usurp any portion of the authority of God, we must obey them only so far as may be done without offending God."* If my conscience is thoroughly subject to God, I am free as regards men; but if I cling to any thing besides heaven, men may easily enslave me. True liberty exists only in the higher regions. The bird that skims the earth may lose it at any moment; but we can not ravish it from the eagle who soars among the clouds.

The great movements in the way of law and liberty effected by the people in the sixteenth and seventeenth centuries, have certain relations with the Reformation of Calvin, which it is impossible to ignore

As soon as Guy de Brès and many others returned from Geneva to the Low Countries, the great contest between the

* Calvin, *Harmonie évangélique*, Matt. xx. 21.

rights of the people and the revolutionary and bloody despotism of Philip II. began; heroic struggles took place, and the creation of the United Provinces was their glorious termination.

John Knox returned to his native Scotland from Geneva, where he had spent several years; then popery, arbitrary power, and the immorality of a French court made way in that noble country for that enthusiasm for the gospel, liberty, and holiness, which has never since failed to kindle the ardent souls of its energetic people.

Numberless friends and disciples of Calvin carried with them every year into France the principles of civil and political liberty;* and a fierce struggle began with popery and the despotism, of the Valois first, and afterwards of the Bourbons. And though these princes sought to destroy the liberties for which the Huguenots shed their blood, their imperishable traces still remain among that illustrious nation.

The Englishmen who, during the bloody persecution of Mary, had sought an asylum at Geneva, imbibed there a love for the gospel and for liberty. When they returned to England, a fountain gushed out beneath their footsteps. The waters confined by Elizabeth to a narrow channel, rose under her successors and swiftly became an impetuous roaring flood, whose insolent waves swept away the throne itself in their violent course. But restored to their bed by the wise hand of William of Orange, the dashing torrent sank into a smiling stream, bearing prosperity and life afar.

Lastly, Calvin was the founder of the greatest of republics. The 'pilgrims' who left their country in the reign of James I., and, landing on the barren shores of New England, founded populous and mighty colonies, are his sons, his direct and legitimate sons; and that American nation which we have seen growing so rapidly boasts as its father the humble reformer on the shores of the Leman.

There are indeed, writers of eminence who charge this man of God with despotism; because he was the enemy of

* Among other political writings of Calvin's disciples see *La Gaule franke*, *Le Réveille-matin des Français et de leurs voisins*, &c.

libertinage, he has been called the enemy of liberty. Nobody was more opposed than Calvin to that moral and social anarchy which threatened the sixteenth century, and which ruins every epoch unable to keep it under control. This bold struggle of Calvin's is one of the greatest services he has done to liberty, which has no enemies more dangerous than immorality and disorder.

Should the question be asked, How ought infidelity to be arrested? we must confess that Calvin was not before his age, which was unanimous, in every communion, for the application of the severest punishments. If a man is in error as regards the knowledge of God, it is to God alone that he must render an account. When men—and they are sometimes the best of men—make themselves the avengers of God, the conscience is startled, and religion hides her face. It was not so three centuries back, and the most eminent minds always pay in one manner or another their tribute to human weakness. And yet, on a well-known occasion, when a wretched man, whose doctrines threatened society, stood before the civil tribunals of Geneva, there was but one voice in all Europe raised in favor of the prisoner; but one voice that prayed for some mitigation of Servetus's punishment, and that voice was Calvin's.*

However inveterate the prejudices against him may be, the indisputable evidence of history places Calvin among the fathers of modern liberty. It is possible that we may find impartial men gradually lending their ear to the honest and solemn testimony of past ages; and the more the world recognises the importance and universality of the Reformation which came forth from Geneva, the more shall we be

* 'Pœnæ vero atrocitatem remitti cupio.' (*Calvin to Farel*, Aug. 26, 1553.) Calvin appears afterwards to have prevailed on his colleagues to join him: 'Genus mortis conati sumus mutare, sed frustra.' 'We endeavored to change the manner of his death, but in vain; why did we not succeed? I shall defer telling you until I see you.' (*Same to same*, Oct. 26, 1553.) Farel replied to Calvin, 'By desiring to soften the severity of his punishment you acted as a friend towards a man who is your greatest enemy.'

excused for directing attention for a few moments to the heroic age of this obscure city.

The sixteenth century is the greatest in Christian times; it is the epoch where (so to speak) every thing ends and every thing begins; nothing is paltry, not even dissipation; nothing small, not even a little city lying unobserved at the foot of the Alps.

In that renovating age, so full of antagonist forces and energetic struggles, the religious movements did not proceed from a single centre; they emanated from opposite poles, and are mentioned in the well-known line—

> Je ne décide pas entre Genève et Rome.*

The Catholic focus was in Italy—in the metropolis of the ancient world; the evangelical focus in Germany was transferred from Wittemberg to the middle of European nations—to the smallest of cities—to that whose history I have to relate.

When history treats of certain epochs, as for instance the reign of Charles V., there may be a certain disadvantage in the vastness of the stage on which the action passes; we may complain that the principal actor, however colossal, is necessarily dwarfed. This inconvenience will not be found in the narrative I have undertaken. If the empire of Charles V. was the largest theatre in modern history, Geneva was the smallest. In the one case we have a vast empire, in the other a microscopical republic. But the smallness of the theatre serves to bring out more prominently the greatness of the actions: only superficial minds turn with contempt from a sublime drama because the stage is narrow and the representation devoid of pomp. To study great things in small is one of the most useful exercises. What I have in view—and this is my apology—is not to describe a petty city of the Alps, for that would not be worth the labor; but to study in that city a history which is in the main a reflection of the history of Europe,—of its sufferings, its struggles, its aspirations, its political liberties, and its re-

* La Henriade.

ligious transformations. I will confess that my attachment to the land of my birth may have led me to examine our annals rather too closely, and narrate them at too great length. This attachment to my country which has cheered me in my task, may possibly expose me to reproach ; but I hope it will rather be my justification. 'This book,' said Tacitus, at the beginning of one of his immortal works, 'was dictated by affection: that must be its praise, or at least its excuse.'* Shall we be forbidden to shelter ourselves humbly behind the lofty stature of the prince of history?

Modern liberties proceed from three different sources, from the union of three characters, three laws, three conquests—the Roman, the German, and the Christian. The combination of these three influences, which has made modern Europe, is found in a rather striking manner in the valley of the Leman. The three torrents from north, south, and east, whose union forms the great stream of civilisation, deposited in that valley which the Creator hollowed out between the Alps and the Jura that precious sediment whose component parts can easily be distinguished after so many ages.

First we come upon the Roman element in Geneva. This city was for a long while part of the empire ; 'it was the remotest town of the Allobroges,' says Cæsar.† About a league from Geneva there once stood an antique marble in honor of Fabius Maximus Allobrogicus, who, 122 years before Christ, had triumphed over the people of this district ;‡ and the great Julius himself, who constructed immense works round the city, bequeathed his name to a number of Roman colonists, or clients at least. More remarkable traces—their municipal institutions—are found in most of the cities which the Romans occupied ; we may be permitted to believe that Geneva was not without them.

In the fifth century the second element of modern liberties appeared with the Germans. The Burgundians—those Teu-

* 'Hic enim liber professione pietatis, aut laudatus erit, aut excusatus.'—Tacitus, *Agricola*, iii.

† 'Extremum oppidum Allobrogum.'—*De Bello Gallico*, i. 6.

‡ Spon, *Hist. de Genève*, livre i.

tons of the Oder, the Vistula, and the Warta—being already converted to Christianity, poured their bands into the vast basin of the Rhone, and a spirit of independence, issuing from the distant forests of the north, breathed on the shores of the Leman lake. The Burgundian tribe, however, combined with the vigor of the other Germans a milder and more civilizing temperament. King Gondebald built a palace at Geneva; an inscription placed fifteen feet above the gate of the castle, and which remains to this day, bears the words, *Gundebadus rex clementissimus*, &c.* From this castle departed the king's niece, the famous Clotilda, who, by marrying Clovis, converted to Christianity the founder of the French monarchy. If the Franks then received the Christian faith from Geneva, many of their descendants in the days of Calvin received the Reformation from the same place.

Clotilda's uncle repaired the breaches in the city walls, and having assembled his ablest counsellors, drew up those Burgundian laws which defended small and great alike, and protected the life and honor of man against injury.†

The first kingdom founded by the Burgundians did not, however, last long. In 534 it fell into the hands of the Merovingian kings, and the history of Geneva was absorbed in that of France until 888, the epoch when the second kingdom of Burgundy rose out of the ruins of the majestic but ephemeral empire of Charlemagne.

But long before the invasion of the Burgundians in the fifth century, a portion of Europe, and Geneva in particular, had submitted to another conquest. In the second century Christianity had its representatives in almost every part of the Roman world. In the time of the Emperor Marcus Aurelius and of Bishop Irenæus (177) some persecuted

* *Inscription de Gondebaud à Genève*, by Ed. Mallet, in the *Mémoires d'Archéologie*, t. iv. p. 305. Professor A. de la Rive, having built a house in 1840 on the site of the old castle, the gate or arcade was pulled down, and the stone with the inscription placed in the Museum of the Academy.

† 'Ordinum Consilium Genevæ habitum est in quo novæ leges ab illo rege (Gondebald) latæ. . . .'—Fragment quoted by Godefroy.

Christians of Lyons and Vienne, in Dauphiny, wishing to escape from the flames and the wild beasts to which Rome was flinging the children of God, and desirous of trying whether their pious activity could not bear fruit in some other soil, had ascended the formidable waters of the Rhone, and, coming to the foot of the Alps—refuge and refugees are of old date in this country—brought the gospel thither, as other refugees, coming also from Gaul, and also fleeing their persecutors, were fourteen centuries later to bring the Reformation. It seems they were only disciples, humble presbyters and evangelists, who in the second and third century first proclaimed the divine word on the shores of the Leman; we may therefore suppose that the Church was instituted in its simplest form. At least it was not until two centuries later, in 381, that Geneva had a bishop, Diogenes,* and even this first bishop is disputed.† Be that as it may, the gospel which the refugees brought into the valley lying between the Alps and the Jura, proclaimed, as it does everywhere, the equality of all men before God, and thus laid the foundations of its future liberties.

Thus were commingled in this region the generating elements of modern institutions. Cæsar, Gondebald, and an unknown missionary represent, so to speak, the three strata that form the Genevese soil.

Let us here sketch rapidly a few salient points of the ancient history of Geneva. The foundations upon which a building stands are certainly not the most interesting part, but they are perhaps the most necessary.

* List of the Bishops of Geneva, according to Bonivard. Gabarel, *Hist. de l'Eglise de Genève*, Pièces justificatives, p. 4.

† M. Baulacre (*Œuvres*, i. p. 37) is of opinion that this Diogenes was a *Genoese* bishop.

CHAPTER II.

FIRST USURPATIONS AND FIRST STRUGGLES.

GENEVA was at first nothing but a rural township (*vicus*), with a municipal council and an edile. Under Honorius in the fourth century it had become a city, having probably received this title after Caracalla had extended the rights of citizenship to all the Gauls. From the earliest times, either before or after Charlemagne, Geneva possessed rights and liberties which guaranteed the citizens against the despotism of its feudal lord. But did it possess political institutions? was the community organized? Information is wanting on these points. In the beginning of the sixteenth century the Genevese claimed to have been free so long that *the memory of man runneth not to the contrary*.* But this 'memory of man' might not embrace many centuries.

The pope having invited Charlemagne to march his Franks into Italy, for the *love of God*, and to fight against his enemies, that prince proceeded thither in 773 with a numerous army, part of which crossed Mount St. Bernard, thus pointing the way to another Charlemagne who was to appear a thousand years later, and whose empire, more brilliant but still more ephemeral than the first, was also in its dissolution to restore liberty to Geneva, which had been a second time absorbed into France.† Charlemagne, while

* 'Tanto tempore, quod de contrario memoria hominis non extitit.'—*Libertates Gebennenses*, *Mém. d'Archéologie*, ii. p. 312.

† 'Cum toto Francorum exercitu ...... Gebennam venit ...... et copiarum partem per montem Jovis ire jussit.'—Eginhardi *Annales*. These words of the ancient annals may be applied to Napoleon I. as well as to Charlemagne. The First Consul Bonaparte passed through Geneva on his way to Marengo, May, 1800.

passing through with his army, halted at Geneva and held *a council*.* This word has led to the belief that the city possessed *liberties* and *privileges*, and that he confirmed them ;† but the council was probably composed of the councillors around the prince, and was not a city council. Be that as it may, the origin of the liberties of Geneva seems to be hidden in the night of time.

Three powers in their turn threatened these liberties.

First came the counts of Geneva. They were originally, as it would seem, merely officers of the Emperor ;‡ but gradually became almost independent princes.

As early as 1091, we meet with an Aymon, count of Genevois.§ The rule of these counts of Genevois soon extended over a wide and magnificent territory. They resided not only at their hereditary manor-seat in Geneva, which stood on the site of Gondebald's palace, but also in various castles scattered in distant parts of their domain—at Annecy, Rumilly, La Roche, Lausanne, Moudon, Romont, Rue, Les Clées, and other places.‖ In those days, the counts lived both a solitary and turbulent life, such as characterized the feudal period. At one time they were shut up in their castles, which were for the most part surrounded by a few small houses, and begirt with fosses and drawbridges, and on whose walls could be seen afar the arms of the warders glittering in the rising sun. At other times, they would sally forth, attended by a numerous escort of officers, with their seneschal, marshal, cup-bearers, falconers, pages, and esquires, either in pursuit of the chase on the heights of the Jura

* 'Genevamque civitatem veniens synodum tenuit.' (See the *Monumenta Historiæ Germanicæ* of Pertz, tom. i. ann. 773 ; the Chronicle of *Regino*, pp. 557, 558 ; Eginhardi *Annales*, p. 150.)

† Spon states this positively, i. p. 59.

‡ 'In Burgundia in pago Genevensi, ubi pater ejus *comes* fuit. Beneficium non grande.'—Eginhardi *Epistolæ*, pp. 26, 27.

§ Comes Genevensium. Guichenon, *Bibl. Geb.* cent. ii.—See also (circa 1140) Peter the Venerable, *de Miraculis*, lib. ii.

‖ Spon's *Histoire de Genève*, i. p. 71. Galiffe, jun. *Introduction à l'Armorial genevois*, p. 9. Hiseli, *Les Comtes de Genève et de Vaud*, pp. 4, 18.

and the Alps; or it might be with the pious motive of visiting some place of pilgrimage; or not unfrequently indeed to wage harassing crusades against their neighbors or their vassals. But during all these feudal agitations another power was growing in Geneva—a power humble indeed at first—but whose mouth was to *speak great things.**

At the period of the Burgundian conquest Geneva possessed a bishop, and the invasion of the Germans soon gave this prelate considerable power. Gifted with intelligence far superior to that of the men by whom they were surrounded, respected by the barbarians as the high-priests of Rome, knowing how to acquire vast possessions by slow degrees, and thus becoming the most important personages in the cities where they resided, the bishops labored to protect the city from abroad and to govern it at home. Finally, they confiscated without much ceremony the independence of the people, and united the quality of prince with that of bishop.

In 1124 Aymon, Count of Genevois, by an agreement made with Humbert of Grammont, Bishop of Geneva, gave up the city to the latter,† reserving only the old palace and part of the criminal jurisprudence, but continuing to hold the secondary towns and the rural district.

The institution of bishop-princes, half religious and half political, equally in disaccord with the Gospel of past ages and the liberty of the future, may have been exceptionally beneficent; but generally speaking it was a misfortune for the people of the middle ages, and particularly for Geneva. If at that time the Church had possessed humble but earnest ministers to hold up the light of the Gospel to the world, why should not the same spiritual power, which in the first century had vanquished Roman polytheism, have been able in later times to dispel the darkness of feudalism? But, what could be expected of prelates who turned their croziers into swords, their flocks into serfs, their pastoral dwellings

* Daniel, vii. 8.

† 'Totas Gebennas episcopo in pace dimisit.' (The document will be found in the *Pièces Justificatives* of Spon, No. 1.)

into fortified castles? *Corruptio optimi pessima.* The prince-bishop, that amphibious offspring of the barbaric invasion, cannot be maintained in Christendom. The petty people of Geneva—and this is one of its titles to renown—was the first who expelled him in modern times; and the manner in which it did this is one of the pages of history we desire to transcribe. It needed truly a powerful energy—the arm of God—to undertake and carry through this first act which wrested from episcopal hands the temporal sceptre they had usurped. Since then the example of Geneva has often been followed; the feudal thrones of the bishops have fallen on the banks of the Rhine, in Belgium, Bavaria, Austria, and elsewhere; but the first throne that fell was that of Geneva, as the last will be that of Rome.

If the bishop, owing to the support of the emperors, succeeded in ousting the count from the city of Geneva, leaving him only the jurisdiction over his rural vassals, he succeeded also, in the natural course of things, in suppressing the popular franchises. These rights, however, still subsisted, the prince-bishop being elected by the people—a fact recorded by Saint Bernard at the election of Ardutius.* The prince even made oath of fidelity to the people. Occasionally the citizens opposed the prelate's encroachments, and refused to be dragged before the court of Rome.†

Christianity was intended to be a power of liberty; Rome, by corrupting it, made it a power of despotism; Calvin, by regenerating it, set it up again and restored its first work.

But what threatened most the independence and liberty of Geneva, was not the bishops and counts, but a power alien to it, that had begun by robbing the counts of their towns and villages. The house of Savoy, devoured by an insatiable ambition, strove to enlarge its dominions with a skill and perseverance that were crowned with the most rapid success. When the princes of Savoy had taken the place of the counts of Genevois and the dukes of Zœhringen in the Pays de

* 'Tanto cleri populique consensu.'—Bernardi *Epist.* xxvii.

† 'Si vos in curia Romana in causam traheret.'—*Conventiones an.* 1286.

Vaud, Geneva, which they looked upon as an *enclave*, became the constant object of their desires. They hovered for centuries over the ancient city, like those Alpine vultures which, spreading their wings aloft among the clouds, explore the country beneath with their glance, swoop down upon the prey, and return day after day until they have devoured each fragment. Savoy had her eyes fixed upon Geneva,—first, through ambition, because the possession of this important city would round off and strengthen her territory; and second, through calculation, because she discovered in this little state certain principles of right and liberty that alarmed her. What would become of the absolute power of princes, obtained at the cost of so many usurpations, if liberal theories should make their way into European law? A nest built among the craggy rocks of the Alps may perhaps contain a brood of inoffensive eaglets; but as soon as their wings grow, they will soar into the air, and with their piercing eyes discover the prey and seize it from afar. The safer course, then, is for some strong hand to kill them in their nest while young.

The relations between Savoy and Geneva—one representing absolutism, the other liberty—have been and are still frequently overlooked. They are of importance, however, to the history of Geneva, and even of the Reformation. For this reason we are desirous of sketching them.

The terrible struggle of which we have just spoken began in the first half of the thirteenth century. The house of Savoy finding two powers at Geneva and in Genevois, the bishop and the count, resolved to take advantage of their dissensions to creep both into the province and into the city, and to take their place. It declared first in favor of the bishop against the count, the more powerful of the two, in order to despoil him. Peter of Savoy, Canon of Lausanne, became in 1229, at the age of twenty-six, Provost of the Canons of Geneva; and having thus an opportunity of knowing the city, of appreciating the importance of its situation, and discovering the beauties that lay around it, he took a liking to it. Being a younger son of a Count of Savoy, he could easily have become a bishop; but under his amice, the canon concealed the arm of a soldier and the genius of a politician. On the death of his father in 1232, he threw off his cassock, turned soldier, married Agnes whom the Count of Faucigny made his heiress at the expense of her elder sister, and then took to freebooting.* Somewhat later, being the uncle of Elinor of Provence, Queen of England, he was created Earl of Richmond by his nephew Henry III., and studied the art of government in London. But the banks of the Thames could not make him forget those of the Leman. The castle of Geneva remained, as we have seen above, the private property of his enemy the Count of Geneva, and this he made up his mind to seize. 'A wise man,' says an old chronicler, 'of lofty stature and athletic strength, proud, daring, terrible as a lion, resembling the most famous paladins, so brave that he was called the valiant (*preux*) Charlemagne'—possessing the organising genius that founds states and the warlike disposition that conquers them—Peter seized the castle of Geneva in 1250, and held it as a security for 35,000 silver marks which he pretended the count owed him. He was now somebody in the city. Being a man of restless activity, enterprising spirit, rare skill, and indefatigable perseverance, he used this foundation on which to raise the edifice of his greatness in the valley of the Leman.† The people of Geneva, beginning to grow weary of ecclesiastical authority, desired to enjoy freely those communal franchises which the clergy called 'the worst of institutions.'‡ When he became Count of Savoy, Peter, who had conceived the design of annexing Geneva to his hereditary states, promised to give the citizens all they wanted; and the latter, who already (two centuries and a half before the Reformation) desired to shake off the temporal yoke of their bishop, put themselves under his guardianship. But ere long they grew alarmed, they

* 'Faisait le *gart*,' in the language of the chroniclers. Wustemberger, *Peter der Zweyte*, i. p. 123.

† 'L'animo irrequieto ed intraprendente del Principe Pietro.—Datta, *Hist. dei Principi*, i. p. 5.

‡ 'Communio, novum ac pessimum nomen.'—*Script. Rev. Franc.* xii. p. 250.

feared the sword of the warrior more than the staff of the shepherd, and were content with their clerical government

De peur d'en rencontrer un pire.*

In 1267 the second Charlemagne was forced to declare by a public act that he refused to take Geneva under his protection.† Disgusted with this failure, weakened by age, and exhausted by his unceasing activity, Peter retired to his castle at Chillon, where every day he used to sail on that beautiful lake, luxuriously enjoying the charms of nature that lay around; while the harmonious voice of a minstrel, mingling with the rippling of the waters, celebrated before him the lofty deeds of the illustrious paladin. He died in 1268.‡

Twenty years later Amadeus V. boldly renewed the assault in which his uncle had failed. A man full of ambition and genius, and surnamed 'the Great,' he possessed all the qualities of success. The standard of the prince must float over the walls of that free city. Amadeus already possessed a mansion in Geneva, the old palace of the counts of Genevois, situated in the upper part of the city. He wished to have more, and the canons gave him the opportunity which he sought of beginning his conquest. During a vacancy of the episcopal see, these reverend fathers were divided, and those who were hostile to Amadeus, having been threatened by some of his party, took refuge in alarm in the Château de l'Ile. This castle Amadeus seized, being determined to show them that neither strong walls nor the two arms of the river which encircle the island could protect them against his wrath. This conquest gave him no authority in the city; but Savoy was able more than once to use it for its ambitious projects. It was here in 1518, shortly after the

* 'For fear of finding a worse.'

† 'Communitatem de Gebennis in gardam non recipiemus.'—Treaty between the count and the bishop; *Mém. d'Archéologie*, vii. pp. 196–258, and 318, 319.

‡ *Monumenta Hist. Patriæ*, iii. p. 74. Mr. Ed. Mallet thinks, but without authority, that Peter died at Pierre-Chatel in Bugey. See also *Pierre de Savoie d'après M. Cibrario*, by F. de Gingins.

appearance of Luther, that the most intrepid martyr of modern liberty was sacrificed by the bishop and the duke.

Amadeus could not rest satisfied with his two castles: in order to be master in Geneva, he did not disdain to become a servant. As it was unlawful for bishops, in their quality of churchmen, to shed blood, there was an officer commissioned in all the ecclesiastical principalities to inflict the punishment of death, *vice domini*, and hence this lieutenant was called *vidomne* or *vidame*. Amadeus claimed this vidamy as the reward of his services. In vain did the citizens, uneasy at the thought of so powerful a vidame, meet in the church of St. Magdalen (November, 1288); in vain did the bishop forbid Amadeus, 'in the name of God, of the glorious Virgin Mary, of St. Peter, St. Paul, and all the saints, to usurp the office of lieutenant,'* the vulture held the vidamy in his talons and would not let it go. The citizens jeered at this sovereign prince who turned himself into a civil officer. 'A pretty employment for a prince—it is a ministry (*ministère*) not a magistry (*magistère*)—service not dominion.' 'Well, well,' replied the Savoyard, 'I shall know how to turn the valet into a master.'†

The princes of Savoy, who had combined with the bishop against the Count of Geneva to oust the latter, having succeeded so well in their first campaign, undertook a second, and joined the citizens against the bishop in order to supplant him. Amadeus became a liberal. He knew well that you can not gain the hearts of a people better than by becoming the defender of their liberties. He said to the citizens in 1285, 'We will *maintain*, *guard*, and *defend* your city and goods, your *rights* and *franchises*, and all that belongs to you.‡ If Amadeus was willing to *defend* the liberties of Geneva, it is a proof that they existed: his language

* 'Quod ullus alius princeps, baro, vel comes habeat in eadem (civitate) aliquam jurisdictionem.'—*Mém. d'Archéologie*, viii. *Pièces Justificatives*, p. 241.

† Savyon, *Annales*, pp. 16–18.

‡ 'Villam vestram, nec non bona et jura vestra et franchisias vestras . . . . manutenebimus, gardabimus, et defendemus.'—Spon, *Preuves pour l'Histoire de Genève*, iii. p. 108.

is that of a conservative and not of an innovator. The year 1285 did not, as some have thought, witness the first origin of the franchises of Geneva, but their revival. There was however at that time an outgrowth of these liberties. The municipal institutions became more perfect. The citizens, taking advantage of Amadeus's support, elected *rectors* of the city, voted taxes, and conferred the freedom of the city upon foreigners. But the ambitious prince had calculated falsely. By aiding the citizens to form a corporation strong enough to defend their ancient liberties, he raised with imprudent hand a bulwark against which all the plans of his successors were doomed to fail.

In the fifteenth century the counts of Savoy, having become dukes and more eagerly desiring the conquest of Geneva, changed their tactics a third time. They thought, that as there was a pope at Rome, the master of the princes and principalities of the earth, a pontifical bull would be more potent than their armies and intrigues to bring Geneva under the power of Savoy.

It was Duke Amadeus VIII. who began this new campaign. Not satisfied with having enlarged his estates with the addition of Genevois, Bugey, Verceil, and Piedmont, which had been separated from it for more than a century, he petitioned Pope Martin V. to confer on him, for the great advantage of the Church, the secular authority in Geneva. But the syndics, councillors, and deputies of the city, became alarmed at the news of this fresh manœuvre, and knowing that 'Rome ought not to *lay its paw* upon kingdoms,' determined to resist the pope himself, if necessary, in the defence of their liberties, and placing their hands upon the Gospels they exclaimed: 'No alienation of the city or of its territory—this we swear.' Amadeus withdrew his petition; but Pope Martin V., while staying three months at Geneva, on his return in 1418 from the Council of Constance, began to sympathize with the ideas of the dukes. There was something in the pontiff which told him that liberty did not accord with the papal rule. He was alarmed at witnessing the liberties of the city. 'He feared those general councils that spoil every thing,' says a manuscript chronicle in the

Turin library: 'he felt uneasy about those turbulent folk, imbued with the ideas of the Swiss, who were always whispering into the ears of the Genevese the *license of popular government*.'* The liberties of the Swiss were dear to the citizens a century before the Reformation.

The pope resolved to remedy this, but not in the way the dukes of Savoy intended. These princes desired to secure the independence of Geneva in order to increase their power; while the popes preferred confiscating it to their own benefit. At the Council of Constance, from which Martin was then returning, it had been decreed that episcopal elections should take place according to the canonical forms, by the *chapter*, unless for some *reasonable and manifest* cause the pope should think fit to name a person more useful to the Church.† The pontiff thought that the necessity of resisting popular liberty was a *reasonable* motive; and accordingly as soon as he reached Turin, he translated the Bishop of Geneva to the archiepiscopal see of the Tarentaise, and heedless of the rights of the canons and citizens, nominated Jean de Rochetaillée, Patriarch *in partibus* of Constantinople, Bishop and Prince of Geneva. Four years later Martin repeated this usurpation. Henry V. of England, at that time master of Paris, taking a dislike to Jean de Courte-Cuisse, bishop of that capital, the pope, of his sovereign authority, placed Courte-Cuisse on the episcopal throne of Geneva, and Rochetaillée on that of Paris. Thus were elections wrested by popes from a Christian people and their representatives. This usurpation was to Geneva, as well as to many other parts of Christendom, an inexhaustible source of evils.

It followed, among other things, that with the connivance of Rome, the princes of Savoy might become princes of Geneva. But could they insure this connivance? From that moment the activity of the court of Turin was employed in making interest with the popes in order to obtain

* Turin Library, manuscript H. Gaberel, *Hist. de l'Eglise de Genève* i. p. 45.

† Harduin, *Concil.* viii. p. 887.

the grant of the bishopric of Geneva for one of the princes or creatures of Savoy. A singular circumstance favored this remarkable intrigue. Duke Amadeus VIII., who had been rejected by the citizens a few years before, succeeded in an unexpected manner. In 1434 having abdicated in favor of his eldest son, he assumed the hermit's frock at Ripaille on the Lake of Geneva; and the Council of Basle having nominated him pope, he took the name of Felix V. and made use of his pontifical authority to create himself bishop and prince of Geneva. A pope making himself a bishop . . . strange thing indeed! Here is the key to the enigma: the pope was a prince of Savoy: the see was the see of Geneva. Savoy desired to have Geneva at any price: one might almost say that Pope Felix thought it an advancement in dignity to become a Genevan bishop. It is true that Felix was pope according to the episcopal, not the papal, system; having been elected by a council, he was forced to resign in consequence of the desertion of the majority of European princes. Geneva and Ripaille consoled him for Rome.

As bishop and prince of Geneva, he respected the franchises of his new acquisition; but the poor city was fated somewhat later to serve as food to the offspring of this bird of prey. In 1451, Amadeus being dead, Peter of Savoy, a child eight or ten years old, grandson of the pope, hermit, and bishop, mounted the episcopal throne of Geneva; in 1460 came John Louis, another grandson, twelve years of age; and in 1482 Francis, a third grandson. To the Genevans the family of the pope seemed inexhaustible. These bishops and their governors were as leeches sucking Geneva even to the bones and marrow.

Their mother, Anne of Cyprus, had brought with her to Savoy a number of 'Cypriote leeches' as they were called, and after they had drained the blood of her husband's states, she launched them on the states of her children. One Cypriote prelate, Thomas de Sur, whom she had appointed governor to little Bishop Peter, particularly distinguished himself in the art of robbing citizens of their money and their liberty. It was Bishop John Louis, the least wicked of the three brothers, who inflicted the most terrible blow on Geneva. We shall tell how that happened; for this dramatic episode is a picture of manners, carrying us back to Geneva with its bishops and its princes, and showing us the family of that Charles III. who was in the sixteenth century the constant enemy of the liberties and Reformation of the city

Duke Louis of Savoy, son of the pope-duke Amadeus, was good-tempered, inoffensive, weak, timid, and sometimes choleric; his wife, Anne of Cyprus or Lusignan, was arrogant, ambitious, greedy, intriguing, and domineering; the fifth of their sons, by name Philip-Monsieur, was a passionate, debauched, and violent young man. Anne who had successively provided for three of her sons by placing them on the episcopal throne of Geneva, and who had never met with any opposition from the eldest Amadeus IX., a youth subject to epilepsy, had come into collision with Philip. The altercations between them were frequent and sharp, and she never missed an opportunity of injuring him in his father's affections; so that the duke, who always yielded to his wife's wishes, left the young prince without appanage. Philip Lackland (for such was the name he went by) angry at finding himself thus deprived of his rights, returned his mother hatred for hatred; and instead of that family affection, which even the poets of heathen antiquity have often celebrated, an implacable enmity existed between the mother and the son. This Philip was destined to fill an important place in history; he was one day to wear the crown, be the father of Charles III. (brother-in-law to Charles V.) and grandfather of Francis I. through his daughter Louisa of Savoy. But at this time nothing announced the high destiny which he would afterwards attain. Constantly surrounded by young profligates, he passed a merry life, wandering here and there with his troop of scapegraces, establishing himself in castles or in farms; and if the inhabitants objected, striking those who resisted, killing one and wounding another, so that he lived in continual quarrels. 'As my father left me no fortune,' he used to say, 'I take my property wherever I can find it.'—'All Savoy was in discord,' say the old annals, 'filled with murder, assault, and riot.'*

The companions of the young prince detested the *Cypriote* (as they called the duchess) quite as much as he did; and in their orgies over their brimming bowls used the most insulting language towards her. One day they insinuated that 'if she plundered her husband and her son it was to enrich her minions.' Philip swore that he would have justice. Duke Louis was then lying ill of the gout at Thonon, on the southern shore of the Lake of Geneva. Lackland went thither with his companions, and entering the chapel where mass was going on, killed his mother's steward, carried off his father's chancellor, put him in a boat and took him to Morges, 'where he was drowned in the lake.' Duke Louis was terrified; but whither could he flee? In his own states there was no place where he could feel himself safe; he could see no other refuge but Geneva, and there he resolved to go.

John Louis, another of his sons, was then bishop, and he was strong enough to resist Philip. Although destined from his infancy for the ecclesiastical estate, he had acquired neither learning nor manners, 'seeing that it is not the custom of princes to make their children scholars,' say the annals. But on the other hand he was a good swordsman; dressed not as a churchman but as a soldier, and passed his time in 'dicing, hawking, drinking, and wenching.' Haughty, blunt, hot-headed, he was often magnanimous, and always forgave those who had rightfully offended him. 'As appears,' says the old chronicle, 'from the story of the carpenter, who having surprised him in a room with his wife, cudgelled him so soundly, that he was left for dead. Nevertheless, the bishop would not take vengeance, and went so far as to give the carpenter the clothes he had on when he was cudgelled.'

John Louis listened favorably to his father's proposals. The duke, Anne of Cyprus, and all the Cypriote officers arrived at Geneva in July 1642, and were lodged at the Fran-

* Savyon, *Annales*, p. 23

ciscan convent and elsewhere; but none could venture outside Geneva without being exposed to the attacks of the terrible Lackland.*

The arrogant duchess became a prey to alarm: being both greedy and avaricious, she trembled lest Philip should succeed in laying hands upon her treasures; and that she might put them beyond his reach, she despatched them to Cyprus after this fashion. In the mountains near Geneva the people used to make very excellent cheeses; of these she bought a large number, wishing (she said) that her friends in Cyprus should taste them. She scraped out the inside, carefully stored her gold in the hollow, and therewith loaded some mules, which started for the East. Philip having received information of this, stopped the caravan near Friburg, unloaded the mules, and took away the gold. Now that he held in his hands these striking proofs of the duchess's perfidy, he resolved to slake the hatred he felt towards her: he would go to Geneva, denounce his mother to his father, obtain from the exasperated prince the Cypriote's dismissal, and receive at last the appanage of which this woman had so long deprived him.

Philip, aware that the bishop would not let him enter the city, resolved to get into it by stratagem. He repaired secretly to Nyon, and thence despatched to Geneva the more skilful of his confidants. They told the syndics and the young men of their acquaintance, that their master desired to speak to his father the duke about a matter of great importance. One of the syndics (the one, no doubt, who had charge of the watch) seeing nothing but what was very natural in this, gave instructions to the patrol; and on the 9th of October, Philip presenting himself at the city gate—at midnight, according to Savyon, who is contradicted by other authorities—entered and proceeded straight to Rive, his Highness's lodging, with a heart full of bitterness and hatred against his cruel mother. We shall quote literally the ancient annals which describe the interview in a picturesque manner:—'Philip knocks at the door; thereupon

* Savyon, *Annales*, pp. 22, 32. Galiffe, i. p. 222, *Chronique Latine de Savoie.*

one of the chamberlains coming up, asks who is there? He answers: "I am Philip of Savoy, I want to speak to my father for his profit." Whereupon the servant having made a report, the duke said to him: "Open to him in the name of all the devils, happen what may," and immediately the man opened the door. As soon as he was come in Philip bowed to his father, saying: "Good day, father!" His father said: "God give thee bad day and bad year! What devil brings thee here now?" To which Philip replied meekly: "It is not the devil, my lord, but God who brings me here to your profit, for I warn you that you are robbed and know it not. There is my lady mother leaves you nothing, so that, if you take not good heed, she will not only make your children after your death the poorest princes in Christendom, but yourself also during your life." '

At these words Philip opened a casket which contained the gold intended for Cyprus, and 'showed him the wherewithal,' say the annals. But the duke, fearing the storm his wife would raise, took her part. Monsieur then grew angry: "You may bear with it if you like,' he said to his father, 'I will not. I will have justice of these thieves.' With these words he drew his sword and looked under his father's bed, hoping to find some Cypriotes beneath it, perhaps the Cypriote woman herself. He found nothing there. He then searched all the lodging with his band, and found nobody, for the Cypriotes had fled and hidden themselves in various houses in the city. Monsieur did not dare venture further, 'for the people were against him,' say the annals, 'and for this cause he quitted his father's lodging and the town also without doing other harm.'*

The duchess gave way to a burst of passion, the duke felt very indignant, and Bishop John Louis was angry. The people flocked together, and as they prevented the Cypriotes from hanging the men who had opened the gate to Monsieur, the duke chose another revenge. He represented to the bishop that his son-in-law Louis XI., with whom he was negotiating about certain towns in Dauphiny, detested the

* Savyon, *Annales*, pp. 24, 25. According to other documents he made some stay in Geneva.

Genevans, and coveted their large fairs to which people resorted from all the country round. He begged him therefore to place in his hands the charters which gave Geneva this important privilege. The bishop threw open his archives to the duke; when the latter took the documents in question, and carrying them to Lyons, where Louis XI. happened to be, gave them to him. The king immediately transferred the fairs first to Bourges and then to Lyons, forbidding the merchants to pass through Geneva. This was a source of great distress to all the city. Was it not to her fairs, whose privileges were of such old standing, that Geneva owed her greatness? While Venice was the mart for the trade of the East, and Cologne for that of the West, Geneva was in a fair way to become the mart of the central trade. Now Lyons was to increase at her expense, and the city would witness no longer in her thoroughfares that busy, restless crowd of foreigners coming from Genoa, Florence, Bologna, Lucca, Brittany, Gascony, Spain, Flanders, the banks of the Rhine, and all Germany. Thus the catholic or episcopal power, which in the eleventh century had stripped Geneva of her territory, stripped her of her wealth in the fifteenth. It needed the influx of the persecuted Huguenots and the industrial activity of Protestantism to recover it from the blow that the Romish hierarchy had inflicted.*

This poor tormented city enjoyed however a momentary respite. In the last year of the fifteenth century, after the scandals of Bishop Francis of Savoy, and his clergy and monks, a priest, whom we may in some respects regard as a precursor of the Reformation, obtained the episcopal chair.

This was Anthony Champion, an austere man who pardoned nothing either in himself or others. 'I desire,' he said, 'to sweep the filth out of my diocese.' He took some trouble to do so. On the 7th of May, 1493, five hundred priests convened by him met in synod in the church of St. Pierre. 'Men devoted to God's service,' said the bishop with energy, 'ought to be distinguished by purity of life;

* Savyon, *Annales*, p. 30. Spon, *Hist. de Genève*, i. p. 199. Pictet de Sergy, *Hist. de Genève*, ii. pp. 175–242. Weiss, *Hist. des Réfugiés*, pp. 217, 218.

now our priests are given to every vice, and lead more execrable lives than their flocks. Some dress in open frocks, others assume the soldier's head-piece, others wear red cloaks or corselets, frequent fairs, haunt taverns and houses of ill fame, behave like mountebanks or players, take false oaths, lend upon pawn, and unworthily vend indulgences to perjurers and homicides.' Thus spoke Champion, but he died eighteen months after the synod, and the priestly corruption increased.*

In proportion as Geneva grew weaker, Savoy grew stronger. The duke, by circumstances which must have appeared to him providential, had lately seen several provinces settled on different branches of his house, reunited successively to his own states, and had thus become one of the most powerful princes of Europe. La Bresse, Bugey, the Genevois, Gex, and Vaud, replaced under his sceptre, surrounded and blockaded Geneva on all sides. The poor little city was quite lost in the midst of these wide provinces, bristling with castles; and its territory was so small that, as they said, there were more Savoyards than Genevans who heard the bells of St. Pierre. The states of Savoy enfolded Geneva as in a net, and a bold stroke of the powerful duke would, it was thought, be sufficient to crush it.

The dukes were not only around Geneva, they were within it. By means of their intrigues with the bishops, who were their fathers, sons, brothers, cousins, or subjects, they had crept into the city, and increased their influence either by flattery and bribes, or by threats and terror. The vulture had plumed the weak bird, and imagined that to devour him would now be an easy task. The duke by means of some sleight-of-hand trick, in which the prelate would be his accomplice, might in the twinkling of an eye entirely change his position—rise from the hospitable chair which My Lords of Geneva so courteously offered him, and seat himself proudly on a throne. How was the feeble city, so hunted down, gagged and fettered by its two oppressors, able to resist and achieve its glorious liberties? We shall see.

* *Constitutiones synodales, eccl. Genev.* Register of canons, May 1493. Gaberel, *Hist. de l'Eglise de Genève*, i. p. 56.

New times were beginning in Europe, God was touching society with his powerful hand; I say 'society' and not the State. Society is above the State; it always preserves its right of priority, and in great epochs makes its initiative felt. It is not the State that acts upon society: the movements of the latter produce the transformations of the State, just as it is the atmosphere which directs the course of a ship, and not the ship which fixes the direction of the wind. But if society is above the State, God is above both. At the beginning of the sixteenth century God was breathing upon the human race, and this divine breath worked strange revivals in religious belief, political opinions, civilisation, letters, science, morals, and industry. A great reformation was on the eve of taking place.

There are also transformations in the order of nature; but their march is regulated by the creative power in an unchangeable manner. The succession of seasons is always the same. The monsoons, which periodically blow over the Indian seas, continue for six months in one direction, and for the other six months in a contrary direction. In mankind, on the contrary, the wind sometimes comes for centuries from the same quarter. At the period we are describing the wind changed after blowing for nearly a thousand years in the same direction; God impressed on it a new, vivifying, and renovating course. There are winds, we know, which, instead of urging the ship gently forward, tear the sails, break the masts, and cast the vessel on the rocks, where it goes to pieces. A school, whose seat is at Rome, pretends that such was the nature of the movement worked out in the sixteenth century. But whoever examines the question impartially, confesses that the wind of the Reformation has wafted humanity towards the happy countries of light and liberty, of faith and morality.

In the beginning of the sixteenth century there was a living force in Geneva. The ostentatious mitre of the bishop, the cruel sword of the duke appeared to command there; and yet a new birth was forming within its bosom. The renovating principle was but a puny, shapeless germ, concealed in the heroic souls of a few obscure citizens; but its future developments were not doubtful. There was no power in Christendom able to stem the outbreak of the human mind, awakening at the mighty voice of the eternal Ruler. What was to be feared was not that the progress of civilisation and liberty, guided by the Divine word, would fail to attain its end; but that on the contrary, by abandoning the supreme rule, the end would be overshot.

Let us enter upon the history of the preparations for Reform, and contemplate the vigorous struggles that are about to begin at the foot of the Alps between despotism and liberty, ultramontanism and the Gospel.

CHAPTER III.

A BISHOP SENT BY THE POPE TO ROB GENEVA OF ITS INDEPENDENCE.

(APRIL TO OCTOBER, 1513.)

On the 13th of April, 1513, there was great excitement in Geneva. Men were dragging cannon through the streets, and placing them on the walls. The gates were shut and sentries posted everywhere.* Charles de Seyssel, bishop and prince of Geneva, had just died on his return from a pilgrimage. He was a man of a mild and frank disposition, 'a right good person,' says the chronicler, 'and for a wonder a great champion of both ecclesiastical and secular liberty.' Duke Charles of Savoy, who was less attached to liberty than this good prelate, had recently had several sharp altercations with him. 'It was I who made you bishop,' haughtily said the angry duke, 'but I will unmake you, and you shall be the poorest priest in the diocese.'† The bishop's crime was having wished to protect the liber-

* Manuscript registers of the Council of Geneva, under 13th April, 1513.

† Savyon, *Annales de Genève*, p. 44.

ties of the city against Charles's usurpations. The prince kept his word, and, if we may believe the old annals, got rid of him by poison.*

When the news of this tragical and unexpected death reached Geneva, the citizens were alarmed: they argued that no doubt the secret intention of the duke was to place a member of his family on the episcopal throne, in order thus to obtain the seigniory of the city. The excited citizens gathered in groups in the streets, and impassioned orators, among whom was Philibert Berthelier, addressed the people. The house from which this great citizen sprang appears to have been of high position, as early as the twelfth century; but he was one of those noble natures who court glory by placing themselves at the service of the weak. No man seemed better fitted to save Geneva. Just, generous, proud, decided, he was above all firm, true, and attached to what was right. His glorious ambition was not revolutionary: he wished to uphold the right and not to combat it. The end he set before himself was not, properly speaking, the emancipation of his country, but the restoration of its franchises and liberties. He affected no great airs, used no big words, was fond of pleasure and the noisy talk of his companions; but there were always observable in him a seriousness of thought, great energy, a strong will, and above all a supreme contempt of life. Enamored of the ancient liberties of his city, he was always prepared to sacrifice himself for them.

'The duke,' said Berthelier and his friends in their animated meetings, 'received immediate news of the death of the bishop, as did the pope also. The messengers are galloping with the news, each wants to have his share of the skin of the dead beast.' The patriots argued that if the pope had long since laid hands on the Church, the Duke of Savoy now desired to lay his upon the State. Geneva would not be the first place that had witnessed such usurpations. Other cities of Burgundy, Grenoble, Gap, Valence, Die, and Lyons, had fallen one after the other beneath a foreign

* Savyon, *Annales de Genève*, p. 44.

power. 'We ourselves,' said the citizens in the energetic and somewhat homely language of the day, 'have had our wings cut so short already, that we can hardly spit from our walls without bespattering the duke. Having begun his conquest, he now wishes to complete it. He has put his *snout* into the city and is trying to get in all his body. Let us resist him. Is there a people whose franchises are older than ours? We have always been free, and there is no memory of man to the contrary.'* The citizens were resolved accordingly to close their gates against the influence of Savoy, and to elect a bishop themselves. They called to mind that when Ardutius, descending from his eyrie in the rocks of the Mole, was named bishop of Geneva, it was by the accord of clergy and people.† 'Come, you canons,' said they, 'choose us a bishop that will not let the duke put his nose into his soup.'‡ This rather vulgar expression meant simply this: 'Elect a bishop who will defend our liberties.' They had not far to seek.

There was among the canons of Geneva one Aimé de Gingins, abbot of Bonmont and dean of the chapter, a man of noble house, and well connected in the Swiss cantons. His father Jacques, seignior of Gingins, Divonne, and other places, had been councillor, chamberlain, and high steward to the Duke of Savoy, and even ambassador from him to Pope Paul II. Aimé, who had been appointed canon of St. Pierre's in Geneva when very young, was forty-eight years old at this time. He was 'the best boon-companion in the world, keeping open house and feasting joyously the friends of pleasure,' fond of hearing his companions laugh and sing, and of rather free manners, after the custom of the Church; but he excused himself with a smile, saying, without blush or shame: 'It is a *slippery* sin.' M. de Bonmont was the most respected of the priests in Geneva, for while his colleagues were devoted heart and soul to the house of Savoy, the dean stood by Geneva, and was no

* 'De libertatibus, franchisiis et immunitatibus sumus cum maxima diligentia informati.'—*Libertates Gebennenses, Mém. d'Archéol.* ii. p. 312.

† 'Credimus electionem tuam, etc.'—Bernardi *Epist.* xxvii.

‡ Bonivard, *Chroniq.* i. p. 22; ii. p. 230.

stranger to the aspirations which led so many generous minds to turn towards the ancient liberties. The people named him bishop by acclamation, and the chapter confirmed their choice ; and forthwith the citizens made every effort to uphold the election. They prayed the Swiss cantons to support it before the pope, and sent to Rome 'by post both letters and agents.'*

If this election by the chapter had been sustained, it is probable that M. de Gingins would have lived on good terms with the council and citizens, and that harmony would have been preserved. But the appointment of bishops, which had in olden times belonged to the clergy and the people, had passed almost everywhere to the prince and the pope. The election of a superior by the subordinates had given way to the nomination of an inferior by a superior. This was a misfortune : nothing secures a good election like the first of these two systems, for the interest and honor of the governed is always to have good governors. On the other hand, princes or popes generally choose strangers or favorites, who win neither the affection nor esteem of their flocks or of the inferior clergy. The last episcopal elections at Geneva, by separating the episcopacy from the people and the clergy, deprived the Church of the strength it so much needed, and facilitated the Reformation.

Duke Charles understood the importance of the crisis. This prince who filled for half a century the throne of Savoy and Piedmont, was all his life the implacable enemy of Geneva. Weak but irritable, impatient of all opposition yet undecided, proud, awkward, wilful, fond of pomp but without grandeur, stiff but wanting firmness, not daring to face the strong, but always ready to be avenged on the weak, he had but one passion—one mania rather : to possess Geneva. For that he needed a docile instrument to lend a hand to his ambitious designs—a bishop with whom he could do what he pleased. Accordingly he looked around him for some one to oppose to the people's candidate, and he soon hit upon the man. In every party of pleasure at

* Manuscript archives of the Gingins family. Froment, *Gestes de Genève*, p. 157. Savyon, *Annales*, pp. 44, 45.

court there was sure to be found a little man, weak, slender, ill-made, awkward, vile in body but still more so in mind, without regard for his honor, inclined rather to do evil than good, and suffering under a disease the consequence of his debauchery. This wretch was John, son of a wench of Angers (*communis generis*, says Bonivard) whose house was open to everybody, priests and laymen alike; sparely liberal with her money (for she had not the means) 'she was over-free with her venal affections.' Francis of Savoy, the third of the pope-duke's grandsons, who had occupied in turn the episcopal throne of Geneva, and who was also archbishop of Aux and bishop of Angers, used to 'junket with her like the rest.' This woman was about to become a mother, 'but she knew not,' says the chronicler, 'whom to select as the father; the bishop being the richest of all her lovers, she fathered the child upon him, and it was reared at the expense of the putative parent.' The Bishop of Angers not caring to have this child in his diocese, sent it to his old episcopal city, where there were people devoted to him.* The poor little sickly child was accordingly brought to Geneva, and there he lived meanly until being called to the court of Turin, he had a certain retinue assigned him, three horses, a servant, a chaplain, and the title of *bastard of Savoy*. He then began to hold up his head, and became the greediest, the most intriguing, the most irregular priest of his day. 'That's the man to be bishop of Geneva,' thought the duke: 'he is so much in my debt, he can refuse me nothing.' There was no bargain the bastard would not snap at, if he could gain either money or position: to give up Geneva to the duke was an easy matter to him. Charles sent for him. 'Cousin,' said he, 'I will raise you to a bishopric, if in return you will make over the temporality to me.' The bastard promised everything: it was an unex-

* It has been supposed that he was brought up at Angers, but I found in the Archives of Geneva a letter addressed to John, dated 2nd September, 1513, by J. A. Vérard, a jurisconsult of Nice, wherein the latter congratulates the new bishop '*inclitæ civitatis Gebennanum in qua cunabulis ab usque nutritus et educatus es.*' *Archives de Genève*, No. 870.

pected means of paying his debt to the duke, which the latter talked about pretty loudly. 'He has sold us not in the ear but in the blade,' said Bonivard, 'for he has made a present of us before we belonged to him.'*

The duke without loss of time despatched his cousin to Rome, under the pretext of bearing his congratulations to Leo X. who had just succeeded Julius II.† John the Bastard and his companions travelled so fast that they arrived before the Swiss. At the same time the court of Turin omitted nothing to secure the possession of a city so long coveted. First, they began to canvass all the cardinals they could get at. On the 24th February the Cardinal of St. Vital, and on the 1st March the Cardinal of Flisco promised their services to procure the bishopric of Geneva for John of Savoy.‡ On the 20th of April the Queen of Naples wrote to the duke, that she had recommended John to her nephew, the Cardinal of Aragon.§ This was not enough. An unforeseen circumstance favored the designs of Savoy.

The illustrious Leo X. who had just been raised to the papal throne, had formed the design of allying his family to one of the oldest houses in Europe. With this intent he cast his eyes on the Princess Philiberta of Savoy; a pure simple-hearted young girl, of an elevated mind, a friend to the poor, younger sister to the duke and Louisa of Savoy, aunt of Francis I. and Margaret of Valois. Leo X. determined to ask her hand for his brother Julian the Magnificent, lieutenant-general of the armies of the Church. Up to this time Julian had not lived a very edifying life; he was deeply enamored of a widow of Urbino, who had borne him a son.

To tempt the duke to this marriage, which was very flat-

* Bonivard, *Chronique*, i. p. 25; ii. pp. 227, 228. Ibid. *Police de Genève*, *Mém. d'Archéologie*, p. 380. Savyon, *Annales de Genève*, p. 45.

† 'Misso legato Johanne de Sabaudia, episcopo postea Gebennensi.' *Monumenta Historiæ Patriæ*, Script. i. p. 848, Turin. The instructions given by the duke to his cousin may be seen in the MSS. of the Archives of Geneva, No. 875.

‡ See the letters in the Archives of Geneva, Nos. 872 and 873.

§ Ibid, No. 876.

tering to the *parvenus* of Florence, the pope made 'many promises,' say the Italian documents.* He even sent an envoy to the court of Turin to tell Charles that he might 'expect from him all that the best of sons may expect from the tenderest of fathers.'†

The affair could only be decided at Rome, and Leo X. took much trouble about it. He received the bastard of Savoy with the greatest honor, and this disagreeable person had the chief place at banquet, theatre, and concert. Leo took pleasure in talking with him, and made him describe Philiberta's charms. As for making him bishop of Geneva, that did not cause the least difficulty. The pope cared nothing for Dean de Bonmont, the chapter, or the Genevans. 'Let the duke give us his sister, and we will give you Geneva,' said he to the graceless candidate. 'You will then make over the temporal power to the duke . . . The court of Rome will not oppose it; on the contrary, it will support you.' Everything was settled between the pope, the duke, and the bastard. 'John of Savoy,' says a manuscript, 'swore to hand over the temporal jurisdiction of the city to the duke, and the pope swore he would force the city to consent under pain of incurring the thunders of the Vatican.'‡

This business was hardly finished when the Swiss envoys arrived, empowered to procure the confirmation of Dean de Bonmont in his office of bishop. Simple and upright but far less skilful than the Romans and the Piedmontese, they appeared before the pope. Alas! these Alpine shepherds

* 'Leo X. Sabaudianum ducem ad affinitatem ineundam *multis pollicitis* invitavit.'—*Monumenta Historiæ Patriæ*, Script. i. p. 814. Turin, 1840.

† 'Omnia expectare quæ ab optimo filio de patre amantissimo sunt expectanda.'—*Letter of Bembo in the pope's name*, 3d April, 1513.

‡ I found this MS. in the library at Berne (*Histoire Helvétique*, v. 12). It is entitled, *Histoire de la Ville de Genève*, by J. Bonivard. The history is not by Bonivard: it was copied at Berne in 1705 from an old MS. in the possession of Ami Favre, first syndic. Although not known at Geneva, it contains many important circumstances that Spon and Gautier have omitted either from timidity or by order, says Haller. I shall call it the Berne MS. v. 12.

had no princess to offer to the Medici. 'Nescio vos,' said Leo X. 'Begone, I know you not.' He had his reasons for this rebuff; he had already nominated the bastard of Savoy bishop of Geneva.

It was impossible to do a greater injury to any church. For an authority, and especially an elective authority, to be legitimate, it ought to be in the hands of the best and most intelligent, and he who exercises it, while administering with zeal, should not infringe the liberties of those he governs. But these are ideas that never occurred to the worthless man, appointed by the pope chief pastor of Geneva. He immediately however found flatterers. They wrote to him (and the letters are in the Archives of Geneva) that his election had been made *by the flock* . . . 'not by mortal favor, but by God's aid alone.' It was however by the favor of the Queen of Naples, of Charles III., and by several other very mortal favors, that he had been nominated. He was exhorted to govern his church with integrity, justice, and diligence, as became his *singular gravity and virtue.** The bastard did not make much account of these exhortations; his reign was a miserable farce, a long scandal. Leo X. was not a lucky man. By the traffic in indulgences he provoked the Reformation of Wittemberg, and by the election of the bastard he paved the way for the Reformation of Geneva. These are two false steps for which Rome has paid dearly.

The news of this election filled the hearts of the Genevan patriots with sorrow and indignation. They assembled in the public places, murmuring and 'complaining to one another,' and the voices of Berthelier and Hugues were heard above all the rest. They declared they did not want the bastard, that they already had a bishop, honored by Geneva and all the league, and who had every right to the see because he was dean of the chapter. They insinuated that if Leo X. presumed to substitute this intrusive Savoyard for their legitimate bishop, it was because the house of Savoy wished to lay hands upon Geneva. They were especially

* 'Pro tua singulari gravitate atque virtute.'—*Archéol. de Genève*, No. 879.

exasperated at the well-known character of the Romish candidate. 'A fine election indeed his Holiness has honored us with!' said they. 'For our bishop he gives us a disreputable clerk; for our guide in the paths of virtue, a dissipated bastard; for the preserver of our ancient and venerable liberties, a scoundrel ready to sell them.' . . . Nor did they stop at murmurs; Berthelier and his friends remarked that as the storm came from the South, they ought to seek a shelter in the North; and though Savoy raised her foot against Geneva to crush it, Switzerland stretched out her hand to save it. 'Let us be masters at home,' they said, 'and shut the gates against the pope's candidate.'

All did not think alike: timid men, servile priests, and interested friends of Savoy trembled as they heard this bold language. They thought, that if they rejected the bishop sent from Rome, the pope would launch his thunders and the duke his soldiers against Geneva. The canons of the cathedral and the richest merchants held lands in the states of Charles, so that (says a manuscript) the prince could at pleasure 'starve them to death.' These influential men carried the majority with them, and it was resolved to accept the bishop nominated at Rome. When the leaders of the independent party found themselves beaten, they determined to carry out forthwith the plan they had formed. On the 4th of July, 1513, Philibert Berthelier, Besançon Hugues, Jean Taccon, Jean Baud, N. Tissot, and H. Pollier petitioned Friburg for the right of citizenship *in order to secure their lives and goods;* and it was granted. This energetic step might prove their ruin; the duke might find the means of teaching them a bloody lesson. That mattered not: a great step had been taken; the bark of Geneva was made fast to the ship that would tow them into the waters of liberty. As early as 1507 three patriots, Pierre Lévrier, Pierre Taccon, and D. Fonte, had allied themselves to Switzerland. Now they were nine, drawn up on the side of independence, a small number truly, and yet the victory was destined to remain with them. History has often shown that there is another majority besides the majority of numbers.*

* Michel Roset, *Histoire manuscrite de Genève,* liv. i. chap. lxix.

While this little band of patriots was on its way to embrace the altar of liberty in Switzerland, the ducal and clerical party was making ready to prostrate itself slavishly before the Savoyard prince. The more the patriots had opposed him, the more the episcopalians labored to give him a splendid reception. On the 31st of August, 1513, the new prince-bishop entered the city under a magnificent canopy; the streets and galleries were hung with garlands and tapestry, the trades walked magnificently costumed to the sound of fife and drum, and theatres were improvised for the representation of miracles, dramas, and farces. It was to no purpose that a few citizens in bad humor shrugged their shoulders and said: 'He is truly as foul in body as in mind.' The servile worshipped him, some even excusing themselves humbly for having appeared to oppose him. They represented that such opposition was not to his lordship's person, but simply because they desired to maintain their right of election. John of Savoy, who had said to himself, 'I will not spur the horse before I am firm in the saddle,' answered only by a smile of his livid lips: both people and bishop were acting a part. When he arrived in front of the cathedral, the new prelate met the canons, dressed in their robes of silk and damask, with hoods and crosses, each according to his rank. They had felt rather annoyed in seeing the man of their choice, the abbot of Bonmont, unceremoniously set aside by the pope; but the honor of having a prince of the ducal family for their bishop was some compensation. These reverend gentlemen, almost all of them partisans of Savoy, received the bastard with great honor, bowing humbly before him. The bishop then entered the church, and standing in front of the altar, with an open missal before him, as was usual, made solemn oath to the syndics, in presence of the people, to maintain the liberties and customs of Geneva. Certain good souls took him at his word and appeared quite reassured; but the more intelligent wore a look of incredulity, and placed but little trust

(Roset was syndic fourteen times during the sixteenth century.) Lévrier, *Chronologie des Comtes de Genevoise*, p. 102. Bonivard, *Police de Genève* (*Mém. d'Archéologie*), v. p. 380. Savyon, *Annales*, p. 46.

in his protestations. The bishop having been recognised and proclaimed sovereign, quitted the church and entered the episcopal palace to recruit himself after such unusual fatigue. There he took his seat in the midst of a little circle of courtiers, and raising his head, said to them: 'Well, gentlemen, we have next to *savoyardise* Geneva. The city has been quite long enough separated from Savoy only by a ditch, without crossing it. I am commissioned to make her take the leap.' These were almost the first words the bastard uttered after having sworn before God to maintain the independence of the city.*

The bishop, naturally crafty and surrounded by counsellors more crafty still, was eager to know who were the most influential men of the party opposed to him, being resolved to confer on them some striking mark of his favor. First he met with one name which was in every mouth—it was that of Philibert Berthelier. The bishop saw this citizen mingling with the people, simple, cheerful, and overflowing with cordiality, taking part in all the merry-makings of the young folks of Geneva, winning them by the animated charm of his manners, and by the important services he was always ready to do them. 'Good!' thought John of Savoy, 'here is a man I must have. If I gain him, I shall have nothing to fear for my power in Geneva.' He resolved to give him one of the most honorable charges at his disposal. Some persons endeavored to dissuade the bishop: they told him that under a trifling exterior Berthelier concealed a rebellious, energetic, and unyielding mind. 'Fear nothing,' answered John, 'he sings gaily and drinks with the young men of the town.' It was true that Berthelier amused himself with the *Enfans de Genève*,† but it was to kindle them at his fire. He possessed the two qualities necessary for great things: a popular spirit, and an heroic character; practical sense to act upon men, and an elevated mind to conceive great ideas.

The bishop, to whom all noble thoughts were unknown,

* Roset MS. liv. i. ch. lxix. Savyon, *Annales*, p. 46. Registers of the Council, MS. 25–30th August, 1513. Bonivard, *Chroniq.* ii. p. 235.

† *Enfans de Genève* is a term applied to the youths of the town capable of bearing arms.

appeared quite enchanted with the great citizen; being always ready to sell himself, he doubted not that the proud Genevan was to be bought. The Castle of Peney, situated two leagues from the city, and built in the thirteenth century by a bishop of Geneva, happened at that time to be without a commandant: 'You shall have the governorship of Peney,' said the prelate to Berthelier. The latter was astonished, for it was, as we have said, one of the most important posts in the State. 'I understand it all,' said he, 'Peney is the apple which the serpent gave to Eve.' 'Or rather,' added Bonivard, 'the apple which the goddess of Discord threw down at the marriage of Peleus.' Berthelier refused; but the bastard still persisted, making fine promises for the future of the city. At last he accepted the charge, but with the firm intention of resigning it as soon as his principles required it. The bishop could not even dream of a resignation: such an act would be sheer madness in his eyes; so believing that he had caught Berthelier, he thought that Geneva could not now escape him. This was not all; the bishop elect, M. de Gingins, whose place the bastard had taken, possessed great influence in the city. John gave him a large pension. Believing he had thus disposed of his two principal adversaries, he used to joke about it with his courtiers. 'It is a bone in their mouths,' said they, laughing and clapping their hands, 'which will prevent their barking.'*

The people had next to be won over. 'Two features characterise the Genevans,' said the partisans of Savoy to the bishop, 'the love of liberty and the love of pleasure.' Hence the counsellors of the Savoyard prince concluded, that it would be necessary to manœuvre so as to make one of these propensities destroy the other. The cue was accordingly given. Parties, balls, banquets, and entertainments were held at the palace and in all the houses of the Savoyard party. There was one obstacle however. The bastard was naturally melancholy and peevish, and his disease by no means tended to soften this morose disposition. But John

* Bonivard, *Chroniq.* ii. pp. 236, 259. Savyon, *Annales*, p. 46. Gautier and Roset MSS. Galiffe, *Notices Généologiques*, i. p. 8.

did violence to himself, and determined to keep open house. 'Nothing was seen at the palace but junketing, dicing, dancing, and feasting.' The prelate leaving his apartments, would appear at these joyous entertainments, with his wan and gloomy face, and strive to smile. Go where you would, you heard the sound of music and the tinkling of glasses. The youth of Geneva was enchanted; but the good citizens felt alarmed. 'The bishop, the churchmen, and the Savoyards,' they said, 'effeminate and *cowardise* our young men by toothsome meats, gambling, dancing, and other immoderate delights.' Nor did they rest satisfied with complaining; they took the young citizens aside, and represented to them that if the bishop and his party were lavish of their amusements, it was only to make them forget their love for the common weal. 'They are doing as Circe did with the companions of Ulysses,' said a man of wit, 'and their enchanted draughts have no other object than to change men into swine.' But the bastard, the canons, and the Savoyard nobles continued to put wine upon their tables and to invite the most charming damsels to their balls. The youths could not resist; they left the old men to their dotage; in their intoxication they indulged with all the impetuosity of their age in bewitching dances, captivating music, and degrading disorders. Some of the young lords, as they danced or drank, whispered in their ears: 'Fancy what it would be if the duke established his court with its magnificent fêtes at Geneva.' And these thoughtless youths forgot the liberties and the mission of their country.*

Among the young men whom the courtiers of Savoy were leading into vice, was the son of the bishop's procurator-fiscal. One of the ablest devices of the dukes who desired to annex Geneva to their states, had been to induce a certain number of their subjects to settle in the city. These Savoyards, being generally rich men and of good family, were joyfully welcomed and often invested with some important office, but they always remained devoted to the ducal interests. Of this number were F. Cartelier of La Bresse, M.

* Bonivard, *Chroniq.* ii. p. 235, &c.

Guillet, seignior of Montbard, and Pierre Navis of Rumilly in Genevois; all these played an important part in the crisis we are about to describe. Navis, admitted citizen in 1486, elected councillor in 1497, was a proud and able man, a good lawyer, thoroughly devoted to the duke, and who thought he was serving him faithfully by the unjust charges he brought against the patriots. Andrew, the youngest of his sons, was a waggish, frolicsome, noisy boy who, if sometimes showing a certain respect to his father, was often obstinate and disobedient. When he passed from boyhood to youth, his passions gained more warmth, his imagination more fire: family ties sufficed him no longer, and he felt within him a certain longing which urged him towards something unknown. The knowledge of God would have satisfied the wants of his ardent soul; but he could find it nowhere. It was at this period, he being twenty-three years old, that John of Savoy arrived in Geneva, and his courtiers began to lay their toils. The birth of Andrew Navis marked him out for their devices, and it was his fate to be one of their earliest victims. He rushed into every kind of enjoyment with all the impetuosity of youth, and pleasure held the chief place in his heart. Rapidly did he descend the steps of the moral scale: he soon wallowed in debauchery, and shrank not from the most shameful acts. Sometimes his conscience awoke and respect for his father gained the upper hand; but some artful seduction soon drew him back again into vice. He spent in disorderly living his own money and that of his family. 'When I want money,' he said, 'I write in my father's office; when I have it, I spend it with my friends or in roaming about.' He was soon reduced to shifts to find the means of keeping up his libertinism. One day his father sent him on horseback to Chambery, where he had some business to transact. Andrew fell to gambling on the road, lost his money, and sold his horse to have the chance of winning it back. He did worse even than this: on two several occasions, when he was short of money, he stole horses and sold them. He was not however the only profligate in Geneva: the bishop and his courtiers were training up others; the priests and monks whom John found at

Geneva, also gave cause for scandal. It was these immoralities that induced the citizens to make early and earnest complaints to the bishop.*

CHAPTER IV.

OPPOSITION TO THE DESIGNS OF THE DUKE, THE POPE, AND THE BISHOP.

(1513—1515.)

The opposition to the bishop was shown in various ways and came from different quarters. The magistrates, the young and new defenders of independence, and lastly (what was by no means expected) the cardinals themselves thwarted the plan formed to deprive Geneva of its independence. Opinion, 'the queen of the world,' as it has been called, overlooked worldliness in priests but not libertinism. Debauchery had entered into the manners of the papacy. The Church of the middle ages, an external and formal institution, dispensed with morality in its ministers and members. Dante and Michael Angelo place both priests and popes in hell, whether libertines or poisoners. The crimes of the priest (according to Rome) do not taint the divine character with which he is invested. A man may be a holy father—nay, God upon earth—and yet be a brigand. At the time when the Reformation began there were certain articles of faith imposed in the Romish church, certain hierarchies, ceremonies, and practices; but of morality there was none; on the contrary, all this framework naturally tended to encourage Christians to do without it. Religion (I reserve the exceptions) was not the man: it was a corpse arrayed in magnificent garments, and underneath all eaten with worms. The Reformation restored life to the Church. If salvation

* Galiffe, *Matériaux pour l'Histoire de Genève.* Interrogatory of Navis, pp. 168-181.

is not to be found in adherence to the pope and cardinals, but in an inward, living, personal communion with God, a renewal of the heart is obligatory. It was within the sphere of morality that the first reforming tendencies were shown at Geneva.

In the month of October, 1513, the complaints in the council were very loud: 'Who ought to set the people an example of morality, if not the priests?' said many noble citizens; 'but our canons and our priests are gluttons and drunkards, they keep women unlawfully, and have bastard children as all the world knows.'* Adjoining the Grey Friars' convent at Rive stood a house that was in very bad repute. One day a worthless fellow, named Morier, went and searched the convent for a woman who lived in this house, whom these reverend monks had carried off. The youth of the city followed him, found the poor wretch hidden in a cell, and carried her away with great uproar. The monks attracted by the noise appeared at their doors or in the corridors but did not venture to detain her. Morier's comrades escorted her back in triumph, launching their jokes upon the friars.† The Augustines of our Lady of Grace were no better than the Franciscans of Rive, and the monks of St. Victor did no honor to their chief. All round their convents were a number of low houses in which lived the men and women who profited by their debauchery.‡

The evil was still greater among the Dominicans of Plainpalais: the syndics and council were forced to banish two of them, Brother Marchepalu and Brother Nicolin, for indulging in abominable practices in this monastery.§ The monks even offered accommodation for the debaucheries of the town; they threw open for an entrance-fee the extensive gardens of their monastery, which lay between the Rhone

* Galiffe, *Matériaux pour l'Histoire de Genève*, ii. vii.

† Registers of Geneva (MS.), 2nd September, 1483; 13th June, 11th and 25th July, 28th November, 1486; 24th June, 1491.

‡ Registers of Geneva, *ad ann.* 1534.

§ 'De iis quæ gesta fuere occasione nefandi criminis Sodomye, de quo diffamantur et nonnulli alii.'—Registers of the Council, 22nd July, 1513.

and the Arve, and whose deep shades served to conceal improper meetings and midnight orgies.* Nobody in Geneva had so bad a reputation as these monks: they were renowned for their vices. In the way of avarice, impurity, and crime, there was nothing of which they were not thought capable. 'What an obstinate devil would fear to do,' said some one, 'a reprobate and disobedient monk will do without hesitation.'†

What could be expected of a clergy at whose head were popes like John XXIII., Alexander VI., or Innocent VIII., who having sixteen illegitimate children when he assumed the tiara, was loudly proclaimed 'the father of the Roman people?'‡ The separation between religion and morality was complete; every attempt at reform, made for centuries by pious ecclesiastics, had failed: there seemed to be nothing that could cure this inveterate, epidemic, and frightful disease:—nothing save God and his Word.

The magistrates of Geneva resolved however to attempt some reforms, and at least to protest against insupportable abominations. On Tuesday, 10th October, the syndics appeared in a body before the episcopal council, and made their complaints of the conduct of the priests.§ But what could be expected from the council of a prelate who bore in his own person, visibly to all, the shameful traces of his infamous debaucheries? They hushed up complaints that compromised the honor of the clergy, the ambition of the duke, and the mitre of the bishop. However the blow was struck, the moral effect remained. One thought sank from that hour deep into the hearts of upright men: they saw that something new was wanted to save religion, morality, and liberty. Some even said that as reforms from below were impossible, there needed a reform from heaven.

It was at this moment when the breeze was blowing to-

* Registers of 22nd May, 1522 et sqq.

† 'Quod agere veretur obstinatus diabolus, intrepide agit reprobus et contumax monachus.'

‡ 'Hunc merito poterit dicere Roma patrem.'

§ 'De putanis sacerdotum.' Public Registers of Geneva, MS. *ad ann.* 1513.

wards independence, and when the liberal party saw its defenders multiplying, that there came to Geneva a brilliant young man, sparkling with wit, and full of Livy, Cicero, and Virgil. The priests received him heartily on account of his connection with several prelates, and the liberals did the same on account of his good-humor; he soon became a favorite with everybody and the hero of the moment. He had so much imagination: he knew so well how to amuse his company! This young man was not a superficial thinker: in our opinion he is one of the best French writers of the beginning of the 16th century, but he is also one of the least known. Francis Bonivard—such was the name of this agreeable scholar—had, in the main, little faith and little morality; but he was to play in Geneva by his liberalism, his information, and his cutting satires, a part not very unlike that played by Erasmus in the great Reformation. As you left the city by the Porte St. Antoine, you came almost immediately to a round church, and by its side a monastery inhabited by some monks of Clugny,* whose morals, as we have seen, were not very exemplary. This was the priory of St. Victor, and within its walls were held many of the conversations and conferences that prepared the way for the Reformation. St. Victor was a small state with a small territory, and its prior was a sovereign prince. On the 7th of December, 1514, the prior, John Aimé Bonivard, was on his death-bed, and by his side sat his nephew Francis, then one-and-twenty. He was born at Seyssel;† his father had occupied a certain rank at the court of Duke Philibert of Savoy, and his mother was of the noble family of Menthon. Francis belonged to that population of nobles and churchmen whom the dukes of Savoy had transplanted to Geneva to corrupt the citizens. He was educated at Turin, where he had become the ringleader of the wild set at the university; and ever carrying with him his jovial humor, he seemed made to be an excellent bait to entice the youth of the city into the nets of Savoy. But it was far otherwise, he chose the path of liberty.

* Near the present Observatory.

† Now in the department of Ain.

For the moment he thought only of his uncle whose end seemed to have arrived. He did not turn from him his anxious look, for the old prior was seriously agitated on his dying bed. Formerly, in a moment of irritation, he had ordered four large culverins to be cast at the expense of the Church in order to besiege the seigniory of Viry, one of his neighbors, in his castle at the foot of Mount Saleve. Old Bonivard had committed many other sins, but he troubled himself little about them, compared with this. These large guns, purchased out of the ecclesiastical revenues, with a view to kill men and batter down the castle of an old friend, gave him a fearful pang.* In his anguish he turned towards his nephew. He had found an expedient, a meritorious work which seemed calculated to bring back peace to his agitated conscience. 'Francis,' he said to his nephew, 'listen to me; you know those pieces of cannon . . . they ought to be employed in God's service. I desire that immediately after my death they may be cast into bells for the church.' Francis gave his promise, and the prior expired satisfied, leaving to his nephew the principality, the convent, and the culverins.

A close sympathy soon united Berthelier and Bonivard. The former had more energy, the latter more grace; but they both belonged to the new generation; they became brothers in arms, and promised to wage a merciless war against superstition and arbitrary power. They gave each other mutual marks of their affection, Bonivard standing godfather for one of Berthelier's sons. Berthelier, having paid his friend a visit of condolence on the very day of his uncle's death, heard from his lips the story of the culverins. 'What!' said he, 'cast cannons to make into bells! We will give you as much metal as you require to make a peal that shall ring loud enough to stun you; but the culverins ought to remain culverins.' Bonivard represented that, according to his uncle's orders, the cannon were to be employed in the service of the Church. 'The Church will be doubly served,' retorted Berthelier; 'there will be bells at

* Bonivard, *Chroniq.* ii. p. 246.

St. Victor, which is the church, and artillery in the city, which is the church land.' He laid the matter before the council, who voted all that Berthelier required.*

But the Duke of Savoy had no sooner heard of this than he claimed the guns from the monastery. The Council of Fifty was convened to discuss the affair, and Berthelier did not stand alone in supporting the rights of the city. A young citizen of twenty-five, of mild yet intrepid temper, calm and yet active, a friend to law and liberty, without meanness and without arrogance, and who had within him deep-seated and vigorous powers,—this man feared not to provoke a contest between Geneva and the most formidable of his neighbors. He was Besançon Hugues, who had just lost his father and was beginning to enter into public life. One idea governed him : to maintain the independence of his country and resist the usurpations of Savoy, even should it draw upon him the duke's hatred. 'In the name of the people,' he said, 'I oppose the surrender of this artillery to his Highness, the city cannot spare them.' The four guns remained at Geneva, but from that hour Charles III. looked with an angry eye upon Berthelier, Hugues, and Bonivard. 'I will be even with them,' said he.—'When I paid him my respects after the death of my uncle,' said Bonivard, 'his highness turned up his nose at me.'†

Charles III., son of Philip Lackland, was not much like that adventurous prince. When Philip reached a certain age, he became reformed ; and after having several natural children, he married Margaret of Bourbon, and on her death Claudine of Penthievre or Brittany, and in 1496 ascended the throne of Piedmont and Savoy. Charles III., his son by the second wife, rather took after his grandfather Duke Louis ; like him he was steady but weak, submissive to his wife, and inherited from Monsieur only his bursts of passion. His understanding was not large ; but his councillors who were very able made up for this. One single thought seemed to possess him : to annex Geneva to Savoy. It was almost his whole policy. By grasping after Geneva

* Registers of Geneva, 8th and 9th December, 1514

† Bonivard, *Chroniq.* ii. p. 247.

he lost his principalities. Æsop's fable of the dog and the shadow has never been better illustrated.

In 1515 everything seemed favorable to the plans of this prince. The marriage of the Princess Philiberta, which had not been solemnised in 1513 in consequence of her youth was about to take place. The Bishop of Geneva, then at Rome for the Lateran Council, backed his cousin's demand touching the temporal sovereignty. The ministers of Charles, the court, nobility, and priests, all of them pressed the annexation of Geneva. Was not that city the market for the provinces neighboring on Savoy? Was it not necessary for the strategic defence of the duchy? Claude de Seyssel, a skilful diplomatist, author of the *Monarchie de France*, 'a bitter despiser of every republic, and soon after made archbishop of Turin, was continually repeating to the duke that if Geneva remained *in* his territory without being *of* it, Savoy would incur great danger.' 'Truly,' said Bonivard, when he heard of Seyssel's arguments, 'there is no need to push his Highness to make him run. He has begun to beat the tabor, and is now going to open the dance.'*

But would the pope take part in the dance? would he surrender up Geneva to Savoy? That was the question. Leo X. loved wealth, the arts, pleasure, and all the enjoyments of life; he was generous, liberal, prodigal even, and did not care much for business. He had prepared a magnificent palace in the city of the popes and of the Cæsars, for Julian and his young wife. Entertainments of unusual splendor celebrated the union of the Medici with the old family of Humbert of the white hand. 'I will spare no expense,' Leo said, and in fact these rejoicings cost him the enormous sum of 15,000 ducats.

How could a pontiff always occupied in plundering others to enrich and exalt his own kindred, compromise so glorious an alliance in order to maintain the independence of an unknown city in the wild country of the Alps? Besides, the situation at Geneva was disquieting; the free institutions of the city threatened the temporal power of the bishop,

* Bonivard, *Chroniq.* ii. pp. 250–253.

and if that were destroyed, what would become of his spiritual power? But if the Duke of Savoy should become sovereign prince there, he would revoke the insolent liberties of the citizens, and thus save the episcopal prerogative. Such had been the history of most cities in the middle ages: was it also to be that of Geneva?* Lorenzo de' Medici had been accustomed to say: 'My son Julian is good; my son John (Leo X.) is crafty; my son Peter is mad.' Leo thought he was displaying considerable tact by sacrificing Geneva to the glory of the Medici and the ambition of Savoy. 'The Duke of Savoy,' says a catholic historian, 'took advantage of this circumstance (the marriage) to procure a bull confirming the transfer of the temporal authority.'† Charles III. triumphed. He had reached the end which his predecessors had been aiming at for centuries: he had done more than Peter, surnamed Charlemagne; more than Amadeus the Great; he fancied himself the hero of his race. 'I am sovereign lord of Geneva in temporal matters,' he told everybody. 'I obtained it from our holy father the reigning pope.' But what would they say at Geneva? Would the ancient republic meekly bow its head beneath the Savoyard yoke?‡

The whole city was in commotion when this important news arrived. Berthelier, Bonivard, Hugues, Vandel, Bernard, even the most catholic of the citizens, exasperated at such a usurpation, hurried to and fro, conversing eagerly and especially blaming the pontiff. 'The power of the popes,' they said, 'is not over principalities but over sins—it is for the purpose of correcting vices, and not to be masters of sovereigns and peoples, that they have received the keys of the kingdom of heaven.' There was at Geneva a small number of scholars (Bonivard was one) who opened the dusty tomes of their libraries in search of arguments

* Thierry, *Lettres sur l'Histoire de France*, passim.

† *Chronique des Comtes de Genevois*, by M. Lévrier, lieutenant-general of the bailiwick of Meullant, ii. p. 110.

‡ *Archives of Geneva*, 9th June, 1515. Savyon, *Annales*, p. 49. Roset and Gautier MSS. Muratori, *Annuli d'Italia*, x. p. 110. Roscoe, *Leo X.* iii. p. 9.

against the papal resolution. Did not St. Bernard say to Pope Eugene: 'To till the vineyard of the Lord, to root out the noxious plants, is your task . . . You need not a sceptre but a hoe.'*

On the 25th of May a deputation from the council waited on the bishop. 'My lord,' said the first syndic, 'we conjure you to leave the community in the same state as your predecessors transmitted it to you, enjoying its rightful customs and ancient franchises.' The bishop was embarrassed; on the one hand he feared to irritate men whose energy was not unknown to him, and on the other to displease his cousin whose slave he was; he contented himself with muttering a few words. The syndics waited upon the chapter next: 'Prevent this iniquity,' they said to the canons, 'seeing that it *touches* you as much as the city.' But the reverend fathers, who possessed fat benefices in the duke's territory, and feared to have them confiscated, replied in such complicated phrases that nobody could understand them. Both bishop and canons surrendered Geneva to the man who claimed to be its master.

The report that the city was decidedly given to Savoy spread farther and farther every day: people wrote about it from every quarter. The syndics, moved by the letters they received, returned to the bishop. 'It is now a general rumor,' said they; 'protest, my lord, against these strange reports, so that the usurpation, although begun, may not be completed.' The bishop looked at them, then fixing his hollow, sunken eyes upon the ground, preserved an obstinate silence. The syndics withdrew without obtaining anything. What was to be done now? The last hour of liberty seemed to have struck in the old republic. The citizens met one another without exchanging a word; their pale faces and dejected looks alone expressed their sorrow. One cry, however, was heard among them; 'Since justice is powerless,' said the most spirited, 'we will have recourse to force, and if the duke is resolved to enter Geneva, he shall pass over our bodies.' But the majority were uneasy;

* 'Disce sarculo tibi opus esse, non sceptro.—Bernardus, *de Consideratione, ad Eugenium papam*, lib. ii. cap. vi.

knowing their own weakness and the power of Savoy, they considered all resistance useless. Old Rome had destroyed the independence of many a people; new Rome desired to imitate her. . . The city was lost. Salvation came from a quarter whence no one expected it.*

The sacred college had assembled, and the princes of the Church, robed in purple, had examined the affair. To deprive a bishop of his temporal principality . . . what a dangerous example for the papacy itself! Who knows whether princes will not some day desire to do as much by his Holiness? To hear them, you would have fancied, that catholicism would decline and disappear if it did not join the sceptre of the Cæsars with the shepherd's crook. The cardinals resolved that for it to be lawful for a prince of the Church to alienate his temporal jurisdiction, it was necessary 'first, that subjects be in rebellion against their prince; second, that the prince be not strong enough to reduce them; third, that he should have a better recompense.' Was this *recompense* to be another *temporality* or simply a pecuniary compensation? This the documents do not say. In any case, the sacred college refused its consent to the papal decision, and the bull was recalled.†

The duke was surprised and irritated. His counsellors reassured him: they pointed out to him that, according to the decision of the cardinals, it only required a revolt in order to withdraw the temporal jurisdiction from the bishop. 'The Genevans, who are hot-headed and big talkers,' said they, 'will commit some imprudence by means of which we shall prove to the sacred college that it needs *a stronger shepherd than a bishop* to bring them back to their duty.' To these representations they proposed adding certain crafty devices. The judicial officers of the ducal party would draw up long, obscure, unintelligible indictments against the citizens; my lords the cardinals at Rome, who are indolence itself, would waive the reading of these tiresome documents,

* MS. Registers of Geneva, 22d and 25th May, 19th June, 1515. Roset MS. bk. i. ch. 72. Savyon, *Annales*, p. 49, &c.

† Roset MSS. bk. i. ch. 72. Savyon, *Annales*, p. 50. Spon, i. p. 261. Bonivard, *Chroniq.* ii. p. 268. Lévrier, *Chroniq.* ii. p. 110.

the matter would be explained to them *viva voce;* they would be told that the only means of saving the bishop was to give the duke the sovereignty over the city. Charles felt comforted and sent his cousin fresh instructions. 'Since I cannot have the tree,' he said, 'I wish at least to taste the fruit. Set about plundering right and left (*ab hoc et ab hac*) to fill my treasury.' By means of this plundering, the Genevans would be irritated; they would be driven to take up arms, and thus the duke would succeed in confiscating their independence with the consent not only of the pope but of the cardinals also.*

CHAPTER V.

BERTHELIER AND THE YOUTH OF GENEVA AROUSED BY THE BISHOP'S VIOLENCE.

(1515—1517.)

THE bishop, the humble servant of the duke, prepared to act according to his instructions. Charles had set a trustee over him, who allowed him only what was absolutely necessary for his bare maintenance. One day, when an eminent citizen asked him a favor, John of Savoy exclaimed: 'I have only my crozier and my mitre, the property belongs to the duke. He is bishop and abbot.' . . . 'For,' adds the chronicler, 'the duke being very rapacious, John was forced to give the reign to his Highness's extortioners.' They imposed excessive fines; where in the inferior courts the penalty should not exceed sixty sols, they exacted fifty livres. No prince ever made such efforts to suppress revolt as the bastard to foment it. He was almost brave in his devices for losing his principality, but it was the result of

* Bonivard, *Chroniq.* ii. p. 253. Roset and Savyon MSS. Galiffe fils, B. Hugues, p. 226.

servility. He deprived the syndics of their judicial functions; he threw men into prison to avenge private or imaginary offences. The people began to murmur: 'A singular shepherd this!' they said. 'He is not satisfied with shearing his flock, but tears and worries them with his dogs.' The partisans of Savoy were delighted. By one of these exploits the bastard very nearly revolutionized Geneva.*

Claude Vandel was one of the most respected citizens of Geneva. A distinguished lawyer, a man of noble character and spotless integrity, of retiring and respectful manners, but also of great courage, he protected at his own expense the weak and poor against the violence of the great. A citizen having been unjustly prosecuted by a bishop's officer, Vandel undertook his defence and so enraged the prelate that he swore to be revenged on him. But how was he to begin? The people respected Vandel; his ancestors had filled the highest offices in the State; his wife, Mie du Fresnoir, belonged to a good family allied to the Chatillons and other Savoyard houses of the best blood. Moreover Vandel possessed four sons, united by the closest affection, full of veneration for their father, and all destined one day to be called to important duties. Robert, the eldest, was a syndic; Thomas, a canon, procurator-fiscal, and one of the first priests that embraced the Reformation; of the two youngest, who were still youths, Hugo was afterwards the representative of the republic in Switzerland, and Peter captain-general. It was known at the bishop's palace that Vandel's sons would not permit a hand to be laid upon their father; and that even the people would take up his defence. Nevertheless it was decided to make the Genevans bend under the yoke of absolute authority. Thomas, who was then incumbent of Morges, hurried to Geneva on hearing of the design that threatened his father. He was a man of most decided character, and 'handled the sword better than his breviary.' When they learned what were the bishop's intentions, his brothers and he had felt in their hearts one of those sudden and unlooked-for impulses that proceed from the noblest of

* Lévrier, *Chron. des Comtes de Savoye*, ii. p. 112. Galiffe, *Matériaux pour l'Histoire de Genève*, ii. pp. 20, 176. Savyon, *Annales*, p. 50.

affections, and they swore to make their bodies a rampart for their father. The bishop and his courtiers had recourse to stratagem. Vandel was in the country, Robert and Thomas keeping guard beside him. A rumor was set afloat that the bishop's bailiffs would come at nightfall and seize the lawyer. Consequently, 'before night came on,' Robert and Thomas went out to watch for the men who were to carry off their father. But these, instead of leaving at the appointed hour, had started earlier and hidden themselves near the house. As soon as it was dark they left their hiding-place, and while Vandel's sons and friends were looking for them in another direction, they seized the republican Claude, bound him, took him into the city by a secret postern, and conducted him along a subterranean passage to the bishop's prison.*

The next morning, Vandel's sons ran in great distress to their friends and appealed to the people whom they met. They represented that the syndics alone had the right of trial in criminal matters, and that by arresting their father the bishop had trampled the franchises of the city under foot. The people were excited, the council assembled; the syndics went to the bishop and called upon him to let Vandel go, or else hand over to them, his lawful judges, the papers in his case.

'My council,' the bishop answered, 'will examine whether this *arrest* is contrary to your liberties, in which case I will amend what is to be amended.' Even the episcopal council decided for Vandel's discharge; but the bastard obstinately refused.

The anger of the people now grew fiercer against the citizens who had accepted the bishop's pensions.

'The bishop knows very well,' they said, 'that some of them prefer his money to the liberties of the city. Why should he fear to infringe our rights, when traitors have sold them to him?' Thomas Vandel, the priest, the most ardent of the family, hastened to Berthelier. 'The irritation is general,' he said, 'and yet they hesitate. Nobody

* Bonivard, *Chroniq.* ii. p. 257. Registers of Geneva, 29th June, 1515. Savyon, *Annales*, p. 51. Roset and Gautier MSS.

dares bell the cat.' Berthelier joined Vandel's sons, and their bold representations, as well as the murmurs of the people, aroused the syndics. The day (June 29) was already far advanced; but that mattered not, and at the unusual hour of eight in the evening the council met, and 'all the most eminent in the city to the number of about three hundred,' joined the assembly. The people gathered in crowds and filled the hall.

Berthelier was present. He was still governor of Peney, the bishop's gift; and the latter made merry with his courtiers at having put 'a bone in his mouth to prevent his barking.' There were some Genevans who looked frowningly upon him, as if that great citizen had betrayed his country. But Berthelier was calm, his countenance determined: he was prepared to strike the first blow. The syndics described the illegal act of the bishop; the sons of the prisoner called upon them to avenge their father; and Berthelier exclaimed: 'To maintain the liberties of the city, we must act without fear; let us rescue the citizen whom traitors have seized.' John Taccon, captain-general, and at the same time a pensioner of the bishop's, stopped him: 'Gently,' said he, 'if we do as you advise, certain inconveniences may follow.' Berthelier in great excitement exclaimed: 'Now the pensioners are showing themselves!' At these words Taccon could not contain himself: 'It was you,' he said, 'yes, you, who showed me the way to take a pension.' On hearing this reproach Berthelier pulled out the bishop's letters appointing him governor of Peney, and which he had brought with him to the council, and tore them in pieces before the meeting, saying: 'Since I showed you the way to take them, look, I now show you the way to resign them.' These words acted like an electric shock. A cry of 'No more pensions!' was raised on all sides. All the pensioners declared themselves ready to tear up their letters-patent like Berthelier. The commotion was very great. 'Toll the bell for the general council,' cried some. 'No, no,' said the more prudent, 'it would be the signal for a general outbreak, and the people would right themselves.'*

* Bonivard, *Chroniq.* ii. p. 258.

Something however must be done. A portion of the assembly went off to the bishop's palace, and began to shout for the prelate: 'Release the prisoner!' But the bishop did not appear; the doors and windows of the palace remained closely barred. The irritation grew general. 'As the bishop will not show himself,' they said, 'we must assemble the people.' Upon this John Bernard, whose three sons played an important part in the Reformation, ran off to the tower of St. Pierre to ring the bell for the general council. But the priests, anticipating what would happen, had fastened the belfry door. Bernard did not renounce his purpose: he caught up a huge hammer and was beginning to batter the door, when some citizens came up and stopped him. They had just learned that the bastard did not appear because, dreading the fury of the people, he had left Geneva in great haste. One thought consoled the bishop in all his terror: 'Surely here is an argument that will convince the sacred college: my people are in revolt!' But the episcopal council thought differently: Vandel's arrest was illegal, and they restored him to liberty. From that hour the bishop's hatred grew more deadly against those who would not bend to his tyranny.*

The energy displayed by the citizens showed the bastard what he would have to expect if he laid hands on their independence. His creatures resolved therefore to set to work in another way: to enervate this proud and resolute people, and with that view to encourage superstition and profligacy in Geneva. Superstition would prevent the citizens from thinking about truth and reform, while profligacy would make them forget their dignity, their rights, and their dearest liberties.

At the commencement of 1517—the year when the Reformation began in Germany—a bare-footed friar, named Thomas, came and preached at Geneva in *Italian*, and the people who did not understand a word listened to him with admiration. The Virgin Mary, the saints, and the departed were his ordinary theme. Bonivard shrugged his shoulders,

* Bonivard, *Chroniq.* ii. p. 271. Galiffe, *Matériaux pour l'Histoire de Genève*, ii. p. 122. Savyon, *Annales*, p. 52.

saying: 'He is a mere idiot with his cock-and-bull stories!' The friar proceeded next to work miracles; sick persons were brought to him after service; he blessed them right and left, and many returned home *cured*. 'What do you say to that?' triumphantly asked some bigots of the sceptical prior. 'Why, *imaginatio facit casum*, it is the effect of imagination,' he replied. 'The fools believe so firmly that he will heal them, that the cure follows; but it does not last long, and many return worse than they came.' The honorable councillors, befooled like the rest, sent the friar 'princely presents.'

As superstition did not suffice, entertainments and debauchery were added. Duke Philibert the Fair, who visited Geneva in 1498 with his bastard brother René, had already employed this means of subduing the Genevans. 'Go,' said he to his noblest lords, 'and win over all these shopkeepers and mechanics by being on the most familiar footing with them.' The Savoyard nobles, affably accosting the Genevans, used to sit down with them in the taverns, drink, laugh, and sing with them, bewildering the simple by their high-flown language and 'grand airs.' They concealed their subtle treachery under fine phrases; and throwing off all shame, they even permitted looks and gestures of abominable lewdness, infecting the hearts with impurity, and corrupting the young. The priests, far from opposing this depravity, were the first to give way to it. A shameful wantonness engendered criminal excesses which would have brought ruin on those who indulged in them and on the city itself. Effrontery stalked in the streets. The strangers who stopped in Geneva exclaimed:—'It is indeed a city sunk to the eyes in pleasure. Church, nobles, and people are devoted to every kind of excess. You see nothing but sports, dances, masquerades, feasts, lewdness, and consequently, strife and contention. Abundance has generated insolence, and assuredly Geneva deserves to be visited with the scourge of God.'*

Philip Berthelier, a man of indomitable courage, untiring

* Bonivard, *Chroniq.* ii. p. 318 and *passim*.

activity, enthusiastic for independence and the ancient rights of liberty, but infected with the general disease, now put the plan he had conceived into execution, and resolved to turn against Savoy the dissolute habits with which she had endowed his country. He took part in all their feasts, banquets, and debaucheries; drank, laughed, and sang with the youth of Geneva. There was not an entertainment at which he was not present: '*Bonus civis, malus homo*, a good citizen, but a bad man,' they said of him. 'Yes, *malus homo*,' he replied; 'but since good citizens will not risk their comforts in an enterprise of which they despair, I must save liberty by means of madmen.' He employed his practical understanding and profound sagacity in winning men over,* and he attained the end he had set before him. The assemblies of the Genevan youth immediately changed in character. Philibert the Fair had made them a school of slavery; Philip Berthelier made them a school of liberty. Those who opposed the usurpations of the Savoyard princes, boldly held their meetings at these joyous and noisy feasts. The great citizen, as if he had been invested with some magic charm, had entirely changed the Genevan mind, and, holding it in his hand, made it do whatever he pleased. Sarcasms were heaped upon the bishop and the duke's partisans, and every jest was greeted with loud bursts of laughter and applause. If any episcopal officer committed an illegality, information was given to these strange parliaments, and these redressors of wrong undertook to see the victim righted. When the Savoyard party put themselves without the law, the Genevan party did the same, and the war began.

Had Berthelier taken the right course? Could the independence of Geneva be established on such a foundation? Certainly not; true liberty cannot exist without justice, and consequently without a moral change that comes from God. So long as 'young Geneva' loved diversion above everything, the bishop and the duke might yet lay hands upon her. Such was the love of pleasure in the majority of these youths, that they would seize the bait with eager impetu-

* 'Ad alliciendum homines ad se.'—Galiffe, *Matériaux pour l'Histoire de Genève.* Interrogations de Pécolat, ii. p. 42.

osity if it were only dropped with sufficient skill. 'They felt that the hook was killing them,' said a writer of the sixteenth century; but they had not strength to pull it out. This strength was to come from on high. The human mind, so inconstant and so weak, found in God's Words the power it needed, and which the light of the fifteenth century could never have given them. The Reformation was necessary to liberty, because it was neeessary to morality. When the protestant idea declined in some countries, as in France for instance, the human mind lost its energy also, profligacy once more overran society; and that highly endowed nation, after having caught a glimpse of a magnificent dawn, fell back into the thick night of the traditional power of Rome and the despotism of the Valois and Bourbons. Liberty has never been firmly established except among the people where the Word of God reigns.*

CHAPTER VI.

THE OPPOSING PARTIES PREPARE FOR BATTLE.

(1516—1517.)

As a new and powerful opposition was forming in Geneva, it became necessary for the duke and the bishop to unite more closely. About this time an incident of little importance was nearly setting them at variance, and thus accelerating the emancipation of the city.

One day as the gouty bastard, stretched on a couch, was suffering cruelly from his disease, he heard a noise in the street. 'What is the matter?' he asked.—'They are taking a thief to be hanged,' replied the old woman that tended

* Bonivard, *Chroniq.* ii. pp. 265, 271. *Police de Genève,* Mém, d'Archéol. v. p. 381. Galiffe, *Matériaux pour l'Histoire de Genève,* pp. 201. 207, 216. Calvin, *passim.*

him, who added: 'If your Lordship would but pardon him, he would pray for your health all the days of his life.' The bishop, carried away by that fancy of sick people which makes them try everything in the hope that it will cure them, said: 'Be it so, let them set him at liberty.' It was the custom—a strange custom—in Geneva for the syndics to hand over to the vidame the men they had condemned; the vidame transferred them to the governor of Gaillard in Savoy, and the governor to the executioner. The executioner, attended by the governor, was about to hang the man when the bishop's officers brought an order to release him. 'I am the servant of my most dread lord the Duke of Savoy,' said the governor, 'and I shall discharge the duty intrusted to me.' It was agreed, however, that the execution should be put off, and the bishop called his council together to examine whether he had not the right to pardon a malefactor even when he was already in the hands of the officer empowered to execute him. There was among the members of the episcopal council a man of noble character destined to take a place in the history of Geneva by the side of Berthelier and even above him. Aimé Lévrier, judge in the criminal court, son of a former syndic, knew no rule but the law, and had no motive but duty. Serious, calm, full of dignity, endowed with the wisdom of a Nestor, he was decided and energetic in carrying the laws into execution, and as soon as his conscience spoke, he obeyed it in his humble sphere with the impetuosity of an Achilles, if one may compare small things with great. The turbulence of the people and the self-will of princes found him equally unbending. He saw in this little incident the great question between the legitimate authority of the bishop and the usurpations of the duke. 'The prince of Geneva,' he said, 'has the right to pardon a criminal, even if he is on the territory of Savoy and at the foot of the scaffold.' And then, wishing to seize the opportunity of showing that the duke was servant in Geneva and not master, he left the hall, went up to the culprit, cut his bonds, took him by the hand, and, leading him to the bishop, said to the poor wretch: 'Give thanks to God and my lord;' and after that, boldly set him at liberty. But the bishop, who had never imagined the existence of such power, began to tremble already.

They had not indeed long to wait for the duke's anger. If he had given his cousin the diocese of Geneva, it was that he might himself acquire the supreme power; and here was the bishop seized with a fit of independence and going so far as to contest his rights as vidame, his functions as executioner! . . . He would take advantage of this strange boldness to put the bastard in his right place, get rid of Lévrier, destroy the remnant of liberty still to be found in the city, and establish the ducal authority therein. The seignior of La Val d'Isère, attended by two other commissioners, arrived at Geneva in order to execute his Highness's pleasure. Striding haughtily into the bishop's palace, he addressed the bastard rudely on the part of the angry duke. The bishop was lavish of salutations, attentions, and respect, but all to no purpose. La Val d'Isère, who had learnt his lesson well, raised his voice still higher: Wretched bastard! (he said) what did he want with pardoning a man they were going to hang? The poor prelate was on the rack and more dead than alive; at last the ducal envoy having finished his severe reprimand, the bishop tremblingly excused himself, 'like our father Adam when he threw the blame on Eve,' says Bonivard. 'It was one Lévrier, a judge and doctor of laws, who did it,' said he. The seignior of La Val d'Isère gave the bishop to understand that instead of indulging any longings for independence, he ought to unite with the duke in combating the spirit of liberty in Geneva.

To a certain extent, however, the ducal envoy admitted the prelate's excuse; he knew his weakness, and saw that another will than his own had acted in this business. He informed the duke of Lévrier's misdeed, and from that hour this intrepid judge became odious to the court of Turin, and was doomed to destruction. The Savoyards said that as he had rescued the thief from the gallows, he ought to be hanged in his place. The duke and his ministers were convinced that every attempt to enslave Geneva would fail, so long as it contained such an energetic defender of the law. The evening of the day when La Val d'Isère had reprimanded the bishop, the ducal envoy, with one of his colleagues and the vidame, supped at the priory of St. Victor: the ambassador was Bonivard's cousin, and had purposely gone to visit him. He desired to make his cousin a devoted agent of Savoy in Geneva, and to employ him, by way of prelude, in the arrest of the recalcitrant judge. After supper, La Val d'Isère took the prior aside, and began to compliment him highly. 'My dear cousin,' said he, 'the duke has not in all his states a man better fitted than you to do him a service. I know you; I observed you when you were studying beyond the mountains, an intelligent fellow, a skilful swordsman, always ready to execute any deed of daring if it would render your friends a service. Your ancestors were loyal servants of the house of Savoy, and my lord expects you will show yourself worthy of them.' The astonished Bonivard made no reply. Then La Val d'Isère explained to him how he could aid the duke in his schemes against Geneva, adding that at this very moment he might do him an important service. There was Aimé Lévrier, a determined malcontent, a rebel like his father, whom it was necessary to arrest. . . La Val d'Isère communicated his plot to Bonivard. Aimé Lévrier went ordinarily to pay his devotions at the church of Our Lady of Grace, near the bridge of Arve. Bonivard would follow him, seize him the moment he came near the church, and, holding him by the throat, cross the bridge with him, and deliver him up to the ducal soldiers, who would be on the other side ready to receive him. 'This will be an easy task for you, dear cousin,' added the ambassador; 'everybody knows your readiness and your prowess.' . . . La Val d'Isère added that Bonivard would thus gain two advantages: first, he would be revenged on the bishop whom he loved but little; and second, he would receive a handsome reward from my lord of Savoy. It was a singular idea to intrust this outrage to the prior of a monastery; yet it was in accordance with the manners of the day. Bonivard's interests and family traditions would have induced him to serve Savoy; but he had an enlightened understanding and an independent spirit. He belonged to the new times. 'Ever since I began to read history,' he said, 'I have always preferred a republican to a monarchical state, and especially to those where the throne is hereditary.' The duke would have given him honors and riches in abundance, whilst he received from the cause which he embraced only poverty and a dungeon: still he never hesitated. The love of liberty had taken possession of that distinguished man, and he was always faithful to it: whatever may have been his weaknesses, this is a glory which cannot be taken from him. Bonivard wished to decline the proposal without however irritating the ambassador too much. He pointed to his robes, his prayer-book, his monks, his priory, and assigning these as a reason, he said: 'Handling the sword is no longer my business; I have changed it for the breviary.' Upon this La Val d'Isère in great disappointment became angry and said: 'Well, then, I swear I will go myself to-night and take Lévrier in his bed, and carry him tied hand and foot into Savoy.' Bonivard looked at him with a smile: 'Will you really make the attempt?' he asked; 'shake hands then.' The ambassador thinking he was won over gave him his hand. 'Are you going to make preparations for the affair?' 'No, cousin,' replied Bonivard with a bow, 'I know the people of Geneva; they are not indulgent, I warn you, and I shall go and set aside thirty florins to have a mass said for your soul to-morrow.' The ambassador left him in great anger.*

Bonivard perceived that Lévrier's life was in danger. At that time people supped early; the prior waited until nightfall, and then leaving his monastery in disguise, he passed stealthily through the streets, and entering the house of his friend the judge, told him everything. Lévrier in his turn ran to Berthelier. 'Oh, oh!' said the latter, who was captain of the city, 'my lords of Savoy want to be masters here! we will teach them it is not so easy.'

At this moment news was brought the syndics that some lansquenets were at the Vengeron (half a league from the city on the right shore of the lake) and preparing to enter

* Bonivard, *Chroniq.* ii. pp. 277, 278.

the faubourg of St. Gervais: it was clear that Savoy desired to carry off the judge. The syndics ordered Berthelier to keep watch all night under arms. He assembled the companies, and the men marched through the streets in close order with drums beating, passing and repassing the house of the vidame, Aymon Conseil, where the ambassadors were staying.

The seignior of La Val d'Isère, with his two colleagues the Sieur J. de Crans and Peter Lambert, expected every moment to be attacked by these armed men. They called to mind the mass for the dead of which Bonivard had spoken, and altogether passed a horrible night. Towards the morning the city grew calm, and it was scarcely light when the envoys of Savoy, ordering their horses to be saddled, rode out by a secret door of which the bishop had the key, and hastened to report to their master.*

Notwithstanding their precipitate retreat one of the objects of their mission was attained. The deputies from Savoy did not quit Geneva alone; the bastard was still more frightened than they; fear drove away the gout, he left his bed, and taking with him the Count of Genevois, the duke's brother, he hurried over the mountains to Turin, in order to pacify his terrible cousin. The latter was extremely irritated. It was not enough to encroach on his rights, they also forced his envoys to flee from Geneva. The bastard spared no means to justify himself; he crouched at Charles's feet. He was the most to be pitied, he said; these Genevans frightened him day and night. 'I will forget everything,' said the prince to him at last, 'provided you assist me in bringing these republicans to reason.' It was what the prior of St. Victor had foreseen. 'Just as Herod and Pilate agreed in their dark designs,' he said, 'so do the duke and the bishop agree for the ruin of Geneva.'—'Cousin,' continued the duke, 'let us understand one another: in your fold there are certain *dogs* that bark very loudly and defend your sheep very stoutly; you must get rid of them . . . I don't mean only Lévrier the son—there is Lévrier the father

* *Chronique du Pays de Vaud*, Bibl. Imp. No. 16720. Bonivard, *Chroniq.* ii. pp. 276–279.

and Berthelier also, against whom you must sharpen your teeth.'—'The elder Lévrier,' answered the bastard, 'is a sly and cunning fox, who knows how to keep himself out of the trap; as for Berthelier, he is hot, choleric, and says outright what he thinks: we shall have a far better chance of catching him; and when he is done for, it will be an easy matter with the others.' In this way the princes of Savoy, meeting in the duke's cabinet in the palace of Turin, conspired the ruin of Geneva, and plotted the death of its best citizens. Charles the *Good* was the cruellest and most obstinate of the three. 'Let us play the game seriously,' he repeated; 'we must have them dead or alive.' The duke, the count, and the bishop arranged their parts, and then the *wolves* (it was the name Bonivard gave them) waited a good opportunity for falling on the *dogs*.*

While they were making these preparations at Turin to crush liberty, others were preparing at Geneva to fight and die for her. Both parties took up arms: the contest could not fail to be severe, and the issue important to Geneva and to society. Two friends especially did not lose sight of the approaching struggle. Berthelier inclined to the revival of Geneva from democratic motives; Bonivard, from a love of learning, philosophy, and light. Seated opposite each other in the priory of St. Victor, with the mild sparkling wine of the country on the table, they discoursed about the new times. Bonivard possessed an indescribable attraction for Berthelier. The young prior whose mind was full of grace, simplicity, poetry, imagination, and also of humor, was waking up with the sixteenth century, and casting an animated glance upon nature and the world. His style indicates his character: he always found the strongest, the most biting expressions, without either the shades of delicacy or the circuitousness of subtlety. There were however elevated parts in him: he could be enthusiastic for an idea. A thought passing through his mind would call up high aspirations in his soul and bring accents of eloquence to his lips. But, generally, men displeased him. A well-bred gentle-

* Bonivard, *Chroniq.* ii. pp. 279, 383. Roset MSS. liv. i. ch. xxvi. *Matériaux pour l'Histoire de Genève*, ii. pp. 111, 119, 136.

man, a keen and graceful wit, a man of the world, he found the townspeople about him vulgar, and did not spare them the sting of his satire. When Berthelier, in the midst of the uproar of a tavern, shook the youths of Geneva warmly by the hand, and enlisted them for the great campaign of independence, Bonivard would draw back with embarrassment and put on his gloves. 'These petty folks,' he said with some contempt, 'only like justice in others; and as for the rich tradesmen, they prefer the feasts and the money of the Savoyard nobles to the charms of independence.' He was inclined to suspect evil: this was one of the disagreeable features in his character. Even Besançon Hugues was, in his eyes, nothing but pride, hidden under the mask of a citizen. Bonivard, like Erasmus, laughed at everybody and everything, except two: like him he was fond of letters, and still more fond of liberty. At Geneva he was the man of the Renaissance, as Calvin was the man of the Reformation. He overcame his antipathies, sat down at table with the young Genevans, scattered brilliant thoughts in their conversations, and kindled in their understanding a light that was never to be extinguished. Frivolous and grave, amiable and affectionate, studious and trifling, Bonivard attacked the old society, but he did not love the new. He scourged the enormities of the monks, but he was alarmed at the severe doctrines of the Reformation. He desired to bury the past joyously, but he did not know what future to set up in its place.

Berthelier, who fancied he knew, explained his plans to his friends in their familiar colloquies. The liberty of the Italian republics—a selfish liberty, full of discord and faction—had come to an end; a more noble, more vital, more durable liberty was destined to appear. But neither the politic Berthelier nor the æsthetic Bonivard thought of the new element which in new times was to give life to modern liberties: this element was a strong faith, it was the authority of God, held up on high, that was destined to consolidate society after the great earthquake it would have to go through. After Berthelier the republican, after Bonivard the classic, another man was to appear, *tertium genus*, a third kind, as they said at the time when paganism and Judaism disappeared before the Gospel. A Christian hero, boldly standing erect above the volcano of popular passions, was called in the midst of the convulsions of popery to lay in Geneva the foundations of enlightened society, inflexible morality, unyielding faith, and thus to save the cause of liberty. The work of Calvin thus coming after that of Berthelier and Bonivard, no doubt presents a very strange juxtaposition; but three centuries have shown its necessity. The Reformation is indispensable to the emancipation of nations.

Berthelier, Bonivard, and their friends turned their eyes in another direction. 'Have done with banquets and dances,' said Berthelier to his friend; 'we must organise young Geneva into a defensive league.' 'Yes, let us march onwards,' replied Bonivard, 'and God will give a good issue to our bold enterprise!' . . . Berthelier stretched out his hand. 'Comrade,' he said, 'your hand.'* Then, as he held Bonivard's hand in his, he was touched with deep emotion: a cloud passed over his face, and he added: 'But know that for the liberty of Geneva, you will lose your benefice, and I . . . I shall lose my head.' 'He told me that a hundred times,' added the prior of St. Victor, who has handed down this conversation to us. The gloomy foreboding was but too amply fulfilled.

CHAPTER VII.

ASSEMBLY, AGITATION, AND COMEDY OF THE PATRIOTS.

(1516—1517.)

WITHOUT delay Berthelier entered upon the work to which he had sworn to devote his life. Wishing to prepare it carefully, he invited the most ardent of the young Genevans to confer with him on the salvation of the country. He did

* Bonivard, *Chroniq.* i. pp. 28, 29, and 238.

not select for this meeting some lonely field, above the shores of the lake, as the Grütli: he had to deal with the inhabitants of a city and not with the children of the mountains. He therefore took a hall in the principal square of the city, la Place du Molard, then almost washed by the waters of the river, and appointed a time for the meeting when the streets were most thronged. About twilight one afternoon, probably in 1516 (it is difficult to fix precisely the date of this important meeting*), Berthelier, and then a few other patriots, set out for the Molard: they came from the Rue du Rhone, la Rive, and from the Cité; those who came from the upper part of the town passed down the Rue du Perron. As they walked, they conversed of the tyranny of the bishop and the plots of the princes of Savoy. One of those who appeared to have the most influence was Amadeus de Joye, the son of distinguished, upright, and honorable parents, who had brought him up virtuously. The public voice, while proclaiming him a 'merry fellow,' added that he was honest and straightforward, and connected with all the good men of the city: he exercised the honorable vocation of druggist and apothecary, and had always enjoyed a good reputation in his business. Not far from him was Andrew Navis: a change had taken place in the son of the procurator-fiscal. The cause of liberty had dawned upon his ardent soul in all its beauty: in it he fancied he had found the unknown good he had sought so eagerly; his imagination had been inflamed, his heart moved, and leaving the Savoyard party, of which his father was one of the chiefs, he rushed with all his natural impetuosity to the side of independence. One of his friends, John Biderman, surnamed Blanchet, had accompanied him, a young man about twenty-four years old. Full of natural wit, disliking work, very fond of fun, Blanchet 'trotted up and down,' picked up all the news, repeated it at random, and meddled in everybody's business. He had, however, at

* Pécolat, in his examination of 5th August, 1517, says: '*About a year ago.*'—Galiffe, ii. p. 41. Blanchet, in his examination of 5th of May, 1518, at Turin, says: '*About two years ago.*'—Ibid. p. 99. Then on 21st of May, he says: '*About a year ago.*'—Ibid. p. 205.

bottom a sensitive heart, and the tyranny of the bishop provoked him. Berthelier, who was among the earliest arrivals, scanned attentively the young people and the earnest men who had joined them, and experienced a feeling of happiness at the sight. There was in him a being superior to the follies of banquets. The daily routine, the small passions, the vulgarity of mind, life such as he had hitherto known it, wearied him. At last he had before him an assembly brought together for the noble cause of independence ; and for that reason he affectionately pressed the hand of all comers. At this moment the bell rang for vespers at Magdalen old church, and was distinctly heard at the Molard. There were present with Berthelier about fifty citizens—a small meeting, and yet more numerous than that of Walter Fürst and his friends. Besides, did not all noble hearts in Geneva beat in harmony with those of the fifty patriots? *

They gathered in a circle round Berthelier, and stood silent; the heroic citizen reminded them that from the most remote times Geneva had been free ; but that for one or two centuries the princes of Savoy had been trying to enslave it, and that the duke only waited for the favorable opportunity to impose his usurped sovereignty upon their country. Then fixing his noble look upon his audience, he asked them if they wished to transmit to their children not liberty but . . . slavery? The citizens answered No, and demanded anxiously how the liberties of the city could effectually be saved? 'How!' said Berthelier. 'By being united, by forgetting our private quarrels, by opposing with one mind every violation of our rights. We have all the same franchises, let us all have the same heart. If the bishop's officers lay hands on one of us, let all the others defend him with their swords, their nails, their teeth!'† Then he exclaimed: '*Who touches one, touches all.*' At these words they all raised their hands and said: 'Yes, yes!

* Galiffe, *Matériaux pour l'Histoire de Genève*, ii. pp. 199, 206, 210, *passim.*

† 'Armis, unguibus, et rostris.'—Galiffe, *Matériaux*, &c. Joye's Exam. ii p. 215.

one heart, one common cause! Who touches one, touches all!'—'Good,' resumed Berthelier, 'let this motto be the name of our alliance, but let us be faithful to the noble device. If the bishop's constables take one of us to prison, let us rescue him from their hands. If they indulge in criminal extortions, let us seek out the abominable plunder even in their houses.' And then he repeated in a loud voice: '*Who touches one, touches all!*' And yet in the midst of this enthusiasm, the marks of fear could be seen on some faces. One citizen asked with considerable uneasiness what they would do if my lord of Geneva, aided by his Highness, should attack the city with a strong army? 'Fear nothing,' answered Berthelier sharply, 'we have good friends;' and he added soon after: 'I will go to the Swiss, I will bring back forces, and then . . . I will settle accounts with our adversaries.' *

From that time the consultations and debates became more and more frequent: the discussions went on in private families, at St. Victor's, in the houses of the principal citizens, sometimes even in the public places: men reminded each other of the customs and franchises of Geneva, and promised to be mutually faithful.

One day Berthelier, Blanchet, and several other citizens meeting at Mugnier's to discourse round the table about the common interest, unfortunately brought with them a vile and corrupt fellow, a creature of the bishop's named Carmentrant. They sat down, the wine circulated, and their heads soon became heated: 'The bishop,' said one of them, 'has sold Geneva to the duke!'—'If he breaks his oath,' said another, 'his treason does not free us from ours. When princes trample the law under foot, the citizens ought to uphold it at any cost.'—'We must let the bishop know,' added Berthelier, 'the resolution we have adopted to defend our independence.'—'That is not easy,' observed one; 'how can we approach my lord and dare tell him all the truth?'—'Let us mask ourselves,' returned he; 'we may say hard things under our masks. . . Let us make a *momon* at the

* Galiffe, *Matériaux*, &c. Exam. of Pécolat, ii. p. 42. Exam. of Blanchet, ib. p. 206.

palace.' The *momon* was a bet made by maskers when playing at dice. Pécolat did not seem convinced. 'Leave that to me,' said Berthelier, 'I shall find a way of speaking to the prelate.' Carmentrant listened in silence; he engraved in his memory every word of the great patriot, ready to add to them his private interpretations. He asserted afterwards that Berthelier proposed attacking the prelate's life; but the contrary was proved, and even the farce of the *momon* was never carried out. That mattered not; the smallest joke at that time was metamorphosed into the crime of high treason.*

Berthelier was not the only person the bishop caused to be watched; Bonivard, ever sparkling with wit, gave opportunities to informers. He had at that time a difference with the bishop about the right of fishing in the Rhone. One day when walking with Berthelier and other friends, he complained of the prelate's avarice; and then indulging in a joke, he said laughingly: 'If ever I meet him near my fishery, one or other of us will catch an ugly fish.' This was made a principal charge against him: he wished to *drown* the bishop. They were mistaken: Bonivard was not a violent character; but he was ambitious, and, without wishing the bishop any harm, he secretly aspired to the bishopric. 'I will go to Rome, said he to one of his intimate friends, 'and will not have my beard shaved until I am bishop of Geneva.'

The court of Turin had not forgotten the famous decision of the cardinals. A few light words were not enough to prove to the sacred college that the people of Geneva were in revolt; an *émeute* (as the Savoyards called it) furnished this party with the arms they sought.

On the 5th of June, 1517, the only talk throughout the city was about Messire Gros' mule, which was dead. This mule was well known, for the judge rode it whenever he went on his judicial investigations. People seriously discussed in the streets and at table the cause of the death of this famous beast. 'It is Adrian of Malvenda,' said some,

* Galiffe, *Matériaux*, &c. Exam. of Pécolat and Blanchet. *Chroniq. des Comtes de Genève*, ii. p. 141.

'that Spaniard whose father came from Valence la Grande, who, having had a quarrel with the judge at a dinner party, has hamstrung the beast.' 'No,' said others, 'some young Genevans meeting the judge on his mule and wishing to frighten him, shouted out and drew their swords: his servants drew also, and one of them awkwardly wounded the mule, so that it died.'*

Messire Claude Gros or Grossi, judge of the three castles (Peney, Thiez, and Jussy) was one of those harsh magistrates who are hated by a whole people. They coupled him in this respect with the procurator-fiscal Peter Navis; and Berthelier, De Lunes, and De la Thoy had often threatened both of them with the vengeance of the patriots. Their hatred against these two magistrates was such that even Andrew Navis suffered from it. In vain had he given himself up heart and soul to the party of liberty; he was regarded with distrust; and men asked if any good could come from the house of the procurator-fiscal. Quite recently Andrew had had a dispute with John Conod on this subject. The two young people were, however, reconciled, and the very evening of the day when the mule died, Conod gave a supper to Navis and thirty 'children of Geneva.' This was the name they gave to the young men of age to bear arms. That evening, however, some citizens of riper years joined them: among whom were Berthelier, J. de Lunes, E. de la Mare, J. de la Porte, J. de la Thoy, and J. Pécolat. 'Gentlemen,' said Berthelier after supper, 'it is a long time since this merry company has had any fun.' They were all agreed. Berthelier delighted in setting his enemies at defiance without any regard for the consequences. 'The mule of the respectable Claude Grossi is dead,' he continued; 'that judge is a wretch continually beating after us and our friends. Let us play him a trick: let us sell his mule's skin by auction to the highest bidder.' The proposal was adopted by acclamation. Two or three, however, appeared to wish to withdraw: 'Let every one follow the drum on pain of being fined a gold crown,' said Berthelier.

* Bonivard, *Chroniq.* ii. p. 265. Galiffe, *Matériaux*, &c., ii. pp. 50, 174.

'Agreed, agreed!' cried the giddiest of the company. At every court and even in the houses of many noblemen it was the custom to keep *fools* who had the privilege of telling the boldest truths with impunity. The Abbot of Bonmont had one named Master Littlejohn Smallfoot. Berthelier, desirous of carrying out the practical joke to the uttermost, sent for Littlejohn. 'Here,' said he, 'here's a proclamation for you to cry through the streets. Forward.' All marched out with drawn swords, and, with the drummer at their head, began to traverse the streets, stopping at every place where the ordinary publications were made. After a roll of the drum, Master Littlejohn blew a horn and cried with his squeaking voice: 'O yes, this is to give notice that whoever wishes to buy the skin of a beast, of the *grossest* ass in Geneva, and will call at the house situate between the keeper's and the Hôtel de Ville, it will be sold to the highest bidder.' 'Is not that where Judge *Gros* lives?' asked a bystander. 'Yes, it's he that is the *gross* ass,' replied another. A general burst of laughter followed this proclamation. Andrew Navis in particular indulged in the most noisy demonstrations; he was bent on showing that he was as good a patriot as the rest.

The oldest of the patriots were however uneasy: the elder Lévrier thought they were going too fast. 'Ah,' said he, 'these young folks will play us a pretty game!' 'Certes, added others spitefully, 'this Berthelier has a singular talent for stirring up quarrels.'* The joke was continued through great part of the night.

The next day the judge of the three castles hastened to lay his complaint before the vidame and the episcopal council. The vidame called for the arrest of the guilty parties, who disappeared. Being summoned by sound of trumpet to appear at the Château de l'Ile under pain of being fined a hundred crowns, they came out of their hiding-places, and Berthelier brought an action against the vidame for having threatened him and his friends with a fine that was not authorised by the law. The partisans of Savoy were still

* 'Ingeniosus suscitando quam plurima debata.'—Galiffe, *Matériaux*, &c., ii. pp. 50, 61, 171, 174. Savyon, *Annales*, p. 64.

more exasperated. 'There is a conspiracy against my lord the bishop-prince of Geneva,' they exclaimed; 'he alone has the right of making proclamations.' They wrote letter after letter to Turin, and metamorphosed a fool's jest into the crime of high treason.*

The princes of Savoy thought that this was a disorder by which they might profit. Charles had the reputation in his hereditary states of being irresolute in deciding and feeble in executing; but whenever Geneva was concerned, he ventured upon daring measures. He gave the order of departure to his court; took with him one of the most learned diplomatists of the age, Claude de Seyssel, whom he thought he should require in the great matters that were to be transacted, and arrived in Geneva. The vidame, still irritated by the story of the mule, immediately presented his homage to the duke, and described the situation in the gloomiest of colors. 'You see,' said Charles to his councillors, 'the citizens of Geneva are in revolt: it needs *a stronger shepherd than a bishop* to bring them back to their duty.' But Seyssel was a man of great judgment: he was no novice either in government or in history; he had studied Thucydides, Appian, Diodorus, and Xenophon, and even rendered them into French. He inquired more particularly into the matter, learned that the notice had been cried by the Abbot of Bonmont's fool, and that it was the same fellow who sang habitually in the streets all the comic songs produced by the satiric vein of the Genevans. The diplomatist smiled. 'This business of the mule is a mere practical joke,' he said to the duke; 'fools, you know, have the privilege of saying and doing everything; and as for the band of wags who surrounded the buffoon, do not let us make these young men into Cethegi and Catilines. The cardinals will never consent to give us the temporal sovereignty of Geneva for such foolery. It would be too much, my lord, for the first stroke; we must mount to the pinnacle of sovereignty by shorter steps. This story will not however be quite useless to us; we will employ it to sow dissension among our enemies.' In

* Reg. du Conseil *ad annum.* Bonivard, *Chroniq.* ii. pp. 267, 268. Savyon, *Annales*, p. 55.

fine, the able Seyssel having come to an understanding with the bishop, the latter summoned to his presence those of 'the band,' that is to say, of the children of Geneva, whom he thought most pliable. 'You will gain nothing,' said Claude de Seyssel to them, 'by following a lot of rioters and rebels. In making this proclamation you committed a wrongful action, and you might justly receive corporeal punishment; but the bishop is a good prince, inclined to mercy; he will pardon all of you except Berthelier and his accomplices. He will even give you office, places, and pensions . . . only do not consort any more with seditious people.' Many, delighted at getting out of the scrape, thanked Seyssel heartily, and promised that they should be seen no more among the disaffected.* The bastard showed himself more difficult with regard to the son of his procurator-fiscal: the bravadoes of Andrew Navis, at the time of the proclamation about the mule, had aroused all the prelate's anger. It would seem that the poor father dared not intercede for his prodigal son; one of his friends obtained his pardon, but only after Navis had promised to reform. He returned to his father's office and might be seen constantly poring over the laws and acts of the exchequer.

This manœuvre having succeeded, and the party of the independents being thus weakened, the bishop, the duke, and their friends thought that its head should be removed: that head was Berthelier. It was not easy, however, to get rid of him: he was a member of council, much looked up to in Geneva, and possessed a skill and energy that baffled all their attempts. 'To catch this big partridge,' said the bishop, 'we must first trap a little decoy-bird.' The advice appeared excellent. The prince determined accordingly to catch some friend of Berthelier's, less formidable than himself, who by his depositions (for the *question* would not be spared) would compromise the best citizens in Geneva. The decoy would by his song draw the large birds into the nets spread to catch them.†

* Bonivard, *Chroniq.* ii. p. 285. Savyon, *Annales*, p. 51. Mignet's Memoir on the *Réformation de Genève*, p. 28.

† Bonivard, *Chroniq.* ii. p. 285.

CHAPTER VIII.

PÉCOLAT TORTURED AND BERTHELIER ACCUSED.

(1517.)

Among the best patriots of Geneva was John Pécolat, whom we have already met at the mule supper. He had not Berthelier's strength of character, but he had spirit. A prey by turns to enthusiasm and fear, at times indulging in the most courageous acts or the most culpable weakness, subject to the blackest melancholy or to fits of the maddest humor, Pécolat was at once a hero and a jester. His social position offered the same contrasts. One of his ancestors had been syndic in 1409, another councillor in 1474; in 1508 his father had exercised the highest functions in the State, and he was himself one of the Council of Fifty; he was well instructed, understood Latin, and yet was a hosier by trade. It is true that at this time we often find traders invested with the highest offices; it is one of the peculiarities of democratic manners; and we meet with examples of it in modern society. An accident which deprived him of the use of his right arm, compelled him to give up his business, reduced him to poverty, and plunged him at first into great dejection. However, that did not last long, and there was no man in Geneva that had such fits of gaiety. At a banquet, nobody was louder than Pécolat; he laughed and joked; pun followed pun, in rapid succession. 'What happy things come into his head!' said everybody, and 'it was these happy things,' adds the chronicler, 'that gave him access to good tables.'* When he entered the room a frank

* Savyon, *Annales*, p. 53.

and hearty greeting, an enthusiasm mingled with laughter, welcomed his arrival. But Pécolat had hardly left his friends when dark thoughts mounted to his brain. Sitting in his narrow chamber, he thought of his maimed arm, his indigence, his dependent life; he thought frequently too of the liberties of Geneva, which he saw sacrificed; and this strange man who made all the city laugh, would burst into tears. It was not long before Pécolat compromised himself in such a manner as to furnish arms against the patriots of Geneva.

The Bishop of Maurienne, precentor of the cathedral and canon of Geneva, who had a suit against the bishop, was then staying in the city and 'feasting' the citizens. Having one day invited several of his friends, and among others his colleague, the Abbot of Bonmont, who always had a grudge against the bishop for depriving him of the diocese, he invited Pécolat also. During the dinner the two prelates worked themselves into a passion against the bastard of Savoy: each tried who could attack him the most bitterly, and indeed he gave them a fair handle. Pécolat began to do as the others, and to let fly his usual epigrams against the bastard. Maurienne had no end of complaints. 'Pray, my lord, said Pécolat, 'do not vex yourself about the bishop's injustice: *non videbit dies Petri*: he will not live as long as St. Peter!' This was a saying they were in the habit of applying to the popes at the time of their coronation; and Pécolat meant to say that the bishop, who, as everybody knew, was suffering under an incurable disease, could not live long. Two Savoyards, creatures of the duke and the bishop, who were of the party, went immediately and repeated these words to the bastard. 'At sumptuous tables,' said the prior of St. Victor, who was probably one of the guests, 'there are always gluttons picking up words that will get them another dinner.' The episcopal court concluded from the Latin proverb that the independents were conspiring against the bishop, and that Pécolat announced the prelate's death as near at hand. This speech was not sufficient, however, to send him to trial: they waited for some act that would serve as a pretence for the charge of assassination.*

The opportunity soon occurred. Not long after, the duke having crossed the mountains to present his homage to Queen Claude of Brittany, whom Francis I. had just married, and who was then at Lyons, invited the bishop to come and see him in this city. The bastard set off immediately: his steward ordered some fish pasties as provision for the journey, and the purveyor, whether from hurry or from desire to make a large profit, used fish that had been kept too long. The bishop did not touch them, but some of his people having eaten of them, fell sick; it was asserted that one of them died. The bastard, whose conscience was none of the easiest, saw an assassin everywhere; and though in this matter of the pasties there was nothing but what was very natural, he thought or seemed to think that it was an attempt at poisoning. The idea occurred to certain Savoyards that they might make use of this story to accuse Pécolat, and show the cardinals that the prince-bishop's subjects were conspiring against him.

Pécolat had so little to do with my lord's kitchen that at first the vidame refused to prosecute; but the affair of Messire Gros' mule having occurred, and greatly annoyed the judges, they hesitated no longer. Pécolat was one of the band who had cried, 'The skin of the gross beast!' On the 27th of July, 1517, a warrant was issued against him.

It was necessary to arrest Pécolat; but that was no easy thing, for the members of the society *Who touches one touches all*, would no doubt rise and defend him. It was resolved to arrange the matter carefully. First they would get the most determined of the young men out of Geneva; then they would entice Pécolat into some lonely place; and finally, as they knew not what might happen, the bishop should go and stay in some castle beyond the reach of the Genevese. This triple stratagem was immediately put into execution. The Count of Genevois, who played the part of a jovial host, organised a grand hunt of wild animals, the

* Savyon, *Annales*, p. 53. Bonivard, *Chroniq.* Roset MSS. Spon, i. p. 267.

rendezvous being at Vouache, two leagues to the west of Geneva: he invited the Abbot of Bonmont, Bonivard, and many young men of the city, whose names were in the *black book*, that is, whom they wished to get rid of. While this joyous company was hunting with hound and horn at the foot of Mont Saleve, the bishop wishing to enjoy a fresher air (it was said) had repaired, escorted by a few gentlemen, to his castle of Thiez between the mountains of Mole, Voirons, and Reposoir, on the road to Mont Blanc, a little above the point where the Giffre torrent joins the Arve. At the same time one Maule, a secret agent of the vidame, invited Pécolat to take a walk with him to Pressinge, a village situated between the lake and the Voirons, where one of them possessed some property. Ten horsemen setting out from the castle of Thiez lay in ambush. They surrounded the two pedestrians, bound and carried them to the castle, where the bishop having released the tempter, threw Pécolat into prison. When the news of this treachery reached Geneva, the irritation was directed against Maule still more than against the bishop. The traitor, who seems to have been a man of debauched life, was loaded with the people's maledictions. 'May the cancer eat Maule up!' they cried; and this saying became a proverb applicable to traitors ever afterwards.*

He had however played his part so well that the imprisoned Pécolat was exasperated not against him but against his most intimate friend Berthelier. His black fit came over him. He said to himself that although a man of the most inoffensive character, he seemed destined to expiate the faults of all his party. With what had they to reproach him? Mere jokes and laughter. . . Berthelier was the real conspirator, and he was at large. . . On the third of April Pécolat was removed from the dungeon into which he had been thrown, and conducted to the top of the castle, under the roof. The bishop had ordered him 'to be examined and forced to speak the truth;' and the torture-room was at the top of the castle. After the usual preliminaries

* Savyon, *Annales*, p. 57. Bonivard, *Chroniq.* p. 284. Spon, i. p. 278. Roset and Gautier MSS.

the examination began. The plot of the *non videbit* and the salt fish was too absurd; M. de Thoire, the examining judge, dwelt but little upon it, and endeavored particularly (for that was the object of the arrest) to obtain such admissions as would ruin Geneva and her principal citizens. As Pécolat deposed to nothing that would inculpate them, he was tied by one hand to the rope, and, as he still refused to answer, was hoisted four feet from the floor. The poor fellow groaned deeply and speaking with difficulty * said: 'Cursed be Berthelier for whom I am shut up!' He made no confession, however.

The next day they resorted to another expedient. The bishop gave himself the pleasure of keeping the wretched man hanging to the cord while he was at dinner. The servants, as they passed backwards and forwards waiting on their master, said to Pécolat: 'You are very stupid to let yourself be put to such torture: confess everything. What will your silence help you? Maule has told everything; he has named So-and-so . . . the Abbot of Bonmont, for instance, whom you want to make your bishop after you have done for my lord.' All these traps were useless—he made no confession. It was next determined to expose Pécolat to a more cruel torture: the executioners tied his hands behind his back, and then pulled the rope so as to raise his arms above his head; lastly they lifted him five or six feet from the floor, which was enough to dislocate his shoulders. Pécolat suffered horribly, and he was not a Regulus. 'Let me down! let me down!' he cried, 'and I will tell all.' . . . The judges, delighted at having vanquished the obstinate rebel at last, ordered him to be lowered. Terror was in his heart, and his features betrayed the trouble of his mind. The man, usually so gay and so witty, was now pale, affrighted, his eyes wandered, and he fancied himself surrounded by hungry dogs. He said all that they wanted him to say. To the falsest imputations against the noblest of his friends he answered 'Yes, yes!' and the satisfied judges sent him back to his dungeon.†

* 'Suspirans et ab imo trahens pectore vocem.'—Galiffe, *Matériaux*, &c. Interrog. ii. p. 40.

† Galiffe, *Matériaux*, &c. Interrog. de Pécolat, ii. pp. 29–49.

This was no comfort to the unhappy Pécolat: more terrible anguish awaited him there. The thought that he had deposed against his best friends and even incurred the guilt of bearing false witness, alarmed him seriously: the fear of God's judgment surpassed all the terrors which men had caused him. 'Gentlemen,' said he to the noble F. de Thoire and others standing round him, 'my declarations were extorted from me only by the fear of torture. If I had died at that moment, I should have been eternally damned for my lies.' *

The bastard, not liking to feel himself within the same walls as his victim, had removed to St. Joire, two leagues from Thiez, and there attentively watched the examination and the torture. He had acquired a taste for it; and accordingly on the 5th of August he ordered another prisoner to be put to the question. 'I have some here who say plenty of good things,' he wrote to Geneva.† These 'good things' were the false witness extorted by pain and which permitted the imprisonment of the innocent. The terror increased in Geneva every day. People kept themselves indoors, the streets were deserted: a few laborers only could be seen in the fields. Bonivard, who feared, and not without cause, that the bishop and the duke wished to carry him off also, did not leave St. Victor's. 'Things are in such a state,' he said, 'that no one dares venture into the country lest he should be treated like Pécolat.' Many of the citizens quitted Geneva. One day two friends happened to meet in a room of the hostelry of St. Germain on the Jura. 'Where are you going?' asked one of them who had just come from Lyons. 'I am leaving Geneva,' answered the other, by name Du Bouchet. 'They have so tortured Pécolat that his arms remained hanging to the rope, and he died upon the rack.' Du Bouchet added: 'The Church not having the right of putting men to death, my lord of Geneva will have to send somebody to Rome to get him absolved. He weeps greatly about it, they say; but I place no trust in such crocodile's tears? . . . I am going to Lyons.' ‡

* Galiffe, *Matériaux*, &c. Interrog. de Pécolat, ii. pp. 77, 80.

† Ibid, ii. p. 275. Letters of Jean of Savoy.

‡ Ibid, p. 81.

The bishop had no notion of excusing himself to the pope: on the contrary, he thought only of pursuing his revenge. The *decoy* was in the cage and some small birds with him; he wished now at any cost to catch the large one,—Berthelier. Most of the youth of Geneva were either out of the way or disheartened; the league *Who touches one touches all* was nearly dissolved, at the moment when it ought to have been ready to save its founder. The bishop thought it superfluous to resort to stratagem or violence and simply required the syndics to surrender the great agitator to him. At eight o'clock in the evening of the 28th of July, 1517, the council was sitting, when the president who was on the bishop's side said: 'It is my lord's pleasure that we take up one of his subjects against whom he possesses sufficient informations which he will communicate in proper time and place; and that when the said subject is in prison, the syndics shall execute justice, if the affair requires it.' * At these words every one looked at a seat which was empty for the first time. Berthelier's friends were uneasy; and as the bishop had adopted a lawful course, the council answered the prelate that they would take up the accused, provided that on his part he maintained the liberties of Geneva.

As the councillors left the Hôtel de Ville in the dark, they said to one another: 'It is Berthelier.' The friends he had among them ran off to tell him the news, conjuring him to escape the vengeance of the prince by flight. Bonivard joined his entreaties to theirs: 'The sword is over your head,' he said.—'I know it,' answered Berthelier, 'yes, I know that I shall die, and I do not grieve at it.' 'Really,' said Bonivard, 'I never saw and never read of one who held life so cheap.' The friends of the noble-minded citizen redoubled their entreaties. They represented to him that there remained in Geneva only a small number of civic guards, imperfectly trained to arms; † that one part of the burgesses would assent through fear to the plots of the Savoyard party, and that another part would aid them.

* Public Registers of Geneva, MSS. *ad diem*.

† Bonivard, *Chroniq.* ii. p. 289.

Berthelier still resisted; 'God,' said he, 'will miraculously take away their power.'* His friends resorted to another argument. There happened to be just then in Geneva some envoys from Friburg; Berthelier's friends begged him to depart with them. 'Out of Geneva,' they said, 'you will serve the city better than within.' That consideration decided him. He went during the night to the hostelry of the Friburgers. 'We leave to-morrow,' they told him; 'here is a livery cloak with the arms of Friburg; put it on, and thus disguised you shall come with us, like one of the state riders. If you are not recognised at the gates of Geneva or in the Pays de Vaud, you are safe.' The Friburgers left the city very early: the guard looked at them for a moment as they passed the gate, but without suspecting that the great republican was with them. He was safe.

The next day the syndic Nergaz having delivered the message of the council to the bastard of Savoy, the latter was exasperated because instead of seizing Berthelier, they simply told him that they intended doing so. 'Do you mean to give him time to escape?' he asked. The council immediately ordered a great display of force to arrest the liberal leader. His friends the councillors, who knew him to be already far away in the country, let his enemies go on. 'Shut all the city gates,' said they. 'Assemble the tithing men and the tens; summon the vidame to assist in executing the laws; let the syndics preside in person over the search for the culprit.'† 'Bravo!' whispered some aside, 'shut the cage . . . the bird has flown.' The most zealous of the bishop's partisans hurried off to close the gates. The syndics and tithing men set out, followed by a great number of citizens, and all went towards Berthelier's house. They searched every chamber, they sounded every hiding-place, but found nobody. Some were angry, others laughed in their sleeves; the most violent, supposing he had escaped to one of his friends, put themselves at the head of the troop and searched every house that Berthelier was in the habit of frequenting. As a six days' search led to nothing,

* Bonivard, *Chroniq.* ii. p. 286.

† Registers of the Council of Geneva, MSS. 29th July, 1517.

they were forced to rest satisfied with summoning the accused by sound of the trnmpet. No one had any more doubts about his escape: the liberals were delighted, but anger and vexation prevailed at the castle.

CHAPTER IX.

BERTHELIER CALLS THE SWISS TO THE AID OF GENEVA HUGUENOTS AND MAMELUKES; THE BISHOP'S VIOLENCE.

Berthelier's flight was more than a flight. He went to Switzerland; and from that day Switzerland turned towards Geneva, and held out the hand to her.

Disguised in the livery of an usher of the city of Friburg, the faithful citizen arrived there without hindrance. No one there felt more affection for Geneva than Councillor Marty, governor of the hospital, who by his energy, rank, and intelligence, possessed great influence in the city. Berthelier went to his house, sat down at his hearth, and remained for some time sorrowful, silent, and motionless. It was thus that an illustrious Roman had formerly sat with veiled head at the hearth of a stranger; but Coriolanus sought among the Volsci the means of destroying his country, Berthelier sought at Friburg the means of saving his. A great idea, which had long since quickened in the hearts of himself and some other patriots, had occupied his mind while he was riding through the Vaudois territory. Times had changed. The long conspiracy of Savoy against Geneva was on the point of succeeding. The obstinate duke, the dishonored bishop, the crafty count—all united their forces to destroy the independence of the city. Switzerland alone, after God, could save it from the hands of the Savoyards. Geneva must become a canton, or at least an ally of Switzerland. 'For that,' said Berthelier, 'I would give my head.' He began to discourse familiarly with his host. He told him that he had arrived in Friburg, poor, exiled, persecuted, and a suppliant; not to save his life, but to save Geneva; that he had come to pray Friburg to receive the Genevans into citizenship. At the same time he described with eloquence the calamities of his country. Marty greatly moved held out his hand, told him to take courage and to follow him into the 'abbeys' where the guilds assembled. 'If you gain them,' he said, 'your cause is won.'

The Genevan and the Friburger immediately set off together to the chief of these 'abbeys' or clubs. They had scarcely entered the hall, when Marty in some confusion whispered into his companion's ear: 'Some of the duke's pensioners are here; veil your meaning, for fear they should stop our work.' Berthelier took the hint, and, rendered cautious by the presence of his enemies, spoke in ambiguous language, concealing his thoughts, but in such a manner that they might be guessed. He spoke of the wars that Burgundy had waged against Switzerland and of Charles the Bold; he intended thus to remind them of the war Savoy was now making upon Geneva and of Charles *the Good.* He hinted that the Swiss ought to distrust the Duke of Savoy, however smiling the face he showed them. Had they not spoiled his country during the Burgundian wars, and did they not still occupy a part of it? 'Your ancestors,' said Berthelier, 'have plundered and ravaged certain provinces—you know which—and in any case *others* do not forget it . . . If *somebody* should become master of Geneva, he would fortify it against you . . . but if Geneva became your ally, you could make it your rampart against all princes and potentates.' Every one knew of whom Berthelier was speaking. But if he saw the angry eye of some pensioner of Savoy fixed upon him, he became more guarded, his language more figurative and interrupted; he spoke lower, and 'as if at random,' said Bonivard. Then remembering Geneva, his courage revived, and his energetic accents burst forth again in the council of Friburg. He then forgot all prudence, and made, says the chronicler, a great *lament* of the oppression under which the city groaned. This speech, which aroused violent storms, was not to remain useless: Berthelier's eloquent words were fruitful thoughts, cast into the hearts of the people of Friburg. Like those seeds which, borne by the tempest, fall here and there among the Alps, they were destined one day to revive in Geneva the ancient tree of her liberties.*

The exile desired that the Friburgers should see the misfortunes of Geneva with their own eyes, and connect themselves with the principal men there. If Geneva and Friburg come together, he thought, the flame will break out and the union will be cemented. He attained his end. Some citizens of Friburg set off, arrived at Geneva, and were welcomed by Besançon, Hugues, Vandel, and all the patriots. They dined sometimes with one, sometimes with the other. They spoke of the liberties of the Swiss; they described their heroic struggles, and in these animated conversations, hearts were melted and united in such a way as to form but one. The deputies, having been received by the council, complained of the violation of the franchises of the city, and demanded a safe-conduct for Berthelier. Three councillors immediately set off for St. Joire, a village in the mountains, a few leagues from Geneva, where the bastard happened to be staying at a castle he possessed there. John did not like to be disturbed in his country retreats; he gave orders, however, that the magistrates should be admitted, when they set before him pretty plainly the complaints of the Friburgers. 'What! *I* violate the franchises!' he exclaimed, with a look of astonishment, 'I had never even thought of it. A safe-conduct for Berthelier . . . why, he does not require one. If he believes himself innocent, let him come; I am a good prince . . . No, no, no! No safe-conduct!' On the 12th of August the syndics communicated this answer to the Friburgers. The Swiss were indignant, and as if the syndics had some share in the matter, they upbraided them: 'Why even the Turks would not refuse a safe-conduct, and yet a bishop dares do it! A safe-conduct useless? . . . Was not Pécolat seized a few days ago beyond the bounds of the city? Did they not expose

* *Histoire de Genève*, by Pictet de Sergy, ii. p. 313. Bonivard, *Chroniq.* Spon, i. p. 287. Savyon, *Annales*, p. 58.

him to such torture that pain extorted from him all they wanted? Citizens have left the town in alarm; others are shut up in their houses. Are they not always bringing one or another into trouble? And yet the bishop refuses Berthelier a safe-conduct? . . . Very well! we will get together all these grievances and see them remedied. Rest assured of this . . . we will risk our persons and our goods. We will come in such force that we will take his Highness's governor in the Pays de Vaud, the friends of Savoy in your city, and then—we will treat them as you have treated our friends.'—Upon this they departed in great anger, say contemporary manuscripts.*

The language of the Friburgers, repeated from house to house, inflamed all hearts. The union between Geneva and Switzerland was, so to speak, accomplished before any public act had rendered it official and authentic. Berthelier had foreseen that Geneva would find in the Helvetic league a mightier protection than in that of the young men enrolled beneath the flag of dissipation.† From that moment a political party was slowly formed, a party calm but firm, which put itself at the head of the movement and replaced the licentious band of the 'children of Geneva.'

The Friburg deputies had hardly left the city, when the duke's party accosting the independent Genevans, and gallicising each in his own way the German word *Eidesgenossen* (confederates) which they could not pronounce, called after them *Eidguenots*, *Eignots*, *Eyguenots*, *Huguenots!* This word is met with in the chronicles of the time written in different ways;‡ Michel Roset, the most respectable of

* Public Registers of Geneva, *ad diem.* Bonivard, *Chroniq.* ii. p. 294.

† M. Mignet's Mémoire, p. 23.

‡ Bonivard places its origin in 1518, and writes *Eiguenots.* (*Chroniq.* ii. p. 331.) The Registers of the Council have it under the date of 3rd of May, 1520, and read *Eyguenots.* In 1521 we find in the trial of B. Toquet, *Ayguinocticæ sectæ.* (Galiffe, *Matériaux*, &c., ii. p. 164.) We come upon it later in 1526: *Traitre Eyguenot.* (Ibid. p. 506.) In the same year: *Tu es Eguenot.* (Ibid. p. 508.) Lastly, Michel Roset in his Chronicle (liv. i. ch. lxxxix.) generally writes *Huguenot.* In the sixteenth century as well as in the nineteenth nicknames have often passed from Geneva to France.

these authorities of the sixteenth century, writes *Huguenots;* we adopt that form, because it is the only one that has passed into our language. It is possible that the name of the citizen, Besançon Hugues, who became the principal leader of this party, may have contributed to the preference of this form over all the others. In any case it must be remembered that until after the Reformation this sobriquet had a purely political meaning, in no respect religious, and designated simply the friends of independence. Many years after, the enemies of the protestants of France called them by this name, wishing to stigmatise them, and impute to them a foreign, republican, and heretical origin. Such is the true etymology of the word; it would be very strange if these two denominations, which are really but one, had played so great a part in the sixteenth century, at Geneva and in French protestantism, without having had any connection with one another. A little later, about Christmas, 1518, when the cause of the alliance was more advanced, its use became more general. The adherents of the duke had no sooner started the nickname than their opponents, repaying them in their own coin, called out: 'Hold your tongues, you Mamelukes! . . . As the Mamelukes have denied Christ to follow Mahomet, so you deny liberty and the public cause to put yourselves under a tyranny.'* At the head of these Mamelukes were some forty rich tradesmen, men good enough at heart despite their nickname, but they were men of business who feared that disturbances would diminish their gains. The term Mamelukes put them into a great passion: 'Yes, continued the Huguenots, 'Sultan Selim conquered the Mamelukes last year in Egypt; but it seems that these slaves, when expelled from Cairo, took refuge at Geneva. However, if you do not like the name . . . stay, since you deliver up Geneva through avarice, we will call you Judases!'*

While the city was thus disturbed, the bishop, proud of having tortured the wretched Pécolat, removed from St.

* Bonivard, *Chroniq.* ii. p. 287. (Some MSS. of the sixteenth century read *Mamelus, Maumelus.*)

† Bonivard, *Chroniq.* ii. p. 888.

Joire to Thonon. He had never experienced to a like degree the pleasure of making his power felt, and was delighted at it; for though servile before the duke, he had in him some of the characteristics of the tyrant. He had made somebody tremble! . . . and he therefore regarded the trap laid for Pécolat as a glorious deed, and desired to enjoy his triumph in the capital of Chablais. At the same time he repeated to every one who would listen to him that he would not return to Geneva: 'They would murder me,' he said. The Genevans, conscientiously submissive to the established order, resolved to display their loyalty in a marked manner. There lived at that time in Geneva an old man, Pierre d'Orsières, respected by all parties, whose family possessed the lordship of that name in Valais, on the way to the St. Bernard pass. Forty years before (in 1477) he had been one of the hostages given to the Swiss; since then he had been six times elected chief magistrate of the State. His son Hugonin had been made a canon out of respect to his father; but he was a fanatical priest and in after days the most hostile of all the clergy to the Reformation. The council resolved to send a solemn deputation to the bishop, and placed the syndic d'Orsières at its head.

It was perhaps carrying rather far their desire to appear loyal subjects, and these good people of Geneva were to learn what it costs to flatter a tyrant. The bastard determined to gain fresh triumphs. Tormented by disease he needed diversion; the sufferings of his enemies made him feel a certain pleasure—it was sympathy after his fashion. He bore a mortal hatred against all the Genevans, even against the most catholic: an opportunity of gratifying it offered itself. The deputation having appeared before him and made every demonstration of respect, he fixed his bloodshot eyes upon the noble old man, whose hoary head bent humbly before him, and ordered him to be seized, to be taken out of his sight and thrown into a dungeon. If he had been proud of his exploits against Pécolat the hosier, he was more so now at having by one bold stroke put out of the way a man whose family shone in the first rank, and whom his fellow-citizens had invested with the sacred character of ambassador. When the news of this outrage reached Geneva, all the city (Huguenot and Mameluke) cried out. The man most respected in the whole State had been seized as a criminal at the very moment when he was giving the bishop proofs of the most loyal fidelity. They doubted not that this crime would be the signal of an attack upon the city; the citizens immediately ran to arms, stretched the chains across the streets, and shut the gates.*

The duke was displeased at these mistakes of the bishop, and they came upon him at a difficult moment. Charles III., a weak and fickle prince, inclined at that time to the emperor's side, and displeased his nephew Francis I., who seemed disposed to give him a roughish lesson. Moreover, the proceedings of the Friburgers disquieted him, for Geneva was lost to Savoy if the Swiss took up its cause. Liberty, hitherto driven back to the German Alps, would plant her standard in that city of the Leman, and raise a platform whence she would act upon all the populations speaking the French tongue. The most skilful politicians of Savoy—Seyssel who had just been appointed archbishop of Turin, and Eustace Chappuis who understood thoroughly the mutual relations of states, and whom Charles V. employed afterwards in his negotiations with Henry VIII.—represented to the duke that he must take care at any cost not to alienate the Swiss. The terrified Charles III. assented to everything, and Chappuis was authorised to patch up the blunders committed by the bishop.

This learned diplomatist saw clearly that the great business was, if possible, to raise an insurmountable barrier between the Swiss and the Genevans. He reflected on the means of effecting it: and resolving to show himself kind and good-natured, he set out for Geneva. By the duke's intervention he had been made official of the episcopal court; as such he was sworn in before the syndics; he then exerted all his skill to alienate the Genevans from the Swiss and attach them to the house of Savoy; but his fine words did not convert many. 'The duke,' said the prior of St.

* MS. Registers of the Council, 8th September, 1517.

Victor, 'seeing that his cats have caught no rats, sends us the sleekest of mousers.' Chappuis immediately set off for Friburg, where he began to *practise* on the pensioners. 'Ha!' said they, 'Berthelier is an instance of what the princes of Savoy can do.' The diplomatist stuck at nothing: he called upon the fugitive and entreated him to return to Geneva, promising him a pardon.—'A pardon!' exclaimed the haughty citizen, 'pardon does not concern good men but criminals. I demand absolution if I am innocent, and punishment if I am guilty.' *

Berthelier's firmness paralysed all the diplomatist's efforts; and it was decided that the duke himself should visit Switzerland. Making a pretence of business at Geneva and Lausanne, Charles III. arrived at Friburg and Berne. He endeavored to win over the cantons, induced them to dissuade the king of France from making war upon him, renewed his alliance with the League, and as they complained of the tyranny of his cousin the bishop, of the illegal arrest of Pécolat, and of Berthelier's exile, he made them all the fairest promises.†

But he reckoned without his host: the bishop who had a meaner character than the duke, had also a more obstinate temper. As his illustrious cousin had visited Switzerland, it was his duty to be there to receive him; he had accordingly returned to Geneva, and as some sensible men had made him understand how deeply he was compromised in D'Orsières' arrest, he set the good old man at liberty. If he consented to yield on this point, he was determined not to give way on others. When the syndics complained to him of the irregularities committed within the city and without, representing to him that citizens were arrested without cause, and that too, not by the officers of justice, but—a thing unprecedented—by his own archers, the prelate was deaf; he turned away his head, looked at what was going on around him, and dismissed the magistrates as politely as he could. Accordingly when the duke returned

* Bonivard, *Chroniq.* ii. pp. 294, 295. Registers of the Council of Geneva, 21st August, 1517. Spon, *Hist. de Genève*, i. p. 278.

† Ibid.

from Friburg, the syndics laid all their grievances before him: 'Our franchises are infringed by the bishop. A citizen cannot be arrested beyond our boundaries, yet Pécolat was seized at Pressinge. All criminal cases fall within the syndics' jurisdiction, yet Pécolat has been tried by the episcopal officers.' Whereupon the bishop and the duke, wishing to have the appearance of giving some little satisfaction to the Swiss and the Genevans, transferred Pécolat from his prison at Thiez to Geneva, and shut him up in the Château de l'Ile. But neither the duke nor the bishop dreamt of letting him go; would they ever have a better opportunity of showing the cardinals that the bishop's life was in danger? But if Pécolat should appear before the syndics, his judges, would he be condemned? The duke's friends shook their heads. 'One of them, the elder Lévrier, an incorrigible dotard,' they said, 'would sooner be put in prison, as in 1506, than give way; another, Richardet, a hot-headed fellow, would wax wroth, and perhaps draw his sword; and Porral, a wag like his elder brother, would turn his back and laugh at the Mamelukes!'

CHAPTER X.

FRESH TORTURES, PÉCOLAT'S DESPAIR AND STRIKING DELIVERANCE.

PÉCOLAT'S condemnation became the chief business of the court of Turin in its relations with Geneva. Archbishop Seyssel, who at that time possessed great influence, was not for despotism: he approved of moderating the royal authority, but hated republics, and wished to take advantage of Pécolat's trial to crush the spirit of liberty, which was displaying so much energy in Geneva, and which might spread farther. Feeling the importance of this case, in combating the Huguenot influence, the archbishop determined to withdraw, if possible, the Genevan from his natural judges, and resorted to a trick unworthy so great a statesman. He represented that high treason, the crime of which Pécolat was accused, was not one of those comprehended under the constitutions of the city, and that the cognisance belonged therefore to the prince; but he could not succeed. 'We have the power,' answered the syndics, 'to take cognisance of every criminal case.' All that Seyssel could obtain was that the bishop should appoint delegates who would sit in court and give their opinion, but not vote.*

The judges met in the Château de l'Ile on the 10th of November, 1517; they were surrounded by the duke's and the bishop's attorneys, the governor of Vaud, and other partisans of Savoy. Among the six councillors who were to sit with the syndics (the judges being thus ten in number), were some decided ducal partisans, upon whom the bishop could rely for a sentence of condemnation. Poor Pécolat, still suffering, was brought in by the vidame. The sight of the syndics—of the elder Lévrier, Richardet, and Porral—revived his courage: he knew that they were just men and enemies of episcopal despotism. 'The confessions I made at Thiez,' he said, 'were wrung from me by torture: the judge dictated the words and I repeated them after him. I knew that if I did not say what they wanted, they would break my arms, and maim me for ever.'†

After this declaration, the examination began: the clearness of Pécolat's answers, his gentleness and candor, showed all present that they had before them an innocent man, whom powerful princes desired to destroy. The syndics having declared that they were bound to acquit him, the bishop said: 'Give him the question, and you will see clearly that he is guilty.' The syndics refused, whereupon the two princes accused them of being partial and suspected men. The episcopal council, therefore, decided, that the

* Registers of the Council, 25th Sept., 30th Oct., 5th, 6th, 9th, 10th November, 1517. Spon, *Hist. de Genève*, i. p. 279. Savyon, *Annales*, p. 59. Bonivard, *Chroniq.* ii. p. 299.

† Galiffe, *Matériaux*, &c. Interrog. ii. pp. 75, 77, 88.

city and the bishop should each appoint four judges—an illegal measure, to which the syndics submitted.

The new examination ought to have taken place on the 20th of January, 1518; but Pécolat, suffering from the torture past and terrified by the torture to come, had fallen seriously ill, and it was necessary to send the doctor to him. This man consented to his being carried before the court. The four episcopal judges immediately called for the question, but the syndics opposed it, and the episcopal delegates began to study this living corpse. After examining him attentively they said: 'He still affords some hold for the torture; he may be examined with *a few torments*' (such is the expression in the report.) Nergaz siding with the Savoyard doctors, the torture was decided upon. Poor Pécolat began to tremble from head to foot; he knew that he should denounce all his friends, and cursed his own weakness. They tied his hands behind his back, they showed him the rack, and interrogated him . . . 'However, they did not torture him,' continues the report, 'considering the weakness of his body and his long imprisonment.' They thought that the fear of the rack would suffice to make him speak; they were deceived; the sick—we might almost call him the dying man, though tied up and bound, having the instrument of torture before him, answered with simplicity and frankness. Even the bishop's judges were struck with his candor, and two of them, 'having the fear of God before their eyes, says Bonivard, rather than the fear of men, declared *roundly*: 'They have done this poor man wrong, *Non invenimus in eo causam.* We find no fault in him.'*

This honorable declaration embarrassed the duke all the more that he had other anxieties on his mind. The news from Piedmont was bad: every day he received letters urging him to return. 'The Marquis of Montferrat,' they told him, 'is committing serious depredations.' But the headstrong prince was ready to lose his own states, if he could but get Geneva—and lose them he did not long after.

* MS. Registers of the Council, 24th December, 1517; 8th, 9th, 15th, 20th January, 1518. Savyon, *Annales*, p. 60. Bonivard, *Chroniq.* ii. p. 300.

Finding himself on the point of discovering a conspiracy, calculated to satisfy the cardinals, he resolved not to yield. His creatures and those of the prelate held conference after conference; at last they found a means—a diabolical means—of putting Pécolat to death. Seeing that lay judges were not to be persuaded to condemn an innocent man, they resolved that he should be tried by priests. To put this plan into execution, it was necessary to change the layman—the ex-hosier, the merry fellow who was at every banquet and every masquerade—into a churchman. They succeeded. 'To gratify their appetite,' said Bonivard, 'they produced a forged letter to the effect that Pécolat was an *ordained clerk* . . . and therefore his case belonged not to the secular, but to the ecclesiastical judge.' The fraud found, or seemed to find belief in the official world. 'Accordingly,' goes on the chronicle, 'they transferred him from the Château de l'Ile, which was the lay prison, to the bishop's palace which was the church court, and he was placed once more in the hands of the Pharisees.' This was a stroke worthy of a celebrated religious order not yet in existence, but which was about to be founded to combat the Reformation. Henceforth we shall see none of that silly consideration, of that delicate circumspection, which the laymen had employed. The bishop, now become judge and party, 'deliberated how to handle him well.' Some persons having asserted that Pécolat could not endure the rack, the doctors again examined his poor body: some said yes and others no, so the judges decided that the first were right, and the instrument of torture was prepared. It was not only heroic men like the Bertheliers and Lévriers, who, by their daring opposition to arbitrary power, were then raising the edifice of liberty; but it was also these wicked judges, these tyrannical princes, these cruel executioners, who by their wheel and rack were preparing the new and more equitable times of modern society.*

When Pécolat was informed of the fatal decision, his terrors recommenced. The prospect of a new torture, the

* Bonivard, *Chroniq.* ii. p. 300. Savyon, *Annales*, p. 60. MS. Archives of Geneva.

thought of the accusations he would make against his friends, disturbed his conscience and plunged him into despair . . . His features were distorted by it, his beard was in disorder, his eyes were haggard: all in him expressed suffering and terror. His keepers, not understanding this state of his mind, thought that he was possessed by a devil. 'Berthelier,' said they, 'is a great *charmer*, he has a familiar spirit. He has charmed Pécolat to render him insensible to the torture; try as we may, he will say nothing.' It was the belief at that time that the *charmers* lodged certain devils in the patients' hair. The prisoner's long rough beard disquieted the bishop's officers. It was resolved that Pécolat should be shaved in order to expel the demon.*

According to rule it should have been an exorcist and not a barber that they should have sent for. Robed in surplice and stole, the priest should have made the sign of the cross over Pécolat, sprinkled him with holy water, and pronounced loud-sounding anathemas against the evil spirit. But no, the bishop was contented to send a barber, which was much more prosaic; it may be that, besides all his other vices, the bastard was a freethinker. The barber came and got his razor ready. The devil whom Pécolat feared, was his own cowardice. 'I shall inculpate my best friends,' he said to himself; 'I shall confess that Berthelier wished to kill the bishop; I shall say all they want me to say. . . . And then if I die on the rack (which was very possible, considering the exhaustion of his strength) I shall be eternally damned for having lied in the hour of death.' This idea alarmed him; a tempest agitated his soul; he was already in agony. 'It is better,' he thought, 'to cut off an arm, a foot, or even the tongue, than fall into everlasting perdition.' At this moment the barber, who had wetted the beard, quitted the room to throw the water out of the basin; Pécolat caught up the razor which the man had left on the table by his side and raised it to his tongue; but moral and physical force both failing him, he made only a gash. He was trying again, when the barber

* Bonivard, *Chroniq.* ii. p. 202. Savyon, *Annales*, pp. 61, 62.

returned, sprang upon him in affright, snatched the razor from his hand, and raised an alarm. The gaoler, his family, and the prince's surgeon rushed in and found Pécolat 'coughing and spitting out blood in large quantities.' They seized him and began to stanch the blood, which it was not difficult to do. His tongue was not cut off, as some have asserted; there was only a deep wound. The officers of the duke and the bishop took extraordinary pains to cure him, 'not to do him good,' say the chronicles, 'but to do him a greater ill another time, and that he might use his tongue in singing whatever they pleased.' All were greatly astounded at this mystery, of which there was great talk throughout the city.* Pécolat's wound having been dressed, the bastard demanded that he should be put to the rack, but Lévrier, feeling convinced that Pécolat was the innocent victim of an illegal proceeding, opposed it. The bishop still persisted in the necessity of obtaining a confession from him: 'Confession!' replied the judge, 'he cannot speak.'—'Well then,' answered, not the executioner but, the bishop, 'let him *write* his answer.' Lévrier, as firm when it was necessary to maintain the respect due to humanity as the obedience due to the law, declared that such cruelty should not be practised before his tribunal. The bishop was forced to give way, but he kept account of this new offence on the part of the contumacious judge.†

All Geneva pitied the unhappy man, and asked if there was no one to deliver him from this den of thieves? Bonivard, a man who afterwards knew in his own person the horrors of a prison, never ceased thinking of the means of saving him. He loved Pécolat; he had often admired that simple nature of his, so impulsive, so strong and yet so weak, and above all his devotion to the cause of the liber-

* Bonivard, *Chroniq.* ii. pp. 301, 304. Roset, *Hist. de Genève,* MS. liv. i. ch. lxxxi. The testimony of these two contemporary authors leaves no doubt as to the reality of Pécolat's attempt. (See also Savyon, *Annales,* p. 61.) This circumstance has been the subject of a long archæological controversy, whose solution is simply this: Pécolat did not cut off, he only cut, his tongue.

† Lévrier, *Chronologie des Comtes de Genevois,* ii. p. 131.

ties of the city. He felt that human and divine rights, the compassion due to the unhappy, his duty towards Geneva, ('although I am not a native,' he said,)—all bound him to make an effort. He left his monastery, called upon Aimé Lévrier, and expressed his desire to save Pécolat. Lévrier explained to him that the bishop had forbidden any further steps, and that the judges could not act without his consent. 'There is however one means,' added he. 'Let Pécolat's relations demand justice of me; I shall refuse, alleging the prince's good pleasure. Then let them appeal, on the ground of denial of justice,* to the metropolitan court of Vienne.' Bonivard, full of imagination, of invention, of resources, heedless of precedents, and energetic, immediately resolved to try this course. The Archbishop of Vienne (he argued) being always jealous of the Bishop of Geneva, would be delighted to humble his powerful colleague. 'I have friends, relations, and influence in Savoy,' said he, 'I will move heaven and earth, and we will teach the bastard a pretty lesson.' He returned to his monastery and sent for Pécolat's two brothers. One of them, Stephen, enjoyed the full confidence of his fellow-citizens, and was afterwards raised to the highest offices; but the tyranny of the princes alarmed everybody: 'Demand that your brother be brought to trial,' said Bonivard to the two brothers.—'No,' they answered, 'the risk is too serious.' . . . Bonivard's eloquence prevailed at last. Not wishing to leave them time for reflection, he took them forthwith to Lévrier; the petition, answer, and legal appeal were duly made; and Stephen Pécolat, who by contact with these two generous souls had become brave, departed for Vienne in Dauphiny with a warm recommendation from the prior. The Church of Vienne had enjoyed from ancient times the title of holy, of *maxima sedes Galliarum*, and its metropolitan was primate of all Gaul. This prelate, delighted with the opportunity of making his authority felt by a bishop who was then more powerful than himself, summoned the procurator-fiscal, the episcopal council, and the bishop of Geneva to appear before

* 'A denegata justitia.'—Bonivard, *Chroniq.* ii. p. 306.

his court of Vienne within a certain term, to hear judgment. In the meanwhile he forbade the bishop to proceed against the prisoner under pain of excommunication. 'We are in the right road now,' said Bonivard to Lévrier. But who would serve this daring summons upon the bishop? These writs of Vienne were held in such slight esteem by the powerful prelates of Geneva, that it was usual to cudgel the bearers of them. It might be foreseen that the bishop and duke would try every means to nullify the citation, or induce the archbishop to recall it. In short, this was not an ordinary case. If Pécolat was declared innocent, if his depositions against Berthelier were declared false, what would become of the scheme of Charles III. and Leo X. at which the bishop himself so basely connived? Geneva would remain free. . . . The difficulties which started up did not dishearten Bonivard; he thought that the devices set on foot to enslave the city were hateful, and that as he wished to live and die there, he ought to defend it. 'And then,' adds a chronicler, 'the commander of St. Victor was more bold than wise.' Bonivard formed his resolution. 'Nobody,' he said, 'dares bell the cat . . . then I will attempt the deed.' . . . But his position did not permit him 'to pass the river alone.' It was necessary that the metropolitan citation should be served on the bishop by an episcopal bailiff. He began to search for such a man; and recollecting a certain poor clerk who vegetated in a wretched room in the city, he sent for him, put two crowns in his hand, and said: 'Here is a letter from the metropolitan that must be delivered to the bishop. The duke and the prelate set out the day after to-morrow for Turin; to-morrow morning they will go and hear mass at St. Pierre; that will be the latest hour. There will be no time after that. Hand this paper to my lord.' The clerk was afraid, though the two crowns tempted him strongly; Bonivard pressed him: 'Well,' said the poor fellow,' 'I will promise to serve the writ provided you assist me personally.' Bonivard agreed to do so.

The next day the prior and the clerk entered the cathedral. The princes were present, surrounded with much pomp: it was high mass, a farewell mass; nobody was absent. Bonivard in his quality of canon had a place of honor in the cathedral which would have brought him near the bishop; but he took care not to go there, and kept himself at a distance behind the clerk in order to watch him; he feared lest the poor man should get frightened and escape. The consecration, the elevation, the chanting, all the sumptuous forms of Roman worship, all the great people bending before the altar, acted upon the unlucky bailiff's imagination. He began to tremble, and when the mass was ended and the moment for action arrived, 'seeing,' says Bonivard, 'that the game was to be played in earnest,' he lost his courage, stealthily crept backwards, and prepared to run away. But Bonivard, who was watching him, suddenly stepped forward, seized him by the collar, and placing the other hand upon a dagger, which he held beneath his robe, whispered in his ear: 'If you do not keep your promise, I swear I will kill you.' The clerk was almost frightened to death, and not without cause, 'for,' adds Bonivard in his plain-spoken 'Chronicles,' 'I should have done it, which I do not say to my praise; I know now that I acted foolishly. But youth and affection carried me away.' He did not kill the clerk, however; he was satisfied with holding him tightly by the thumb, and with a firm hand held him by his side. The poor terrified man wished in vain to fly: Bonivard's dagger kept him motionless; he was like a marble statue.*

Meanwhile the duke, his brother the count, and the bishop were leaving the church, attended by their magnificent retinue, and returning to the episcopal palace, where there was to be a grand reception. 'Now,' said Bonivard to the clerk, 'no more delay, you must discharge your commission;' then he put the metropolitan citation into the hand that was free, and still holding him by the thumb, led him thus to the palace.

When he came near the bishop, the energetic prior letting go the thumb, which he had held as if in a vice, and pointing to the prelate, said to the clerk: 'Do your duty.' The

* Bonivard, *Chroniq.* pp. 307, 308.

bishop hearing these words, 'was much afraid,' says Bonivard, 'and turned pale, thinking I was ordering him to be killed.' The cowardly prelate turning with alarm towards the supposed assassin cast a look of distress upon those around him. The clerk trembled as much as he; but meeting the terrible eye of the prior and seeing the dagger under his robes, he fell on his knees before the bishop, and kissing the writ, presented it to him, saying: 'My lord, *inhibitur vobis, prout in copia.*'* He then put the document into his hand and ran off: 'Upon this,' adds the prior, 'I retired to my priory of St. Victor. I felt such juvenile and silly arrogance, that I feared neither bishop nor duke.' Bonivard had his culverins no longer, but he would yet have stood a siege if necessary to bring this matter to a successful issue. The bishop never forgot the fright Bonivard had caused him, and swore to be even with him.

This energetic action gave courage to others. Fourscore citizens more or less implicated with Pécolat in the affair of the rotten fish—'all honest people'—appeared before the princes, and demanded that if they and Pécolat were guilty, they should be punished; but if they were innocent that it should be publicly acknowledged. The princes, whose situation was growing difficult, were by no means eager to have eighty cases in hand instead of one. 'We are sure,' they answered, 'that this poisoning is a thing invented by certain wicked men, and we look upon all of you as honest people. But as for Pécolat, he was always a naughty fellow; for which reason we wish to keep him a short time in prison to correct him.' Then fearing lest he should be liberated by force during their absence, the princes of Savoy had him transferred to the castle of Peney, which was contrary to the franchises of the city. The transfer took place on the 29th of January, 1518.†

A division in the Church came to Pécolat's assistance. Since the struggles between Victor and Polycrat in the second century, between Cyprian and Stephen in the third, dissensions between the Catholic bishops have never ceased;

* 'You are inhibited, as in the copy.'—Bonivard, *Chroniq.* ii. p. 309.

† Galiffe, Bonivard, Council Registers.

and in the middle ages particularly, there were often severe contests between the bishops and their metropolitans. The Archbishop of Vienne did not understand yielding to the Bishop of Geneva, and at the very moment when Luther's Theses were resounding throughout christendom—in 1517 and 1518—the Roman Church on the banks of the Rhone was giving a poor illustration of its pretended unity. The metropolitan, finding his citations useless, ordered the bishop to liberate Pécolat, under pain of excommunication;* but the episcopal officers who remained in Geneva, only laughed, like their master, at the metropolitan and his threats.

Pécolat's friends took the matter more seriously. They feared for his life. Who could tell whether the bastard had not left orders to get rid of the prisoner, and left Geneva in order to escape the people's anger? These apprehensions were not without cause, for more than one upright man was afterwards to be sacrificed in the castle of Peney. Stephen Pécolat and some of his brother's friends waited on St. Victor: 'The superior metropolitan authority has ordered Pécolat to be released,' they said; 'we shall go off straight in search of him.' The acute Bonivard represented to them that the gaolers would not give him up, that the castle was strong, and they would fail in the attack; that the whole people should demand the liberation of the innocent man detained by the bishop in his dungeons, in despite of the liberties of the city and the orders of his metropolitan. 'A little patience,' he continued; 'we are near the beginning of Lent, holy week is not far off; the interdict will then be published by the metropolitan. The christians finding themselves deprived of the sacrament will grow riotous, and will compel the bishop's officers to set our friend at liberty. Thus the inhibition which we served upon the bishop in his palace, will produce its effect in despite of him.' The advice was thought sound, they agreed to it, and everybody in Geneva waited with impatience for Easter and the excommunication.

Anthony de la Colombière, official to the metropolitan of

* 'Mandamus relaxari sub pœna excommunicationis.'—Savyon, *Annales*, p. 63.

Vienne, arrived to execute the orders of his superior, and having come to an understanding with the prior of St. Victor and judge Lévrier, he ordered, on the 18th of March, that Pécolat should be released within twenty-four hours. He waited eight days, but waited in vain, for the episcopal officers continued to disobey him. Then, on Good Friday, the metropolitan officers, bearing the sentence of excommunication and interdict, proceeded to the cathedral at two o'clock in the afternoon, and there, in the presence of John Gallatin, notary, and three other witnesses, they posted up the terrible monition; at four o'clock they did the same at the churches of St. Gervais and St. Germain. This was not indeed the thunder of the Vatican, but it was nevertheless the excommunication of a prelate who, at Geneva, filled the first place after the pope in the Roman hierarchy. The canons, priests, and parishioners, as they went to evening prayers, walked up to the placards and were quite aghast as they read them. 'We excommunicate,' they ran, 'the episcopal officers, and order that this excommunication be published in the churches, with bell, book, and candle. Moreover, we command, under pain of the same excommunication, the syndics and councillors to attack the castles and prisons wherein Pécolat is detained, and to liberate him by force. Finally we pronounce the interdict against all places wherein these excommunicates are found. And if, like the deaf adder, they persist in their wickedness, we interdict the celebration not only of the sacraments, but also of divine service, in the churches of St. Pierre, Notre Dame la Neuve, St. Germain, St. Gervais, St. Victor, St. Leger, and Holy Cross.'* After the canons and priests had read this document, they halted in consternation at the threshold of the church. They looked at one another, and asked what was to be done. Having well considered, they said: 'Here 's a barrier we cannot get over,' and they retired.

As the number of devout catholics was still pretty large in Geneva, what Bonivard had foreseen came to pass; and the agitation was general. No more services, no more

* Galiffe, *Matériaux*, &c., ii. p. 91.

masses, no baptisms, no marriages . . . divine worship suspended, the cross hidden, the altars stripped.* . . . What was to be done? The chapter was sitting, and several citizens appeared before them in great irritation. 'It is you,' they said to the terrified canons, 'that are the cause of all this.' . . . Nor was this all. The excommunicates of the Savoyard parishes of the diocese used to come every year at the approach of Easter and petition the bishop's official for letters of *consentment*, in order that their parish priests might give them the *communion*. 'Now of such folks there chanced to be a great number at Geneva. Heyday, they said, it is of no use putting one obstacle aside, when another starts up immediately, all owing to the fault of these episcopal officers!' . . . The exasperated Savoyards united with the Genevans, and the agitated crowd assembled in front of the cathedral gates; the men murmured, the women wept, even priests joined the laity. Loud shouts were heard ere long. The people's patience was exhausted; they took part against their bishop. 'To the Rhone,' cried the devout, 'to the Rhone with the traitors! the villains who prevent us from receiving our Lord!' The excommunicated episcopal officers had a narrow escape from drowning. All the diocese fancied itself excommunicated, and accordingly the confusion extended beyond the city. The syndics came up and entreated the citizens to be calm; and then, going to the episcopal council, the bishop being still absent, they said: 'Release Pécolat, or we cannot protect you against the anger of the people.' The episcopal officers seeing the bishop and the duke on one side, the metropolitan and the people on the other, and impelled in contrary directions, knew not whom to obey. It was reported to them that all the city was in an uproar, that the most devout catholics wished at any cost to communicate on Easter Sunday, and that looking upon them as the only obstacle which prevented their receiving the host, they had determined to throw them over the bridge. 'The first of you that comes out shall go over,' cried the crowd. They were

* 'Altaria nudentur, cruces abscondantur.'

seized with great alarm, and fancying themselves half drowned already, wrote to the governor of Peney to release Pécolat forthwith. The messenger departed, and the friends and relations of the prisoner, not trusting to the episcopal court, accompanied him. During the three-quarters of an hour that the walk occupied, the crowd kept saying :—suppose the governor should refuse to give up his victim ; suppose the bastard's agents have already carried him away—perhaps put him to death ? None of these suppositions were realised. Deep in a dungeon of the castle, the poor man, heavily chained, in utter darkness, wrecked both in mind and body, was giving way to the blackest melancholy. Suddenly he hears a noise. He listens ; he seems to recognise well-known voices : it was his brothers and his friends arriving noisily under the walls of the castle, and giving utterance to their joy.

Their success was, however, less certain than it appeared to them. Strange things were, in fact, taking place at that moment in Geneva. The bishop and the duke had not been so passive as had been imagined, and at the very instant when the messenger bearing the order from the episcopal court, and accompanied by a body of Genevans, was leaving by the French gate, a courier, with an order from the Roman court, entered by the Savoy gate. The latter went with all speed to the bishop's representatives, and handed them the pontifical letters which the princes had obtained, and by which the pope *annulled the censures of the metropolitan.* This Roman messenger brought in addition an order from the bishop forbidding them *on their lives* to release Pécolat. The bastard had shuddered at the thought that the wretch whom he had so successfully tortured, might escape him : he had moved heaven and earth to keep him in prison. We may imagine the emotion and alarm which fell upon the episcopal councillors when they read the letters handed to them. The coincidence of the moment when these two contradictory orders left Geneva and arrived there is so striking, that we may ask whether these letters from Rome and Turin were not supposed—invented by the episcopal officers themselves ; but there is nothing in the narrative to indicate a trick. '*Immediately* on reading the letters, the episcopal officers *with all diligence* countermanded the release.' These words in the 'Annals' show the precipitation with which they endeavored to repair the mistake they had committed. There was not, in fact, a moment to lose, if they wished to keep Pécolat. Several officers got on horseback and set off full gallop.

The bearers of this order were hardly halfway, when they met a numerous jubilant and noisy crowd returning from Peney. The friends of Pécolat, preceded by the official letters addressed to the governor, had appeared before that officer, who, after reading the despatch over and over, had thought it his duty to obey. Pécolat's friends hurried after the gaoler, who, carrying a bunch of keys in his hand, went to open the cell; they entered with him, shouting release! They broke the prisoner's chains; and, finding him so weak, carried him in their arms and laid him in the sunshine in the castle yard. Without loss of time they placed him in a peasant's cart and all started for Geneva. This was the crowd met by the episcopal officers. The Genevans were bringing back their friend with shouts of joy. In vain did the episcopal officers stop this joyous band, and require that the prisoner should be led back to Peney; in vain did they speak of the bishop and even of the pope; all was of no use. Despite the *rogations* of the pope, the prelate, and the messengers, the people carried Pécolat back in triumph. This resistance offered to the Roman pontiff, at the moment he was lending assistance to the bastard in his oppression of a poor innocent man, was, as it were, an affair of outposts; and the Genevans were thus training themselves for more notable battles. 'Forward,' they shouted, 'to the city! to the city!' and the crowd, leaving the episcopal officers alone in the middle of the road, hastened to the gates.

At last they approached Geneva, and there the excitement was not less great than on the road. Pécolat's return was the triumph of right over injustice, of liberty over despotism; and accordingly it was celebrated with enthusiasm. The poor man, dumb (for his wound was not yet healed), shattered by the torture, and wasted away by his long captivity, looked silently on all around him, and experienced an emotion he could hardly contain. After such trials he was returning into the old city amid the joyous cries of the population. However, his friends did not forget the orders of the pope and the bishop; and fearing lest the vidame should again seize the poor fellow, they took him to the convent of the Grey Friars of Rive, an asylum reputed inviolable, and quartered him in the cell of his brother, the monk Yvonnet. There the poor invalid received all the affectionate attendance he required; he remained some time without saying much; but at last he recovered his speech, 'by the intercession of *a saint*,' said the priests and Pécolat himself, as it would appear. Was it devoutly or jestingly that he spoke of this pretended miraculous cure? We shall not decide. Bonivard, who perhaps no longer believed in the miracles of saints, assigns another reason: 'The surgeon dressed the wound in his tongue;' and he adds: 'He always stuttered a little.' If Bonivard had doubts about the saints, he believed in the sovereign justice of God: 'Then came to pass a thing,' he said, 'which should not be forgotten; all the judges who condemned Pécolat to be tortured died this year, one after another, which we cannot suppose to have happened except as a *divine punishment*.'

The remembrance of Pécolat's torture long remained in the memory of the citizens of Geneva, and contributed to make them reject the rule of the Romish bishops.* In fact the interest felt for this victim of episcopal cruelty was manifested in every way. The cell of brother Yvonnet, in the Grey Friars' convent, was never empty; everybody wished to see the bishop's victim. The prior of St. Victor was one of the first to come, attended by several friends. The poor man, being tongue-tied, told 'the mystery of his sufferings with his fingers,' says Bonivard. It was long since there had been such an interesting sight in Geneva. The citizens, standing or sitting around him, could not turn their eyes away from his thin pale face. By his gestures

* Bonivard, *Chroniq.* ii. pp. 310, 315, 316. Savyon, *Annales*, p. 65. Spon, *Hist. de Genève*, i. p. 286. Roset MSS.

and attitudes Pécolat described the scenes of the examination, the torture, and the razor, and in the midst of these remembrances which made the tears come to his eyes, he from time to time indulged in a joke. The young men of Geneva looked at each other and trembled with indignation . . . and then sometimes they laughed, at which the episcopal officers 'were terribly enraged.' The latter were in truth both vexed and angry. What! they receive an order from the bishop, an order from the pope, and only a few minutes before they have issued a contrary order! Strange mishap! Not knowing whom to blame, they imprisoned the governor, who had only released Pécolat by their command, and to cover their responsibility were actually planning to put him to death.

Some timid and alarmed citizens dared not go and see Pécolat; one of these was Blanchet, the friend of Andrew Navis, who had been present at the famous meeting at the Molard and the *momon* supper, and who, falling not long after beneath the bishop's violence, was doomed to expiate his errors by a most cruel death. Blanchet is the type of a character frequent at this epoch. Having learnt, shortly after the famous *momon* banquet, that a certain individual whose name even he did not know, but who, he said, 'had given him the lie to his face,' was in Burgundy, Blanchet set off after him, gave him a box on the ears, and returned. He came back to Geneva, thence he went into Faucigny, and afterwards to Italy; he took part in the war between the pope and the Duke of Urbino (who so terribly frightened Leo X.); returned to Pavia, thence to Turin, and finally to Geneva. His cousin Peter, who lived in Turin, had told him that during his travels Pécolat had been arrested for plotting against the bishop. 'I shall not go and see him,' he said, 'for fear of compromising myself.' In spite of his excessive precaution, he could not finally escape the barbarous vengeance of the prelate.*

* Bonivard, *Chroniq.* ii. pp. 316, 317. Galiffe, *Matériaux*, &c., ii. pp. 196, 197.

CHAPTER XI.

BERTHELIER TRIED AT GENEVA; BLANCHET AND NAVIS SEIZED AT TURIN; BONIVARD SCANDALISED AT ROME.

(1518.)

No one embraced Pécolat with so much joy as Berthelier, who had returned to Geneva within these few days. In fact the duke, desirous to please the Swiss by any means, had given him, and also made the bishop give him, a safe-conduct which, bearing date February 24, 1518, extended to Whitsunday, May 23, in the same year. The favor shown the republican hero was not great, for permission was granted him to return to Geneva *to stand his trial;* and the friends of the prelate hoped that he would not only be tried, but condemned and put to death. Notwithstanding these forebodings, Berthelier, a man of spirit and firm in his designs, was returning to his city to accomplish the work he had prepared in Switzerland: namely, the alliance of Geneva with the cantons. He had taken great trouble about it during his residence among the confederates. He was seen continually 'visiting, eating, drinking in the houses of his friends or at the guilds (called abbeys), talking with the townsfolk, and proving to them that this alliance would be of great use to all the country of the League.' Berthelier was then full of hope; Geneva was showing herself worthy of liberty; there was an energetic movement towards independence; the people were wearied of the tyranny of princes. Free voices were heard in the general council. 'No one can serve two masters,' said some patriots. 'The man who holds any pension or employment from a prince, or has taken an oath to other authorities than the republic, ought not to be elected either syndic or councillor.' This resolution was carried by a large majority. And better still, the citizens chose for syndics three men capable of guarding the franchises of the community; they were Ramel, Vandel, and Besançon Hugues. A mameluke, 'considering the great credit of the party,' had also been elected, but only one, Montyon; he was the premier syndic.*

Whilst the patriots were thus making efforts to save the independence of the city, the duke, the bishop, the count, Archbishop Seyssel, and other councillors, meeting at Turin, were pursuing contrary schemes. Would they succeed? Seyssel, the illustrious author of the *Grande Monarchie*, might tell them that in the eleventh and twelfth centuries, in France, Burgundy, and Flanders, the bishop and the lay lord had combined against the liberties of the towns, and aided by arms and anathemas had maintained a war against the communes which had ended in the destruction of the rights and franchises of the citizens. Then the night was indeed dark in the social world. At Geneva, these rights existed still: you could see a flickering light glimmering feebly in the midst of the darkness. But would not the bishop and the duke succeed in extinguishing it? If so, despotism would hold all Europe under its cruel hand, as in the Mahometan and other countries of the world. Why should the operation carried through at Cambray, Noyon, St. Quentin, Laon, Amiens, Soissons, Sens, and Rheims, fail on the shores of the Leman? There was indeed a reason for it, but they did not take it into account. We do not find this reason—at least not alone—in the fact that the heroes of liberty were more intrepid at Geneva than elsewhere. The enfranchisement was to come from a higher source: God then brought forth light and liberty. The middle ages were ending, modern times were beginning. The princes and bishops of Roman Catholicism, in close alliance, had everywhere reduced to ashes the edifice of communal liberties. But in the midst of these ashes some embers were found which, kindled again by fire from heaven, lighted up once more in the world the torch of

* Council Registers of 7th February, 1518. Savyon *Annales*, p. 66. Bonivard, *Chroniq.* ii. p. 311.

lawful liberty. Geneva was the obstacle to the definite annihilation of the popular franchises, and in Geneva the strength of the obstacle was Berthelier. No wonder then that the Savoyard princes agreed that in order to check the triumph of the spirit of independence, it was absolutely necessary to get rid of this proud, energetic, and unyielding citizen. They began to prepare the execution of their frightful project. A strange blindness is that which imagines that by removing a man from the world it is possible to thwart the designs of God!

Berthelier calm because he was innocent, provided besides with an episcopal safe-conduct, had appeared before the syndics to be tried. The duke and the bishop had given orders to their agents, the vidame Conseil and Peter Navis, the procurator-fiscal, to manage his condemnation. The trial began: 'You are charged,' said these two magistrates, 'with having taken part in the riotous amusements of the young men of Geneva.'—'I desired,' answered Berthelier frankly, 'to keep up the good-will of those who were contending for liberty against the usurpations of tyrants.' The justification was worse than the charge. 'Let us seize him by the throat, as if he were a wolf,' said the two judges. 'You have conspired,' they continued, 'against the life of the prince-bishop,' and they handed in Pécolat's depositions as proof. 'All lies,' said Berthelier coldly, 'lies extorted by the rack and retracted afterwards.' Navis then produced the declarations of the traitor Carmentrant, who, as we have seen at the *momon* supper, undertook the office of informer. 'Carmentrant!' contemptuously exclaimed the accused, 'one of the bishop's servants, coming and going to the palace every day, eating, drinking, and making merry . . . a pretty witness indeed! The bishop has prevailed upon him, by paying him well, to suffer himself to be sent to prison, so that he may sing out against me whatever they prompt him with . . . Carmentrant boasts of it himself!' When they sent the report to the bishop, he perceived, on reading it, that this examination, instead of demonstrating the guilt of the accused, only revealed the iniquity of the accuser; the alarmed prelate therefore wrote to the vidame and Navis to 'use every imaginable precaution.' It was necessary to destroy Berthelier without compromising the bishop.

Navis was the man for that. Of a wily and malicious character, he understood nothing about the liberties of Geneva; but he was a skilful and a crafty lawyer. 'He so mixes retail truth with wholesale falsehood,' people said, 'that he makes you believe the whole lump is true. If any iniquity of the bishop's is discovered, straight he cuts a plug to stop the hole. He is continually forging new counts, and calling for adjournments.' Navis, finding himself at the end of his resources, began to turn and twist the safe-conduct every way: it expressly forbade the detention of Berthelier's person. That mattered not. 'I demand that Berthelier be arrested,' he said, 'and be examined in custody; for the safe-conduct, if you weigh it well, is not opposed to this.'* —'The first of virtues,' said Berthelier, 'is to keep your promise.' Navis, little touched by this morality, resolved to obtain his request by dint of importunity; the next day he required that 'Berthelier should be shut up closely in prison;' on the 20th of April, he moved that 'he should be incarcerated;' and on the following day he made the same request; about the end of May he demanded, on two different occasions, not only that 'the noble citizen should be arrested but tortured also.' . . . All these unjust prayers were refused by the court.† Navis, being embarrassed and irritated, multiplied his accusations; his plaint was like an overflowing torrent: 'The accused,' he said, 'is a brawler, fighter, promoter of quarrels, illegal meetings, and seditions, rebellious to the prince and his officers, accustomed to carry out his threats, a debaucher of the young men of the city, and all without ever having been corrected of his faults and excesses.'—'I confess that I am not corrected of these faults,' answered Berthelier with disdain, 'because I never was guilty of them.'‡ It was determined to associate with the

* 'Si bene ruminetur.'—Galiffe, *Matériaux*, &c. Berthelier documents, ii. p. 105.

† Galiffe, *Matériaux*, &c. Berthelier papers, ii. pp. 113, 114, 116, 125, 132.

‡ Galiffe, *Matériaux*, &c. Berthelier papers, ii. pp. 124, 125.

syndics some commissioners devoted to the bishop ; but the syndics replied that this would be contrary to law. The vidame and Navis, not knowing what to do next, wrote to the duke and the prelate to find some good grievances. 'You shall have them,' they answered ; 'we have certain witnesses to examine here, this side the mountains.' . . . Who were these witnesses ? Navis little imagined that one of them was his own son, and that the inquiry would end in a catastrophe that would extort from him a cry of anguish. Let us now see what was going on at Turin.*

Blanchet, disgusted with his condition since he had been to the wars, cared little for Geneva. During his sojourn at Turin, in the house of the magnificent lord of Meximieux, the splendor of the establishment had dazzled him. His love for liberty had cooled down, his taste for the luxuries and comforts of life had increased. 'I will seek patrons and fortune,' he often repeated. With this object he returned from Geneva to Turin. It was the moment when the bishop was on the watch to catch one of the 'children of Geneva.' Blanchet was seized and thrown into prison ; and that was not all.†

Andrew Navis, who, since the affair of the mule, had led a more regular life, was dreadfully weary of his father's office. One Sunday, M. de Vernier gave his friends a splendid breakfast, to which Navis and Blanchet had been invited. Andrew was never tired of hearing 'the wanderer' talk about Italy, its delightful landscapes, the mildness of its climate, its fruits, monuments, pictures, concerts, theatres, beautiful women, and of the war between the pope and the Duke of Urbino. A desire to cross the Alps took possession of Andrew. 'As soon as there is any rumor at Geneva of a foreign war,' he said, 'some of my companions hasten to it : why should I not do the same ?' The Duke of Urbino, proud of the secret support of France, was at that time a cause of great alarm to Leo X. An open war against a pope tempted Navis. The vices from which he suffered were not those base errors which nullify a man ; but those

* Ibid. p. 133. Bonivard, *Chroniq.* ii. pp. 311–318.

† Galiffe, *Matériaux*, &c. Blanchet's Exam. ii. p. 197, &c.

ardent faults, those energetic movements which leave some hope of conversion. Leaning on his father's desk, disgusted with the pettifogging business, he felt the need of a more active life. An opportunity presented itself. A woman named Georgia with whom he had formerly held guilty intercourse, having to go to Turin, to join a man who was not her husband, asked Andrew to be her escort, promising him 'a merry time of it.' Navis made up his mind, and without his father's knowledge left Geneva and his friends, and reached Turin at noon of Saturday, the 8th of May. One Gabriel Gervais, a Genevan, was waiting for him: 'Be on your guard,' he said; 'Blanchet has been taken up for some misunderstandings with the bishop.' The son of the procurator-fiscal thought he had nothing to fear. But on the morrow, about six o'clock in the evening, the same Gabriel Gervais came and told him hastily: 'They are going to arrest you: make your escape.' Andrew started off directly, but was caught as he was about to leave the city and taken to the castle.*

The bishop and the duke wished, by arresting these young Genevans, to punish their independent spirit, and above all to extort from them confessions of a nature to procure the condemnation of Berthelier and other patriots. On the 26th of April the bishop of Geneva had issued his warrant to all the ducal officers, and, in his quality of peaceful churchman, had concluded with these words: 'We protest we have no desire, so far as in us lies, that any penalty of blood or death should result, or any mutilation of limbs, or other thing that may give rise to any irregularity.'† We shall see with what care the bishop avoided *mutilation of limbs*. The duke issued his warrant the same day.

Blanchet's examination began on the 3rd of May in the court of the castle of Turin. He believed himself accused of an attempt upon the life of the bishop, and doubted not that torture and perhaps a cruel death were reserved for

* Galiffe, *Matériaux*, &c., ii. pp. 169, 171, 177, 179. Savyon, *Annales*. Bonivard, *Chroniq.* ii. p. 320. Roset and Gautier MSS.

† 'Ex qua possit contrahi irregularitas.'—Galiffe, *Matériaux*, &c., ii. p. 166.

him ; accordingly this young man, of amiable but weak disposition, became a prey to the blackest melancholy. On the 5th of May, having been brought back to the court of the castle, he turned to the lieutenant De Bresse, who assisted the procurator-fiscal, and without waiting to be interrogated, he said : 'I am innocent of the crime of which I am accused.'—'And of what are you accused?' said the lieutenant. Blanchet made no answer, but burst into tears. The procurator-fiscal then commenced the examination, and Blanchet began to cry again. On being skilfully questioned, he allowed himself to be surprised, and made several depositions against Berthelier and the other patriots ; then perceiving his folly, he stopped short and exclaimed with many groans : 'I shall never dare return to Geneva ! my comrades would kill me . . . I implore the mercy of my lord duke.' Poor Blanchet moved even his judges to pity. Navis, when led before the same tribunal on the 10th of May, did not weep. 'Who are you?' they asked. 'I am from Geneva,' he replied, 'scrivener, notary, a gentleman's son, and twenty-eight years old.' The examination was not long. The bishop, who was then at Pignerol, desired to have the prisoners in his own hand, as he had once held Pécolat ; they were accordingly removed thither.*

On the 14th, 15th, and 21st of May, Navis and Blanchet were brought into the great hall of the castle before the magnificent John of Lucerne, collateral of the council, and Messire d'Ancina. 'Speak as we desire you,' said the collateral, 'and then you will be in his Highness's good graces.' As they did not utter a word, they were at first threatened with two turns of the cord, and that not being sufficient, they were put to the rack ; they were fastened to the rope, and raised an arm's length from the floor. Navis was in agony ; but instead of inculpating Berthelier, he accused himself. The commandment which says : 'Honor thy father and thy mother,' was continually in his mind, and he felt that it was in consequence of breaking it, that he had fallen into dissipation and disgrace. 'Alas !' said he, when

* Galiffe, *Matériaux*, &c., ii. pp. 95, 168, 196, 199, 202.

put to the question, 'I have been a vagabond, disobedient to my father, roaming here and there, squandering my own and my father's money in taverns . . . Alas! I have not been dutiful to my parents . . . If I had been obedient, I should not have suffered as I do to-day.' On the 10th of June, says the report, he was again put to the torture and pulled up the height of an ell. After remaining there a moment, Navis begged to be let down, promising to tell everything. Then sitting on a bench, he accused himself bitterly of the crime of which he felt himself guilty; he confessed . . . to having *disobeyed his parents.** Peter Navis was a passionate judge in the opinion of many; Andrew saw only the father in him; and contempt of paternal authority was the great sin that agonised the wretched young man. Looking into himself, foreseeing the fatal issue of the trial, he did not give way, like Blanchet, to the fear of death, but bewailed his faults. Family recollections were aroused in his heart, the most sacred of bonds recovered their strength, and the image of his father followed him night and day.

The bishop had got thus far in his prosecutions when he learnt that Bonivard had just passed through Turin on his way to Rome. Delighted at seeing the prior of St. Victor fall into his net, the prelate gave orders to seize him on his return. Was it not Bonivard who had caused him such alarm in the palace on the occasion of the metropolitan summons? Was it not this man who had robbed him of Pécolat, and who even aspired to sit some day on his episcopal throne? . . . It is the nature of certain animals to carry their prey into their dens to devour it. The bastard of Savoy had already dragged Navis and Blanchet into his dungeons, and was preparing to mutilate their limbs; but it would be much better still if he could catch and rend the hated Bonivard with his claws.†

The latter so little suspected the impending danger, that he had come into Italy to solicit the prelate's inheritance.

* Galiffe, *Matériaux*, &c. Interrog. ii. pp. 162, 168, 179, 180, 185, 186, 205.

† Bonivard, *Chroniq.* ii. p. 320.

It was evident that the sickly bastard had not long to live. 'I will go to Rome,' said Bonivard to his friends, 'to obtain the bishop's benefices by means of a *cardination*' (an intrigue of cardinals).* He desired eagerly to be bishop and prince of Geneva; had he succeeded, his liberal catholicism would perhaps have sufficed for the citizens, and prevented the Reformation. Bonivard reached Rome without any obstacle six years after Luther, and like the reformer was at once struck by the corruption which prevailed there. 'The Church,' he said, 'is so full of bad humors, that it has become dropsical.'† It was in the pontificate of Leo X.; all that priests, monks, bishops, and cardinals thought about was being present at farces and comedies, and of going masked to courtesans' houses.‡ Bonivard saw all this with his own eyes, and has left us some stories into which he has admitted expressions we must soften, and details we must suppress. 'Having business one day with the concubinary of the pope's cubicular (we leave these unusual expressions, the meaning of which is not very edifying), I had to go and find him at a courtesan's. . . . She wore smart feathers, waving over a fine gold coif, and a silk dress with slashed sleeves; you would have taken her for a princess.'§ Another day, while walking in the city, he met one of these 'misses,' disguised as a man, and riding on a Spanish jennet; on the crupper behind her was a *janin* wrapped in a Spanish cape, which he drew carefully over his nose so that he might not be recognised. 'Who is he?' asked Bonivard. 'It is Cardinal So-and-so with his favorite,' was the reply. 'We say in my country,' he rejoined, 'that all the madmen are not at Rome; and yet I see you have them in abundance.'‖

The prior of St. Victor did not lose sight of the object of his journey, and canvassed unceasingly; but began to despair of success. 'Do you wish to know,' he was asked, 'what you must do to obtain a request from the pope and cardinals? Tell them that you will kill any man whom

* 'Cardinationis.'—Galiffe, *Matériaux*, &c., ii. p. 184.

† *Advis et Devis de la Source de l'Idolatrie Papale*, published by M. Revillod, p. 134.

‡ Ibid, p. 78. § Ibid, p. 79. ‖ Ibid, p. 80.

they have a grudge against; or that you are ready to serve them in their pleasures, to bring them *la donna*, to gamble, play the ruffian, and rake with them—in short, that you are a libertine.' Bonivard was not strict; yet he was surprised that things had come to such a pass in the capital of catholicism. His mind, eager to learn, asked what were the causes of this decline. . . . He ascribed it to the disappearance of christian individualism from the Church, so that a personal conversion, a new creature, was required no longer. 'That in the first place,' he said, 'because when princes became christians, their whole people was baptised with them. Discipline has been since then like a spider's web which catches the small flies, but cannot hold the large ones. And next it comes from the example of the popes. . . I have lived to see three pontiffs. First, Alexander VI., a *sharp fellow*,* a ne'er-do-well, an Italianised Spaniard,—and what was worst of all,—at Rome! a man without conscience, without God, who cared for nothing, provided he accomplished his desires. Next came Julius II., proud, choleric, studying his bottle more than his breviary; mad about his popedom, and having no thought but how he could subdue not only the earth, but heaven and hell.† Last appeared Leo X., the present pope, learned in Greek and Latin, but especially a good musician, a great glutton, a deep drinker; possessing beautiful pages whom the Italians style *ragazzi;* always surrounded by musicians, buffoons, play-actors, and other jesters; accordingly when he was informed of any new business, he would say: *Di grazia, lasciatemi godere queste papate in pace; Domine mio me la ha date. Andate da Monsignor di Medici.*‡ . . . Everything is for sale at the court: red hats, mitres, judgeships, croziers, abbeys, provostries, canonries. . . . Above all do not trust to Leo the Tenth's word; for he maintains that since he dispenses others from their oaths, he can surely dispense himself.'§

* *Advis et Devis*, p. 34. † Ibid. p. 42.

‡ 'Pray let me enjoy the papacy in peace. The Lord has given it me. Go to my Lord of Medici.'

§ *Advis et Devis*, pp. 67–74.

Bonivard, astonished at the horrible state into which popes and cardinals, priests and monks, had sunk the Church, asked whence could salvation come. . . . It was not six months since Prierias, master of the sacred palace, had published a book entitled: *Dialogue against the presumptuous Propositions of Martin Luther.** 'Leo X. and his predecessors,' said Bonivard, 'have always taken the Germans for beasts: *pecora campi*, they were called, and rightly too, for these simple Saxons allowed themselves to be saddled and ridden like asses. The popes threatened them with cudgelling (excommunication), enticed them with thistles (indulgences), and so made them trot to the mill to bring away the meal for them. But having one day loaded the ass too heavily, Leo made him jib, so that the flour was spilt and the white bread lost. That ass (he added) is called *Martin*, like all asses, and his surname is *Luther*, which signifies *enlightener*.'†

They found at Rome that Bonivard had not the complaisance necessary for a Roman bishop; and the prior, seeing that he had no chance of success, shook the dust off his feet against the metropolis of catholicism, and departed for Turin. His journey had not, however, been useless: he had learnt a lesson which he never forgot, and which he told all his life through to any one that would listen to him. When he reached Turin, he went to visit his old friends of the university, but they cried out with alarm: 'Navis and Blanchet are within a hair's-breath of death, and it has been decided to arrest you. Fly without losing a moment.' Bonivard remained. Ought he to leave in the talons of the vulture those two young men with whom he had so often laughed at the noisy banquets of 'the children of Geneva?' He resolved to do what he could to interest his friends in their fate. For a whole week he went from house to house, and walked through the streets without any disguise. Nothing seemed easier than to lay hands on him, and the ducal police would have attempted it, but he was never

* 'Dialogus in præsomptuosas M. Lutheri conclusiones de potestate papæ.' December, 1517.

† *Advis et Devis*, p. 80.

alone. The scholars, charmed with his spirit and independence, accompanied him everywhere, and these thoughtless headstrong youths would have defended him at the cost of their blood. Bonivard, wishing to employ every means, wrote by some secret channel to Blanchet and Navis; the gaoler intercepted the letter, and took it to the bishop, who, fancying he saw in it a conspiracy hatching against him, even in Turin, pressed the condemnation of the prisoners, and ordered Bonivard to be seized immediately. Informed of what awaited him, the intelligent prior displayed great tranquillity. 'I shall stay a month longer at Turin,' he told everybody, 'to enjoy myself with my old friends.' Many invitations being given him, he accepted them all; but the next day, before it was light, he took horse and galloped off for Geneva.*

CHAPTER XII.

BLANCHET AND NAVIS EXECUTED. THEIR LIMBS SUSPENDED TO THE WALNUT-TREE NEAR THE BRIDGE OF ARVE.

(OCTOBER, 1518.)

THE bastard was staggered when he was informed that Bonivard had escaped. He consoled himself, however, with the thought that he had at hand the means of gratifying his taste and his revenge, and concentrated all his attention on Navis and Blanchet. What should he do with these two young men who had so thoughtlessly fallen into his net? How, in striking them, could he best strike the independent men of Geneva? For he was not thinking merely of getting rid of these two adventurers, but of filling all the city with terror by means of their death. To no purpose was he reminded that the father of one of the prisoners was the most

* Bonivard, *Chroniq.* ii. pp. 320, 321. Galiffe, *Matériaux*, &c. ii. p. 184. *Mém. d'Archéol.* iv. pp. 152, 153.

zealous of his officers; the bastard cared little for a father's grief, and thought that Peter Navis would serve him still better, when he had given him a striking example of the manner in which he desired to be served. He pressed the court to hasten on the trial. Ancina, judge in criminal matters; Caracci, seignior of Farges, and attorney-general of Savoy; aud Licia, his deputy, constituted by ducal letters judges of Navis and Blanchet, declared them solemnly convicted, first, of having been present at the meeting at the Molard, and of having promised, they and their accomplices, to be 'unanimous against the bishop's officers, to rescue out of their hands any of their number whom these episcopal agents might take into custody; second, of having proposed, in case the duke should take part against them, to flee and place themselves under a foreign government (Switzerland), abandoning thus the sôvereignty of Savoy and the splendor of the white cross.' The two prisoners were condemned to be beheaded, and then quartered, according to the bishop's desire. They prepared for execution immediately.*

Navis breathed not a murmur; the feeling of his disobedience to his father closed his lips; it appears also that Blanchet recovered from his terror, dried his tears, and acknowledged his folly. Nothing indicates that the repentance of these two Genevan youths was truly christian; but it would be unjust to overlook their noble confession at the hour of death. The provost and his men, having received them from the hands of the magistrates, led them to the place of execution. Their appearance was becoming, and their look serious; they walked between their guards, calm, but without weakness or alarm. When they had mounted the scaffold, Navis spoke: 'Wishing before all things to make amends for the evil we have done, we retract all that we have said touching certain of our countrymen, and declare that such avowals were extorted from us by the fear of torture. After proclaiming the innocence of others, we acknowledge ourselves guilty. Yes, we have lived in such a way that we justly deserve death, and we pray God, in this

* Galiffe, *Matériaux*, &c., ii. pp. 189–195.

our last hour, to pardon our sins. Yet understand, that these sins are not those of which we are accused; we have done nothing contrary to the franchises and laws of Geneva: of that we are clean . . . The sins which condemn us are our debaucheries.' Navis would have continued, but the provost, vexed at what he had said already, ordered the executioner to do his duty. The man set to work instantly: the two young men knelt down, he raised his sword, and 'thus they were beheaded, and then quartered.'*

At last the bishop saw his desires satisfied; he had in his possession the heads and the quarters of two of the 'children of Geneva.' This little man, so frail, livid, hideous, reduced almost to a shadow, without genius and without will, had nevertheless the will and the genius of evil. Notwithstanding his protest against *the mutilation of limbs*, he decided that three of the quarters of the two bodies should be exposed over the gates of Turin, and reserved for his own share a quarter of Navis and of Blanchet, with the two heads. He had the flesh pickled, for he intended to keep them as long as possible; and when this savage operation, worthy of the Mohawks, was completed, he placed the heads and limbs in two barrels on which were marked the arms of the count, the duke's brother. The bishop wished to show his flock a sample of his cleverness; and as the execution did not take place at Geneva, he intended at least to send the limbs of the victims 'to stir up and terrify the scoundrels.' The bearers of these two pickle-tubs started from Turin, crossed Mont Cenis, arrived in the basin of the Leman on Saturday, October 2, 1518, and lodged on 'the other side of the Arve.'†

On the bank of this river, which then separated the ducal states from those of Geneva, at the foot of the bridge on the Savoy side, stood a fine walnut-tree, whose leafy branches

* Savyon, *Annales*, p. 72. Galiffe, *Matériaux*, &c., ii. pp. 26, 145. Spon, *Hist. de Genève*, i. pp. 293, 294. Bonivard, *Chroniq.* ii. p. 323.

† Galiffe, *Matériaux*, &c. (Instructions pour les réponses à faire à Soleure), ii. p. 135. Savyon, *Annales*, p. 72. Registers of the Councils of Geneva, Oct. 3, 1518. Spon, *Hist. de Genève.* Roset and Gautier MSS.

spread opposite the church of Our Lady of Grace on the Genevan side. The bishop's agents, who had received orders to make an exhibition of the mutilated limbs for the benefit of the Genevans, proceeded to the bridge on Saturday night in order to discharge their disgraceful commission under cover of the darkness. They carried with them, in addition to their casks filled with flesh, brine, and blood, a ladder, a hammer, some nails and cord. On reaching the tree, they opened the barrels and found the features well preserved and easily recognisable. The bastard's agents climbed the tree, and nailed the heads and arms to the branches in such a manner as to be seen by all the passers-by. They fixed a placard underneath, bearing these words: 'These are the traitors of Geneva;' and the white cross of Savoy above. They then withdrew, leaving the empty casks at the foot of the tree. 'It was done by order of your bishop,' said the duke, in a letter written three days later, (October 5) to his very dear, beloved, and trusty citizens of Geneva, 'your bishop, whom we have in this supported and favored, which ought to be to your contentment.'*

The day broke, the people arose, opened their windows, and went out of their houses; some were going to the city. One man was about to cross the bridge, when, fancying he saw something strange, he drew near, and discovered with astonishment human limbs hanging from the tree. He shuddered, supposing that this had been done by some murderers in mere bravado; and, wishing to make the extraordinary occurrence known, he quickened his steps. 'The first who saw this mystery did not keep it secret, but ran and told the news all through the city. "What 's the matter?" people asked . . . and then everybody hurried thither,' adds the chronicler. In truth, an immense crowd of citizens—men, women, and children—soon gathered round the tree. It was Sunday, a day which the bastard had probably selected for this edifying sight; every one was free from his ordinary occupations, and during all that

* Galiffe, *Matériaux*, &c., ii. p. 151. Registers of the Council of Geneva, Oct. 3, 1518. Savyon, *Annales*, p. 72. Bonivard, *Chroniq.* ii. p. 325. Roset and Gautier MSS.

holy day an agitated multitude pressed continually around the tree where the blood-stained remains of the two victims were hanging. They looked closely at them and examined the features: 'It is Navis,' they said; 'it is Blanchet.' . . . 'Ah!' exclaimed a huguenot, 'it is not difficult to penetrate the mystery. It is one of my lord bishop's messages come to us by the Turin post!' Bonivard, who had returned to Geneva, thought himself fortunate that the swiftness of his horse had carried him beyond the prelate's reach, and rejoiced that his head was not between those of Blanchet and Navis; but he was at the same time filled with indignation and anger against the monster who had so treated his two young friends. The Genevan youth indulged in bitter irony. 'A fine maypole they have raised us this morning on the city boundary!' they said; 'they have put up a flag already, it only wants a few ribands and flowers to make the show complete?' But the sight of these bloody fragments, swinging in the air, was no fit subject for jesting; there was great mourning in the city; groans and weeping were heard in the crowd; women gave vent to their horror, and men to their indignation.

Navis's father, a man detested by the Genevans, was not the last to be informed; some people ran to tell him of the tragic event that was stirring up the whole city. 'Come,' said they, 'come and see the reward the bishop sends you for your faithful services. You are well paid; the tyrants recompense you right royally for the disfavor you have won from all of us; they have sent from Turin, as your pay, the head of your son.' . . . Peter Navis might be an unjust judge, but he was a father; at first he was overwhelmed. Andrew had been disobedient, but the ingratitude of the child had not been able to extinguish the love of the parent. The unhappy man, divided between affection for his son and respect for his prince, shed tears and endeavored to hide them. Prostrated by grief and shame, pale and trembling, he bent his head in sullen silence. It was not the same with the mother, who gave way to the most violent affection and most extravagant despair. The grief of Navis's parents, which was expressed in such different ways, struck all the spectators. Bonivard, who at this tragic moment mingled in the agitated groups of the citizens, was heart-stricken by all he saw and heard, and on returning to his priory exclaimed: 'What horror and indignation such a spectacle excites! even strangers, whom it does not affect, are disgusted at it . . . What will the poor citizens do now? the poor relations and friends? their father and mother?' . . .

The Genevans did not confine themselves to useless lamentations; they did not turn their eyes to the blow they had just received, they looked to the hand that struck it; it was the hand of their bishop. Everybody knew the failings of Navis and Blanchet, but at this moment no one spoke of them; they could only see two young and unhappy martyrs of liberty. The anger of the people rose impetuously, and poured itself out on the prelate more than on the duke. 'The bishop,' they said, 'is a wolf under a shepherd's cloak. Would you know how he feeds his lambs, go to the bridge of Arve!' Their leaders thought the same: they said, it was not enough for the prince-bishop to plunge families and a whole city into mourning, but his imagination coldly calculated the means of increasing their sorrow. These suspended heads and arms were a notable instance of that cruel faculty of invention which has always distinguished tyrants. To torture in Piedmont the bodies of their young friends did not satisfy the prelate, but he must torture all hearts in Geneva. What is the spirit that animates him? What are the secret motives of these horrible executions? . . . Despotism, self-interest, fanaticism, hatred, revenge, cruelty, ambition, folly, madness . . . It was indeed all these together. Think not that he will stop in the midst of his success: these are only the first-fruits of his tenderness. To draw up proscription lists, to butcher the friends of liberty, to expose their dead bodies, to kill Geneva,—in one word, to take pattern by Sylla in everything,*—such will henceforward be the *cure of souls* of this son of the pope.

The resistance of the citizens to the encroachments of the

* 'Si fut exercé lors une cruauté presque *Sylleine*,' says Bonivard, *Chroniq.* ii. p. 324.

prelate assumed from that hour a character that must necessarily lead to the abolition of the Roman episcopacy in Geneva. There is a retributive justice from which princes cannot escape, and it is often the innocent successors who are hurled from their thrones by the crimes of their guilty predecessors; of this we have seen numerous examples during the past half-century. The penalty which has not fallen on the individual falls on the family or the institution; but the penalty which strikes the institution is the more terrible and instructive. The mangled limbs hanging on the banks of the Arve left an indelible impression on the minds of the Genevan people. If a mameluke and a huguenot happened to pass the bridge together, the first, pointing to the walnut-tree, would say to the second with a smile: 'Do you recognise Navis and Blanchet?'—the huguenot would coldly reply: 'I recognise my bishop.'* The institution of a bishop-prince, an imitation of that of a bishop-king, became every day more hateful to the Genevans. Its end was inevitable—its end at Geneva: hereafter the judgments of God will overtake it in other places also.

The agitation was not confined to the people: the syndics had summoned the council. 'This morning,' they said, 'before daybreak, two heads and two arms were fastened to a tree opposite the church of Our Lady of Grace. We know not by whose order.'† Everybody guessed whose heads they were and by whose order they had been exposed; but the explosion was not so great in the council as in the crowd. They must have understood that this cruel act betokened sinister designs; they heard the thunder-clap that precedes the storm: yet each man drew a different conclusion. Certain canons, monks, and other agents of the Roman Church, accomplices of the tyrant, called for absolute submission. Certain nobles thought that if they were freed

* MS. Registers of the Council, Oct. 3 and Nov. 26, 1518. Bonivard, *Chroniq.* ii. p. 326. Roset and Gautier MSS., *Les Maumelus* (Mamelukes) *de Genève.* The latter MS., as well as many others collected by M. Mallet-Romilly, are now in the possession of Professor Cellérier, to whose kindness I am indebted for their perusal.

† Registers of the Council, Oct. 3, 1518.

from the civic councils, they could display their aristocratic pretensions more at their ease. Certain traders, Savoyards by birth, who loved better 'large gains in slavery than small gains in liberty,' amused themselves by thinking that if the duke became master of the city, he would reside there with his court, and they would get a higher price for their goods. But the true Genevans joyfully consented that their country should be small and poor, provided it were the focus of light and liberty. As for the huguenots, the two heads were the signal of resistance. 'With an adversary that keeps any measure,' they said, 'we may relax a little of our rights; but there are no considerations to be observed with an enemy who proceeds by murder . . . Let us throw ourselves into the arms of the Swiss.'

The bishop's crime thus became one of the stages on the road to liberty. No doubt the victims were culpable, but the murderers were still more so. All that was noble in Geneva sighed for independence. The mameluke magistrates strove in vain to excuse an act which injured their cause; they were answered rudely; contrary opinions were bandied to and fro in the council, and 'there was a great disturbance.' At last they resolved to send an ambassador to the princes to inquire whether this barbarous act had been perpetrated by their orders, and in that case to make remonstrances. This resolution was very displeasing to the mamelukes, who endeavored to soften the harsh message by intrusting it to pleasing messengers. 'To obtain what you desire from princes, you must send them people who are agreeable to them,' said the first syndic. The assembly accordingly named the vidame Aymon Conseil, an unblushing agent of Savoy; the ex-syndic Nergaz, a bad man and personal enemy of Berthelier; and Déléamont, governor of Peney, against whom the huguenots had more than once drawn the sword. The duke, being at that time in his Savoy provinces, received the deputation coldly at a public audience, but made much of them in private. The ambassadors returned in three days with an unmeaning answer.*

* MS. Registers of the Council, Oct. 3, 6, and 22, 1518. Roset and Gautier MSS., *Les Maumelus de Genève.*

The bishop was at Pignerol, where he had presided over the terrible butchery. The council were content to write to him, considering the distance; and as he was still proud of his exploit, he replied by extolling the mildness of his government: "You have never had prince or prelate with such good intentions as myself,' he wrote from Turin on the 15th of October; 'the execution done the other side the bridge of Arve is to give those a lesson who desire to lead evil lives.' Accordingly the bastard exhorted the Genevans to show themselves sensible of his kindness by returning him a double share of love. These executions, far from causing him any remorse, gave him a longing for more; he invited the Genevans to acknowledge his tender favors by granting him the head of Berthelier and a few others besides. Making confession to the council of his most secret anguish, he expressed a fear that if these heads did not fall before his return, it would prevent his enjoying the pleasures of the table. 'Discharge your duty,' said he, 'so that when I am with you, there may be nothing to do but to make *good cheer*.' To live merrily and to put his most illustrious subjects to death were the two chief points of his episcopal cure of souls. To be more sure of obtaining these heads, he threatened Geneva with his vengeance: 'If you should refuse,' said he in conclusion, 'understand clearly that I shall pray my lord (the duke) and his brother (the count) to preserve my good rights; and I have confidence in them, that they will not let me be trampled upon; besides this, I will risk my life and my goods.' This mild pastoral was signed: THE BISHOP of Geneva.*

Thus everybody was leaguing against Geneva. Would it be crushed? Was there in this small republic strength enough to resist the twofold lay and clerical opposition, which had crushed so many free cities in the dark ages? There were influences at work, as we have seen, in the formation of modern liberties, and we find in Geneva the representatives of the three great schools in which Europe has learnt the principles of government. The characteristic of

* Galiffe, *Matériaux*, &c., ii. pp. 270–273.

the German liberties was an energetic love of independence; now Berthelier and many of his friends were true Germans in this respect. The characteristic of the Roman liberties was legality; we find this strongly marked in Lévrier and other eminent men. The third element of the independence of this people was to be that christian principle which, subjecting the conscience to God, and thus giving man a firmness more than human, makes him tread in the path of liberty and walk along precipices without his head turning or his feet stumbling. Yet a few years more, and a great number of Genevans will find this latter element in the Gospel. To this Geneva owes principally the maintenance of her existence.

After the murder of Blanchet and Navis, the passion of independence became dominant. 'From that time,' said a magistrate of the seventeenth century, 'the duke and bishop were looked upon in Geneva as two tyrants who sought only the desolation of the city.'*

CHAPTER XIII.

THE HUGUENOTS PROPOSE AN ALLIANCE WITH THE SWISS, AND THE MAMELUKES AMUSE THEMSELVES AT TURIN.

(OCTOBER TO DECEMBER, 1518.)

THE moment had come when men of decision were about to apply themselves to the work. The patriots learnt that the encroaching designs of Savoy were irrevocable, and that it was consequently necessary to oppose them with an energetic and unbending resistance. Berthelier, 'the great despiser of death,' smiled coldly at the bishop's threats; magnanimous, firm, and resolute, he fancied he saw the happy

* Document addressed to Lord Townsend by M. Chouet, Secretary of State. Berne MSS.

moment approaching when his fondest dream would be realised—the giving his life to save Geneva. If he wished to escape from the cruelties of the princes which threatened him on every side, he must sink himself, retire, give up his noblest plans: he shrank with horror from the thought. To resist the conspiracy directed against the liberties of Geneva was his duty; if he neglected to discharge it, he would degrade himself in his own eyes, he would expose himself to remorse; while if he accomplished this task, he would feel himself in his proper place; it seemed to him that he would become better and more acceptable to God. But it was not only imperious, invincible duty which impelled him: it was passion, the noblest of passions; nothing could calm the tempests struggling in his bosom. He therefore threw himself energetically into the midst of dangers. In vain did Bonivard show symptoms of discouragement, and say to his generous friend in their meetings at St. Victor: 'You see the pensions and threats of the prince are inducing many reputed sensible men to *draw in their horns*.' Bonivard could not check Berthelier's decision. Caring for nothing, not even for his life, provided he saved the liberties of Geneva, the intrepid citizen went through the city, visiting from house to house, remonstrating with the citizens 'one by one;' exhorting them in private.*

His exhortations were not unavailing: a strong fermentation began to stir men's minds. They called to remembrance how these Swiss, from whom they expected deliverance, had conquered their liberty. A hat set up in Altorf on the top of a pole; an apple placed by a cruel order on the head of a child: were, according to the old traditions of that people, the signal of their independence. Was the bastard less tyrannous than Gessler? Those two heads, those two arms,—were they not a still more frightful signal? The remains of Navis and of Blanchet were long left exposed: in vain did the unhappy father, judge Navis, address frequent and earnest appeals to the bishop to have them removed; the prelate took delight in this demonstration of

* Bonivard, *Chroniq.* ii. p. 328.

his power.* It was a strange blindness on his part. Those dead limbs, those closed eyes, those blood-stained lips preached to the citizens that it was time to defend their ancient liberties. . . . The great agitator took advantage of the bastard's cruelty, and employing the energetic language of the times, he said: 'The same pin hangs on the cloak of every one of us. We must resist. Let us unite, let us give our hand to the League, and fear nothing, for nobody dares touch their allies . . . any more than St. Anthony's fire.* . . . Let us help ourselves, and God will help us.'

The young, the poor, all generous hearts listened to Berthelier's words; 'but the great and the rich,' says Bonivard, 'were afraid on account of their riches which they preferred to their life.'† These great and rich folk, Montyon and the ducal faction, seeing the dangers that threatened the princes of Savoy in Geneva, resolved to send a second embassy with orders to go this time even to Turin and Pignerol. The same three mamelukes were intrusted with the mission. The patriots were indignant: 'What!' they said, 'you want to save the sheep, and yet select wolves to do it?'—'Do you not understand,' replied Montyon, 'that if you wish to *tame* princes, you must take care not to send men who are disagreeable to them?' The deputation arrived at Turin, where the duke then was. They demanded an audience to present their homage to his Highness, and as their sentiments were known, their prayer was easily granted. They timidly stated their grievances. 'It was not I who did it,' said Charles; 'it was my lord of Geneva; go to the bishop at Pignerol.' The deputation proceeded to this town, situated in the neighborhood of the schismatic Waldenses, whom the prelate hated as much at least as he did the Genevans. Having obtained an audience, they repeated the lesson they had been taught: 'The city is much astonished that you have put two of our citizens to death and sent their quarters to the frontiers of Geneva. If any private individuals had offended against you, say our

* Council Registers, May 3, 1519.

† A contagious carbuncle. Bonivard, *Chroniq.* ii. p. 327.

‡ Ibid. p. 328.

citizens, you had only to accuse them, they would have been punished at Geneva.' *—'It was not I who did that,' said the bishop, 'it was my lord the duke.' The mameluke deputies were strongly inclined to admit one half of the assertion of the two princes, and to believe that probably the murder came neither from John nor Charles. The official mission being ended, the prelate, who knew well with whom he had to deal, gave directions for the ambassadors to be entertained. The latter desired nothing better. The bishop 'accordingly entertained them,' say the chronicles, 'treated, feasted, and made merry with them.' Pleasure parties followed each other rapidly, and the three mamelukes, forgetting their diplomatic business, found the wines of Italy excellent, and the bastard and his court quite captivating.†

All good cheer however comes to an end: the politicians of the court of Turin wished to profit by the embassy, and, although it had been directed against the usurpations of the princes of Savoy, to turn it skilfully against the liberties of the people of Geneva. This was not difficult, for their representatives were betraying them. The three ambassadors, the bishop, his officers, and the ducal councillors deliberated on the answer to be sent to the council of Geneva. The princes, trusting in their pensioners, despised the liberal party; but the three envoys, the vidame, Nergaz, and Déléamont, who had seen the danger closely, far from doing the same, were alarmed at this carelessness. 'There are loyal subjects in Geneva,' they said; 'but there are also rascals, rebels and plotters who, in order to escape the punishment of their misdeeds, urge the people to contract an alliance with Friburg. The evil is greater than you imagine; the Helvetic republics will establish their accursed popular government in Geneva. You must therefore punish very sharply the advisers of such matters, and crush the rebels.'‡ The two cousins desired nothing better. Charles had no wish to see liberal principles come nearer to Savoy and perhaps to Turin; but he preferred making only a verbal answer to the council. The deputies, alarmed at the responsibility thus

* Savyon, *Annales*, p. 74.

† Ibid. p. 75. *Archives de Genève*, No. 888. ‡ Ibid. p. 75.

laid upon them, insisted on a written answer, and a letter was accordingly drawn up. In it the duke and the bishop informed the council 'that they would hold them loyal subjects if they would assist in *unhesitatingly putting to death Berthelier and ten or twelve others*,' whom they named. 'We hand you this letter,' said the duke and the bishop to the deputies; 'but you will not deliver it to the syndics and council of Geneva unless they promise on their oaths (before reading it) to execute without delay the orders it contains.' Never had monarch put forward such enormous pretensions. God first disorders in mind those whom He intends to ruin. The servile ambassadors took care to make no objections, and delighted with the success of their embassy and particularly with the brilliant fêtes of the court of Turin, they departed with the strange instructions which the two princes had given them.*

While the mamelukes and Savoyards were conspiring at Turin and Pignerol against the liberties of the city, Berthelier and his friends were thinking how to preserve them. The iniquity of the duke and the bishop showed them more and more every day the necessity of independence. They resolved to take a decisive step. Berthelier, Bernard, Bonivard, Lévrier, Vandel, De La Mare, Besançon Hugues, and some others met in consultation. 'Hitherto,' said Berthelier, 'it is only in parlors and closets that we have advised an alliance with the Swiss; we must now proclaim it on the house-tops; simple conversations are no longer enough: it is time to come to a common decision. But alas! where, when, and how? . . . The princes of Savoy have accustomed us to assemble only for our pleasures. Who ever thinks in our meetings of the safety of the city?' Bonivard then began to speak: 'The house of M. de Gingins and mine at St. Victor have often seen us assembled in small numbers for familiar conversation. We now require larger larger rooms and more numerous meetings. This is my proposition. Let us employ to do good the same means we have hitherto used to do evil. Let us take advantage of the

* Savyon, *Annales*, p. 75. Bonivard, *Chroniq.* ii. pp. 332. Roset and Gautier MSS. Spon, *Hist. de Genève*, i. pp. 296, 298.

meetings where until now nothing was thought of but pleasure, to deliberate henceforth on the maintenance of our liberties.' This proposition met with a favorable reception.

Since the murder of Blanchet and Navis, it had become more difficult to hold these huguenot meetings. The threats of Savoy were such that men were afraid of everything that might give an excuse for violent measures. 'There was in former times at Geneva,' observed one of the company, 'a brotherhood of St. George which is now degenerated but not destroyed; let us revive it and make use of it; let us employ it to save the franchises threatened by the Savoy princes.' *

Berthelier set to work as soon as the meeting broke up. When he desired to assemble his friends, he used to pass whistling under their windows. He began to saunter through the streets with a look of unconcern, but with his eyes on the watch, and gave a whistle whenever he passed the house of a devoted citizen. The huguenots listened, recognized the signal of their chief, came out, and went up to him: a meeting was appointed for a certain day and hour.

The day arrived. 'We were about sixty,' said Bonivard. It was not a large number, but they were all men of spirit and enterprise. It was no meeting of conspirators: the worthiest members of the republic had assembled, who had no intention to go beyond the rights which the constitution gave them. In fact Berthelier and Besançon Hugues proposed simply an alliance with the Swiss. 'This thought is not a fancy sprung from an empty brain,' they said: 'the princes of Savoy force us to it. By taking away our fairs, by trampling the laws under foot, by breaking off our relations with other countries, they compel us to unite with the Swiss.' When they found Savoy violently breaking the branches of the tree, and even trying to uproot it, these patriots were determined to graft it on the old and more vigorous stock of Helvetic liberty.†

* Bonivard, *Chroniq.* ii. pp. 328, 330.

† Bonivard, *Chroniq.* ii. p. 330. Galiffe, *Matériaux*, &c. ii. p. xxxii. Spon, *Hist.* i. p. 299.

The rumor of this decision, which they tried however to keep secret, reached Turin. Nothing in the world could cause more anger and alarm to the bishop and the duke. They answered immediately, on the 13th of October, by sending an order to bring Berthelier to trial in the following month before the episcopal commissioners; this was delivering him to death. Councillor Marti of Friburg, a blunt man, but also intelligent, warm, devoted and ready, being informed of what was going on, hastened to Geneva. The most sacred friendship had been formed between him and Berthelier when, seated at the same hearth, they had conversed together about Geneva and liberty. The thought that a violent death might suddenly carry off a man so dear, disturbed Marti seriously. He proceeded to the hôtel-de-ville, where the Council of Fifty had met, and showed at once how full he was of tenderness for Berthelier, and of anger for his enemies. 'Sirs,' he said bluntly, 'this is the fifth time I have come here about the same business: I beg that it may be the last. Protect Berthelier as the liberties of your city require, or beware! Friburg has always desired your good; do not oblige us to change our opinion. . . Do not halt between two sides: decide for one or the other. The duke and the bishop say one thing, and they always do another: they think only of destroying your liberties, and Friburg of defending them.' The council, who found it more convenient to give the right hand to one and the left to another, to keep on good terms with Friburg and the bishop, thought this speech a little rude. They thanked Marti all the same, but added that, before giving a decisive answer, they must wait the return of the deputies sent to the bishop and the duke. 'Nevertheless,' added the syndics, 'as regards Berthelier we will maintain the liberties of the city.' *

The deputies whom they expected from Turin—Nergaz, Déléamont, and the vidame—soon arrived. When they returned to the free city, they were still dazzled by the pomp of the Piedmontese court, and filled with the ideas

* Registers of the Council, Nov. 10 and 11, 1518.

which the partisans of absolute power had instilled into them. 'Everything is in the prince,' they had said, 'and the people ought to have no other will but his.' Thinking only of claiming absolute authority for the bishop, they appeared on the 29th of November before the Council of State, and said in an imperative tone: 'We have orders from my lord bishop not to discharge our mission until you have added to your number twenty of the most eminent citizens.' In this way the princes of Savoy wished to make sure of a majority. The council assented to this demand. 'We require them,' added Syndic Nergaz, 'to make oath in our presence that they will reveal nothing they may hear.'—'What means all this mystery?' the councillors asked each other; but the oath was taken. The ambassadors then advanced another step: 'Here is the letter in which my lord makes known his sovereign will; but before it is opened, you must all swear to execute the orders it contains.' This strange demand was received in sullen silence; such open despotism astonished not only the friends of liberty but even the mamelukes. 'Hand us the letter addressed to us, that we may read it,' said Besançon Hugues and other independent members of the council. 'No,' replied Nergaz, 'the oath first, and then the letter.' Some partisans of Savoy had the impudence to second this demand; but 'the friends of independence' resisted firmly, and the meeting broke up. 'There must be some secret in that letter dangerous to the people,' they said. It was resolved to convene the general council in order that the ambassadors might deliver their message in person. This appeal to the people was very disagreeable to the three deputies; yet they encouraged one another to carry out their mission to the end.*

On Sunday, December 5, the sound of a trumpet was heard, the great bell of the cathedral tolled, the citizens put on their swords, and the large hall of Rive was 'quite filled with people.' The deputies were desired to 'deliver their message.'—'Our message is found in the letter,' said Ner-

* Council Registers, Nov. 29 and Dec. 2, 1518. Savyon, *Annales*, p. 78. Roset and Gautier MSS.

gaz, 'and our only instructions are that before the council of Geneva open it, they shall swear to carry out its orders.' These words caused an immense agitation among the people. 'We have so good a leader,' said they with irony, 'that we ought to follow him with our eyes shut and not fear to fall into the ditch with him! How can we doubt that the secret contained in this mysterious paper is a secret of justice and love? . . . If there are any sceptics among us, let them go to the walnut-tree at the bridge of Arve, where the limbs of our friends are still hanging.'—'Gentlemen,' said the more serious men, 'we return you the letter unopened, and beg you will send it back to those who gave it you.' Then Nergaz, feeling annoyed, exclaimed bitterly: 'I warn you that my lord of Savoy has many troops in the field, and that if you do not execute the orders contained in this letter, no citizen of Geneva will be safe in his states. I heard him say so.' The people on hearing this were much exasperated. 'Indeed!' they exclaimed, 'if we do not swear beforehand to do a thing without knowing it, all who possess lands in Savoy or who travel there, will be treated like Navis and Blanchet.' . . . Thereupon several citizens turned to the three deputies and said: 'Have you remained five or six weeks over the mountains, feasting, amusing yourselves, exulting and living merrily, in order to bring us such despatches? To the Rhone with the traitors! to the Rhone!' The three mamelukes trembled before the anger of the people. Were they really to be flung into the river to be cleansed from the impurities they had contracted in the fêtes at Turin? . . . Lévrier, Besançon Hugues, and other men of condition quieted the citizens, and the servile deputies got off with their fright. Calm being restored, the councillors returned the prince's letter to Nergaz and his colleagues, saying: 'We will not open it.' They feared the influence of the creatures of Savoy, of whom there were many in the Great Council. We give this name to the body established in 1457, which consisted at first of only fifty persons, and which being frequently increased became somewhat later the Council of Two Hundred. The people withdrew from this assembly a privilege they had given it in 1502, and decreed that the general council alone should henceforward decide on all that concerned the liberties of Geneva.*

CHAPTER XIV.

THE HUGUENOTS DEMAND AN ALLIANCE WITH FRIBURG: THE MAMELUKES OPPOSE IT. BERTHELIER IS ACQUITTED.

(DECEMBER 1518 TO JANUARY 1519.)

THE cruel butchery of Navis and Blanchet, and the insolent sealed letter, were acts ruinous to those who had committed them. If the bishop had possessed only the spiritual power, he would not have been dragged into such measures; but by wishing to unite earthly dominion with religious direction, he lost both: a just punishment of those who forget the words of Christ: 'My kingdom is not of this world.' The bishop had torn the contract that bound him to the free citizens of the ancient city. The struggle was growing fiercer every day, and would infallibly end in the fall of the Roman episcopate in Geneva. It was not the Reformation that was to overthrow the representative of the pope: it was the breath of liberty and legality that was to uproot that barren tree, and the reformers were to come afterwards to cultivate the soil and scatter abroad the seeds of life. Two parties, both strangers to the Gospel, stood then face to face. On the one side were the bishop, the vicar and procurator-fiscal, the canons, priests, monks, and all the agents of the popedom; on the other were the friends of light, the friends of liberty, the partisans of law, the representatives of the people. The battle was between clerical and secular society. These struggles were not new; but while in the middle ages clerical society had always gained the victory,

* Council Registers, Dec. 5, 1518. Savyon, *Annales*, p. 77. Berne MSS. v. 12.

at Geneva, on the contrary, in the sixteenth century the series of its defeats was to begin. It is easy to explain this phenomenon. Ecclesiastical society had long been the most advanced as well as the strongest; but in the sixteenth century secular society appeared in all the vigor of youth, and was soon to gain the victories of a maturer age. It was all over with the clerical power: the weapons it employed at Geneva (the letter and the walnut-tree) indicated a thorough decline of human dignity. Out of date, fallen into childishness, and decrepid, it could no longer contend against the lay body. If the duel took place on open ground, without secret understandings, without trickery, the dishonored clerical authority must necessarily fall. The Epicurean hog (if we may be permitted to use an ancient phrase), at once filthy and cruel, who from his episcopal throne trampled brutally under foot the holiest rights, was unconsciously preparing in Geneva the glorious advent of the Reformation.

The meeting of the 5th of December was no sooner dissolved than the citizens dispersed through the town. The insolent request of the princes and the refusal of the people were the subject of every conversation: nothing else was talked of 'in public or in private, at feast or funeral.' The letter which demanded on behalf of Geneva an alliance with Friburg was not sealed like the bishop's; it was openly displayed in the streets, and carried from house to house; a large number of citizens hastened to subscribe their names: there were three hundred signatures. It was necessary to carry this petition to Friburg; Berthelier, who was still under trial, could not leave the city; besides, it would be better to have a new man, more calm perhaps, and more diplomatic. They cast their eyes on the syndic Besançon Hugues, who in character held a certain mean between Berthelier the man of action, and Lévrier the man of law. 'No one can be more welcome among the confederates than you,' they said; 'Conrad Hugues, your father, fought at Morat in the ranks of Zurich.'—'I will go,' he replied, 'but as a mere citizen.' They wished to give him a colleague of a more genial nature, and chose De la Mare. He had resided for some time on a property his wife possessed in Savoy; but the gentry of the neighborhood 'playing him many tricks,' because he was a Genevan, he had returned to the city burning with hatred against the Savoyard dominion.

The two deputies met with a warm reception and great honor at Friburg. The pensioners of Savoy opposed their demand in vain; the three hundred Genevans who had signed the petition received the freedom of the city, with an offer to make the alliance general if the community desired it. On Tuesday, December 21, the two deputies returned to Geneva, and on the following Thursday the proposal of alliance was brought before the people in general council. It was to be a great day; and accordingly the two parties went to the council determined, each of them, to make a last effort. The partisans of absolutism and those of the civic liberties, the citizens attached to Rome and those who were inclined to throw off their chains, the old times and the new, met face to face. At first there were several eloquent speeches on both sides: 'We will not permit law and liberty to be driven out of Geneva,' said the citizens, 'in order that arbitrary rule may be set up in their place. God himself is the guarantee of our franchises.' They soon came to warmer language, and at last grew so excited that deliberation was impossible. The deputy from Friburg, who had returned with Hugues and De la Mare, strove in vain to calm their minds; the council was compelled to separate without coming to any decision. Switzerland had offered her alliance, and Geneva had not accepted it.*

The friends of independence were uneasy; most of them were deficient in information and in arguments; they supplied the want by the instinct of liberty, boldness and enthusiasm; but these are qualities that sometimes fail and fade away. Many of them accordingly feared that the liberties of Geneva would be finally sacrificed to the bishop's good pleasure. The more enlightened thought, on the contrary, that the rights of the citizens would remain secure; that neither privilege, stratagem, nor violence would overthrow them; but that the struggle might perhaps be long,

* Registers of the Council, Dec. 7, 21, 23, 1518; Feb. 6, 1519. Galiffe, *Matériaux*, &c., ii. p. 217.

and if, according to the proverb, Rome was not built in a day, so it could not be thrown down in a day. These notable men, whose motto was, 'Time brings everything,' called upon the people to be patient. This was not what the ardent Berthelier wanted. He desired to act immediately, and seeing that the best-informed men hesitated, he said : 'When the wise will not, we make use of fools.' He had again recourse to the young Genevans, with whom he had long associated, with a view of winning them over to his patriotic plans. He was not alone. Another citizen now comes upon the scene, a member of one of the most influential families in the city, by name Baudichon de la Maison-Neuve, a man of noble and exalted character, bold, welcome everywhere, braving without measure all the traditions of old times, often turbulent, and the person who, more perhaps than any other, served to clear in Geneva the way by which the Reformation was to enter. These two patriots and some of their friends endeavored to revive in the people the remembrance of their ancient rights. At the banquets where the young men of Geneva assembled, epigrams were launched against the ducal party, civic and Helvetic songs were sung, and among others one composed by Berthelier, the unpoetical but very patriotic burden of which was :

Vivent sur tous, Messieurs les alliés !

Every day this chorus was heard with fresh enthusiasm. The wind blew in the direction of independence, and the popular waves continued rising. 'Most of the city are joining our brotherhood,' said Bonivard ; 'decidedly the townsfolk are the strongest.' The Christmas holidays favored the exultation of the citizens. The most hot-headed of the Genevan youths paraded the streets ; at night they kindled bonfires in the squares (which they called *ardre des failles*), and the boys, making torches of twisted straw, ran up and down the city, shouting : 'Hurrah for the League ! the huguenots for ever !' Armed men kept watch throughout the city, and as they passed the houses of the mamelukes, they launched their gibes at them. 'They were very merry,' said Bonivard, 'and made more noise than was necessary.' The two parties became more distinct every day, the huguenots wearing a cross on their doublets and a feather in their caps, like the Swiss ; the mamelukes carrying a sprig of holly on their head. 'Whoever touches me will be pricked,' said they, insolently pointing to it. Quarrels were frequent. When a band of the friends of Savoy happened to meet a number of the friends of the League, the former would cry out : 'Huguenots !' and the latter would reply : 'We hold that title in honor, for it was taken by the first Swiss when they bound themselves by an oath against the tyranny of their oppressors ! . . . But you mamelukes have always been slaves !' —'Beware,' said the vidame, 'your proceedings are seditious.'—'The necessity of escaping from slavery makes them lawful,' replied Berthelier, Maison-Neuve, and their followers. The mountain torrent was rushing impetuously down, and men asked whether the dykes raised against it would be able to restrain its fury.*

The party of Savoy resolved to strike a decisive blow. No one was more threatened than Berthelier. The two princes might perhaps have spared the lives of the other citizens whose names were contained in the letter ; but as for Berthelier, they must have his head, and that speedily. This was generally known : people feared to compromise themselves by saluting him, and timid men turned aside when they saw him coming, which made Bonivard, who remained faithful to him, exclaim with uneasiness : 'Alas ! he is abandoned by almost everybody of condition !' But Berthelier did not abandon himself. He saw the sword hanging over his head ; he knew that the blow was coming, and yet he was the most serene and animated of the citizens of Geneva ; it was he who 'by word and by example always comforted the young men.' He asked simply that *right should be done.* 'I am accused of being a marplot because I ask for justice ;—a good-for-nothing, because I defend liberty against the enterprises of usurpers ;—a conspirator against the bishop's life, because they conspire against mine.' His case was adjourned week after week. His friends,

* Bonivard, *Chroniq.* ii. pp. 330, 331. Savyon, *Annales*, p. 79. Roset and Gautier MSS.

touched by the serenity of his generous soul, loudly demanded a general council. The people assembled on the 19th of January: 'All that I ask,' said Berthelier, 'is to be brought to trial; let them punish me if I am guilty; and if I am innocent, let them declare it.' The general council ordered the syndics to do justice.*

They hesitated no longer: they carefully examined the indictment; they summoned the vidame and the procurator-fiscal three times to make out their charges. The vidame, knowing this to be impossible, got out of the way: he could not be found. Navis appeared alone, but only to declare that he would give no evidence. All the formalities having been observed, the Grand Council, consisting at that time of 117 members, met on the 24th of January, 1519, and delivered a judgment of acquittal. The syndics, bearing their rods of office and followed by all the members of the council, took their station (according to the ancient custom) on the platform in front of the hôtel-de-ville. An immense crowd of citizens gathered round; many were clinging to the walls; all fixed their eyes with enthusiasm on the accused, who stood calm and firm before his judges. Then Montyon, the premier syndic, a mameluke yet a faithful observer of the law, said to him: 'Philibert Berthelier, the accusations brought against you proceeding, not from probable evidence but from violent and extorted confessions, condemned by all law human and divine, We, the syndics and judges in the criminal courts of this city of Geneva, having God and the Holy Scriptures before our eyes,—making the sign of the cross and speaking in the name of the Father, Son, and Holy Ghost,—declare you, Philibert, by our definitive sentence, to be in no degree attaint or guilty of the crime of conspiring against our prince and yours, and declare the accusations brought against you unreasonable and unjust. Wherefore you ought to be absolved and acquitted of these, and you are hereby absolved and acquitted.' This judgment, delivered by a magistrate devoted to the duke and the bishop, was a noble homage paid to the

* Bonivard, *Chroniq.* ii. p. 344. Savyon, *Annales*, p. 91. Spon, *Hist. de Genève*, i. p. 303.

justice of the cause defended by Berthelier. A solemn feeling, such as accompanies a great and just deliverance, pervaded the assembly, and the joyful patriots asked if Berthelier's acquittal was not the pledge of the liberation of Geneva.*

But if the joy among the huguenots was great, the consternation of the mamelukes was greater still. This *mystery*—for such they called the acquittal of an innocent man—terrified them. They had fancied their affairs in a better position, and all of a sudden they appeared desperate. That noble head, which they desired to bring low, now rose calm and cheerful in the midst of an enthusiastic people. To complete their misfortune, it was one of their own party that had delivered that abominable verdict of acquittal. They sent the news to their friends in Piedmont, adding that their affairs had never been in a worse position. Berthelier's acquittal created a deep sensation at the court of Turin. It was a triumph of law and liberty that compromised all the plans of Savoy. By seizing Berthelier, they had hoped to extinguish that fire of independence and liberty, which they could discern afar on the Genevan hills; and now the fire which they hoped had been stifled, was shooting out a brighter and a higher flame. . . . The Archbishop of Turin, who had sworn to destroy all republican independence, represented to his sovereign the true meaning of the sentence that had just been delivered. The feeble duke, who knew not how to carry out his enterprises and feared spending money more than losing his dominions, had remained until this moment in a state of foolish confidence. He now awoke: he saw that the alliance with Switzerland would deprive him of Geneva for ever, and considered Berthelier's acquittal as an outrage upon his honor. He determined to break the alliance, to quash the judgment, and to employ, if necessary, all the force of Savoy. He began, however, with diplomatic measures.†

On the 30th of January his ambassadors, the president of

* Galiffe, *Matériaux*, &c., ii. pp. 137–139. Registers of the Council for January 11, 19, and 24, 1519. Savyon, *Annales*, p. 82. Roset and Gautier MSS. Archives of Geneva, No. 998.

† Bonivard, *Chroniq.* ii. p. 332. M. Mignet's *Mémoire*, p. 24.

Landes, the seignior of Balayson, Bernard of St. Germain, and the skilful and energetic Saleneuve, arrived in Geneva, and, having been introduced to the general council, made at first loud protestations of friendship. But soon changing their tone and wishing to terrify by their threats, they said: 'Nevertheless his highness learns that some of you are conspiring against him.' At these words there was a great commotion in the assembly: 'Who are the conspirators? name them,' was the cry from every side. The seignior of Landes, who had let the word escape him, corrected himself, and assured them that the duke was delighted to hear that the people had refused to favor those who were opposed to him. But the ambassador changed his tone to no purpose—the Genevan susceptibility was roused: that unlucky word *conspire* spread through the city. 'To conspire against the duke he must first be our prince,' said some. 'Now, whatever he may say, he is only *vidame*, that is, a civil officer, and as such, subordinate to the supreme council. We will make no reply to the ambassadors of Savoy so long as they do not name the conspirators.' The Savoyards increased their attentions, and showed the tenderest regard for the purses of the Genevans. 'We are quite alarmed,' they said, 'at the quantity of gold florins you will have to pay Friburg for its alliance.' They carefully hid themselves under sheep's clothing; but do what they would, the wolf's fangs peeped out unexpectedly now and then; and while the chiefs were enshrouding themselves in diplomacy, sharp disputes occurred between the citizens and the ambassadors' attendants. 'All the Genevans are traitors!' exclaimed a servant belonging to the treasury of Chambéry. The varlet was reprimanded, but the ambassadors thought it prudent to leave the city. They were exasperated, and on their return to Turin told the duke: 'You will gain nothing by reasoning with these citizens. If you say you are their prince, they will maintain that you are their vassal.'—'Well, then,' said the duke, 'let us settle the matter not with the pen but with the sword.' That was just what the energetic Saleneuve desired.*

* MS. Registers of Geneva, Jan. 30 and 31, 1519. Bonivard, *Chroniq.* ii. p. 333. Savyon, *Annales*, p. 82.

CHAPTER XV.

THE PEOPLE IN GENERAL COUNCIL VOTE FOR THE ALLIANCE. THE DUKE INTRIGUES AGAINST IT.

(FEBRUARY AND MARCH, 1519.)

THE Genevans knew what sort of report would be made of them at Turin; they therefore resolved to forestall the duke and to conclude as soon as possible an alliance with the Swiss, which would permit them vigorously to repel the Savoyards. Nothing could be more lawful. Liberty was of old date in Geneva: the despotism of the princes was an innovation. The people having met according to custom on Sunday, February 6, 1519, to elect the four syndics for the year, Besançon Hugues came forward. At first he seemed to be speaking in personal explanation, but one only thought filled his heart—he wished to see Geneva united to Switzerland. To propose this openly would endanger his life, and perhaps give an advantage to the enemy; he therefore proceeded artfully to work. 'Sovereign lords,' said he, 'the ambassadors of Savoy spoke of conspirators; I think they meant me, and had my journey to Friburg in their mind. Now, I declare that I have done nothing contrary to the duty of a citizen. . . . Besides,' added he, as if parenthetically, 'if you desire to know all about it, you will find it explained at length in a letter from the council of Friburg.'—'The letter, read the letter,' they cried out. This was just what Hugues wanted: Friburg would thus make the proposal which he dared not bring forward himself. The letter was read before all the assembly. 'When it shall please the entire community of Geneva to join in friendship and citizenship with the people of Friburg,' said the writer, 'the latter will agree cheerfully, without prejudice either to the rights of the bishop and prince of Geneva, or to the liberties and franchises of the city, and neither of the parties shall pay tribute to the other.' *

When they heard this loyal and generous letter, the people were enraptured. The Swiss themselves were stretching out their hands to them. The joy was universal; there was a cry for the offer of these noble confederates to be put to the vote. Montyon, the mameluke syndic, was alarmed; he was taken unawares; that immense affair against which the bishop and Savoy were uniting their forces was about to be carried as if by storm. Even the patriotic Vandel was intimidated, and proposed that they should proceed immediately to the election of the syndics conformably to the order of the day. It was too late. Since the 22nd of December, Berthelier and his friends had displayed unwearied activity: in six weeks the huguenot party had made immense progress. Desire, hope and joy animated the citizens. Another feeling, however, was mingled with this enthusiasm, and it was indignation. The ambassadors of Savoy had insinuated, it will be remembered, that Geneva would have to pay tribute to Friburg. 'Where are those famous gold florins, with which they frightened us?' said the citizens. 'The duke who is only a civil officer among us, in his desire to become prince, condescends to vile falsehoods in order that he may succeed!' . . . From every quarter rose the cry: 'A poll, a poll! citizenship with Friburg! A poll, a poll!' As the two first syndics obstinately refused, Hugues remembered that there are moments when audacity alone can save a people. He laid aside his habitual scruples, and acting solely on his own responsibility, he proposed the alliance. 'Yes, yes,' replied the majority of the assembly with uplifted hands. A few mamelukes, surprised, disconcerted, and disheartened, remained silent and still.†

Thus, at the very moment when the court of Turin was expressing its discontent at the acquittal of Berthelier, the

* Council Registers, Feb. 6, 1519.

† Bonivard, *Chroniq.* ii. p. 333. Registers of the Council, Feb. 6, 1519.

people replied by a resolution which threatened still more the ambitious designs of Savoy. The citizens of Geneva opened their gates to the Swiss. By turning their backs on the south, they forsook despotism and popery; by turning towards the north, they invited liberty and truth.

The nomination of the syndics, which came next, seemed to confirm this solemn vote: it was the most huguenot election ever known. Three of the new syndics were devoted partisans of independence, namely, Stephen de la Mare, a connection of the Gingins, who had accompanied Hugues to Friburg; John Baud, Hugues' brother-in-law; and Louis Plongeon, seignior of Bellerive. Guiges Prévost, the premier syndic, had indeed very close relations with the ducal party, but he was a man of good intentions. Many old councillors had to make way for devoted patriots. Geneva was beginning to soar: it desired to be free. Ambassadors set off immediately to announce to Friburg that the people had voted the alliance.*

Then burst forth one of those great transports that come over a whole nation, when after many struggles it catches a glimpse of liberty. In all the city there were bonfires, cheering, songs, processions, and banquets. But here and there, in the midst of this great joy, there were gloomy faces to be seen; the mamelukes strove in vain to keep down their anger; it broke out suddenly in insults and riots. The reaction was indeed prompt: in the presence of the simple joy of the people, the duke's friends drew closer together, and their party was organized. The house of Savoy had still many adherents in Geneva, capable of opposing the desire for independence and truth. There were old Savoyard families devoted to the duke; persons who were sold to him; young men of birth, enthusiasts of absolute power; priests and laymen enamored of Rome; traders averse to a war that would injure their business; weak men, trembling at the least commotion, and many low people without occupation, who are easily excited to riot. The party felt the necessity of calculating their strength and

* See the letter from the council in the Registers, Feb. 6, 1519, and in the fragments of Grenus, p. 109.

coming to some understanding; but it was not its most prominent leaders who placed themselves in the front. Francis Cartelier, a native of Bresse, and syndic in 1516, a lettered, prudent, and cunning but mean man, convened its principal members in a room at the convent of Rive, which was called 'the little stove.' Thither came in succession, besides Montyon and Nergaz, whom we know already, other mamelukes young and full of zeal: Messieurs de Brandis, who were at the head of Genevan society; the two De Fernex, who derived their name from a lordship which became famous in after years; Marin de Versonex, whose family was distinguished by its good works, a young man of limited understanding but ardent imagination, of a disposition easily led away, and passionately devoted to the Church of Rome, which alone he thought able to save him; by his side was his cousin Percival de Pesmes, united to him by a sincere friendship, and whose ancestors had been among the crusading barons who followed St. Louis; lastly, many other noble mamelukes, determined to oppose even to death the triumph of the party of liberty and Switzerland. These old magistrates and these young nobles found themselves out of their element in Geneva. Sincere for the most part in their convictions, they believed they saw in the new day that was rising over the world, a day of tempest which destroying what existed would put nothing in its place. What must be done to avert so dire a misfortune? They resolved to inform the duke of the alliance which had just been voted, and urge him to make every exertion to prevent its being carried out.*

All these efforts were to prove useless. Liberty was beginning to raise her head in one of the smallest but most ancient cities of the Empire and the Church. It is a strange thing that the city bearing on its flag the symbols of these two absolute powers—the key of the popes and the eagle of the emperors—raised this very significant banner, and thus proclaimed, as if in a spirit of contradiction, liberty in Church and State. While other nations (if we except the

* Galiffe, *Matériaux*, &c., ii. pp. 246, 262, 264.

Swiss League) were sleeping under the feudal sceptre of their masters, this little republic in the centre of Europe was awaking. Like a dead man lying in a vast cemetery, it began to stir and alone came forth triumphant from its tomb. In all the neighboring countries, in Switzerland, Savoy, France, and places more remote, people talked of the strange movements taking place at Geneva, and of the daring resistance opposed by a few energetic citizens to a prince who was brother-in-law to Charles V. and uncle to Francis I. Men of the old times grew alarmed. True, it was but a cloud, small as a man's hand, but it might grow into a fierce tempest in which the two ancient buttresses of feudal and Roman society—absolute power in spiritual and in temporal matters—might be shattered. What would happen then? Might not this emancipatory movement extend through Europe? At Geneva men talked of political liberty; at Wittemberg of religious reform: if these two streams should chance to unite, they would make a formidable torrent which would throw down the edifice of the dark ages and sweep away its ruins into the great abyss. 'People spoke everywhere,' Bonivard tells us, 'of huguenots and mamelukes, as they once did of Guelfs and Ghibelines.' The prior of St. Victor, to whom these things were reported, reflected on them and said in his musings: 'Geneva is beginning to be a member in the body of christendom of which strange things are said.' In examining them, however, he thought there was room for abatement both of hopes and fears:—'Fame, as Virgil sings, is a goddess who makes things greater than they are.' * These things were greater than Bonivard thought. Geneva, by setting out in search of liberty, was to find the Gospel.

The duke, the count, and the bishop, informed successively by their ambassadors, the vidame, and lastly by the mamelukes of 'the little stove,' 'drank of these bitter waters,' and asked themselves if they were going to lose that city from which the house of Savoy had derived such great profit for centuries. They began to understand the impru-

* Bonivard, *Chroniq.* ii. p. 344.

dence of their rough policy; they began to regret the arrests and the murders; they would have liked that 'the work was to be done over again.' That seemed difficult; yet after many conferences, the three princes agreed upon certain plans, one or other of which they thought must succeed.

First: They sought to break the alliance by means of their pensioners at Friburg. The latter wishing to earn their money began to intrigue, to declaim, and to discuss. But the Friburgers, devoted to the cause of Geneva and liberty, resisted them, and the people, discovering the intrigues of the pensioners, rose against them. There were great disturbances in the streets, and blows were exchanged. 'What! does even Friburg take side with the new ideas?' people said at the court of Turin. It was not because they were new, but because they were old, that Friburg adopted them. The pensioners of Savoy were obliged to strike their sails, and they wrote to the duke: 'All who do not dance to the tune the people play, incur the risk of a beating.* . . . Will your Highness pray excuse us?'

This attempt having failed, the court of Turin passed to another, and endeavored to win over the leaders of the opposition in Geneva. 'They open their mouths very wide,' said the Savoyards; 'stuff them with gold.' Much skill was required to carry out this new manœuvre. The Bishop of Maurienne, precentor of the cathedral of Geneva, a supple, able, insinuating man, and tolerably esteemed by the friends of liberty, was selected by the duke for this delicate mission. The prince declared to him with the strongest oaths (in order that it might be repeated) that he had nothing to do with the deaths of Navis and Blanchet. 'It was done by my lord of Geneva alone without my knowledge,' said he. 'Ah, I should be very glad it had never happened, let it cost me ever so much. Repeat all I say to Berthelier. Offer him gold and silver; in a word, do anything to attach him to my service.' Maurienne arrived in Geneva. Nobody doubted at that time that every man had

* 'S'exposent à recevoir de la pantoufle.'—Bonivard, *Chroniq.* ii. p. 335.

his price. 'His Highness,' said the bishop to Berthelier, 'is aware that the crimes of which you are accused are the inventions of your enemies.' Then came promises of gold and silver. 'Only,' added Maurienne, 'let Geneva renounce her alliance with the Swiss.' Berthelier, who awaited with unflinching heart the hour when he would pour out his life for the independence of Geneva, smiled disdainfully at these words; then he shuddered, and putting aside the gilded yet poisoned cup which Maurienne presented to him, he answered coldly: 'A vile interest will never make us render up an innocent people to the vengeance of your prince.' Maurienne, rejected by Berthelier, 'frequented every place of meeting,' says a manuscript, 'in order to prevail upon the chief supporters of the alliance to give it up; but he only lost his pains.' All whom he tried to seduce wished to be free and to join hands with Switzerland.*

The duke, seeing that he was laboring in vain, made one more heroic effort. 'Well, then,' he said, 'let us raise all Switzerland.' The energetic Saleneuve, the able Chappuis, and the diplomatic Lambert were sent as ambassadors from Savoy to the deputies of the cantons then sitting in diet, and complained bitterly of Geneva. Would that little city weigh as much in the balance as the powerful house whose states enclosed the two sides of the Alps? 'Friburg,' said president Lambert, 'treats with *enclavés*, without the consent of the most serene prince in whose states they are placed.' This new name given to the Genevans amused Bonivard greatly. 'Oh, oh!' he said: 'no longer daring to call us his subjects, for the word is used up, the duke styles us his *enclavés!*' This time Charles III. and his government had taken the right course. The cantons, offended that Friburg had acted alone in this matter, desiring to humor the duke, and not being acquainted with the facts, promised to exhort 'certain headstrong and rebellious Genevans to desist from their enterprise.'† This little republic, at the moment of

* Council Registers, March 1, 1519. Bonivard, *Chroniq.* ii. p. 336. Berne MSS. v. 12. Gautier MS.

† 'Exhortamur obstinatos et rebelles, pacis corruptores, ab incepto ut desistant.'—Archives of Geneva, No. 912.

her awakening, found ranged against her both the neighboring princes and a large majority of the cantons. The diet declared in favor of the duke, and sent the Sieur d'Erlach to Geneva to support the ducal protest. What could little Geneva do, when pressed at once by Savoy and Switzerland? It was as if two ships in full sail should come up in opposite directions, threatening to crush a frail boat that floated between them. But the poor little bark carried a ballast which was its salvation, namely, liberty and the protection of God. Such vessels, even if they are run down, come to the surface again sooner or later. The Friburgers did not desert the cause of independence, but sent John Fabri to Geneva on their behalf. The two deputies met almost about the same time on the shores of the Leman, one bringing peace, the other war.

The general council having met on the 1st of March, 1519, the generous Fabri, faithful to a desperate cause, spoke first, and did not conceal from the assembly the large majority that had declared against Geneva. 'Consider the matter and see for yourselves what ought to be done,' he said. 'As for us, we will preserve the alliance to the last drop of our blood.' These words electrified the audience. 'And we too!' they shouted all around. The citizens were stirred: they shook hands, they blessed Friburg and embraced Fabri: everybody swore to be true to the alliance. The Friburgers quitted the hall touched with the noble sight of a nation ready to brave the greatest dangers in the maintenance of its rights.

The deputy from the League was admitted next. Cold and diplomatic, a stiff patrician and inflexible magistrate, D'Erlach spoke with an imperious voice: 'Obey the duke,' he said. 'Be henceforward his faithful subjects; break off your alliance with Friburg. The League require it from you under pain of their deep resentment; and as for Friburg, they command it.' This short and rough speech amazed the Genevans. How long had they been the subjects of Savoy? . . . Had the Swiss League broken their own yoke only to impose it on others? Had they lighted the torch of liberty on their own mountains only to extinguish it elsewhere? . . . What! shall the representatives of the ancient liberties draw up in battle array against the new liberty? The proudest of the Genevans, with heads upraised, said haughtily that even the Swiss could not make them bend. Yet all the citizens were not so brave. Could Geneva be saved if Switzerland forsook her? Many became uneasy, some were grieved: the mamelukes alone rejoiced and triumphed. The place of assembly reëchoed with weeping, groans, and curses. The confusion continued to increase.

When the deputy from Berne had withdrawn, the deputy from Friburg, animated with the most heroic sentiments, returned to reassure the people; and notwithstanding the declarations of the Bernese commissioner he affirmed stoutly that Berne would not abandon Geneva. 'Fear nothing,' he said; 'my lords of Berne and Friburg are brothers; they will not quarrel with each other for the love of Savoy. And though Berne should forsake you, we are strong enough with God's help, and we will not permit either you or ourselves to be trampled on . . . Declare frankly whether you desire the alliance: say Yes or No.' Then with a loud shout the people exclaimed: 'Yes! yes! Better see our wives and children slain, better die a thousand deaths ourselves, than cancel the alliance with Friburg!' The general council desiring to give an energetic proof of its will, and to make the resolution irrevocable, decreed that if any should propose the rupture of the alliance, he should be forthwith beheaded. The syndics returned to the inn where D'Erlach coldly awaited their answer. It was as becoming and proud as D'Erlach's speech had been imperious. 'We will send a deputation to the next diet,' they said, 'when we will prove that we are not the duke's subjects, and that we have done nothing to his prejudice.'*

The greatness of a people does not depend upon the extent of its territory. There was a soul in this little nation, and in that soul dwelt lofty aspirations. Had all the powers of the earth risen against Berthelier, Lévrier, and Hugues, these energetic men would not have quailed. At the meet-

* Registers of the Council *ad diem.* Bonivard, *Chroniq.* ii. p. 338.

ing of the general council on the following day (March 2, 1519) the alliance was confirmed; Hugues and Malbuisson started immediately for Friburg with instructions to sign the engagement, which the Helvetic diet had just ordered to be cancelled. Such was the answer made by Geneva to the Swiss. The faithful devotedness of Friburg should be for ever inscribed as an example in the records of history. But it is not to the Swiss in general, as is commonly believed, that the Genevans substantially owe their independence. but to God and to the strong will that God gave them.*

CHAPTER XVI.

THE CANONS JOIN THE DUKE, AND THE PEOPLE RISE AGAINST THEM.

(MARCH, 1519.)

THE duke hesitated no longer. Pacific and diplomatic means were exhausted; he must now draw the sword and with its trenchant edge hew down the pride of Geneva. Nevertheless, to save appearances, he desired that some influential body would decare against the alliance; for it would then seem as if he were supporting a Genevese party, and his intervention with an armed force would look less odious. To attain his end he turned his eyes on the chapter of St. Pierre, the bishop's natural council, and in his absence representing the catholic church. Its members being all noble or graduates in law (which at that time amounted almost to nobility), this body might be considered as the house of lords in the Genevan constitution.† The duke instructed his agents to work upon the canons, and they might have been seen

* Registers of the Council *ad diem.* Bonivard, *Chroniq.* ii. p. 338. Spon, *Hist. de Genève,* i. p. 314. Berne MSS. v. p. 12. Roset and Gautier MSS.

† Galiffe, *Matériaux pour l'Histoire de Genève.*

going from door to door in the street that still bears their name. They advised the canons to be on their guard; that this alliance with the Swiss compromised everything, and particularly their functions and benefices. They were conjured to write to my lords of the League, stating that the chapter did not assent to the alliance in question. The canons, flattered by the importance which his Highness of Savoy attached to their opinion, hastily put on scapulary and amice and assembled in chapter. The success of this ducal manœuvre could not be doubtful. Only one canon was a native of Geneva; and this was Michael Navis, brother of him whom the bishop had murdered—a man as servile as his brother was independent. Two only were liberals: De Gingins, abbot of Bonmont, and Bonivard, prior of St. Victor, who was the youngest of the chapter, and who had no vote because he was not in holy orders. All the other canons were devoted to the duke—all worthy gentlemen, much impressed with their own dignity, like those canons of St. John of Lyons who, having produced their quarterings of nobility, demanded the privilege of not kneeling at the elevation of the host. The chapter opened their deliberations; and 'the stout master-courtiers who had the right to speak first began to say *amen*.' Bonivard, who saw these fat canons one after another bending low their bloated faces, grew alarmed at the turn matters were taking. What would be the consequence if the Church said No, while the people said Yes? What disorders at home, what weakness abroad! He saw that the opposition in the chapter fell to his share; he performed his duty valiantly, and paid dearly for it. He had not been asked for his vote, and the secretary was preparing to commit the resolution to writing, when the prior rose and said: 'Stop a little, Mr. Secretary, although I am not *in sacris* (in orders) and have no vote in the chapter, I have a duty here. Now it seems to me that before granting the illustrious duke his request, you should consider the purport of it a little better.* It tends to break off that alliance with Friburg which the people of this city have so much

* 'Vous devriez un peu mieux en mâcher la teneur.' (Bonivard has preserved his speech, *Chroniq.* ii. pp. 339, 340.)

at heart that they would lose their wives and children sooner than renounce it. Think of what you are doing . . . Very reverend sirs, you cannot return an answer to the duke without that answer being known to our people with whom you have promised to live and die. What will they say of you? With your permission I will tell you. They will say that you are playing the scorpion's trick—that you pretend to be friends in front, and behind you inflict a mortal wound with your tail . . . Fear their anger. Rest assured that if they say nothing at the moment, they will bear you in mind another day.' The 'stout masters,' who were far from brave, began to feel uneasy and to turn in their stalls. They were in an awkward dilemma. 'There is one way of satisfying both parties,' continued Bonivard; 'that is, reply to my lord of Savoy, and to the people also, that your business does not extend to alliances and other like civil matters, but to spiritual things only: that it does not concern you to make or unmake treaties; and that your function is only to pray to God and to pray principally for peace among all men. If you do this, no one will have reason to be dissatisfied with you.'

Thus did Bonivard, at the beginning of the sixteenth century, lay down a categorical distinction between the spiritual and the temporal government, and maintain that the Church and the State had each its own sphere. The canons thought this theory very strange, and stranger still that a young man of twenty-five should presume to teach it them.

The Bishop of Maurienne, who fancied himself a great diplomatist, was seriously offended. 'Do you think, M. de St. Victor,' he said, 'that we do not know how to write a letter?' . . . The Savoyard canons were exasperated that one of their countrymen should desire anything but what the duke wished. 'The house of Savoy,' said M. de Monthoux, 'has conferred many favors on your predecessors, and is it thus you show your gratitude?' . . . 'I would willingly render service to the duke,' answered Bonivard, 'but before all I will observe my oath to Geneva and the Church.' At these words, which resembled a reproach, murmurs arose from all quarters. Bonivard was not intimidated. Upright in heart, noble in intention, wise in counsel, of extraordinary intelligence and superior talent, he was far above the anger of his venerable colleagues. 'Very well, then, gentlemen,' said he, 'do as you please, but I protest that I do not agree.' Then turning to the clerk, he said: 'Write down that, Mr. Secretary,' and left the chapter. The canons were too full of the sense of their own importance to heed the protest. Persuaded that it was their duty to check a political movement, which might besides lead to a religious revolution, these churchmen, desirous of displaying a courage similar to that of the Roman senators, peremptorily drew up their declaration against the Swiss alliance, without regard to the resistance of the people which Bonivard had predicted.

At the dawn of the canonical institution, when the scattered priests of a church were assembled by the bishop into one body, these priests or canons led at first a life so regular and so strict that the people were enraptured with them. But that did not last long, and the lives of these ecclesiastics too often became so disorderly that the laity turned away from them with disgust and hatred. It had been so at Geneva. The decision of the canons was soon known in the city, and the people immediately assembled in great numbers in the Place Molard. They described the scene in the chapter, of which Bonivard may perhaps have given some hints; and complained that lazy priests should dare to declare their opinions on public matters and take sides with the enemies of Geneva. They said that churchmen were always wanting to meddle with politics, and striving, by flattering authority, to gratify their avarice and increase their power. It was proposed to pay these reverend men a visit, and request them to mind their own affairs and leave state matters alone. In fact, the patriots were stirring, and ready, says Bonivard, 'to proceed in great rage to assault the canons.' Aimé de Gingins, abbot of Bonmont and episcopal vicar, who lived with his colleagues in the street still known as the Rue des Chanoines,* sent in all haste for his friend the prior of St. Victor, that he might stop the people. Would he consent? As

* In the house afterwards occupied by Calvin, where the Maison Naville now stands.

the canons had rejected his advice, might he not leave them to get out as they could from the evil strait into which they had fallen? Bonivard in truth hated despotism, and was one of the most honestly liberal men of the sixteenth century. 'Monarchical princes are always enemies of the liberty of the people,' he said, 'and the servants whom they keep are the same, because they can live in greater licence under king than under law. This nearly caused the ruin of Rome, when the young men conspired to restore the kings, as Livy bears witness in his second book.'*

But if Bonivard was opposed to the despotism of princes, he was equally so to the disorders of the people. Accordingly he did not hesitate, but hurried to the episcopal vicar's. De Gingins, who was waiting for the return of his messenger in the keenest anxiety, flew to meet the prior, exclaiming: 'Ah, St. Victor, if you do not give orders, some disaster will happen to the canons. Our folks have done a foolish thing, and the people have heard of it: see if you can quiet them.'†

Bonivard hastily lighted a torch (for it was night) and ran to meet the people. He found them at the top of the Perron, a steep street, which opens between the cathedral and the Rue des Chanoines. Berthelier and the ex-syndic Hugues 'were in front,' he tells us. The former of the two, seeing his friend Bonivard at the top of the street, with a furred amice upon his head, holding a torch in one hand, and with the other making eager signs for them to stop, exclaimed with an oath: 'Ah! you *Bouche-Coppons*, you make a fair show in front with treachery behind.'—'Bouche-Coppon (or hooded friar) was a name they gave us,' says the prior, 'because we carried the amice on our heads in winter.'‡

The moment was critical: the trembling canons expected to see the people fall upon them; some of their servants,

* Bonivard, *Chroniq.* ii. p. 343.

† Ibid. p. 342.

‡ The amice was a furred hood with which the canons sometimes covered their head, but generally carried on the arm. Bonivard, *Chroniq.* ii. p. 342.

peering anxiously down the Perron, from the top of the street watched the movements of the crowd, and of a sudden shrank back with terror on hearing the shouts of the advancing huguenots. In fact the people were exasperated and demanded that the priests should be brought to account for meddling with politics. Bonivard did not flinch: 'Gently, good sirs,' he said to the citizens; 'do not be vexed at trifles; there is not so much harm done as you think.' Then ascribing to the canons his own ideas, he continued: 'These reverend gentlemen have written, that they will not live under other protection than that of God and St. Peter, and that as for the alliance with Friburg, they do not mean either to accept or refuse it . . . The letter is not sent yet . . . you shall see it!' Upon this Besançon Hugues motioned the people to halt, and the crowd obeyed a magistrate so respected. On his side Bonivard hastily despatched a messenger to the Bishop of Maurienne, the most intelligent of the canons, instructing him to 'change promptly the purport of the letter.' Maurienne privately sent for the secretary and dictated to him a new despatch such as Bonivard required. Berthelier, Hugues, and Pécolat, deputed by the people, arrived shortly after, conducted by Bonivard, when Maurienne showed them the new document. They suspected the trick. 'Oh no! the ink is still quite wet,' they said. However, as the contents satisfied them, they would not examine the letter too narrowly, and the people, unwilling to make a disturbance to no purpose, were satisfied also. 'Let the business be settled this once,' they said; 'but let us keep a kick in store for the other courtiers.' They meant, no doubt, that having given a smart lesson to the canons, they reserved the honor of giving another to the mamelukes. 'I have inserted this,' says Bonivard, concluding his account of this incident, 'to caution all republics never to give credit or authority to people bred in the courts of princes.'*

* Bonivard, *Chroniq.* ii. pp. 339–343. Gautier, *Hist.* MSS.

CHAPTER XVII.

THE DUKE AT THE HEAD OF HIS ARMY SURROUNDS GENEVA.

(March and April, 1519.)

The duke was at the end of his resources, and the affair of the chapter had raised his indignation to its utmost. There had been comedy enough—it was time now to come to the tragedy. Everything must be prepared to crush Geneva and liberty.

The duke raised an army 'this side the mountains (that is, in Savoy) as secretly as he could.' Then fearing lest the Friburgers, if they were warned, should hasten to the support of the city, and wishing 'to catch the fish without wetting his paws,' he sent M. de Lambert into Switzerland to amuse the cantons with fine speeches. While the ambassador was thus occupying the attention of Messieurs de Friburg, the Savoyard nobles hastily summoned their vassals to arms. The duke placed his forces under the command of the Sieur de Montrotier, Bonivard's cousin and an excellent captain. The latter marched off his troops during the night and assembled them in silence round Geneva; so that the duke reached St. Jullien, a league from the city, with seven thousand soldiers, before anything was known of his enterprise. The Savoyards had never done so well before. In a short time the people of the neighborhood, hurrying in crowds to his standard, raised the ducal army to ten thousand men.*

Then the duke no longer concealed his intentions. He kept his court at St. Jullien, and there gathered round the prince an ever-increasing number of nobles in rich dresses

* Bonivard, *Chroniq.* ii. pp. 343, 346. Savyon, *Annales*, p. 82. Spon, *Hist. de Genève*, i. p. 311. Gautier MSS.

and splendid armor; and especially of young gentlemen brimful of insolence, who longed to make a campaign against the noisy shopkeepers. Never before had this little town witnessed so much display, or heard so many boasts. 'We must put them down with our riding-whips,' said some. No sooner said than done. On the 15th of March, 1519, fifteen of these cavaliers started from St. Jullien to carry out their plan of campaign; they arrived in Geneva, proceeded straight to the hôtel-de-ville, leaving their horses with their servants in the streets, and with a swaggering air entered the council-room, all booted and splashed with mud. Not waiting to be offered chairs, they rudely sat down, and without any preface said: 'My lord, desiring to enter this city, orders you to lay down your arms and to open the gates.' The Genevan senators, seated in their curule chairs, looked with astonishment at this singular embassy; they restrained themselves, however, and replied at once firmly and moderately that the duke would be welcome at Geneva provided he came with his ordinary retinue, and only to enjoy himself as he had often done before. 'In that case,' added the syndics, 'the arms we carry will be used only to guard him.' This seemed to imply that another use might be made of them; and accordingly the gentlemen answered haughtily: 'My lord will enter your city with whom he pleases and do in it as he pleases.'—'Then,' answered the syndics bluntly, 'we will not let him enter.' At these words the fifteen cavaliers rose up like one man: 'We will enter in spite of your teeth,' they said, 'and we will do in your city whatever we please.' Then striding noisily across the flagstones with their spurred boots, they left the hall, remounted their horses, and galloped off along the St. Jullien road.*

As they were seen riding hastily along, fear came over the population. In truth the moment was critical. Geneva was from that time for more than a century under arms, and on repeated occasions, especially at the epoch of the famous escalade in 1602, repelled the attacks of Savoy. But the Reform gave it a strength afterwards which it did not now

* Bonivard, *Chroniq.* ii. pp. 348, 349.

possess. The Swiss diet ordered them to receive the duke; there were only from ten to twelve thousand souls in the city, including women and children; and the prince of Piedmont, duke of Savoy, was at their gates with ten thousand soldiers. They fancied that Charles was going to enter, to burn and massacre everything: many families fled in alarm with the most valuable of their property. But their flight was useless, for the armed men of Savoy occupied the roads, so that the fugitives came upon them everywhere. Some returned to the city: 'All the country of Savoy is in arms,' said they; 'and many of our people have been taken and put to the torture.' It was then three o'clock in the afternoon.* The patriots assembled: Berthelier, Hugues, Bonivard, and many others met in order to come to some understanding. They resolved that it was expedient to send an embassy to Friburg to inform their allies of this incident, and to ask for a garrison, as the duke would not dare to fire a gun at the walls guarded by the League. But whom should they send? Many reasons,—the question of expense being one,—restrained the citizens, for they were poor. Bonivard grew warm: 'You have exasperated the wolf; he is at your gates ready to devour you,' he said, 'and you prefer to let him eat up your milk, your butter, and your cheese—what am I saying? you would sooner let him eat yourselves up than give a share of your pittance to the mastiff that would guard you.' There was one man in the meeting who never calculated when the object was to save his country: this was Besançon Hugues. He was ill, he had already incurred debt in the cause of Geneva; but that mattered not! 'I will go,' said he, and he departed.†

During this time the fifteen gentlemen had returned to St. Jullien and made a report of their visit to the council. Charles and his advisers did not consider their proceedings very diplomatic, and resolved to act more officially but more insolently. The next day, Friday, April 1, the king-at-arms, Provena de Chablais (he derived this name from the province where he was born) arrived in Geneva, and was intro-

* Registers of the Council, April 2, 1519.

† Bonivard, *Chroniq.* ii. p. 347. Galiffe, *Notices Généalogiques,* i. p. 4.

duced to the council with the usual ceremony. A cuirass covered him down to the waist; on his left arm he wore his casaque or coat of arms, and his right hand held a rod,—a *gaulé*, says a manuscript. He entered with head erect, without uncovering or making any bow to the council. 'Sit down by my side,' politely said the premier syndic to him, 'and unfold your message.' Chablais remained standing, with sneering lip and silent, although the invitation was repeated thrice. This mute embassy considerably astonished the Genevan senate. At last, the king-at-arms quitted his fixed posture and took a seat of his own accord, not by the side of, but above the syndics who remained impassive. Then he said: 'Worshipful syndics and councillors, do not marvel if I did not sit down when you desired me, and if I sit down now without being invited; I will tell you the reason. I am here in behalf of my most dread prince and lord, the Duke of Savoy, my master and *yours*. It does not become you to tell him to sit down—it is his privilege to do so when and where he pleases:—not beside you but *above* you, as your sovereign prince; and as representing his person, I have done so myself. Now from my seat I unfold my commission, and it is this. My lord and yours charges and *commands* you to prepare his lodging in your hôtel-de-ville with the sumptuousness and magnificence that belong to such a prince. Likewise he orders that you will get ready provisions for him and his company, which will be ten thousand infantry without including cavalry; for his intention is to lodge here with this retinue to administer justice in Geneva.'*

The king-at-arms was desired to retire, the council wishing to deliberate on the answer to be returned. The discussion was not a long one, all being unanimous to maintain firmly the liberties of Geneva. The herald was called in again, and the first syndic said to him: 'Sir Chablais, we are equally surprised at what you *do* and at what you *say*. At what you do; for after we offered you a seat, you refused it; and when you had refused it, you took it. . . . At

* For this speech see Bonivard, *Chroniq.* ii. p. 349. MS. *Mamelouks de Genève.* Spon, *Hist. de Genève*, i. pp. 314–320.

what you say; for you say that my lord of Savoy is your prince and *ours* . . . a thing unheard of until this time. He may be your prince—that we believe; but ours . . . no! We are his very humble servants, but we are neither his subjects nor his vassals. . . . It therefore does not belong either to you or to him to sit in the place where you are. . . . As for what you say respecting our hôtel-de-ville, we know not what you mean; the duke may choose any lodging he pleases except our hôtel-de-ville, which we cannot spare. He will be treated as in former times—better if possible. He desires to administer justice; it is the place of the bishop and council to do so, according to the franchises which he himself has sworn. If any one among us has offended him, let him inform us. Lastly, as to the large train with which he desires to be attended, it is a singular company for the administration of justice! Let him please to come with his usual retinue, nay, with five hundred men; but ten thousand men and cavalry besides. . . . We have not supplies for so many.' *

Chablais listened coldly and disdainfully. 'Will you or will you not obey the orders of my lord?' he said. The first syndic answered bluntly: 'No.' The herald then rose, put on his coat of arms, and with a loud voice said: 'On his behalf then I pronounce you rebellious to *your* prince—and I declare war against you with fire and sword.' Then flinging his rod into the middle of the hall, he continued: 'I defy you on the part of my lord, in sign of which I throw down this rod (gaule); let him take it up who pleases.' So saying, he left the hall.†

The news of this singular challenge was immediately carried to the people, who were dismayed at it. The huguenots, seeing that they must die or be slaves (say the annals), chose the first alternative and prepared for death, resolving, however, to sell their lives and not to throw them away. Feeling themselves the strongest body in the city, they called the people together. 'Let every one take up arms!' they

* 'Nous n'avons pas mis cuire pour tant de gens.'—Bonivard, *Chroniques.*

† See note, p. 165.

said. They even forced the mamelukes to do so. The gates were shut, the chains stretched across the streets, the artillery manned, the watch set: 'they made all the preparations for war according to the skill and experience they had in that business.'*

The duke, knowing that right was not on his side, resolved to draw the sword. Advised by Montrotier, a daring officer, he had a fit of courage, and, closing all the roads, sent out his troops in every direction. It was Saturday, April 2, and market day at Geneva. The market was held 'without a word said;' they allowed everybody to go in and out who wished;† but about noon a report of the duke's manœuvre having reached the city, the inhabitants took up arms. The peasants, returning from market, described to the Savoyards, with some exaggeration perhaps, the war preparations made by the Genevans. Immediately the duke's fit of courage was succeeded by one of fear. Bonivard had expected this, and on hearing that the prince was at the head of an army, had shrugged his shoulders. 'The duke knows as much of war,' he said, 'as a monk bred in a convent since he was seven years old.' This display of ten thousand men, assembled a league from Geneva, these troops sent out in every direction—all ended in a pitiful retractation. M. de Lucinge, appearing before the council, said: 'His Highness has ordered me to inform you, most honored lords, that he desires to come and sup with you in a friendly way. If he cannot lodge in the hôtel-de-ville, be so good as to prepare a lodging elsewhere for him, his great suite,‡ and two or three hundred infantry only . . . He desires to do violence to nobody.' The mamelukes proposed that the gates should be opened to the duke immediately, but the syndics replied that they would consult the general council on the morrow. The mameluke councillors, who thought that the duke did Geneva a great honor by coming to it, looked around with astonishment at the answer: their greatest happiness was to approach a prince and pay court to his Highness, and these

* Bonivard, *Chroniq.* ii. p. 350. Savyon, *Annales.*

† *Les Mamelouks de Genève*, MS.

‡ '*Magnus status*,' his court. Registers of the Council, April 2.

inflexible huguenots turned their backs upon him. 'Well,' said they, 'if they will not let the duke come to us, we will go to him.' Accordingly Montyon and several others of his party left the council-room. The court-yard of the hôtel-de-ville was full of citizens waiting to learn the result of the meeting: they saw the mamelukes pass with astonishment. The spectators whispered in each other's ears: 'They are going to join the Savoyards.' . . . Presently a loud shout was raised, and several huguenots, catching up some spears that were resting against the wall, ran after the mamelukes to seize them; they were almost overtaken when the councillors, deputed by the syndics, entreated them, for the safety of the city, to avoid a strife between citizens. The angry patriots returned to the hôtel-de-ville. Every one was distressed at knowing that there were among them men capable of forsaking Geneva for the Duke of Savoy.*

The disloyalists (as they were called) hastened along the St. Jullien Road. Besides Montyon, there were Cartelier, Déléamont, Nergaz, Ray, the two De Fernex, and others, making in all between thirty and forty. 'Our interview with the duke must be private,' said the cunning Cartelier, who felt how criminal was the step they were taking. The duke let them know that at a certain hour of the night he would be under a particular tree in the Falcon orchard. Thither they resorted one by one, and were all soon gathered round the tree without being able to recognize each other except by the voice. The intriguing Cartelier was spokesman. Political views influenced Montyon, De Versonex, and others; but in him, it was the hatred he bore against the huguenots and the desire to be revenged on them. He assured the duke that the majority of the people were ready to acknowledge him for their sovereign. 'But,' he added, 'the bad ones have shut the gates, stretched the chains, placed guards . . . Enter Geneva, my lord, sword in hand.' They then discussed their guilty projects, and it was agreed in whispers what the mamelukes should do in order to facilitate the entrance of the Savoyards into the city. 'The

* 'Obviaverunt ne irent alicubi.'—Galiffe, *Matériaux pour l'Histoire de Genève*, Exam. of de Joye, ii. p. 218.

traitors,' says Bonivard, 'entered into a plot with the duke.'*

Early on Sunday Charles took up a better position and went to his strong castle of Gaillard on the Arve, three quarters of a league from Geneva. The report of his intentions having spread through all the valley of the Leman, the gentlemen and the companies of the Pays de Vaud, Chablais, and Faucigny came thronging in. Nay, more: the canons and priests of the city, quickly forgetting the lesson they had received, hurried off to Gaillard. Bonivard, who was almost the only cleric remaining in Geneva, saw all his theories confirmed. It was his maxim that 'people bred up in the courts of princes always remember their first food.'—'And now,' said he, 'of all the canons and folks of the long robe, there are left in Geneva only De la Biolée, Navis, and myself. All are gone to visit the duke at Gaillard, even M. de Bonmont, who was considered the principal friend of the public weal.'† Ere long the castle was filled with an imposing crowd, more numerous than at St. Jullien.

The storm was approaching, the danger increasing from hour to hour: the little band of patriots was still full of courage; but alas! it was an ant-hill on which a rock from the Alps was about to fall. They had watched the priests with anxious eye, but without desiring to stop them. 'These birds have so keen a scent,' it was said, 'that they hasten wherever there is any flesh.' If Friburg would only send a few valiant warriors to assist those of Geneva, that Savoyard army would soon be dispersed; but Friburg remained dumb. The uneasiness spread from one to another; desponding faces were met in the streets . . . On a sudden two horsemen are seen on the Swiss road . . . O joy! they wear the Friburg colors! . . . At eleven o'clock in the forenoon of Sunday, April 3, 1519, Berthelier's friend, Councillor Marti, accompanied by a herald, entered Geneva. 'And your armed men?' they said to him, and were informed in

* Bonivard, *Chroniq.* ii. p. 346. Galiffe, *Matériaux*, Exam. of Cartelier, ii. pp. 234, 246, 262, 264.

† Bonivard, *Chroniq.* ii. p. 354. *Les Mamelouks de Genève*, MS

answer that, for the present at least, there were none. The general council happening to be assembled in order to reply to M. de Lucinge, Marti instantly proceeded thither, but was not received so well as he had expected. 'We want ambassadors in doublets and not in long robes,' said the huguenots to him; 'not diplomats, but soldiers.' Marti started for Gaillard, but the Genevans saw him depart without hope; in their opinion, arquebuses should be the only answer for the Savoyards.*

The Friburger, as he drew near Gaillard, was struck with the large number of troops around the castle. At this moment the duke was giving audience to the canons, who were making all the bows and compliments learnt in former days at court; he hoped to be able to draw them into the plot, and was therefore much annoyed at seeing this mediator arrive. Turning impatiently towards his officers, he vented in an under tone some contemptuous words against him. Nevertheless, a few minutes later, when he had examined him more closely, Charles took courage, doubting not that his political skill would easily manage this shepherd of the Alps. 'He seems a good plain man, easy to be deceived,' said the duke, who, commencing his manœuvres, added: 'Sit down, Mr. Ambassador,' and thereupon feasted him liberally, and gave him all kinds of good words. But the plain man, who was in reality a bold and crafty Friburger, replied in his Romane tongue: 'My lord, you have already told my friends so many lies, that I do not know if they will believe you any more.'† The duke, offended at this rude language, spoke more sharply: 'I shall enter Geneva as a friend,' he said; 'or, if they do not like it, as an enemy. My artillery is all ready to *lather* (savonner) the city in case of refusal.' Marti in alarm demanded a truce, at least for the night, so that he might speak to the people of Geneva and settle the matter, which the duke granted.‡

All the citizens were afoot: the guards at the gates, the

* Savyon, *Annales*, p. 87. Bonivard, *Chroniq* ii. p. 351, &c.

† 'Monseigneu, vos avi ja dict à Messieurs tant de iangles, que je ne say si vo vudront ple crerre.'—Bonivard, *Chroniq*. ii. p. 351

‡ Ibid, p. 352.

cannon on the walls, the watch day and night in the streets. At ten o'clock Marti arrived, and went straight to the council, whose sittings were declared permanent. 'Gentlemen,' said he to the syndics, 'I think you must trust the duke and let him enter the city.'—'And the assistance of Friburg?' asked some; to which Marti replied: 'My lords are far away!'* He seemed to have lost all hope. He added, however: 'There is a truce until to-morrow morning.' It was agreed to convene the Great Council the next morning before daybreak in order to deliberate on the course to be taken in this terrible crisis; and as the citizens had been on foot for three nights, they were permitted in consideration of the truce to go and take some repose. It was then eleven o'clock.

It struck twelve. No sound was heard but the measured steps of the sentinels; a dark night covered the city with its curtain, and all were asleep. Suddenly the flash of a torch gleamed from the top of one of the three towers of St. Pierre; it was the signal agreed upon between Cartelier and the duke at the nocturnal conference held under the tree in the Falcon orchard: that flash announced that the Swiss could enter without resistance. The noise of horses was heard almost immediately without the city, in the direction of St. Antoine, and a loud blow was struck on the gate. It was Philip, count of Genevois, the duke's brother, at the head of his cavalry: having knocked, he waited for the mamelukes to open according to their promise. But the sentry at the St. Antoine gate, who had seen the torch and heard the knock, suspecting treachery, fired his arquebus and gave the alarm. Immediately the tocsin sounded; the citizens awoke, grasped their arms, and hurried in the direction of the attack. 'All were much frightened and vexed, and great uproar was made in the city.' Everybody was running about shouting and ordering. The count, who was listening, began to fear that the plot had failed. In the midst of the confusion, a clap of thunder was heard, which terrified both sides. The count and his followers hesitated

* Bonivard, *Chroniq.* ii. p. 352.

no longer, but retired; the Genevans did the same, and a few angry patriots, as they passed Marti's house on their way home, went in and asked him angrily: 'Is this the fine truce you brought us?'*

The Grand Council met before daybreak on Monday, April 4. The mamelukes made an excuse for the night affair: it was no doubt a patrol of cavalry which had advanced too far. But Marti did not conceal the danger: 'The duke is at your gates with his whole army,' he said: 'if you comply with his demands, he told me you would be satisfied with him; if not, he will enter by force this very afternoon. Make a virtue of necessity; or, at the least, send him a deputation.' The syndics started for Gaillard immediately. The duke received them most graciously and affectionately. 'I will enter Geneva with none but my ordinary retinue,' he told them; 'I will take only five hundred footmen for my guard and dismiss all the rest of my army. I will do no injury either to the community or to individuals, and my stay shall not be long.' His Highness made so many promises and oaths that entrance was at last yielded to him.

When this resolution of the council was known, the indignant patriots threw away their arquebuses; all laid down their arms, and a profound dejection came over men's minds. Cries of vexation and of sorrow were heard, but there still lingered here and there a hope that God would finally deliver the city.†

On the morning of Tuesday, April 5, the duke set all his army in motion. *All!* . . . When they heard of this, the Genevans hastened to remonstrate with him. 'My people will only pass through Geneva,' he answered; 'fear nothing, but open your gates.'—'Certainly,' added some mamelukes; 'be easy: they will come in at one gate and go out at another.' The triumph of violence and craft was about to be achieved. A people, too simple and confiding, were now to be crushed under the feet of a powerful prince

* Bonivard, *Chroniq.* ii. p. 352. *Les Mamelouks de Genève,* MS. Savyon, *Annales*, p. 88.

† Ibid.

and of his numerous satellites. All the gates were opened, and those which had been walled up were broken down. The huguenots, who had voted unhesitatingly against the admission of Charles into the city, looked on with indignation at this sad sight; but they were determined to be present to the end at the humiliation of Geneva. Bonivard was the most provident; he took the alarm: he had no culverins now in his priory, and he could not have resisted the Savoy army with his ten monks. 'Consent to the duke's entrance . . . what madness!' he exclaimed. Certainly those who know *his honesty*, of whom I am one, are aware of what will happen.' And this, in Bonivard's opinion, was, that he would be the first victim sacrificed by the duke, and that there would be many others. 'Wishing,' he tells us, 'to be wiser and cleverer than the rest,' he hastily escaped into the Pays de Vaud. Berthelier who was more exposed than his friend, and who saw clearly his end approaching, was not frightened. He knew that the defenders of law and liberty serve their cause by their deaths as well as by their lives, and determined to await the attacks of Charles and the bastard.*

CHAPTER XVIII.

THE ARMY OF SAVOY IN GENEVA.

(April and May, 1519.)

The army of Savoy approached the St. Antoine gate: it was like a triumphal progress. Monarchy, according to politicians, was about to gain the victory over republicanism. 'In front marched the Count of Genevois, in complete steel armor,' say the chronicles, 'wearing a long plume, and riding on a stout stallion, who curvetted about so that it was pleasant to see.' He was followed by the cavalry in

* Bonivard, *Chroniq.* ii. p. 353. Savyon, *Annales.*

breast-plates. Then came the main body, to the number of about eight thousand infantry, headed by six Genevan mamelukes. Last appeared the duke, followed by all his guard; he had laid aside his gracious humor, and desired that his entrance should have something warlike and alarming. 'Montrotier,' he said to his principal captain, 'I have sworn that I will only enter Geneva *over* the gates.' Montrotier understood him, and, going forward with a body of men, knocked down the St. Antoine gate and the adjoining wall. The satisfied duke now resumed his triumphal march. He was armed from head to foot and rode a handsome hackney: two pages carried before him his lance and his helmet. One of these was J. J. de Watteville, afterwards *avoyer* of Berne. The weak-minded Charles, inflated with his success, pulled up his courser, and made him paw the rebellious stones. 'A true Don Quixote,' says a catholic historian, 'he showed the same pride as a conqueror loaded with glory who at the cost of much blood and fatigue had reduced a fortress after a long and dangerous siege.' And if we may believe contemporary documents, 'Charles advanced more like a Jupiter surrounded with his thunders than a conqueror; his head was bare in order, said his courtiers, that his eyes, flashing with wrath, should blast the audacity of the Genevans who should be rash enough to look in his face.' All the army having passed the gate after him marched through the city in order to parade its triumph in the streets and defy the citizens.*

In conformity with the engagements made by the duke, his soldiers entering by one gate ought, after crossing the city, to have gone out by the other. Bonivard on hearing of this had shaken his head. 'It will be with Geneva as with Troy,' said the classical prior; 'the Savoyards, entering by stratagem like the Greeks of Sinon, will afterwards remain by force.' And so it happened, for the whole army took up its quarters immediately in the city. The bands of Faucigny, which were the most terrible, established them-

* Lévrier, *Hist. Chronol. des Comtes de Genevois*, ii. p. 166. *Les Mamelouks de Genève*, MS. Bonivard, *Chroniq.* ii. p. 553. Savyon, *Annales*, p. 89.

selves at St. Gervais by order of the duke; those of the Pays de Vaud at St. Leger, up to the Arve; those of Chablais at the Molard and along the Rhone; those of Savoy and Genevois in the Bourg de Four and the upper part of the city. The nobles were lodged in the best houses situated principally between Rive and the Molard. The duke took up his quarters also on the left bank, near the lake, in the Maison de Nice which belonged to Bonivard. The count, appointed by his brother governor of the city, fixed his head-quarters at the hôtel-de-ville. Geneva was taken; the Duke of Savoy had made himself master of it by perjury, and there he intended to remain. Many citizens thought their country for ever lost. The plans formed during so many years and even centuries, were realised at last; despotism, triumphant in Geneva, was about to trample under foot law, constitution, and liberty. The Savoyards had seen from their mountain-tops a fire in this city which disquieted them—a fire whose flames might extend and consume the time-worn edifices their fathers had raised. They were now going to stifle these flames, to extinguish the embers, and scatter the ashes; the duke, the emperor his brother-in-law, and his nephew Francis I. might henceforth at their pleasure oppress their subjects, put martyrs to death, wink at the disorders of nobles and monks, and sleep quietly on their pillows.

The Savoyard princes behaved as in a city taken by assault. The very evening of the 5th of April, the Count of Genevois removed the cannon from the ramparts, placed them round his quarters, and had them loaded that they might be ready to fire upon the people, the hôtel-de-ville thus becoming a citadel to keep Geneva in obedience. Notwithstanding these precautions the count was uneasy; he had violated his oaths, and knew that he had to deal with men of energy. He did not lie down, and at two in the morning his officers went by his orders and knocked at the doors of the four syndics, commanding them to proceed immediately to the hôtel-de-ville. 'Hand me the keys of the gates,' said the count, 'the ramparts, the arsenal, and the provision magazines.' If the magistrates had really fancied that the Savoyards would come as friends, their foolish delusion must now have ceased and the bandage have fallen from their eyes. But how could they resist? The army filled all the city, and the citizens were divided: the syndics did what was required of them. The fanaticism of the disloyal mamelukes was not yet satisfied. Cartelier, Pierre Joly, Thomas Moyne, and others, taking a lesson from the terrible Montrotier, who desired to *muzzle* the Genevans completely, visited all the streets, squares, and churches, and began to wrench off the staples and locks from the city chains and gates, and even the clappers from the bells. The syndics strove in vain to stop this violence. The wretches did not forget a street, and having thus disarmed Geneva, they carried all these trophies to the duke. 'It is a sign,' said they, laying them before him, 'of the real transfer of the jurisdiction of the city, to intimidate the rebels and deprive them of all hope of succor. Geneva lies at the feet of your Highness.' This occurred before daybreak.*

At length Wednesday, 6th April, dawned, and that day was not less mournful than its predecessor. The Savoyard soldiers, forgetting that they owed their success to the scandalous violation of the most sacred promises, intoxicated alike with hatred and pride, began to show the insolence of conquerors. We know the disorders in which the undisciplined armies of that period were accustomed to indulge in cities taken by storm. The ducal soldiers, not less cruel but more fantastical, exhibited in the sack of Geneva some of those farces which the imperialists played eight years later at the sack of Rome. The citizens, taking refuge in the garrets, had given up their feather beds to the soldiers. The latter slept soundly, and next morning, to make up for the battle which had not been fought, indulged in one of a different kind. Instead of balls they flung the bolsters at each other's heads; taking the beds for enemies, they thrust their swords up to the hilt in the feathers:—these were the hardest blows struck in this war by the soldiers of Charles

* *Les Mamelouks de Genève*, MS. Galiffe, *Matériaux*, &c., ii. pp. 234, 264. Spon, *Hist. de Genève*, i. p. 327

III.—Then, eager to prolong their coarse jests, they shook the beds out of the windows, watching, with roars of laughter, the evolutions made by the feathers in the air. They next called for the keys of the cellars, and forming a circle round the casks, tapped them in various places, singing their loudest as they drank their fill. 'Lastly,' says a chronicle, 'they pulled out the spigots, so that the cellar was filled with wine; and stumbling upstairs again into the house, they insulted everybody they met, ran shouting through the streets, made boasting speeches, and committed a thousand acts of violence.' At Rome, the imperialists made a jest of the papacy; at Geneva, the ducal soldiers, drunk with wine and joy, trampled independence under foot and exulted over liberty. But on a sudden, an alarm was sounded: the braggarts imagined that the Genevans were going to defend themselves, and, the noisiest talkers being generally the greatest cowards, they all scampered away—some ran to the right, others to the left; many fled towards the river and hid themselves under the mills; the more cunning sought other retreats.* It was only a false alarm; the Count of Genevois, being displeased at their behavior, had given it that it might serve as a lesson to the marauders.

During this time the mamelukes were sitting night and day in 'the little stove,' consulting on the best means of repressing for ever the spirit of national independence in Geneva. They believed the city could never belong to Savoy whilst those who had voted for the alliance with Friburg were alive. A king of Rome, while walking in his garden, struck off with his stick the heads of the tallest poppies. The conspirators, resolving to profit by the lessons of history, began to draw up a proscription list, and placed on it the four syndics, the twenty-one councillors, and other notable citizens so as to make up forty. Wishing to end the affair promptly, certain mamelukes went to the executioner and asked him 'how much he would take for forty heads?' It seems that he required more than the heads were worth, according to the value which had been set upon them, for

* 'Jusque dans les lieux privés qui étaient sur le Rhone.'—Savyon, *Annales*, p. 90.

contemporary documents tell us that they 'haggled' about it. Three chronicles of the time, all worthy of trust, describe this disgusting visit to the headsman.* The rumor got abroad, and all Geneva trembled. Some who knew they were on the list, hid themselves. 'A very foolish thing,' said others. 'Without God, the most secret hiding-places are but as the fancies of children, who put their hands before their eyes and think nobody can see them.' The boldest huguenots were filled with indignation: instead of concealing themselves, they girded on their swords, raised their heads, and walked proudly in the streets. 'But they were made to *feel the cord* (sentir la corde).' We do not know whether this means that they were beaten or only threatened. 'After this,' continues Savyon, 'there was no other resource but to commend ourselves to God.'†

Berthelier and his friends hurried to Marti. They represented to him that at the moment when the duke had made such fine promises, he was thinking only of breaking them; they added that assuredly this perjured prince would have to answer for his crime. The Friburger, at once ashamed and indignant, went to the duke and said: 'What do you mean, my lord? Do you wish me to be accounted a traitor? I have your word. You bade me give the people of Geneva assurance of your good will; they consequently opened their gates in good faith; otherwise you would not have entered without hard knocks. But now you break your promise . . . My lord, you will certainly suffer by it.' The duke, embarrassed and annoyed, and unable to justify himself, got into a passion, and offered the Friburg ambassador the grossest insult: 'Go,' said he, addressing Marti with an epithet so filthy that history cannot transcribe his words, 'get out of my presence.'‡

This incident, however, made Charles reflect, and resolve to give a color to his violence. Having drawn out all his men-at-arms, he summoned a general council.* Only the

* Bonivard, *Chroniq.* ii. p. 356. Michel Roset, *Chron.* MS. liv. i. ch. xcix. *Les Mamelouks de Genève*, MS. p. 140.

† Bonivard, *Chroniq.* ii. p. 356. Savyon, *Annales*, p. 90.

‡ Ibid.

mamelukes attended, and not all of them ; but notwithstanding their small number, these ducal partisans, surrounded by an armed force, did not scruple to renounce, in the name of Geneva, the alliance with Friburg.

The duke immediately followed up his victory ; and, wishing to make the hand of the master felt, ordered, in the morning of Thursday, April 7, that the usher and men-at-arms should attend the city herald and make proclamation with an increased display of force. 'O yes ! O yes ! O yes !' said the herald, 'in the name of our most dread prince and lord, Monseigneur the Duke of Savoy. No one, under pain of three blows of the strappado, shall carry any offensive or defensive weapon. No one shall leave his house, whatever noise there may be, or even put his head out of the window, under pain of his life. Whoever resists the order of Monseigneur shall be hanged at the windows of his own house.' Such were the order and justice established by Duke Charles.* It might be said that, with a view to frighten the Genevans, he wished that they might not be able to leave their houses without walking in the midst of his victims. The proclamation was repeated from place to place, and the crowd gradually increased. On a sudden, a certain movement was observed among the people. A few men appeared here and there, whose look had something mysterious ; they spoke to their friends, but it was in whispers. The agitation soon increased ; it spread from one to another : here a man made signs of joy, there of terror. At last the mystery was explained. 'Friburg !' exclaimed several voices ; 'the Friburg army is coming !' At these words the city herald, the men-at-arms, the mamelukes, and the Savoyards who accompanied him, stopped, and, on learning that a courier had just arrived from the Pays de Vaud, they dispersed. . . . Huguenots and mamelukes spread through the city and circulated the good news : 'The Swiss ! the Swiss !' and the cry was answered from all quarters with 'Long live the huguenots !' 'Thus the said proclamation

* *Les Mamelouks de Genève*, MS. p. 142. *Chronique de Roset*, MS. liv. i. chap. xcix. Galiffe, *Matériaux*, Interrogatoire de Cartelier, ii. p. 255.

could not be finished throughout the city,' says a contemporary manuscript.*

Besançon Hugues, having escaped all the perils of the road, had arrived at Friburg, and, without giving himself time to take breath, appeared immediately before the council. He described the perfidy and violence of Charles, the dangers and desolation of Geneva; he showed that the city was on the point of being annexed to Savoy, and the chiefs of the republic about to be put to death. If Friburg did not make haste, it would find nothing but their heads hanging at the gates, like those of Navis and Blanchet.

The look of the generous citizen, the animation of his whole person, the eloquence of his appeal, inflamed every heart. Their eyes were filled with tears, and the men of Friburg laid their hands upon their swords.† A regiment, fully armed, marched out immediately for Geneva: and that was not all; the flower of the young men flocked in from every quarter, and the army soon amounted to 5,000 or 6,000 men. Having entered the Pays de Vaud, they seized his Highness's governor, the Sire de Lullins. 'Write to your master,' said the chiefs of Friburg, 'that he do no harm to our fellow-citizens; your head shall answer for theirs: besides, we are going to give him a treat at Geneva.' Their liberating flags soon floated on the hills above the lake. A great number of the young men of the Pays de Vaud joined them, and the army mustered before Morges 13,000 to 14,000 strong. At their approach, the terrified inhabitants of that town, who were devoted to the duke, threw themselves into their boats, and fled to Savoy. The Friburgers entered their deserted houses, and waited for his Highness's answer.‡

Governor de Lullins failed not to warn his master, and it was this message that had interrupted the proclamation. The duke, at once violent and pusillanimous, was frightened, and suddenly became as humble as he had been insolent be-

* *Les Mamelouks de Genève*, MS. p. 143. Michael Roset says the same, MS. liv. i. chap. c.

† Galiffe, *Matériaux*, ii. p. 294. Spon, *Hist. Genève*, i. p. 328.

‡ *Les Mamelouks*, p. 143. Savyon, *Annales*, p. 91.

fore. Sending for the ambassador of Friburg, he spoke to him as to a dear friend : 'Haste to the camp at Morges,' he said, 'and stop this : prevail upon your lords to return.' Marti, who had not forgotten Charles's gross insult, answered him bitterly : 'Do you think that a —— like me can make an army retreat? Commission your own people to carry your lies.'* Then the duke, still more terrified, sent M. de Maglian, a captain of cavalry, to guard the pass at Nyon, and, 'changing his song,' he had it cried through all the city 'that no one should dare do harm or displeasure to any person of Geneva, under pain of the gallows.' At the same time, the Sieur de Saleneuve and another of his Highness's councillors went to the general council, but this time without riding-whips or wands, and with a benevolent smile upon their faces. There, after assuring the people of the love the duke bore them, they were asked to send two citizens to Morges to declare to the Friburgers that the duke would do no injury to Geneva. Two mamelukes, Taccon and De Lestilley, departed.†

Everything was changed in Geneva. The proposal to cut off forty heads was abandoned, to the great regret of Cartelier, who afterwards said: 'What a pity! but for these —— Friburgers it would have been done.'‡ The huguenots, regaining their courage, 'mocked at the Faucignerans and the other men-at-arms.'§ The inhabitants of the Faubourg St. Gervais, strongly inclined to raillery, attacked their guests with songs, epigrams, and sarcasms. The huguenots imposed on their visitors a strict fast (it was the season of Lent), and gave them for rations only some small fish called *bésolles* (now *féras*). 'You are too good christians,' they said ironically to the Savoyards, 'to eat meat now.' And hence they derisively called the expedition

* 'Manda li de votre gen, qui porton votre jangle,' he said in his Friburg *patois*. Savyon, *Annales*, p. 91.

† *Les Mamelouks*, MS. p. 143. Savyon, *Annales*, p. 91. Bonivard, *Chroniq.* ii. p. 357. Gautier MSS. *Le Citadin de Genève.*

‡ Galiffe, *Matériaux*, Interrogatoire de Cartelier, ii. p. 247. Savyon, *Annales*, p. 92.

§ Bonivard, *Chroniq.* ii. p. 357.

'the Bésolles war,' a name recorded in contemporaneous chronicles.

They could not come to an understanding at Morges. Besançon Hugues and Malbuisson were urging the Friburg troops to advance; Taccon and De Lestilley were urging them to retire. And while the leaders hesitated, the deputies of the cantons arrived and proposed a middle course: that Savoy should withdraw her troops, and Friburg her alliance. It was Zurich, Berne, and Soleure that sought thus to take advantage of the opportunity to withdraw from Geneva the only help which, after God, could save her. The huguenots, abandoned by the cantons, stood stupefied. 'Renounce your alliance with Friburg,' repeated the League, '*without prejudice to your liberties.*' 'But they would not,' said Bonivard, 'for they had the majority of votes.' The real majority did not therefore consent to this fatal proposition; but it seems that it was again carried by the phantom of a general council, at which none but mamelukes were present. When that was done, the duke hastened to leave Geneva, but with less pomp than when he entered; and the plague took his place.*

When Charles quitted the city, he left behind him sad forebodings. The Swiss accused the Genevans of violence and insults, declaring them guilty of disgraceful conduct to the duke, their most illustrious ally.† The bishop, who was at Pignerol, wrote to the citizens: having recovered from my serious illness, I am thinking of passing the mountains, for the benefit and good of my city.'‡ Now every one remembered that he had made use of the same words when he had put Navis and Blanchet to death. The signs were threatening: the sky was thick with storm. The citizens trembled for those who were most precious to them, and frightful deeds were about to increase and prolong their

* Registers of the Council, April 11, 1519. Bonivard, *Chroniq.* ii. p. 360. Savyon, *Annales*, p. 93. Archives de Genève, Nos. 913 and 918.

† 'Insultus et tumultuationes . . . auctoritati ducis damnum nobis extraneum et indignum apparet.'—Archives de Genève, MS. No. 912.

‡ Ibid. No. 886.

terror. 'From the war of 1519 until 1525,' says the learned Secretary of State, Chouet, 'the people of Geneva was in great consternation.'*

CHAPTER XIX.

ARREST OF BONIVARD AND BERTHELIER.

(APRIL TO SEPTEMBER, 1519.)

NEITHER the duke nor the bishop had exhausted their plans. The heads of Blanchet and Navis, suspended seven months before on the walnut-tree, were there still, tossed by every wind, and telling the passers-by that the wrath of the princes was not yet appeased. The bishop asked himself whether these commoners, who claimed liberty in the State, would delay much longer before demanding liberty in the Church . . . People spoke of extraordinary things that were happening in Germany. A Wittemberg doctor had appealed from the pope to a general council, and was preparing to maintain certain propositions at Leipsic in which the primacy of the Roman Church was denied as being opposed to the history of eleven centuries and to the text of Scripture. Would these strange notions, worthy of the Germans, spread to countries nearer Rome? Would Wittemberg and Geneva, those two little corners of the earth, be two volcanoes to shake the ground around them? A remedy must be applied at any cost, and those principles of civil and religious liberty be stifled, which, if not seen to in time, might work strange revolutions in the world.

The bishop on his return from Turin had merely passed through Geneva; and fleeing from the plague, had taken refuge at Ripaille, near Thonon, whence he made the most

* Document addressed to Lord Townsend (seventeenth century). Berne MS. H. vi. 57.

serious complaints to the Genevans. 'You are always conspiring,' he wrote, 'in order that you may satisfy the appetites of a *heap* of individuals who are plotting against their honor and against me.'* About the end of June he removed to the château of Troches, near Dovaine. The principal mamelukes hastened to this ancient manorial house.† They had no very clear ideas of what was going on in Germany, and of the consequences that might result to Europe; their attachment to the ducal and episcopal cause depended rather upon motives of interest and family tradition: but they instinctively felt that a struggle had begun in Geneva between the old and the new times, and that the partisans of the former must combine all their strength against the latter. They made the halls of the château reëcho with their loud voices; they entered into cowardly conspiracies; these supporters of feudalism, however honorable they might be in other matters, shrank not from any crime to check the advent of liberty. There was one citizen in particular whom they hated—one life that must be sacrificed. 'First,' said they to the bishop, 'we require Berthelier's death, and pray, my lord, let the blow be prompt. Second, the rebellious councillors must be dismissed. Third, your grace must come into the city . . . with *good swords!*' The mamelukes undertook to find employment for these swords, and the bishop said 'Amen.'

The cruelties of the princes of Savoy had already fallen upon Bonivard. The very day when the duke entered the city, the prior of St. Victor left it, 'disguised as a monk,' accompanied by two friends of the Pays de Vaud with whom he was very familiar, the Sieur de Voruz and the Abbot of Montheron. 'Fear nothing,' said the latter to him; 'we will go first to my abbey; then we will conduct you to Echallens, a town dependent on Berne, where you

* Galiffe, *Matériaux*, &c., p. 274. M. Galiffe refers this letter to the year 1517, at the time of Pécolat's trial; but it is clear from the contents and from the Council Registers of May 24, 1519, that it belongs to the time of which we are speaking.

† This château still exists, and is inhabited, I believe, by the Marquis de Dovaine.

will be in safety.' But they were leading him to a very different place of safety. The priest and the gentleman had made their account together. They had said that no one in Geneva was more hated by the bishop and the duke than Bonivard, that in their eyes he was not a Genevese, but a Savoyard who had betrayed his prince; so that, to get him into their power, these princes would give his weight in gold. The priory of St. Victor was a good benefice; the two perfidious friends had therefore determined to propose an exchange: they would put the duke in possession of the prior, while the duke should put them in possession of the priory. This establishment would naturally fall to the abbot; but the latter engaged to pay the Sieur de Voruz an annual pension of two hundred florins out of the stipend. The flashing of the gold dazzled these wretches, and they concluded their infamous bargain. The gentleman and the abbot appeared to redouble their vigilance lest any harm should befall the prior. When the three travellers reached Montheron, in the forest of Jorat, between Lausanne and Echallens, the prior was courteously conducted into a room, which, without his suspecting it, was to be his prison. The next morning Voruz, whom Bonivard trusted like a brother, entered the chamber, sat down opposite him, and, laying a sheet of paper on the table, said: 'Resign your priory of St. Victor in favor of the abbot.'—'What!' exclaimed the startled Bonivard, 'is it under a show of friendship that you lay these plots?'—'You are our prisoner,' Voruz answered coldly; 'all attempts to escape will be useless.' Bonivard now understood into what hands he had fallen. 'So, then, instead of taking me to Echallens,' he said, 'you will prevent my going there.' He declared that he would set his hand to no such robbery, and bluntly refused to resign his priory. 'The duke is going to put Berthelier and his companions to death,' resumed Voruz coldly; 'be careful. If you will not do what we tell you, we will deliver you into his hands, and there will be one huguenot the more for the scaffold. You are free; make your choice—resignation or death!' Bonivard had no wish to die. Could he leave so soon this world that he loved so passionately? Could he see rudely interrupted that beautiful dream of liberty, philosophy, and poetry, in whose chimeras he had so long indulged? He consented to everything. 'Good!' said Voruz, as he took away with him the renunciation the prior had signed, and locked the door behind him.

Bonivard, who thought himself free now that he had become poor, had to learn that the tender mercies of the wicked are cruel. He was immediately given up by Voruz and the abbot to the duke, who had him conveyed to Gex by the captain of his guards. He asserted in vain that his only fault was being a friend of the huguenots and of the Swiss; Charles, in whose eyes that was a great crime, imprisoned him in the castle of Grolée, on the banks of the Rhone, two leagues from Belley.* This first imprisonment, which lasted two years, was a foretaste of his harsher and longer captivity in the castle of Chillon. The duke put the abbot in possession of the priory of St. Victor; Voruz received his two hundred florins; the wicked triumphed, and Bonivard in his solitude gave way to gloomy thoughts. Was it at the bottom of an obscure dungeon that the new times of light and liberty were to begin?

The duke having struck the first blow, it was now the bishop's turn. He was taking his holiday, travelling from Ripaille to Troches, from Troches to the castle of Bonne, thence to other adjoining places, and employing all his episcopal zeal in raising soldiers. On the 16th of August the peasants of these districts, who came to the market at Geneva, mentioned that the bishop was assembling armed men for his entrance into the city. The syndic de la Mare and one of his colleagues, alarmed for the future of the republic, set out immediately for Bonne, and commended the city to John's episcopal tenderness. 'Alas!' they said, 'it is stricken with the double scourge of the plague and the sword.' The prelate, as false as his cousin, replied: 'You have been deceived, gentlemen; I shall certainly enter Geneva to-morrow, but only with a hundred or a hundred and fifty footmen for

* Grolée is now in the department of Ain. Savyon, *Annales*, p. 89. Bonivard, *Chroniq.* ii. p. 353. 'Notice' by Chaponnière, *Mem. d'Archéol.* iv. p. 54. Bonivard MSS.

my guard. I desire to live there merrily with the citizens and protect each one in his rights.'* De la Mare and his friend believed what John of Savoy told them, and made their report. The people of the city were somewhat reassured: that little weak and starveling bishop, who looked so like a corpse, seemed not a very formidable appearance to them. They resolved at least to hide the discontent and fears that they felt at heart. 'The shops will be closed, as on a holiday,' said the council, 'and those who have horses will go out to meet his lordship.'

On Saturday, April 20, 1519, the syndics and a great part of the city were afoot. At four in the afternoon the bishop's escort came in sight; the perfidious prelate, who was coming for the purpose of putting the noblest of the citizens to death, noted with a cunning look the handsome reception made him. Six hundred soldiers, stout rough men, surrounded the pastor of Geneva; 'the bishop had thought that number necessary,' say the annals, 'to take Berthelier.' The Genevans, remembering that John was only to bring with him one hundred or one hundred and fifty men-at-arms, counted . . . and found six hundred. They saw that the prelate's entrance was only a second edition of that of the duke. The bastard, satisfied with the welcome he received, proceeded immediately to his palace and without delay convened the general council for the next day. Sadness was in all men's hearts.

On Sunday morning, when the people were assembled, the bishop appeared, surrounded by his councillors and courtiers. He seemed scarcely alive, but his sullen fierce look announced severe measures. 'My lord not having many days to live,' said the official, 'desires that all things be put in order before his decease. He has therefore brought some soldiers with him that he may correct any who shall be mad enough to resist him.'†

After delivering this threatening message, the bishop returned hastily to his palace, where he remained shut up for two days without giving any signs of life. He had selected

* MS. Registers of the Council, Aug. 19, 1519.

† *Les Mamelouks de Genève*, MS. p. 149.

his first victim and was ruminating in silence on the means of sacrificing him. 'He kept still,' said Bonivard, 'watching for Berthelier, whom he considered the leader of the flock.' During this time his satellites, however, did not keep quiet. Being quartered on the huguenots, they stole all they could carry off; if resistance was made, they used insulting language; they went about marauding. But the bishop still gave no word or sign. This silence alarmed all the city, and every one expected what was going to happen.*

One man alone in Geneva preserved a tranquil heart and serene look; it was Berthelier. He had not wished to escape either when Charles or when the bastard entered; he was vainly entreated to withdraw to Friburg; all was useless. He waited for death; the 'cheat' of hope (to use the common expression) did not deceive him. 'The wolf is in the fold,' said his friends, 'and you will be the first victim.' Berthelier listened, smiled, and passed on. In his opinion there could be no evil in life to him who has learnt that the privation of life is not an evil. He awaited calmly that tragical end which he had himself foretold, every day exposing himself to the attacks of his enemies. After the bishop's arrival, 'he went and came just as before; one would have said that, instead of fleeing death, he was running after it.'†

Without the city, in a solitary place then called Gervasa (now corrupted into *Savoises*), was a quiet meadow, which the Rhone bathed with its swift waters: this was Berthelier's favorite retreat. Remote from the noise of the city, seated on the picturesque bank of the river, watching its blue waves gliding rapidly past, he dwelt on the swiftness of time, and casting a serious glance into the future, he asked himself when would Geneva be free? 'Every day he was in the habit of taking his pleasure there,' say the annals, 'and never omitted doing so, although at the time he had so many enemies in Geneva.'‡

* *Les Mamelouks de Genève*, MS. p. 149.

† Bonivard, *Chroniq.* ii. p. 362. Galiffe, *Notices Biographiques*, i. p. 10. Savyon, *Annales*, p. 96.

‡ Savyon, *Annales*, p. 97, where this place is called Pericua.

On Tuesday, August 23, he went out between six and seven to breathe the morning air in his favorite retreat.* Berthelier was now forty years of age; everything foretold him that his end was near; but he preferred, without passion and without fear, to make the passage from life to death. This active and much-dreaded citizen began to sport, but with a serious gentleness, upon the brink of the grave. He had a little weasel which he was very fond of, and 'for the greater contempt of his enemies,' he had taken the tame 'creature in his bosom, and thus walked out to his garden, playing with it.' The vidame, who knew of these morning walks, had given orders for a certain number of soldiers to be posted outside the walls of the city, whilst he remained within, in order to take Berthelier from behind. Just as the latter was about to pass the gates, the troop that awaited him came forward. Berthelier, 'always *booted* and ready to depart for the unknown shores of eternity,' had no thought of returning to the city and arousing the youth of Geneva; he did not turn aside from the road, but continued gently caressing his weasel, and 'walked straight towards the armed men, as proudly as if he was going to take them.'†

'They met,' says a manuscript, 'under the trellis in front of the hostelry of the Goose,'‡ and the vidame, who was descending the hill on his mule, coming up with him at the same time, laid his hand upon his shoulder, saying: 'In the name of my lord of Geneva, I arrest you,' and prepared to take away his sword. Berthelier, who had only to sound his terrible whistle to collect enthusiastic defenders, stood calm, without a thought of resistance, and quietly handed his sword to the vidame, contenting himself with the words: 'Take care what you do with this sword, for you will have to answer for it.'

* The Registers of the Council state, under the date of *Tuesday*, Aug. 23, that the arrest was made on this day; Bonivard speaks of *Monday*, at six o'clock. The arrest may have taken place on Monday night, but we have followed the Registers, whose accuracy should be superior to Bonivard's, who was absent from Geneva.

† Bonivard, *Chroniq.* ii. p. 369.

‡ *Les Maumelus de Genève*, MS. p. 149.

The vidame placed him in the middle of his soldiers, and Berthelier marched off quietly, still carrying the weasel with him. The little timid animal thrust its pretty head into its master's bosom, while the latter encouraged it by gentle caresses. In this way he arrived at the Château de l'Ile, and the vidame, stationing guards everywhere, even in the prisoner's chamber,* shut him up in Cæsar's tower. On the spot where walls had formerly been erected by the destroyer of the liberties of Rome, a humble and almost unknown citizen, one of the founders of modern liberty, was to find a bloody prison.†

Berthelier, shut up in the fortress, and surrounded by guards pacing up and down his chamber and round the castle, felt more free than all of them. We do not say that he possessed the freedom that christianity gives; perhaps it was rather from the *Tusculans* of Cicero than from the Gospel that he had derived the calm with which his soul was filled; yet it is almost impossible not to recognise a noble, serious—we could almost say christian, sentiment in him. As he saw death approaching, he said that all he had to do was to remove its mask, for underneath was the face of a friend. To die . . . what was that? Does not the meanest soldier expose himself to it on the battle-field? Was not the death he was about to suffer for the independence of his country a thousand times sweeter and more glorious than that of a mercenary?

Dulce et decorum pro patria mori.‡

Yet his soul was agitated. Those smiling fields he loved so well, those graceful banks of the lake and river, those mountains where the setting sun fired the everlasting snows, those friends whose idol he was, his country above all, and the liberty which he desired to win for her . . . all these images rose before him in his prison, and deeply stirred his heart. But he soon returned to calmer thoughts. He hoped that

* Registers of the Council, Aug. 23. Bonivard, *Chroniq.* ii. p. 362.

† 'A lacu Lemano, qui in flumen Rhodanum influit . . . . præsidia disponit, castella communit.'—Cæsar, *De Bello Gallico*, lib. i.

‡ Horatius, *Carm.* lib. iii.

his death would lead to the deliverance of Geneva, and then his courage returned. Yet he was without bravado, and to the soldiers around him he showed only a simple and candid soul. His little favorite animal still played in his bosom; surprised at everything about it, the weasel at the least noise would prick up its short wide ears. Berthelier smiled and caressed it. 'The better to mock his guards,' says the prior of St. Victor, 'he played with his weasel.'* Bonivard, inclined to take things by the wrong side, saw mockery where there was only good-nature. In fact, the guards, rough and violent men, touched by so much patience and courage, said to Berthelier: 'Ask my lord's pardon.'—'What lord's?'—'My lord duke of Savoy, your prince and ours.'—'He is not my prince,' he said, 'and if he were, I would not ask for pardon, because I have done no wrong. It is the wicked who should beg for pardon, and not the good.'—'He will put you to death, then,' said the guards. Berthelier made no reply. But a few minutes after, he went up to the wall and wrote: '*Non moriar sed vivam et narrabo opera Domini*—I shall not die but live and declare the works of the Lord.' This quotation from the hundred and eighteenth Psalm, where the Messiah speaks by the mouth of David, shows that Berthelier possessed a certain knowledge of Scripture; perhaps it shows us, too, that his soul had cast all its burdens on the Lord.†

At that time (1519), when christians, trusting in the Bible, were rising at Wittemberg against absolute power in spiritual things, citizens, trusting in the ancient charters of liberty, were rising at Geneva against absolute power in temporal things. At that time there was no fusion of these two principles. Perhaps Luther did not become liberal; Berthelier certainly did not become protestant. But in the presence of death this great citizen sought consolation in the Word of God and not in the ceremonies of the priest, which is the essence of protestantism. The passage he wrote on the wall has reference to the Saviour's resurrection. Did

* Bonivard, *Chroniq.* ii. p. 369.

† Bonivard, *Chroniq.* ii. p. 363. Savyon, *Annales*, p. 97. Spon, *Hist. de Genève*, i. p. 343.

Berthelier find in this transformation of the King of believers a solid reason for expecting for himself a resurrection, a glorious transformation? Did he hope, after this world, for a glorified world of imperishable felicity, the everlasting abode of the children of God?—We believe so.

CHAPTER XX.

PHILIBERT BERTHELIER THE MARTYR OF LIBERTY. TERROR AND OPPRESSION IN GENEVA.

(AUGUST AND SEPTEMBER, 1519.)

THE prisoner was soon diverted from these wholesome thoughts by the arrival of the officers of justice. According to the privileges of Geneva, he could only be tried by the syndics; but the bastard suspected this lawful tribunal, and finding no honest man that would undertake to act against the law, he issued a provost's commission to Jean Desbois, a man of Chambéry, then living at Geneva, and 'formerly a tooth-drawer,' say contemporary documents. This extemporised judge, vain of his functions, wished to begin the examination. 'When the syndics, who are my judges, question me, I will answer them,' said Berthelier, 'but not you, who have no right to do so.'—'I shall come again,' said Desbois after this futile attempt, 'and shall compel you to answer me then.' The provost went and reported to the bishop the unsatisfactory commencement of his high functions.*

The emotion was universal in Geneva. The friend of its liberties, the founder of the league *Who touches one touches all*, was about to pay with his life for his enthusiasm in the cause of independence. The bold spirits, who braved the

* Bonivard, *Chroniq.* ii. p. 363. Spon, *Hist. de Genève*, i. p. 344. Savyon, *Annales*, p. 98.

papal tyrant, proposed that they should consider this act of the bishop's as mere brigandage (which it was in fact), and that they should support the laws by rescuing Berthelier. But the magistrates preferred a more moderate course. The Great Council was hastily assembled, and at their order the syndics waited upon the bishop. 'My lord,' said they, 'Berthelier has been acquitted according to law; and now he is arrested without accuser, and without a preliminary information. If he is innocent, let him be set at liberty; if he is guilty, let him be tried by us; do not permit an infringement of the franchises in your city.'—'It is true there is no accuser,' said the bishop, 'but common rumor stands in his stead; there is no preliminary information, but the notoriety of the deed supplies its place; as for what judges it concerns, the injury having been committed against the prince, it is the business of his officers to prosecute.' Having thus dragged the sheep into his den, the wolf would not let it go.'*

When they were informed of this denial of justice, the more energetic party protested loudly. They asked if there was any duty more sacred than to deliver innocence? Could the people see with indifference the rights which belonged to them from time immemorial trodden under foot by a prince who had sworn to defend them? The bishop and his creatures, fearing lest the storm should burst, resolved to put the rebel speedily out of the way. The proceedings did not last two days, as Bonivard writes; all was done in one, (August 23) between six and seven in the morning and four in the afternoon.† Berthelier saw what was preparing, but his calmness never failed him. He remembered that, according to the sages of antiquity, the voluntary sacrifice which men make of their lives, out of love for their fellow-countrymen, has a mysterious power to save them. Had this not been seen among the Greeks and the Romans?

* MS. Registers of the Council, Aug. 23, 1519. Galiffe, *Matériaux*, i. p. 146.

† Compare the Council Registers of Aug. 23, 1519, and 1526. M. Galiffe, junior, had already pointed out this mistake of Bonivard's. *Besançon Hugues*, p. 245.

And among those very leaguers whom Berthelier had so loved, was it not by thrusting the lances of the enemy into his bosom that Arnold of Winkelried delivered Switzerland? . . . But if Berthelier desired to save Geneva, Geneva desired to save him. Good men, the friends of right and maintainers of the sworn franchises of the citizens, felt that the ancient laws of the State deserved more respect than the despotic will of a perjured and cruel prince. The castle where the liberator was confined (a private possession of the house of Savoy) had long since been put into a condition to resist surprise; but Champel, the usual place of execution, was at a little distance from the city; the moment when Berthelier was conducted there would be the favorable opportunity. He will hardly have taken a hundred steps beyond the bridge when the huguenots, rising like one man and issuing from every quarter, will rescue him from the executioners, who are nothing but murderers before the laws of men and the justice of God.

These rumors reached the ears of the bastard, who took his measures accordingly. Six hundred men-at-arms were drawn out, and all the mamelukes joined them. The vidame posted a detachment on the side of St. Gervais (right bank) to cut off the inhabitants of the faubourg from all access to the island; he stationed the greater part 'under arms and in line of battle,' along the left bank, so as to occupy the bridge, the Rue du Rhone, and the cross streets. Among the Savoyard captains who gave the sanction of their presence to this legal murder was François de Ternier, seignior of Pontverre, a violent and energetic man, and yet of a generous disposition. The blood of Berthelier, which was about to be shed, excited a thirst in his heart which the blood of the huguenots alone could quench; from that hour Pontverre was the deadliest enemy of Geneva and the Genevans. But (as pagan antiquity would have said) the terrible Nemesis, daughter of Jupiter and Night, goddess of vengeance and retribution, holding a sword in one hand and a torch in the other, was one day to overtake him, a few steps only from the spot where the blood of Berthelier was about to flow, and divine justice commissioned to punish crime would avenge this unjust death in his own blood.*

All was ready. Desbois entered the prison with a confessor and the headsman. 'I summon you a second time to answer,' said he to Berthelier. The noble citizen refused. 'I summon you a third time,' repeated the ex-dentist, 'under pain of losing your head.' Berthelier answered not a word; he would reply only to his lawful judges, the syndics. He knew, besides, that these appeals were empty forms, that he was not a defendant but a victim. Then, without other formality, the provost pronounced sentence: 'Philibert Berthelier, seeing that thou hast always been rebellious against our most dread lord and thine, we condemn thee to have thy head cut off to the separation of the soul from the body; thy body to be hung to the gibbet at Champel, thy head to be nailed to the gallows near the river Arve, and thy goods confiscated to the prince.' The provost then introduced the confessor, 'with whom Berthelier did not hold long discourse.' After that the third personage, the headsman, came forward and pinioned him.†

In every quarter of Geneva men's eyes were fixed on the Château de l'Ile. Its old gates fell back, the guards marched out first, the provost came next, followed by the headsman holding Berthelier. The martyr's countenance proclaimed the greatness of his soul. There was and still is, between the castle and the river, a narrow space so protected by the Rhone and the fortress, that fifty men could hold it against all the inhabitants of Geneva. The prince-bishop, so learned in the art of tyranny, was not ignorant that if the victim to be sacrificed is loved by the people, the death-blow must be given in prison, in a court-yard, on a narrow beach, or in a castle moat. Berthelier having advanced a few steps, found himself between the château and the river. 'Say thy prayers,' said the provost. The hero knew he was about to be murdered: he made 'a short prayer,' and, rising from his knees, was preparing 'to utter a few words before dying,'

* Bonivard, *Chroniq.* ii. p. 365. Savyon, *Annales*, p. 98. Spon, *Hist. de Genève*, i. p. 344.

† Savyon, *Annales*, p. 98. Bonivard, *Chroniq.* ii. p. 366.

to give a last testimony to the liberties of Geneva; but the provost would not permit him. Turning to the executioner, he said: 'Make haste with your work.'—'Kneel down,' said the man to his victim. Then Berthelier, whether he desired to express his sorrow at the gloomy future of his fellow-citizens, or was moved at seeing himself sacrificed and none of his friends appearing to defend him, exclaimed as he fell on his knees: 'Ah! . . . Messieurs of Geneva.' . . . It was all he said; he had no sooner uttered the words 'than the executioner cut off his head; it was the 23rd of August, 1519.' The bishop had managed matters well. That cruel man was more like the wild beast that devours the flock than the shepherd who protects them; he had shown himself truly *tremendæ velocitatis animal*, 'an animal of terrible swiftness,' as Pliny says of the tiger; but unlike that animal, he was cowardly as well as cruel. The Genevans, whose father he should have been, turned from him with horror, and the avenging angel of the innocent prepared to visit him with a terrible retribution at his death. Vainly would the waters of the Rhone flow for ages over this narrow space—there are stains of blood that no waters can ever wash out.*

The bishop intended, however, that Berthelier should be conveyed to the place of execution for criminals; he only found it more prudent to have him taken thither dead than alive, being sure that in this way the 'youths of Geneva' could not restore him to liberty. The lifeless body of the martyr was placed on a wagon; the executioner got in and stood beside it, holding the victim's head in his hand. A universal horror fell upon the people, and many, heart-broken at being unable to save their friend, shut themselves up in their houses to veil their hatred and their shame. The long procession, starting from the castle, moved forward, preceded and closed by foreign soldiers; in the middle was the wagon bearing the dead body, and close behind followed many

* Galiffe, *Matériaux pour l'Histoire de Genève*, ii. p. 297. Pliny, *Hist. Nat.* viii. p. 18. Bonivard, *Chroniq.* ii. p. 366. Savyon, *Annales*, p. 99. A plain inscription on Cæsar's tower (in the island) marks the place of Berthelier's death.

mamelukes, 'not the least of their party, in great insolence, mocking at their own calamity; but good men dared not breathe, seeing that when force reigns, the good cause must keep still.'* A few huguenots, however, mournful and indignant, appeared in the streets or at their doors. Meanwhile the executioner, parading in his triumphal car, swung derisively to and fro the martyr's bleeding head, and cried: 'This is the head of the traitor Berthelier; let all take warning by it.' The procession continued its march as far as Champel, where the executioner suspended the body of the father of Genevese liberty to the gibbet. Thence, by a singular refinement of cruelty, they proceeded to the bridge of Arve, and the head of the dead man, who had so often terrified the bishop, was fastened up in the place where those of Blanchet and Navis had hung so long. The prelate seemed to take pleasure in reviving the recollection of his former butcheries.

Thus that kind-hearted man whom everybody loved, that heroic citizen around whom were concentrated all the hopes of the friends of liberty, had been sacrificed by his bishop. That death so hurried, so illegal, so tragical, filled the Genevans with horror. The fate of his widow and children moved them; but that of Geneva moved them more profoundly still. Berthelier had fallen a victim to his passion for his country; and that passion, which made many other hearts beat high, drew tears even from the most selfish. The body hanging from the gibbet, the head nailed up near the bridge of Arve, the memory of that sad procession, did not speak to the senses only; men's hearts were rent as if by a violent blow, and many refused all consolation. There were also some proud firm spirits who, unable to weep, gave vent to maledictions. They might be met silent, frowning in the streets, and their air, the tone of their voice, their gait, their ironical and bitter words, expressed an indescribable contempt for the murderers. They retraced in their minds that strange struggle, between cruel princes and

* 'Il faut que le bon droit tienne chambre.'—Bonivard, *Chroniq.* ii. p. 368.

a generous, simple-minded, poor but free man. On one side were the splendors of the throne, the majesty of the priesthood, armies, executioners, tortures, scaffolds, and all the terrors of power; on the other, a humble man, opposing his enemies by the nobleness of his character and the unshrinking firmness of his courage. . . . The combat was unequal, and the head of the great citizen had fallen. A bishop looked with an ecstasy of joy on the blood of one of his flock, in which he bathed his feet while impudently violating all the laws of the country. But—and it was the consolation of these proud citizens—the blood that had been shed would awaken a terrible voice. Outraged justice and bleeding liberty would utter a long and mournful cry, which would reach the ears of the Swiss League. Then would mountain and valley, castle and cottage, city and hamlet, and every echo of the Alps repeat it one to another, and thousands of arms would one day unite to defend that little city so unworthily oppressed.*

Berthelier's death was to have still more serious consequences. His enemies had hoped to stifle liberty by killing him. Perhaps . . . but it was one of those deaths which are followed by a glorious resurrection. In the battle which had just been fought noble blood had been spilt, but it was blood that leads to victory at last. *Except a corn of wheat fall into the ground and die, it abideth alone; but if it die, it bringeth forth much fruit.* Religious liberty had many victims three centuries ago in all the countries of the Reformation; but the noblest martyrs of political liberty, in modern times, have fallen at Geneva (if my judgment does not mislead me), and their death has not been useless to the universal cause of civilization. *Cruciate, torquete, damnate . . . sanguis christianorum, semen.* The blood of the martyrs is a seed—a seed which takes root and bears fruit, not only in the spot where it has been sown, but in many other parts of the world.

Berthelier's friends were struck by his contempt of death and assurance of eternal life. They still seemed to hear the

* Galiffe, *Matériaux*, &c., ii. pp. 297, 298.

noble testimony he had borne to immortality. Hence one of them wrote this noble epitaph for him :—

> Quid mihi mors nocuit? Virtus post fata virescit;
> Nec cruce nec gladio sævi perit illa tyranni.*

As we see, the idea of a resurrection, of a life after death, over which man has no power, seems to have been uppermost in the mind of Berthelier as well as of his friends. This man was not a common martyr of liberty.

'Verily,' said some, 'the maxim lately set forth is a true one: Heroes and the founders of republics and empires have, next to God, the greatest right to the adoration of men.'†

The bishop hastened to take advantage of his victory. 'Berthelier's death,' said his friend Bonivard, 'gives the tyrant great comfort, for the watch-dog being killed, he can easily manage the scattered sheep.' The bishop began, therefore, to move onwards, and undertook to revolutionise Geneva. At first he resolved to change the magistrature. Four days after the execution he assembled the general council, and, assuming the airs of a conqueror, appeared at it with a numerous train. 'We John of Savoy,' said he in the document which has been preserved, 'bishop and prince of Geneva, being informed of the dissensions of this city, have not feared to come hither at great expense to administer by force of arms the most effectual remedy; and we have behaved like a good shepherd. My lord the Duke of Savoy, who singularly loves this city, having desired to enter it, the syndics and the seditious have with incredible annoyance rebelled against a prince so gentle;‡ and if this illustrious prince had not been touched with compassion, if he had not surpassed by his clemency the charity of the Redeemer § . . . we should all have been destroyed.' After

* 'What harm has death done me? Virtue flourishes beyond the grave; it perishes neither by the cross nor the sword of the cruel tyrant.'

† Machiavelli.

‡ 'Tam mansuetum principem.'

§ 'Nisi fuisset princeps ipse illustrissimus misericordia plenus, suaque

these strange words from a bishop, who placed the duke above Jesus Christ, at the very time when this prince had made himself the accomplice in a murder, Master Chappuis, the official, called out: 'Say is it not so?' None but mamelukes were present at the assembly, and among them several persons who had no right to be there. Many voices shouted, 'Yes, yes!' for it was then the reign of terror. The syndics, 'more ready to yield the bishop their maces than their heads,' says Bonivard, laid down before him the insignia of their office. The next day another general council elected four mameluke syndics: P. Versonay, P. Montyon, P. de Fernex, and G. Danel, 'who everywhere and in everything did what the bishop and the duke desired.' The same day all huguenots were excluded from the two councils; and the bishop forbade the citizens to carry arms or to assemble by night, under penalty of a fine of twenty-five livres and ten stripes of the cord.

Sorrow and dismay filled men's hearts. Geneva lay as it were under one of those funeral palls which are stretched over the dead. No one stirred out, no one spoke; all was motionless and silent; the air of despotism could be felt, as it hung over and benumbed the soul. Besançon Hugues, A. Lévrier, and the other patriots retired to their homes; but they had not lost hope; they waited in silence until God should make the cause of liberty to triumph again in their country.* Erelong, however, a few courageous spirits awoke and began to stir. The patriots felt the need of pouring out their sorrows together; and it was told the bishop 'that several persons of the huguenot sect† were in the habit of meeting secretly in various places.' Then the persecutions began afresh: 'They spared the good as little as the bad,' says Bonivard, 'and accused them of false crimes to be revenged on them.'

clementia vicisset pietatem Redemptoris.' The document will be found entire among the *Pièces Justificatives*, appended to *Besançon Hugues*, by M. Galiffe jun.

* Bonivard, *Chroniq.* ii. pp. 270, 273. Savyon, *Annales*, p. 101. Galiffe, *Matériaux*, ii. p. 277.

† 'Ayguinocticæ sectæ.'—Galiffe, *Matériaux pour l'Histoire de Genève*, ii. p. 164.

A short time before the period we are describing, Amadeus de Joye, one of Berthelier's friends, had committed an act of little importance in itself, but which was the first sign of opposition in Geneva to the Romish superstitions. Two years earlier Luther had written to Spenlein his beautiful letter on justification by faith; he had expounded the epistle to the Galatians, and probably posted up his theses. Zwingle, who had been appointed preacher at Einsiedeln, was declaiming against pilgrimages, offerings, images, and the invocation of the Virgin and the saints. Had the report of these sermons reached Geneva? It is possible, for, as we have seen, there was constant intercourse between this city and the German cantons. However that may be, many Genevans were already asking if the glory of God 'was not defiled by so foolish and lifeless a thing as an image?' Amadeus de Joye, whom we have met before at the Molard assembly, and whom his enemies accused of being the friend of Berthelier, Pécolat, 'and many other villains,' felt little respect for the bishop's *dolls*. Now there was at Geneva a famous black image of wood, between two and three feet high, called St. Babolin. Certain catholics held it in great devotion, carrying it in long processions, and rendering it every sort of honor. One night when the worshippers of St. Babolin had assembled in the house of Ami Motey, one of their number, De Joye, indignant at their idolatry and thinking the ugly figure was more like a devil than a god, carried it off, and, with the intention of giving a lesson to the partisans of the idol, took it to Motey's house. The window was open; he listened to the conversation of this devout little circle, and taking courage raised the image as high as the casement and flung it into the midst of its worshippers. It must be acknowledged that this was not controversy of the right sort; but it was the sixteenth century, and the Genevans were of a bold and scoffing humor. The startled followers of Babolin looked with astonishment at their saint, which appeared to have fallen from heaven. All of a sudden the door was opened and a loud voice called out: 'It is the devil . . . he will eat you all!' At these words, Motey jumped up, caught hold of a javelin and prepared to hurl it at the intruder; but De Joye hastily retired. There were no blows given, and no blood was shed.*

This incident had been almost forgotten when the bishop's agents, who were resolved to be severe upon the friends of liberty, shut up De Joye in the Château de l'Ile, where Berthelier had been imprisoned, and asked the syndics' permission to question and to torture him in order to get at the truth (7th September, 1519). Besides this affair of the image, he was charged with 'having been present at illegal meetings where the citizens bound themselves by oath to resist any infringement of their liberties by word or by deed.'† The syndics ordered that De Joye should be examined in prison, *pede ligato*, with the feet bound. The proceedings commenced.

'I was born of worthy, upright, and distinguished parents,' said De Joye when he appeared before the syndics, 'and by them trained up virtuously until the age of manhood. Since then I have associated with all the good men of the city, and in the profession which I follow I have always borne a good reputation. Far from picking quarrels, I have carefully avoided them, and have reconciled many. Finally, I have been all my life faithful and obedient to my lord the bishop.'‡ These words, which we transcribe from the documents in the trial, were of a nature to inspire the judges with a certain respect; but they did not. First Claude du Bois, the vidame's lieutenant, and next the governor of the castle, proposed that De Joye should be put to the torture to force him to confess the crimes imputed to him;§ but it was decided to begin by examining the witnesses, who told what they had *heard say* by persons *whose names they could not remember*. Fine evidence on which to put a man to the torture!‖ The governor did not abandon his project; the vidame came in person to urge the syndics to *do him this pleasure*.¶ Could they be denied, when it concerned only a

* Galiffe, *Matériaux*, ii. pp. 225–228.

† Ibid, ii. p. 214.

‡ Ibid, Interrog. de Joye, ii. p. 224.

§ 'Ut veritas ex ore delati eruatur.'—Ibid, ii. pp. 221, 224.

‖ Ibid, ii. p. 227.

¶ Ibid.

contemner of St. Babolin? Amadeus knew not the Gospel; his opposition to the black image proceeded merely from the disgust which superstition inspires in intelligent minds, and there was in his character more fire than firmness, more impetuosity than perseverance. The mild, weak, and infirm man, who was scared by the idea of torture, fancied his limbs already dislocated, and beginning to weep, he offered to make oath of his innocence on the relics of St. Anthony. To all the questions put to him he replied only by groans and tears. The vidame, whose heart was hardened, again demanded that he should be put to the torture. 'My right arm is crippled,' exclaimed the poor wretch; 'the sinews are contracted.' Two surgeons declared, after examination, that he might be able to bear the strappado, but could not support the torture of the *chatte* without fainting.* There were in the executioner's list punishments for all temperaments, for the sick and crippled as well as for the strong. De Joye, who, after he had sown his wild oats, had become a respectable citizen, was neither a hero nor a revolutionist. The embarrassed judges, not finding sufficient cause in the Babolin joke to put a man to death, helped him to escape during the night, and so saved appearances. The persecutions of the bishop were not limited to a single individual. John of Savoy took delight in power, and wished to show the cardinals that he was strong enough to put down revolt. 'They imprisoned,' says Bonivard, 'they beat, they tortured, they beheaded and hanged, so that it was quite pitiful.'† Geneva was crushed.

As it was not enough to lay their hands upon men, the princes of Savoy laid their hands upon the constitution. War was made against principles still more than against persons. It was necessary to stifle those strange aspirations which carried men's minds towards new ideas, and to put an end to imaginations which denied the lawfulness of absolute power. The duke, in accord with the bishop, published, although he was a foreign prince, an act restricting the liberties of Geneva, which banished from the general council

* Galiffe, *Matériaux*, &c.

† Bonivard, *Chroniq.* ii. p. 374.

all young men (for they were suspected of independence), and deprived the people of the direct election of syndics. On the 3rd of September, the general council, at which few but mamelukes were present, accepted these articles in silence. Thus did the Duke of Savoy, with the bishop's help, triumph over principles, rights, and liberties, and think he had strangled in their nest the young eagles whom he had once feared to see soaring into the heavens. Geneva, humbled and silenced by a bad prince and a maimed constitution, was no longer to be feared.

The sorrow was general, and it might have been supposed that the community only possessed strength enough to yield its last breath. But as was seen formerly in Israel, in moments of crisis, how prophets and prophetesses arose, so voices were heard in Geneva—voices of the weakest creatures—proclaiming the ruin of the people and denouncing the awful judgments of God. A poor girl for three days walked up and down the city, neither eating nor drinking, but crying everywhere as she went: *Le maz mugnier! le maz molin! le maz molu! . . . tout est perdu.* 'Wicked miller! wicked mill! wicked meal! . . . All is lost!' The miller was the prince, the mill was the constitution, the meal was the people . . . It seems that this monotonous and doleful voice affected everybody, even the mamelukes; the world readily believed in the marvellous in those days; and the vidame dared not arrest the prophetess. Syndic Balard, one of the most enlightened men in Geneva at that time, saw a deep meaning in the poor girl's mission.*

* *Journal* (contemporain) *de Balard*, p. 309. Gautier MS.

CHAPTER XXI.

STRUGGLES OF LIBERTY. LUTHER. DEATH OF THE BISHOP. HIS SUCCESSOR.

(1520–1523.)

The prophetess was mistaken: the *meal* was good. On a sudden the sky hitherto so dark cleared up, and there was a gleam of sunshine. The duke, who was thinking of marriage, returned to Turin; the bishop, who was seriously ill and needed a warmer air, withdrew to his abbey of Pignerol, and the huguenots, freed from their two oppressors, raised their heads. Ramel, Hugues, Taccon, Baudichon de la Maison-Neuve, and two others, waited upon the episcopal vicar, prothonotary of the holy see, and demanded the revocation of the decrees contrary to the liberties of the city, and the liberation of all citizens imprisoned by the bishop. 'In case of refusal,' they said, 'we shall appeal to the metropolitan see of Vienne.'* The vicar, remembering the excommunication incurred in the affair of Pécolat, was alarmed, and granted all they demanded. This concession raised the courage of the most timid, and the patriots immediately held meetings to provide for the safety of the city. Aimé Lévrier, the judge, was especially prominent. Berthelier had been the man of action, Lévrier was the man of right: he had seen with sorrow force substituted for law. In his opinion, every idea hostile to right ought to be combated; and the government of the bishop was not that of the laws, but of arbitrary power and terrorism. Lévrier had examples in his own family: the prelate had caused his brother-in-law (the procurator Chambet) to be thrown into prison because he was a huguenot, and to be tortured so

* 'Ad sanctam sedem metropolitanam Viennensem.'—*Pièces Justificatives de Besançon Hugues*, par M. Galiffe fils.

severely that his limbs remained out of joint. 'God made man free,' said Lévrier, 'ages have made Geneva free; no prince has the right to make us slaves.' Despairing of ever seeing the bishop reign with justice, he proposed an effectual remedy: 'Let us petition the pope for the prelate's destitution.' The daring motion was agreed to, and Lévrier was commissioned to go to Rome to see to its execution. The princes of Savoy succeeded in stopping him, and parried the blow, in part at least. Leo X., however, acknowledging how shameful the bishop's conduct had been, ordered the bastard never to return to Geneva, and to select a coadjutor to replace him. This was a cruel disgrace to the prelate.

Nor was this all: the people reasserted their ancient rights. The time had come for electing the syndics for the year; the duke and the bishop, as it will be remembered, had deprived the citizens of the right to elect, and accordingly the Great Council nominated these magistrates; but immediately loud protests were heard. The aged John Favre* and his two sons, with De la Mare, Malbuisson, Vandel, Richardet, and others, protested vigorously against this illegal act, and declared that the election ought to take place according to the ancient franchises. The people were at that time assembled in general council. The mamelukes unwilling to restore the liberties which their chiefs had taken away from the citizens, resisted stoutly; and there was an immense uproar in the assembly. The huguenots, ever prompt, immediately organized the bureau, not troubling themselves about the protests of their adversaries, and the popular elections began. At this news the ministers of the bishop and the duke hurried to the council, exclaiming: 'Stop! it is a great scandal; the Great Council has already named the syndics!' The huguenots resisted; they declared they would resume the ancient privileges of which a foreign prince had deprived them; and the ministers of the two cousins (Charles and John), finding their only resource was to gain time, demanded and obtained the adjournment

* The Registers of the Council say John Fabri; the words *Favre* and *Fabri*, being both derived from *Faber*, are frequently confounded.

of the election until the morrow. The huguenots felt themselves too strong not to wait. The next day, which was Monday, the citizens poured from every quarter towards St. Pierre's, full of enthusiasm for the constitutions handed down by their ancestors. Violence could not annul right; the election was made by the people in conformity with the liberties of Geneva. But the huguenots, having recovered their liberties, gave a proof of a moderation still more surprising than their energy. They knew that by being patient they would be strong; they thought that the election of huguenot syndics might, under present circumstances, cause the storm to burst, and bring down incalculable disasters upon the city; they therefore returned the same syndics as the Great Council had done. After having conquered absolutism, they conquered themselves. To construct with haste a scaffolding that might afterwards be easily thrown down was not their object; they desired to lay a solid foundation for the temple of liberty.*

They did more: they attempted a reconciliation. Three of them, headed by Robert Vandel (who was syndic in 1529), called upon the mameluke syndic Danel, and said: 'Let us forget our mutual offences and make peace; let us drop the names mameluke and huguenot, and let there be none but Genevans in Geneva. Bring the matter before the council.' The huguenots, like true citizens, desired union in their country; not so the mamelukes, who were sold to the foreigner. They referred the proposition to the vicar and episcopal council, and then to the bishop and the duke—a sure means of insuring its failure.† Moderation, concord, respect for the rights of all, were on the side of liberty. The only thought of the priests and mamelukes was how to separate themselves from the public cause. Of this a striking proof was seen at that time.

Money to pay the expenses of the war (known as the war *des Bésolles*) had to be raised. The clergy, notwithstanding their wealth, refused to pay their quota, little suspecting

* Registres du Conseil des 3, 5 et 6 février 1520. Bonivard, *Chroniq.* ii. p. 377.

† Ibid. 3 mai 1520.

that by their avarice they were preparing the way for the Reformation.* To no purpose did the huguenots, who had shown themselves so magnanimous in the election of the syndics, make an earnest movement to reconcile all parties; the priests, thinking only of their purses, replied by one of those violent measures customary with the papacy. A citation from Rome fell suddenly into the midst of Geneva; the pope summoned the chief magistrates of the republic to appear before him, to render an account of the tax they had dared to levy upon the priests; and on the 30th of April the agents of the court of Rome posted the citation on the gates of the church of St. Pierre. The citizens ran up to read it. What! the priests must always keep themselves apart! Poor men who gain their living painfully by the sweat of their brow, must stint their children's bread in order to pay this debt; and these debauched monks, these indolent priests, still abundantly enjoy the delights of the flesh, and are not willing to make the smallest sacrifice? The public conscience was stirred, the city thrilled with indignation, 'everybody was much vexed;' the next day the anger excited by this new act of meanness, this crying selfishness, burst out, and 'there was some rioting.'

Had the Reformation anything to do with this opposition to the selfishness of the priests and the despotism of Rome? It is possible, nay, probable; but it is a mistake to mix up the Reformer of Wittemberg with it. 'Luther,' says Bonivard, 'had already given instruction at this time to many in Geneva and elsewhere.'† The *instruction*, mentioned by the prior of St. Victor, clearly refers to christian truth in general, and not to the conduct of the Genevese under present circumstances. Had Luther done more? Had he addressed to Geneva any of his evangelical teachings, as Bonivard seems to indicate? Had he begun in this city the work that Calvin completed, as one of Bonivard's editors thinks?‡ This seems to us more than doubtful. The influ-

* Registers of the Council, Feb. 25 and Oct. 5, 1520.

† Bonivard, *Chroniq.* ii. p. 382. The words *donné des instructions* are not legible in the MS. but the context requires them.

‡ 'Luther, qui avait déjà de ce temps travaillé les esprits à Genève,

ence exercised by Luther over Geneva is indisputable; but it proceeded solely from his writings; it was the general influence of the evangelical ideas scattered through the world by the great Reformer.

It was the year 1520. Luther was known at Geneva. A few huguenots, indignant at the bull from Rome, asked whether this monk, who was already spoken of throughout christendom, had not shown that the pope had been often mistaken, and was mistaken every day? When the pope had condemned him, had not Luther appealed from the pope? Had he not said that the power of the sovereign pastor ought not to be employed in murdering 'Christ's lambs and throwing them into the jaws of the wolf?' . . . When the pope had launched a bull against this bold doctor, as he now launched a citation against Geneva, had not Luther asked how it was that you could not find in all the Bible one word about the papacy, and that while the Scriptures often mention little things, they positively say nothing of what we are assured are the greatest in the church?* . . 'We are no longer so frightened at the pope's bulls,' said the Genevans, 'and will not let ourselves be caught in his nets.'† Such was the first echo in Geneva of the cry uttered at Wittemberg. On those hills which rise so gracefully at the extremity of that beautiful lake, there was a soil ready to receive the seed which Luther was scattering in the air. It came borne on the winds from the banks of the Elbe even to the banks of the Rhone. Geneva and Wittemberg began to shake hands.

The Genevan priests, hearing the name of Luther, were alarmed; they fancied they already saw the dreaded face of the arch-heretic in Geneva, and began to make long processions to avert the wrath of heaven. One day, wishing at

fit preuve d'une grande sagacité en fécondant, dans l'intérêt de sa cause, un terrain aussi bien préparé que l'était cette ville pour adopter la Réformation.'—Note 3, p. 383, vol. ii. of the *Chroniques*, Genève, 1831.

* Luther's Works: *Against the Bull of Antichrist—Appeal to a Free Council—Foundation of the Articles condemned by the Bull.* 1520.

† Bonivard, *Chroniq.* ii. p. 382.

any cost to save their purses and their faith, they organised a procession on a greater scale than usual. Issuing from the city they proceeded with loud chants towards Our Lady of Grace on the bank of the impetuous torrent of Arve, whose turbid waters descend from the glaciers. All were there—canons, priests, monks, scholars in white surplices, while clerks, proud of their office, bore in front the image of St. Peter, the symbol of the papacy. The spectacle was very displeasing to the townspeople. If, they thought, we can do without the pope, like Luther, may we not also do without these canons, monks, and priests? Has not Luther said that 'a christian elected by christians to preach the Gospel is more truly a priest than if all the bishops and popes had consecrated him?'* It is scarcely probable that the Genevans would have had the idea of putting into practice this theory of the Reformer; but some of them desired to get quit of this army of Rome, in the pay of the duke of Savoy. 'All the priests had gone out,' said they; 'let us profit by the opportunity to shut the gates of the city, and prevent them from returning!' As the priests placed their interests in opposition to those of the city, it seemed logical to put them quietly out of Geneva. 'All those black coats,' says Syndic Roset, 'were very nearly shut out, through separating themselves from the republic.'† We may imagine the fright of the priests when they learnt what had been proposed. There was nothing, they thought, of which these huguenots were not capable, and such an off-hand way of getting rid of the clergy at one stroke was very much in keeping with their character. The citizens were not however bold enough for this. 'The prudent averted that,' says Bonivard. The startled monks and priests returned hastily and without opposition to their nests, and lived once more at their ease: they escaped with a good fright. This strange proposal, made by a few men of decision, has been considered a prelude to the Reformation in Geneva. That is saying too much; it required the Gospel to be first preached in the city: and that was the real prelude. The hour of the Re-

* Luther to the German nobles, 1520.

† Roset, *Chroniq.* liv. i. chap. cvi. Bonivard, *Chroniq.* ii. p. 383.

formation had not yet come; still the lesson was not lost, and an arrangement was made with the clergy, who paid a portion of the expenses of the war.

Other events gave some hope to the Genevans, whose franchises were so rudely trodden under foot; their greatest friend came out of prison, and their greatest enemy quitted this world. Bonivard was still in confinement, but his relations, who had great influence at court, solicited the duke to restore him to liberty. 'I dare not,' said Charles, 'for fear of offending the pope.' They then applied to Rome: Leo X. commissioned the Bishop of Belley to investigate the matter, and the friends of the prior entreated this prelate to set the prisoner at large: 'I dare not,' he replied, 'for fear of offending the duke.' At last the duke consented, and Bonivard recovered his liberty but not his priory. The Abbot of Montheron, to whom Charles had given it, having gone to Rome to arrange his affairs, was invited by certain ecclesiastics who coveted his benefice to a banquet 'after the Roman manner, and there,' says Bonivard, 'they gave him some cardinals' powder, which purged the soul out of his body.'* It was by having recourse to this 'romanesque' fashion that the guilty soul of Pope Alexander VI. had been hurried from the world. A deed was found by which the repentant Montheron resigned to Bonivard whatever rights he had over the priory;† but Leo X. gave St. Victor to one of his cousins, who leased the revenue for 640 gold crowns; and Bonivard, the amiable and brilliant gentleman, brought up in abundance, at one time prior and even prince, was left in poverty. It is true that he succeeded for a time in being put in possession of his priory; but the duke soon made him regret in a horrible dungeon the liberty and goods that had been restored to him. Geneva's day of agony was not yet ended, and at the very time when the citizens hoped to be able to breathe a purer air, oppression once more came and stifled them.

Another event which seemed likely to be favorable to

* Bonivard, *Chroniq.* ii. p. 180.

† Dr. Chaponnière has printed the deed. *Mém. d'Archéologie*, iv. p. 156.

Geneva was approaching. The pope, as we have said, had forced a coadjutor upon the bishop, and the latter had chosen Pierre de la Baume, an ecclesiastic of high family, a scion of the illustrious house of the counts of Montrevel, whom he looked upon as a son. Pierre, who was abbot of Suze and St. Claude, and bishop of Tarsus *in partibus*, came to Geneva about the time of Bonivard's liberation in 1521 to take possession of his charge. On the 25th of January a *Te Deum* was sung for that purpose at St. Pierre's by the Bishop of Maurienne. Everybody knew that the coadjutor would soon be bishop and prince; accordingly all passions were aroused, and after mass, the mamelukes endeavored to gain over the future bishop to their side. Besançon Hugues, who desired to see Geneva catholic and episcopal, but free, waited upon the prelate; reminded him, to pave the way for a good reception, that one Hugues, his great-uncle, had been cardinal, and perceiving that he had to deal with a frivolous, vain, pleasure-seeking man, and who, as a younger son, was ambitious to rise at least as high as his elder brothers, he strove to make him understand that, far from submitting to the duke, he should remember that the Bishop of Geneva was *prince*, while the duke was only vassal. Pierre de la Baume, a weak man, ever halting between two opinions, carried away by the honesty and eloquence of the Genevan citizen, gave him his confidence. Besançon Hugues remained ever after his most confidential adviser.*

Ere long another scene was enacted beyond the Alps. The miserable John of Savoy lay at Pignerol on his deathbed. Given during his life to the pleasures of the table and of debauchery, he was now paying the penalty of his misdeeds. He suffered from the gout, he was covered with filthy ulcers, he was little more than skin and bone. He had thought only of enjoying life and oppressing others; he had plotted the ruin of a city of which he should have been the pastor; he now received the wages of his iniquity. Near the bed where this prelate lay languishing stood his coadjutor, who had hastened from Geneva to Pignerol.

* Registres du Conseil du 25 janvier, 1521. *Besançon Hugues*, par Galiffe fils, p. 253.

With eyes fixed upon the dying man, Pierre sought to buoy him up with false hopes; but John was not to be deceived. Soon the dreaded moment approached; an historian, whom Romish writers quote habitually with favor,* describes all that was horrible in the end of this great sinner. Hirelings surrounded the dying bishop, and turned their eyes from time to time on him and on the objects they might be able to carry off as soon as he was insensible. Pierre de la Baume contemplated the progress of the disease with ill-dissembled satisfaction, eagerly anticipating the moment when, relieved from his hypocritical cares, he would enter into possession of all that he had coveted for so many years. Jean Portier, the dying man's secretary, the confidant of his successor, watched that criminal impatience, that sordid cupidity, and that perverse meanness, which he already hoped to turn to his advantage. The shadows of the victims of the expiring man were traced on the walls of the room by an avenging hand, and when at last the priests desired to administer extreme unction, he imagined they were covering him with blood. They presented him the crucifix; he seemed to recognise the features of Berthelier, and asked with a wild look; 'Who has done that?' Far from embracing with respect and submission this emblem of eternal salvation, he rejected it with horror, heaping foul abuses on it. Blasphemy and insult mingled with the foam that whitened his trembling lips. Thus wrote an author less Romanist, we perceive, than is imagined.† Repentance succeeded despair in the guilty soul of the prelate before his death. Turning a last look on his adopted son, he said to him: 'I wished to give the principality of Geneva to Savoy . . . and to attain my object, I have put many innocent persons to death.' The blood that he had shed cried in his ears: Navis, Blanchet, and Berthelier rose up before him. Pursued by remorse, weighed down by the fear of a Judge, he would have desired to save La Baume from the faults he

* M. Galiffe. I do not know what documents justify the picture drawn by this vigorous writer.

† Galiffe, *Matériaux*, &c., ii. p. 303. Galiffe's work is often quoted with approbation by Roman Catholics.

had committed himself. 'If you obtain this bishopric,' continued he, 'I entreat you not to tread in my footsteps. On the contrary, defend the franchises of the city . . . In the sufferings I endure, I recognise the vengeance of the Almighty . . . I pray to God for pardon from the bottom of my heart . . . In purgatory . . . God will pardon me!'* It is gratifying to hear this cry of an awakening conscience at the termination of a criminal life. Unfortunately Pierre de la Baume did not profit by this solemn advice. The bastard died after horrible sufferings, 'inflicted by the divine judgment,' says Bonivard, 'and he went into the presence of the Sovereign to plead with those whose blood he had shed.'—'At the time of his death, he was so withered,' adds the prior of St. Victor, 'that he did not weigh five and twenty pounds.' The prophecy of Pécolat was fulfilled: *Non videbit dies Petri.* Instead of twenty-five years, the episcopacy of John of Savoy had only lasted nine.

Geneva was about to change masters. The struggle which had characterised the episcopacy of John of Savoy could not fail to be renewed if, instead of a shepherd, the Genevese received a hireling. Who would come off victorious in this new combat? Would the old times be maintained; or, thanks to a prelate who understood the wants of the age and the nature of the Gospel, should we witness the commencement of a new era? There was little hope that it would be so. The episcopal see of Geneva, which gave the rank of temporal prince, was much coveted by nobles, and even, as we have seen, by members of the sovereign families. These worldly bishops thought only of getting rich and of living in pomp and pleasure, careless of the good government of the Church or of feeding their flock. The thrones of such princes could not but totter and fall ere long. Pierre de la Baume, certain good qualities notwithstanding, could not prevent this catastrophe; on the contrary, he accelerated it. He had wit and imagination; but was weak, vain, and inclined to the same habits of servility as his predecessor,

* 'Si perveneris huic episcopatui, noli, oro te, gressus meos insequi.' —*Mém. du Diocèse de Genève*, par Besson, p. 61. Savyon, *Annales*, p. 108.

'incapable,' says an historian, 'of comprehending any other happiness than sleeping well, after he had eaten and drunk well.'*

The bastard having breathed his last, Pierre, kneeling by the side of his bed, rose up a bishop. He took immediate steps to secure his new property from pillage, and on the 7th of February, 1522, wrote a letter to 'his dearly beloved and trusty syndics, councillors, citizens, and community of Geneva,' which gave no promise that the reign of truth would be witnessed during his episcopacy. He began with the falsehoods usual in such cases, and informed the Genevans that his predecessor had 'made as holy an end as ever prelate did, calling upon his Creator and the Virgin Mary with his latest breath.' He reminded them at the same time 'of the great love and affection which John had felt while alive for them and for all his good subjects.' . . . 'Witness the chestnut-tree at the bridge of Arve,' said some.†

A year elapsed before the new bishop came to Geneva. Was it from fear; or did his temporal occupations keep him away? It was probably the latter motive. He had to come to an understanding with the duke and the pope touching his episcopacy, and he visited Rome in order to obtain his briefs. At last, on the 11th of April, 1523, his solemn entry took place.‡ A great multitude flocked together from all the surrounding districts. The syndics, the councillors, and the people went as far as the bridge of Arve to meet the bishop, who, accompanied by his gentlemen, priests and friends, and having by his side the Countess of Montrevel his sister-in-law, the Marquis of St. Sorlin his second brother, and two of his nephews, advanced 'riding on a mule beautifully harnessed and gilt, and wearing a green hat, after the fashion of the bishops of Rome.' The four syndics carried a handsome canopy over his head, which a pelting rain rendered very necessary. 'More than a hundred horses crept at a snail's pace before him.' Four companies of archers, arquebusiers, bowmen, and spearmen marched by

* Galiffe, *Matériaux*, &c., ii. p. 26.

† Ibid, pp. 304, 305.

‡ Registres MS. du Conseil, mars et avril, 1523.

with firm steps. In every street of the city 'young men well mounted, equipped, and accoutred, rode à l'albanaise.' Dramas, farces, mysteries, games and pastimes were given in the open air in spite of the rain, and the Genevans were full of hope. It might have been said that this branch, so severely shaken and almost separated from the Roman papacy, was about to be restored. Geneva, by welcoming the bishop so cordially, seemed to be welcoming the pope who sent him. This was, however, in the year 1523. Luther had burnt the bull from Rome; he had said before the Diet of Worms, *I cannot do otherwise.* The Reformation was advancing with great strides at Wittemberg, and was spreading over all Germany. And yet it was just at this time that Geneva received a Roman bishop almost with enthusiasm; but if the energetic city should be disappointed in its expectations, we shall see it rise up against all the framework of Rome and overthrow it without leaving a single piece in its place.

For the moment men indulged in the most flattering hopes. La Baume bore a tree (in German *baum*) on his shield; the Genevese presented him a poem, the first lines of which ran thus:

> But for this tree which God has planted,
> Geneva would have had no gladness;
> No branch and no support had I
> To lean upon in time of sadness.
> But God be praised for his good work
> In planting here this goodly tree,
> Beneath whose shade the poor shall dwell
> In peace and unity.*

These verses are a proof of the pacific intentions which the patriots then entertained; for they were written by Ami Porral, a most decided huguenot, who afterwards became one of the first supporters of the Reformation. The Roman episcopacy did not correspond to their hopes; Porral and his friends soon discovered that they must plant *another tree in the orchard*, the tree of the Gospel, in whose branches

* Gaberel, *Hist. de l'Eglise de Genève. Pièces Justificatives*, p. 28.

the birds of the air might come and lodge. A priest representing St. Peter, and dressed as a pope, presented to the bishop the golden key of his cathedral, and the prelate, standing in the church in front of the high altar, swore to observe the franchises of the city.* But he had scarcely taken this oath before he imprisoned a citizen unlawfully; and when the syndics humbly reminded him of their liberties, he exclaimed petulantly: 'You always smell of the Swiss.'† However, he set the prisoner at large.

Between 1519 and 1525 there were few days of energy and enthusiasm in Geneva; her liberty was expiring, tyranny hovered over the city, a funeral pall seemed to hang upon its walls. This was a time of bitter trial and depression in the city. In the midst of citizens who slumbered, of some who paid court to an illegitimate power, and of others who thought of nothing but amusement, there were many who shed tears over the loss of their glorious hopes. We feel ill at ease in Geneva now, and still more ill in the midst of merrymakings than in the midst of trials. Would the duke and the bishop really succeed in stifling the new life which animated this little state? A great event will arise to give strength to liberty. She descended to the tomb with Berthelier, though still young; she will come forth again when, the gates of Switzerland opening wide, Geneva shall grasp the hand of the ancient champions of independence, and receive the words of Him who said: *The truth shall make you free.*

* Bonivard, *Chroniq.* ii. p. 388. Registres du Conseil des 27 février; 17 mars: 9, 10, 11 avril.

† 'Vos semper sentitis Allemanos.'—Gautier MS.

CHAPTER XXII

CHARLES DESIRES TO SEDUCE THE GENEVANS. THE MYSTERIES OF THE CANONS AND OF THE HUGUENOTS.

(AUGUST, 1523.)

THE duke, seeing that the Genevese commune was seriously weakened, had formed new plans for definitively seizing the sovereignty, and of expelling both liberty and the tendencies towards the Reformation, with which, according to Charles III. and Charles V., this restless city was infected. Magnificence, fêtes, grandeur, flattery, seduction and perfidy were all to be brought into play, and for that end Charles possessed new resources. He had just married Beatrice of Portugal, whose sister was about to be united to the Emperor Charles V. Beatrice, a woman of great beauty, proud, ambitious, and domineering, required everything to bend before her; Charles, a man of no will, found one in this princess; and the conspiracy of Savoy against Genevan independence entered into a new phase, which threatened to be marked by great reverses. After a few months of wedlock, the duke expressed a desire to present the beautiful duchess to his good friends of Geneva, and made preparations for displaying all the pomps and seductions of a court in order to win them over. And more than this: the duchess expected to be brought to bed in December: it was now August (1523); if she had a boy in Geneva, would not these worthy burgesses be happy, nay proud, to have for their prince a son of Savoy born within their walls? And would not the child's uncle, the mighty emperor, have a word to say then in his favor in that ancient imperial city which still bore the eagle on its shield? Every means was set to work to carry out this court manœuvre.

The duke had calculated rightly when reckoning on republican vanity. Every one was busied in preparing to receive the prince, with his wife and courtiers, for the Genevese desired that the pomps of this fête should infinitely surpass those of the bishop's reception. There were (so to say) two men in these citizens : one, full of lofty aspirations, longed for truth and liberty ; but the other, full of vanity and fond of pleasure, allowed himself to be seduced by luxury and the diversions of a court. The duke and the bishop would never have succeeded in ruining Geneva ; but if Geneva united with them, her ruin seemed inevitable. All heads were turned. 'I shall be dressed more expensively than you on the day of the duchess's entrance,' said Jean de Malbuisson to Jean Philippe, afterwards first syndic. Upon which, Philippe, one of the proudest huguenots, ordered a magnificent dress of satin, taffeta, velvet, and silver, which cost him forty-eight crowns of the sun. Malbuisson was filled with jealousy and anger, and the syndics were compelled to interfere to appease this strife of vanity.* These vain republicans charmed at the honor to be done them by the daughter of the king of Portugal, wished to strew her path with roses. Portugal, governed by the famous dynasty of Aviz, renowned by the expeditions of Diaz, Vasco de Gama, and Cabral, and by the conquests of Albuquerque, was then overflowing with riches, was a naval power of the first order, and was at the height of its greatness. It was no small thing in the eyes of the burgesses of the city of the Leman that the glory, which filled the most distant seas with its splendor, should shed a few sparks of its brilliancy on the shores of an unknown lake. The duke had no doubt that these citizens, so fond of pleasure, would quietly submit to the claims which beauty laid upon them, and that Geneva would be his.

At last the 4th of August arrived, and all the city hastened to the banks of the Arve to meet the young and charming duchess ; the women had the foremost place in this Genevese procession. A battalion of amazons, composed of three hundred of the youngest and most beautiful persons

* Registres du Conseil du 2 août.

in Geneva, appeared first. They wore the colors of the duchess, blue and white; their skirts, as was the fashion with the warlike damsels of antiquity, were tucked up to the knee; and each one carried in her right hand a javelin, and in her left a small shield. At the head as captain was the wife of the Seignior d'Avully, who, being a Spaniard, could speak to the duchess in her own language: in the middle was the standard-bearer, 'a tall and beautiful woman, waving the colors like a soldier who had done nothing else all his life.'

The duchess appeared, seated in a triumphal chariot drawn by four horses, and so covered with cloth of gold and jewels that all eyes were dazzled. The duke rode by her side on a mule richly caparisoned, and a multitude of noblemen followed them in magnificent attire, smiling and talking to one another: the good-humored simplicity of these republicans charmed them. They said that if they had failed with the sword, they would succeed with jewellery, feathers, and display; and that this rebellious city would be too happy, in exchange for the amusements they would give, to receive the duke and pay court to the pope. Everything had been arranged to make the poison enter their hearts by mild and subtle means. The triumphal car having halted at Plainpalais, the queen of the amazons approached the duchess and said:

En ce pays soyez la bienvenue! . . .

with other verses which we spare the reader. When the princess arrived before the chapel of the Rhone, where stood an image of the Virgin with the child Jesus in her arms, a sibyl appeared and said:

For thee I have obtained a boon divine:—
The Son of God before thine eyes shall shine. . .
Look up . . . see him to Mary's bosom pressed,
The Virgin who hath borne him for our rest;
With great devotion Mary's son adore,
And he shall open wide to thee heaven's door.

The procession passed successively under six triumphal

arches, dedicated to illustrious princesses, before each of which Beatrice had to stop and hear a new compliment. But it was labor lost: the haughty Portuguese woman, far from thanking the ladies, did not even look at them; and when the men came forward in their turn in those magnificent dresses which had cost them so much money and contention, the duchess received the *shopkeepers* with still greater contempt. A deep feeling of discontent immediately replaced the general enthusiasm: 'She takes us for her slaves, in Portugal fashion,' exclaimed one of the proudest of the huguenots. 'Let us show her that we are free men. Come, ladies, I advise you to return to your spinning; and as for us, my friends, we will pull down the galleries and destroy the theatres.' And then he whispered to one of his neighbors: 'Better employ our money in fortifying the city, and compelling these Savoyards to keep outside. You entice them in . . . take care they do not burn you in your own straw.' The duke's counsellors began to feel alarmed. The mine which they fancied had been so skilfully dug, threatened to blow them all into the air. Yet a few more mistakes of this kind and all was lost. . . . Some of the courtiers endeavored to excuse the haughty manners of Beatrice by telling the citizens: *Che eran los costumbre de Portugal.* 'They were the fashions of Portugal.' The duke conjured his wife to make an effort to win back their hearts.*

Doubts were beginning at that time to be circulated concerning the attachment of Geneva to the papacy. Charles and his courtiers had heard something of this; and the desire to keep the city in the fold of Rome for ever had a great share, as we have remarked, in their chivalrous enterprise. The mamelukes and the canons, ashamed of these rumors, had prepared a mystery-play calculated to make the duke and duchess believe that the Genevans thought much more of seeking crosses and other relics than of finding that New Testament so long unknown, and about which they were talking so much in Germany. Accordingly, when the

* *Mém. d'Archéol. de Genève,* i. p. 191. Bonivard, *Chroniq.* ii. p. 391. Savyon, *Annales,* p. 111. Spon, *Hist. de Genève.*

procession arrived at the Place du Bourg de Four, they saw a large scaffold, a kind of house, open on the side next the spectators, and divided into several stories. The triumphal car halted, and the people of Geneva who were afterwards to show the world another spectacle, began to perform the 'Invention of the Cross.'

The first scene represents Jerusalem, where the Emperor Constantine and Helena, his mother, have arrived to make search for the precious relic.

CONSTANTINE *to the Jews.*

Come tell me, Jews, what did you do
With the cross whereon by you
Christ was hanged so cruelly?

THE JEWS, *trembling.*

Dear emperor, assuredly
We do not know.

CONSTANTINE.

You lie.
You shall suffer for this by-and-by.

(*To his guards.*)

Shut them in prison instantly.

The Jews are put into prison; and this is a lesson to show what ought to be done to those who pay no respect to the wood that Helena had come to worship.

A JEW *from the window.*

Judas the president am I,
And if you will let me go
I by signs most clear will show
Where my father saw it hid.

CONSTANTINE.

Out then; we the cross will seek,
And they shall linger here the while.

The next scene represents Golgotha. The emperor, Helena, and their train follow the Jew.

JUDAS.

Mighty emperor, here's the spot
Where the cross by stealth was put
With other two.

CONSTANTINE.

Good!
Let the earth be dug around,
And the cross be quickly found.

A LABORER *digs up three crosses.*

This is all.

CONSTANTINE, *puzzled to know which is the true cross.*

To prove the story true
Still remains. . . What shall we do?

HELENA.

My dear son, pray hold your tongue.

(*She orders a dead body to be brought.*)

To this corpse we will apply
These three crosses carefully,
And, if I be not mistaken,
At the touch it will awaken.

(*The three crosses are applied, and when the third touches the body it is restored to life.*)

HELENA.

O wonderful!

(*Helena takes the true cross in her arms.*)

CONSTANTINE *kneels and worships it.*

O cross of Christ, how great thy power!
In this place I thee adore;
May my soul be saved by thee!

HELENA.

The cross hath brought to us God's grace,
The cross doth every sin efface.
Here's the proof. . . .

Thus, therefore, the Genevese believed in the miracles

worked by the wood of the cross. How, after such manifest proof, should not the world see that Geneva was free from heresy?*

The procession and the princess resumed their march. They stopped before the hôtel-de-ville, and there the syndics made Beatrice a present from the city, which she received *pleasantly* according to the lesson the duke had given her. However, she could hold up no longer: exhausted with fatigue, she begged to be conducted to her lodging. They proceeded accordingly towards the Dominican convent, where apartments had been prepared for the duke and duchess. This monastery, situated without the city, on the banks of the Rhone, was one of the most corrupt but also one of the richest in the diocese. Here they arrived at last, Charles as delighted as Beatrice was wearied. 'The flies are caught by the honey,' said the duke; 'yet a few more fêtes, and these proud Genevans will become our slaves.'

He lost no time, and, full of confidence in the *prestige* of Portugal, the brilliancy of his court, and the graces of his duchess, he began to give 'great banquets, balls, and fêtes.' Beatrice, having learnt that it was necessary to win hearts in order to win Geneva, showed herself agreeable to the ladies, and entertained them with 'exquisite viands,' followed by ballets, masquerades, and plays. On his part the duke organised tournaments with a great concourse of noble cavaliers, assembled from all the castles of the neighboring provinces, and in which the youth of Geneva contended with the lords of the court. 'We have never been so well amused since the time of Duke Philibert,' said the young Genevans. To the allurements of pleasure Savoy added those of gain. The court, which was 'large and numerous,' spent a great deal of money in the city, and thus induced all those to love it who had given up their minds to the desire for riches. Finally the attractions of ambition were added to all the rest. To souls thirsting for distinction Geneva could offer only a paltry magistracy, whilst, by yielding themselves to Savoy, they might aspire to the greatest

* This mystery-play will be found at length in the *Mémoires d'Archéologie de Genève*, i. pp. 196–203.

honors; accordingly the notables and even the syndics laid themselves at the feet of the duke and duchess. 'The prince was better obeyed at Geneva than at Chambéry,' says Bonivard. Everything led the politicians to expect complete success. That bold soaring towards independence and the Gospel, so displeasing to the duke, the king of France, and the emperor, was about to be checked; and those alarming liberties, which had slept for ages, but which now aspired after emancipation, would be kept in restraint and subjection.*

The calculations of the princes of Savoy were not, however, so correct as they imagined. A circumstance almost imperceptible might foil them. Whilst the cabinet of Turin had plotted the ruin of Geneva, God was watching over its destinies. Shortly before the entry of the bishop and the duke, another power had arrived in Geneva; that power was the Gospel. Towards the end of the preceding year, in October and November, 1522, Lefèvre published his French translation of the New Testament. At the same time the friends of the Word of God, being persecuted at Paris, had taken refuge in different provinces. A merchant named Vaugris, and a gentleman named Du Blet, were at Lyons, despatching thence missionaries and New Testaments into Burgundy and Dauphiny, to Grenoble and Vienne.† In the sixteenth century as in the second, the Gospel ascended the Rhone. From Lyons and Vienne came in 1523 to the shores of Lake Leman that Word of God which had once destroyed the superstitions of paganism, and which was now to destroy the excrescences of Rome. 'Some people called evangelicals came from France,' says a *Memoir to the Pope on the Rebellion of Geneva* in the archives of Turin. The names of the pious men who first brought the Holy Scriptures to the people of Geneva have been no better preserved than the names of the missionaries of the second century: it is generally in the darkness of night that beacon fires are kindled. Some Genevans 'talked with them and

* Bonivard, *Chroniq.* ii. p. 395. Savyon, *Annales*, p. 113. Gautier MS.

† See my *Hist. of the Ref.*, vol. iii. bk. xii. chaps. 7 and 11.

bought their books,' adds the MS. Thus, while the canons were assisting in the representation of time-worn fables, and holding up as an example the piety of those who had sought for the cross in the bowels of the earth, more elevated souls in Geneva were seeking for the cross in the Scriptures. One of the first to welcome these biblical colporteurs was Baudichon de la Maison-Neuve, a man bold and ardent even to imprudence, but true, upright, and generous. He was enraptured to find in the Gospel the strength he needed to attack the superstitions of old times, which filled him with instinctive disgust. Robert Vandel did the same. Syndic in 1529, and employed in all the important affairs of the time, he found in these works which had come from Lyons a means of realising his ideal, which was to make Geneva a republic independent in religion as well as in politics. These noble-hearted men and many besides them read the Scriptures with astonishment. They sought, but they could find no Roman religion there—no images, no mass, no pope; but they found an authority and power above prelates and councils and pontiffs, and even princes themselves—a new authority, new doctrine, new life, new church . . . and all these new things were the old things which the apostles had founded. It was as if the quickening breath of spring had begun to be felt in the valley after the rigors of a long winter. They went out into the open air; they basked in the rays of the sun; they exercised their benumbed limbs. Priests and bigot laymen looked with astonishment at this new spectacle. What! they had hoped that the pompous entrance of Charles and Beatrice would secure their triumph, and now an unknown book, entering mysteriously into the city, without pomp, without display, without cloth of gold, borne humbly on the back of some poor pedlar, seemed destined to produce a greater effect than the presence of the brother-in-law of Charles V. and of the daughter of the kings of Portugal . . . Was the victory to slip from their hands in the very hour of success? Was Geneva destined to be anything more than a little city in Savoy and a parish of the pope's? . . . Disturbed at this movement of men's minds, some of the papal agents hastened to write to Rome:

'What a singular thing! a new hope has come to these dejected rebels . . . And to those books which have been brought from France and which they buy of the evangelicals, the Genevans look for their enfranchisement.'*

In fact, the triumph of the duke, the duchess, and their court, who had succeeded in leading certain Genevans into dissipation and servility, exasperated the huguenots: they never met without giving vent, as they grasped each other's hands, to some expression of scorn or sorrow. Among them was Jean Philippe, several times elected captain-general. He was not one of those whom the Holy Scriptures had converted; he was a rich and generous citizen, full of courage and a great friend of liberty; but loving better to pull down than to build up, and carrying boldness even to rashness. He proposed that they should give a lesson to the mamelukes and priests, 'and undertook to bear all the expenses.' Other huguenots, more moderate, and above all more pious, held it of importance to make known the impressions they had received from the Gospel. The Word of God having touched their hearts, they desired to show that it was a remedy for all the ills of humanity. Seeing that everybody was eager to entertain the duke and duchess, they resolved to add their dish also to the banquet, seasoning it however with a few grains of salt. Instead of the discovery of the cross by Helena, they will celebrate the discovery of the Bible by the Reformation. The subject was not ill-chosen, as it brought out strongly the contrast between the old and the new times. The huguenots therefore informed the duke that they were desirous of performing a mystery-play in his honor in the open air on the Sunday after a certain holiday called Les Bordes. Jean Philippe having generously provided for all the expenses, the young men learnt their parts, and everything was ready for the representation.

It was fair-time at Geneva, and consequently a great crowd of Genevans and strangers soon gathered round the

* Archives de Turin, paquet 14, 1re catégorie. *Mémoire au Pape sur la Rébellion de Genève.* M. Gaberel, who has examined this memoir, assigns it (*Hist. de l'Eglise de Genève*, i. p. 84) to the year 1520; but it seems to me more probable that it relates to 1523.

theatre: the Bishop of Maurienne arrived; lords and ladies of high descent took their seats; but they waited in vain for the duke, who did not appear. 'We shall not go, neither the duchess nor myself,' he said, 'because the performers are huguenots.' Charles, knowing his men well, feared some snake in the grass. The huguenot who had composed the piece represented the state of the world under the image of a *disease*, and the Reformation as the *remedy* by which God desired to cure it; the subject and title of his drama was, *Le Monde Malade*, the Sick World, and everything was to appear—priests, masses, the Bible and its followers. The principal character, *Le Monde* (the World), had heard certain monks, terrified at the books which had lately come from France, announce that the last days were at hand, and that the World would soon perish. It was to be burnt by fire and drowned by water . . . This was too much for him; he trembled, his health declined, and he pined away. The people about him grew uneasy, and one of them exclaimed:

> The World grows weaker every day;
> What he will come to, who can say?

He had however some friends, and each of them brought him a new remedy; but all was useless—the World grew worse and worse. He decided then to resort to the sovereign universal remedy, by which even the dead are saved, namely, masses. The Romish worship, assailed by the reformers, was now on its trial in the streets of Geneva.

THE WORLD.

> Come, Sir Priest, pull out your wares—
> Your masses, let me see them all.

PRIEST, *delighted to see the World apply to him.*

> May God give you joy! but how
> You like them I should wish to know.

THE WORLD.

> I like them just as others do.

PRIEST.

Short?

THE WORLD.

Yes, short.

PRIEST, *showing him some masses.*

Then here 's the thing for you.

THE WORLD, *rejecting them with alarm.*

Than these no sermon can be longer.

PRIEST, *showing others.*

Here are others.

THE WORLD, *refusing them.*

No! no! no!

PRIEST, *finding that the World wants neither long nor short masses.*

What you want you do not know.

Then *Le Conseiller* (the Counsellor), a wise and enlightened man, recommends a new remedy, one both harmless and effectual, which is beginning to make a great noise.

What is it, say?

asks the World; the Counsellor answers:

A thing which no man dares gainsay . . .
THE BIBLE.

The World does not know what this new medicine means: another character strives in vain to inspire him with confidence:

Believe me, Mr. World, there's not a fool
But knows it.

The World will not have it at any price. It was known already at Geneva in 1523 that the World was giving a bad reception to the Gospel: 'They shall say all manner of evil against you, and shall persecute you.' As he could not be cured by the priests, and would not be cured by the Bible, the World called in the Doctor (*le Médecin*), and carefully described his disease:

I am so troubled, and teased, and tormented,
With all the rubbish that they have invented . .
That flat here on my bed I lie.

DOCTOR.

What rubbish?

THE WORLD.

That a *deluge* by-and-by
Will come, and that a *fire* to boot
Will burn us all both branch and root.

But the Doctor happens to be (as was often the case in the sixteenth century) one of those who believe the text of the Bible to be infallible; he begins to paint the liveliest picture of the disorders of the clergy, in order to induce his patient to take the remedy prescribed for him:

Why are you troubled, Sir World, at that?
Do not vex yourself any more
At seeing these rogues and thieves by the score
  Buying and selling the cure of souls . . .
Children still in their nurses' arms
Made abbots and bishops and priors. . .
. . . .
For their pleasure they kill their brothers,
Squander their own goods and seize another's;
  To flattering tongues they lend their ear;
For the merest trifle they kindle the flame
Of war, to the shame of the christian name.*

The World, astonished at a description so far from catholic, becomes suspicious, thinks the language heretical, and exclaims:

. . . Mere fables these:
From the land of LUTHER they came.

DOCTOR.

Upon Luther's back men lay the blame,
If you speak of sin . . .

At Geneva, therefore, as well as in all the catholic world,

* The original of this *sottie* will be found in the *Mémoires d'Archéologie de Genève*, pp. 164–180.

Luther was already known as the man who laid bare sins. The Doctor did not allow himself to be disconcerted by this charge of Lutheranism :

World, would you like to be well once more ?

THE WORLD, *with firmness.*

Yes !

DOCTOR.

Then think of abuses what a store
Are daily committed by great and small,
And *according to law* reform them all.

This was demanding a Reformation. The huguenots (*Eidguenots*) applauded ; the foreign merchants were astonished ; the courtiers of Savoy, and even Maurienne himself, smiled. Still Maison-Neuve, Vandel, Bernard, and all those who had 'talked with' the evangelicals, and especially the author of the drama, knew the difficulties the Reformation would have to encounter in Geneva.

The World, irritated against these laymen who turn preachers, exclaims :

This impudent doctor so mild of speech,
I asked him to *cure* me, not to *preach.*
The fool !

Another personage, alarmed at so unprecedented a thing :

Good heavens ! it can't be true.

THE WORLD.

True enough ; but as for his preaching now,
I'd rather be led by a fool, I vow,
Than a preacher.

FRIENDS OF THE WORLD.

That's quite right·
Live by the rule of your appetite.

THE WORLD.

That will I ! . . .

Whereupon the World puts on a fool's dress, and the burlesque ends.

It is too true that the world, after the Reformation, put on a fool's dress in various places, particularly in France. What was the house of Valois but a house of fools? And yet a divine wisdom had then entered the world, and remains in it still, for the healing of nations. From the beginning of 1523, the great principle of protestantism which declares Scripture to be the only source and rule of truth, in opposition to that of Roman Catholicism, which substitutes the authority of the Church, was recognised in Geneva. The 'text of the Bible' was publicly declared 'an irreproachable thing' and the only remedy for the cure of diseased humanity. And what, at bottom, was this burlesque of the huguenots but a lay sermon on the text: *The law of the Lord converteth the soul?* It is good to observe the date, as it is generally thought that the Reformation did not begin till much later in the city of Calvin. This 'mystery' of a new kind did not remain without effect; the evangelicals had taken up their position; the ram, armed with its head of brass, that was to batter and throw down the walls of Rome—the infallible Bible, had appeared. Jean Philippe felt that the piece had not cost him too dear.

The stage of the *Monde Malade* had scarcely been pulled down, when the citizens had to think of something else besides plays. The Savoyards, who did not like the dish served up to them, and thought they smelt the poison of heresy in it, resolved to avenge themselves by making the weight of their yoke felt. Two words comprehend the whole policy of these soldiers and courtiers: despotism of the prince, servility of the people. They undertook to mould the Genevans to their system. With haughty mien and arrogant tone they were continually picking quarrels with the citizens; they called everything too dear that was sold them, they got into a passion and struck the shopkeepers, and the latter, who had no arms, were obliged at first to put up with these insults. But erelong every one armed himself, and the tradesmen, raising their heads, crossed swords with these insolent lords. There was a great uproar in the city. Irritated at this resistance, the grand-master of the court hastened to the council: 'The duke and duchess came here,' he said, 'thinking to be with friends.' The council ordered the citizens to be arrested who had struck the gentlemen, and the Savoyard quarter-master undertook to lock them up, which the Genevan quarter-master resisted. The duke, in a passion, threatened to bring in his subjects 'to pillage the place.' There was some reason, it must be confessed, to desire a little tranquillity. 'The duchess is willing to do us the honor of being brought to bed in this city,' said Syndic Baud to the people; 'please do not make any disturbance; and as soon as you hear the bells and trumpets, go in procession with tapers and torches, and pray to God for her.'

The 'honor' which the duchess was about to confer on Geneva did not affect the Genevans. The most courageous citizens, Aimé Lévrier, John Lullin, and others, were superior to all such seductions. Faithful interpreter of the law, calm but intrepid guardian of the customs and constitutions, Lévrier continually reminded the council that Charles was not sovereign in Geneva. While avoiding a noisy opposition, he displayed unshrinking firmness; and accordingly the duke began to think that he could only become prince of the city by passing over his body. Lullin was not a jurist like Lévrier, but active, practical, and energetic; at every opportunity he manifested his love of liberty, and sometimes did so with rudeness. Although prior of the confraternity of St. Loup, he was at the same time landlord of the *Bear* inn, which, according to the manners of those days, was not incompatible with a high position in the city. One day when his stables were full of horses belonging to a poor Swiss carrier, some richly-dressed gentlemen of Savoy alighted noisily before the inn and prepared to put up their horses. 'There is no room, gentlemen!' said Lullin roughly. 'They are the duke's horses,' replied the courtiers. 'No matter,' returned the energetic huguenot. 'First come, first served. I would rather lodge carriers than princes.' At that time Charles was raising six thousand men, to be present in Geneva at his child's christening, and the cavaliers probably belonged to this body. But the huguenots thought it too much to have six thousand godfathers armed from head to foot, and it was probably this that put Lullin in bad humor. Charles was weak but violent; he stamped his foot when told of the insult offered to his servants, cast a furious glance over the city, and exclaimed with an oath: 'I will make this city of Geneva smaller than the smallest village in Savoy.'* Many trembled when they heard of the threat, and the council, to pacify the prince, sent Lullin to prison for three days.

At length the great event arrived on which the hopes of Savoy reposed. On the 2nd of December one of the duke's officers informed the syndics that the duchess had been delivered at noon of a prince. Immediately the bells were rung, the trumpets sounded: bishop, canons, priests, monks, confraternities, boys and girls dressed in white and carrying tapers in their hands, all walked in long procession. Bonfires were lighted in every open place, and the cannons on the esplanade (La Treille) which looks towards Savoy announced to that faithful country that the duke had a son.† 'As he was born in Geneva,' said the courtiers to one another, 'the citizens cannot refuse him for their prince.'‡ The duchess had the matter very much at heart, and erelong, richly apparelled and seated in her bed, as was the custom, she would say in the frivolous conversations she had with the persons admitted to pay their court to her: 'This city is a *buena posada*' (a very good inn). The delighted duke replied: 'Geneva shall be yours,' which she was very pleased to hear.§

Everything in Geneva and even in Europe seemed to favor the designs of Savoy. Charles V. the duke's brother-in-law, and Francis I. his nephew, were preparing for the war in Lombardy. The struggle between the pope and

* 'Minimum villagium suæ patriæ.'—Reg. du Conseil, 18 décembre. Bonivard, *Chroniq.* ii. p. 392.

† 'Debandata fuit artilleria in porta Baudet.'—Registers of the Council, Dec. 2.

‡ Bonivard, *Chroniq.* ii. p. 392.

§ Bonivard, *Police de Genève. Mém. d'Archéol.* iv. p. 382.

Luther occupied men's minds. The Swiss were 'in great care and discord, city divided against city, and one against another in the same city.' Bishop Pierre de la Baume was fickle, worldly, fond of gambling, of feasting, of waiting upon the ladies, and of pursuing other pleasures which diverted him from better occupations. Timid and even fearful, changing like a weathercock with every wind, he dreaded above all things to lose the benefices he possessed in the territory of his Highness. All this permitted Charles—at least he thought so—quietly to invade Geneva and to unite it to Savoy without Europe's saying a word. To have his hands still freer, he persuaded De la Baume that his presence in Italy was necessary for the emperor's service.* That done, and thinking the fruit ripe and ready to fall, the duke and duchess made preparations for striking the final blow. They clearly saw the hostile disposition of many of the Genevans; but that was only an additional reason for increased exertions. If, now that a prince of Savoy was born in Geneva, the duke failed in his projects, everything would be lost for many a day. The cue was therefore given to all the Savoyard nobility. The beauty of their gold pieces dazzled the shopkeepers; sports, dinners, balls, masquerades, plays, tournaments, pomp, finery, pleasures, luxuries, and all the allurements which seduce men (say contemporary writers), captivated the worldly and particularly the youth. Some few huguenots talked loudly of independence; some old Genevans still strove to retain their sons; some venerable mothers, seeing their children setting out for the court dressed in their gayest clothes, asked them if they did not blush for the old manners of their fathers,—if they desired to sell their free souls and become the servants of princes? . . . But all was useless. 'It is like throwing water on a ball,' said the afflicted parents; 'not a drop stays there.'—'What would you have?' replied these giddy youths. 'It is stronger than us. As soon as the charms of the world appear, our appetites carry us away, like runaway horses.'

The monks did not remain behind in this work of corrup-

* Bonivard, *Chroniq.* ii. p. 395. Savyon, *Annales*, p. 114.

tion. On the 20th of May the Dominicans celebrated the Feast of St. Ives, and invited the youth to one of those notorious vigils where all sorts of abominations were practised. The syndics complained ineffectually to the vicar-general of the scandalous lives (*sceleratæ vitæ*) of these friars. 'Go to the convent and remonstrate with them,' said this ecclesiastic. And when the syndics went there, the prior acknowledged that the monks led a dissolute life, but, he added, 'it is to no purpose that I speak to them of correction; they answer that, if I do not hold my tongue, they will turn me out of the monastery.'* By their vices the clergy were digging a gulf beneath their feet, into which they would drag everything—doctrine, worship, and Church. All appeared to combine for the enslavement of Geneva. Neither the emperor, nor the king, nor the pope, nor the bishop, nor the Swiss, nor even the Genevese themselves, watched over the independence of the city. The living waters of the Gospel alone could purify these Augean stables. 'God only remained,' said Bonivard; 'but while Geneva slept, He kept watch for her.'†

Geneva was indeed about to wake up. The enervating dreams of the 'golden youth' were beginning to fade away. Not only those to whom the New Testament had been brought, not only the friends of independence, but thoughtful men of order and of law were going to oppose the duke. A new martyr was to fertilise a generous soil with his blood, and prepare the final victory of right and liberty.

* Council Registers, May 20; June 30 and 23, 1522; and July 22, 1523.

† Bonivard, *Chroniq.* ii. p. 395. Gautier MS.

CHAPTER XXIII.

AIMÉ LÉVRIER, A MARTYR TO LIBERTY AND RIGHT AT THE CASTLE OF BONNE.

(MARCH, 1524.)

THERE was one citizen in Geneva who greatly embarrassed the duke, and this was Lévrier. It was neither from pride, resentment, nor envy that he resisted the usurpations of the prince, but from an ardent love of justice and respect for the old charters of liberty. He had less spirit than Berthelier, but more gravity; less popularity, but severer manners; more prudence, and quite as much courage. He was not a declaimer; he did not, like the energetic Philibert or the impetuous Maison-Neuve, make his voice heard in the streets: it was in the councils where he calmly put forward his inflexible *veto*. The more violent huguenots reproached him with his moderation; they said that 'when men are too stiff to yield to the breath of persuasion, we must strike them heavily with the hammer; and when flaming brands are kindling a conflagration everywhere, we must rush upon them like a torrent and extinguish them.' But Lévrier, firm in regard to right, was mild in regard to men. An intrepid preserver of the law, he upheld it without clamor, but without hesitation or fear. Never has there lived, in ancient or in modern republics, a citizen of whom it could be better said than of him:

> Non vultus instantis tyranni,
> Mente quatit solida.*

The moment approached when Lévrier would say in Geneva for liberty what Luther had lately said in Worms for truth: 'I can do no otherwise.' But, less fortunate than

* Horace, *Odes*, bk. iii. 3.

the monk of Wittemberg, he will hardly have uttered these words before he will receive his death-blow. These martyrs of liberty at the foot of the Alps, who were to be followed in so many different places by the martyrs of the Gospel, lit up a new flame upon the earth. And hence it is that a grateful posterity, represented by the pious christians of the New World, places a triumphal garland on the humble tombs of Berthelier and of Lévrier, as well as of Luther and of Calvin.*

As the office of vidame belonged to the duke, it was always through the vidamy that the princes of Savoy interfered with the affairs of Geneva; and accordingly they nominated to this post only such men as were well known for the servility of their character. The duke had replaced the wretched Aymon Conseil by the Sieur de Salagine; and when the latter died, he nominated Verneau, sire of Rougemont and one of his chamberlains, in his place.† 'Oh, oh!' said the citizens, 'the duke knows his men. If Conseil knew so well the sound of his tabor, this man knows it better still, and we shall have a pretty dance.'‡ Charles, dissatisfied with the inferior jurisdiction that belonged to him, proposed to make the conquest of Geneva, and to accomplish it in two movements. By the first, he would take possession of all the courts of law; by the second, of the sovereignty. And then his sojourn in Geneva would have attained its end.

By way of beginning, Charles desired that the vidame should make oath to him and not to the bishop—a pretension opposed to the constitution, for in Geneva the prince of Savoy was only an inferior officer of the bishop: and the duke in this way substituted himself for the prince of the city. They were nearly giving way, for the Marquis of St. Sorlin, the prelate's brother, intrusted with the bishop's temporal interests while he was in Italy, and even the epis-

* 'The Swiss republics first came forward; and to the spirit of the Reformation, as the remote cause, is the American Revolution to be itself attributed.'—Smyth, *Eccl. Republicanism*, p. 102, Boston.

† Council Registers, Feb. 19, 1524.

‡ Bonivard, *Chroniq.* ii. p. 353.

copal council, desired to please the duke and grant something to so mighty a lord. But that vigilant sentinel Lévrier immediately placed himself in the breach. He represented to the episcopal council that the bishop was not free to sacrifice the rights of the state; that he was only the simple administrator, and had to render an account 'to the empire, the chapter, the republic, and posterity.' The vidame was forced to make oath to the bishop's representatives, whereupon the irritated duke ordered his chamberlain to give an account of his office to none but him. Lévrier saw that Savoy was planting her batteries against Geneva—that the war was beginning; and determining to save the independence of his country, he resolved to oppose, even at the risk of his life, the criminal usurpations of the foreign prince.*

The struggle between the duke and the judge threatened to become terrible, and could only be ended by the death of one of the combatants or the expulsion of the other. Everything was favorable to the duke. 'Who can hinder him,' said his courtiers, 'from becoming sovereign of Geneva?—The bishop? Although he may make a great fuss, he will easily be quieted, for he has benefices without number in his Highness's states.—Pope Clement? The duke is in alliance with him.—The emperor? His marriage with the duchess's sister is in progress.—The Swiss League? They are in great anxiety about the house of Austria, and they too are divided city against city on account of religion.—The people of Geneva? The court, by spending its money freely, has gained them.—Berthelier? He is dead.—The other huguenots? They were so roughly handled at the time of the former enterprise, that they are afraid of getting into hot water again. . . . What remains to prevent the duke from accomplishing his undertaking?'—'There remains but God,' said the patriots.†

It was Charles's disposition to seek to triumph by stratagem rather than by force. In that age princes imagined

* Council Registers, Feb. 19, 1524. Lévrier, *Chronologie des Comtes de Genevois*, ii. p. 198.

† Bonivard, *Chroniq.* ii. p. 395.

that no one could resist them; he therefore attempted to win over Lévrier by means of those favors of which courtiers are so greedy. But in order to succeed, it was necessary to have a little private talk with him away from Geneva and the Genevans. 'What glorious sunshine!' said they one morning at the ducal court: let us take advantage of this fine winter weather to visit the castle of Bonne and spend a few days at the foot of the soft and smiling slopes of the Voirons mountain.' The duke, and the duchess, and the court made their preparations, and, as a special mark of his good-will, Charles invited Lévrier to accompany him. Arrived at this charming retreat, surrounded by snow-clad mountains gilded by the bright sunshine, the duke led the worthy man aside, addressed him in friendly language, and as Lévrier answered with respect, Charles profited by what he thought to be a favorable moment, and said to him in an insinuating tone: 'You know that I am sovereign lord of Geneva, and that you are my subject.'—'No, my lord, immediately replied the judge, 'I am not your subject, and you are not sovereign of Geneva.' The duke dissembled his anger, but Lévrier seeming impatient to return to Geneva, Charles allowed him to depart, and as he saw that inflexible man disappear, he swore that he should pay dearly for his boldness . . . at the foot of that very mountain, in that very castle where he had dared tell the Duke of Savoy that he was not his sovereign.*

The duke returned, and being resolved to put his hand to the task, he communicated to the episcopal council, with all suitable precautions, his firm intention to assume henceforward the rights of sovereignty. Charles knew the weakness, the venality even of the prince-bishop's councillors, who were unwilling at any price to displease Savoy. As soon as the report of this demand was known in the city, everybody exclaimed against it; they said that the superior jurisdiction belonged only to the sovereign, and that if the duke should obtain it, he would have to take but one step more to be recognised as lord of Geneva. The weakest thought their

* Galiffe, *Matériaux*, ii. p. 242.

independence lost. 'Be easy,' said wiser men, 'there is a certain "child of Geneva" in the council, who will shut all their mouths.' They were not deceived; determined to oppose an inflexible resistance to Charles's demand, Lévrier began to strengthen the weak, to win over the cowards, and to intimidate the traitors. 'Neither the duke nor the senate of Savoy,' he said, 'has any authority in Geneva. The jurisdiction belongs to the city and to its head, the bishop: the duke, when within our walls, is a vassal, and not a sovereign.'* These bold but true words made a deep impression; Gruet, the vicar-episcopal, resolved to join Lévrier in defending the rights of his master. The opposition was not less energetic among the citizens. It was the time for nominating syndics; the alarmed huguenots resolved to place one of the warmest friends of independence among the chief magistrates. They elected Claude Richardet, a man of steady principles and decided character, 'tall, handsome, powerful, and very choleric,' says a chronicle.

When Charles and his counsellors saw the episcopal and the popular authorities uniting against them, they did not lose heart, but preached openly in Geneva the system which the dukes of Savoy had long adopted—the necessity of separating Church and State. What did it matter if Lévrier, and even Gruet, the vicar-episcopal, made a show of defending the bishop's temporal rights?—the duke believed that Pierre de la Baume would be found tractable. The most advanced huguenots desired to have a free church in a free state; but the duke wanted a church enslaved by the pope in a state enslaved by the duke. 'Let the bishop keep his clerical authority,' said the ducal officers, who were irritated by the opposition of the episcopal officers; 'let him keep his amulets, chaplets, and all such wares; let his parishioners indulge, some in sensuality, others in mortifications; let them, with all the monks, black, white, and grey, debauchees, gamblers, inquisitors, mountebanks, flagellands, women of lewd life, and indulgence-sellers, go on a pilgrimage to Loretto, to St. James of Compostella, to Mecca if the bishop

* Bonivard, *Chroniq.* ii. p. 395.

likes . . . well and good . . . that is the priests' department, and we abandon it to them. But the civil power belongs to the laity; the courts of secular justice, the municipal liberties, and the command of the troops ought to be in the hands of a secular prince. Souls to the bishop, body and goods to my lord of Savoy!' This great zeal for the separation of the religious from the political order had no other object than to satisfy the ambition of Savoy. But Geneva profited by these interested homilies, and emancipated herself even beyond Charles's wishes. Yet a few more years, and this city will be enfranchised from both kinds of despotism. The temporal and spiritual power will be taken from the hands of the bishop nominated by Rome; and while the former will be restored to the hands of the citizens, the latter will be in the hands of the Head of the Church and of his Word of truth.

The day after the election, the duke held a grand reception. The new syndics came to pay their respects to him; Gruet, the vicar, and other episcopal officers were present. Charles on a sudden unmasked his battery: 'Mr. Vicar, I have heard that the episcopal officers of this city interfere in profane matters; I mean to reform this abuse; the State and the Church are two distinct spheres. Hitherto my officers, the vidames, have not had sufficient power.* Having recently nominated one of my chamberlains to this post, a man much esteemed and of good repute, the noble Hugh de Rougemont, I shall no longer permit the bishop to interfere in civil causes.' The vicar, who had been prepared by Lévrier for this attack and remembered the lesson well, made answer: 'Your Highness is aware that my lord of Geneva is both bishop and prince; he possesses the two jurisdictions in this city.' The irascible duke, who did not expect any opposition from a vicar, grew angry: 'I intend that it shall be so no longer,' he continued; 'and if the bishop pardons when my vidame has condemned, I will hang up with their letters of grace all to whom he grants them.' Everybody trembled. The pusillanimous vicar held his

* 'Cum non essent magnæ facultatis.'—Registres du Conseil du 9 février, 1524.

tongue, while the syndics endeavored to pacify the prince, although at the same time backing up Gruet's remarks. Then the courtiers of Savoy came forward, and, playing the part that had been assigned them in this wretched comedy, magnified the favors which the duke would heap on the city. There would be signal advantages for commerce, merchandise at half price, great rejoicings, magnificent feasts, fête after fête for the ladies of the city,* graceful and friendly combats in presence of their highnesses, dances and tournaments.† Geneva would become a little paradise. The duke was such a good prince, what folly to reject him! Notwithstanding all this coaxing, the huguenots thought to themselves that the prince's mule, be he ever so richly harnessed, none the less carries a saddle that galls him.

The duke took counsel again. He thought he had made an important step at the time of the syndics' reception. He had now resided eight months in Geneva, as if he had no other capital; now or never he must realize the hereditary schemes of his family. He must hurry on the conclusion, and with that view get rid of the obstacle. That obstacle was Lévrier. This Mordecai, who refused to bow before him, thwarted the projects of Turin and exasperated the weak Charles and the haughty Beatrice. All the courtiers rose against him: they hesitated no longer. Sometimes bold strokes are necessary, and Machiavelli had taught the princes of Italy what was to be done in such cases. They thought that the annexation of Geneva to Savoy was of too great importance not to require the sacrifice of a victim. This man was as a rock in their path, obstructing their advance: it was necessary to remove it. Lévrier's death was decided upon.

The bishop's council, which was regarded by the episcopalians as the sovereign council, was summoned to appear before the duke; all the members, except Lévrier, attended. The episcopal councillors had hardly entered Charles's pres-

* 'De festinationibus factis dominabus civitatis.'—Council Registers, Feb. 9, 1524.

† 'De recolluctione graciosa et amicabili sodalium in tripudiis.'—Ibid.

ence, 'when, unable to contain himself, he waxed very wroth.' 'Do you presume,' he exclaimed, 'to disobey my orders?' Then by his gestures, indicating his cruel intentions, he addressed them in such savage language 'as to put them in fear of their lives.' The councillors, who were almost frightened to death, 'They did like the stag, which (says a chronicle) casts his horns to the dogs in order to save himself.'* 'My lord,' they said, 'it is not our fault; it is Lévrier that has done it all; he maintains stoutly that Monsieur of Savoy has no authority in Geneva.' Whereupon the duke, pretending not to know him, exclaimed: 'What! another Lévrier in my path! Why his father opposed the surrender of the artillery of Geneva to me in 1507! Bring the son here!' The judge's colleagues consented, provided the duke would engage on his side to do him no injury, which Charles promised.

Lévrier knew that his life was at stake, and everybody advised him to leave Geneva; but he resolved not to go out of his way. Two days after the first conference, the episcopal council, accompanied by Lévrier, appeared again before the duke, who had scarcely caught sight of him, when, fiercely scowling at them, he said: 'There are some of you who say that I am not sovereign of Geneva.' . . . He stopped short, but finding that they all remained silent, he continued: 'It is one Lévrier.' . . . Then fixing his angry eyes upon him, he called out with a threatening voice: 'Is that fellow Lévrier here?' Consternation fell upon all the spectators: 'they huddled together, but said not a word.' Charles, who knew Lévrier very well, observing that terror had so far answered, repeated in a still louder tone: 'Is that fellow Lévrier here?'—The judge modestly stepped forward and said calmly: 'Here I am, my lord.' The duke, whom such calmness irritated still more, burst out: 'Have you not said that I am not sovereign of Geneva?'—'My lord,' he answered, 'If I have said anything, it was in the council, where every one has the right to speak freely. You ought not to know of it, and I ought not to be molested about it.'—'Go,'

* Bonivard, *Chroniq.* ii. p. 401.

said the duke, not heeding this just remark, 'prepare to prove to me within three days that what you say is true. Otherwise I will not answer for your life . . . wherever I may be. Leave my presence!'* And they all went out.

'Lévrier departed in great trouble,' said Bonivard. The death with which he was threatened was inevitable. There were plenty of authentic acts, the *Franchises* in particular, by which he could prove that the duke possessed no authority in Geneva; but many of these documents were in the hands of the canons, devoted to the duke; and the syndics refused to lay before the prince such as were in their care, for fear he should throw them into the fire. It is not improbable that such was Charles's intention when he called for them.† 'He has set a condition upon my life,' said Lévrier, 'which it is impossible to fulfil . . . Do what I may, there is nothing left for me but to die.'

His friends wished to save him at all hazards. Bonivard, who was less courageous than Lévrier, and under similar circumstances had taken to flight, continually reverted to the subject: 'There is no escape,' he said, 'except you leave the country.' But Lévrier was not to be moved. Faithful preserver of the ancient customs, he was determined to oppose the usurpations of Savoy to the very last. According to the Genevese, St. Peter—they did not mean the pope—was the prince of their city. Had they not the key of this apostle in their escutcheon? Lévrier replied to the entreaties of his friends, and especially of Bonivard: 'I would rather die for the liberty of the city and for the authority of St. Peter, than confess myself guilty by deserting my post.' The prior of St. Victor was greatly distressed at the answer. He insisted, he conjured his friend, but all to no purpose. 'Is it imprudence on his part?' said he then. 'Is it envy that urges him to be the rival of Berthelier? Is it that he desires to be a champion of the commonwealth at the price of his blood? I know not what motive impels him; but be it what it may, he will no longer confide in our

* Bonivard, *Chroniq.* ii. p. 402. Gautier MS. Spon, *Hist. de Genève*, &c.

† Bonivard, *Chroniq.* ii. p. 403. Gautier MS.

advice.' Lévrier, indeed, went about just as before, even after the term (three days) prescribed by the duke; he waited tranquilly for the blow to fall upon him.*

Charles the Good—such is the name he bears in the history of Savoy—was plotting the death of this just man. His steward and favorite, the Sieur de Bellegarde, was an enemy of Lévrier's, and all the more violent because he had long been his friend. The prince and his steward deliberated over the means best calculated to make away with him. At Geneva it seemed impossible; and as a second edition of Berthelier's death was out of the question, it became necessary to draw Lévrier into some lonely spot, where he might easily be put to death. Bellegarde undertook to carry him off, and the duke ordered him to be brought to the castle of Bonne, where Lévrier had dared to say him *No!* Bellegarde came to an understanding with some Savoyard gentlemen, and being informed that on Saturday, the 12th of March, the judge would attend mass as usual in the cathedral of St. Pierre, the steward arranged with these infamous courtiers that they should lie in ambush near the church, and seize him as he came out.

Everything was prepared for the ambuscade. The person who should have prevented it, and the person who commanded it, both left the city. The cowardly Marquis of St. Sorlin, who, as representative of the bishop, ought to have defended Lévrier, having 'smelt the wind,' went out to Rumilly, where he amused himself with some ladies while men were preparing to kill the defender of his brother's rights. Charles did pretty nearly the same. The appointed day having arrived (it was the eve of the Sunday before Easter, 1524), this prince, poor in courage, trembling at the idea of the daring deed about to be attempted, fearing lest the people should rise and come to his residence and demand the just man about to be torn from them, stealthily quitted his apartments in the lower part of the city near the Rhone, 'went out by a back door,' crossed the lonely meadows which the Arve bathes with its wift waters, and 'retired with

* Bonivard, *Chroniq.* ii. p. 403.

his family to Our Lady of Grace, pretending that he was going there to hear mass.' This church being near the bridge of Arve, the duke, in case a riot should break out, would only have to cross the bridge to be in his own territory. Having thus provided for his own safety, he waited in great agitation for the news of his victim.

Mass was over in the cathedral, the priest had elevated the host, the chants had ceased, and Lévrier quitted the church. He wore a long camlet robe, probably his judicial gown, and a beautiful velvet cassock. He had hardly set foot outside the cemetery (the site is now occupied by the hall of the Consistory) when Bellegarde and his friends, surrounding him with drawn swords, 'laid their hands roughly upon him; and Bressieu, the most violent of them, struck him so severely on the head with the pommel of his sword,' that he was stunned. There was not a moment to lose, lest the people should rise. Some of the gentlemen armed cap-à-pie went in front, others came behind, and they dragged the prisoner rapidly to Plainpalais, where all had been got ready to complete the abduction. Lévrier was put upon a wretched horse, his hands were tied behind his back, his legs were fastened below the belly of his steed; and the escort set off full gallop for the castle of Bonne, where he had formerly dared to deny that the duke was sovereign of Geneva.

On they went, the horsemen loading Lévrier with abuse: 'Huguenot, rebel, traitor!' But in the midst of these insults the judge, pinioned like a murderer, remained calm and firm, and endured their indignities without uttering a word. He was grieved at the injustice of his enemies, but as he thought of the cause for which he suffered, joy prevailed over sorrow. He had been accustomed all his life to struggle with affliction, and now that 'the cross was laid on his shoulders,' it was easier for him to bear it. 'To give his life for right and liberty,' said a contemporary, 'afforded him such great matter for joy as to counterbalance all sadness.' The ferocious, cruel, and passionate Bellegarde, who hated this just man more than he had loved him when both were young, kept his eyes fixed on him: an obstacle appeared, his horse reared, and Bellegarde fell; it was thought that he had broken his leg. There was great confusion; they all stopped. Some men-at-arms alighted, picked up the steward, and placing him on his horse, the escort continued their way, but at a foot-pace. They still went on, and as they advanced, the magnificent amphitheatre formed to the south by the Alps spread out more grandly before them. To the left eastward the graceful slopes of the Voirons extended as far as Bonne; a little further on was seen the opening of the valley of Boëge, and further still the Aiguille Verte and other glaciers, and then much nearer the Mole proudly raised its pyramidal form; immediately after, but in the distance, Mont Blanc rose majestically above the clouds, and the mountains of the Bornes, running towards the west, completed the picture. Lévrier's escort, after descending into a valley, came in sight of the castle of Bonne, seated on a lofty crest and commanding the landscape; they climbed the steep road leading to it, and drew near the castle, leaving below them a narrow ravine, at the bottom of which rolls the torrent of Menoge. At last the old gates were thrown back, they entered the court, and Lévrier was handed over to the governor, who shut him up in a dark cell. As soon as Charles learnt that all had passed off well, he quitted his retreat and returned joyful to his lodging. He was confident that no human power could now deprive him of his victim.*

During this time the city was in great agitation. Men described with consternation the kidnapping of the heroic defender of Genevese independence, and all good citizens gave vent to their indignation. The deed was an insult to the laws of the state—it was an act of brigandage; and hence two sentiments equally strong—love for Lévrier and respect for right—moved them to their inmost souls. The council assembled immediately. 'About an hour ago,' said Syndic La Fontaine, a zealous mameluke, 'Aimé Lévrier was seized by the duke's orders, and carried to Plainpalais.' 'Yes,' exclaimed several patriots, 'the duke is keeping him

* Gautier MS. *in loco*. Bonivard, *Chroniq.* ii. p. 406. Spon, *Hist. de Genève*, i. p. 367. Savyon, *Annales*, pp. 117, 118.

in the Dominican convent; but we know how to get him out of that den.' 'Resolved,' say the Minutes, 'to consider what steps are best to be taken under the circumstances.' When they heard that Lévrier had been carried from Plainpalais to Savoy, the syndics went in a body to the bishop's vicar, and required him to convene the episcopal council, and to lay before it this unprecedented act of violence. Nobody doubted that the duke would yield to the remonstrances made to him. Gruet promptly summoned the members of the bishop's council; but these venal men, devoted to the duke, refused to appear. The next day, the syndics made another attempt. 'Since your colleagues forsake you,' said they to the vicar-episcopal, 'go to his Highness yourself, and make him understand that he is trampling under foot both the sovereignty of the bishop and the liberties of the citizens.' Gruet was timid, and to appear alone before this powerful noble terrified him; he applied to two of his colleagues, De Veigy and Grossi, begging them to accompany him; but they refused. 'I will not go alone,' exclaimed the frightened man, 'no . . . not at any price! The duke would kidnap me like Lévrier.' Charles's violent proceeding struck terror into all those who enjoyed the privilege of free access to him. Nevertheless Geneva was in danger. If the most respected of its citizens were put to death and no one took up their defence, there would be nothing sacred from the Savoyard tyrant. Lévrier's death might be the death of the republic. What was to be done? They remembered one person, the bishop of Maurienne, who was both a friend of the city and a friend of the duke. The cold La Fontaine and the impetuous Richardet hastened to him: 'Save Lévrier, or we are all lost!' they said. The prelate, who was fond of mediating, and knew very well that he had nothing to fear, immediately waited upon his Highness.*

Charles was not a hero; the emotion of the people disturbed him, the energy of the patriots startled him. He determined to make an advantageous use of his perfidy by

* Registres du Conseil du 13 mars 1524, MS.

proposing an exchange: he would spare Lévrier's blood, but Geneva must yield up her liberties. 'Go,' he said to Maurienne, 'and tell the syndics and councillors of Geneva that, full of clemency towards them, I ask for one thing only: let them acknowledge themselves my subjects, and I will give up Lévrier.'* The Savoyard bishop carried this answer to the syndics, the syndics laid it before the council, and Charles calmly awaited the result of his Machiavellian plot.

The deliberations were opened in the council of Geneva. When there are two dangers, it is generally the nearest that affects us most: every day has its work, and the work of the day was to save Lévrier. The ducal courtiers flattered themselves with the success of this well-laid plot. But the citizens, in this supreme hour, saw nothing but their country. They loved Charles's victim, but they loved liberty more; they would have given their lives for Lévrier, but they could not give Geneva. 'What! acknowledge ourselves the duke's subjects!' they exclaimed; 'if we do so, the duke will destroy our liberties for ever.'† Lévrier himself would reject the proposal with horror.'—'To save the life of a man,' they said one to another in the council, 'we cannot sacrifice the rights of a people.' They remembered how Curtius, to save his country, had leaped into the gulf; how Berthelier, to maintain the rights of Geneva, had given his life on the banks of the Rhone; and one of the citizens, quoting the words of Scripture, exclaimed in Latin: '*Expedit ut unus moriatur homo pro populo, et non tota gens pereat.*'‡ 'The duke calls for blood,' they added: 'let him have it; but that blood will cry out for vengeance before God, and Charles will pay for his crime.' The council resolved to represent to the duke, that by laying hands on Lévrier he robbed the citizens of their franchises and the prince of his attributes. Maurienne carried this answer to

* Registres du Conseil du 13 mars 1524, MS.

† Ibid.

‡ John xi. 50: 'It is expedient for us that one man should die for the people, and that the whole nation perish not.'

his Highness, who persisted in his cruel decision: 'I must have the liberties of Geneva or Lévrier's life.'

During these official proceedings, certain noble-hearted women were greatly agitated. They said to themselves that when it is necessary to touch the heart, the weaker sex is the stronger. It was well known that the haughty Beatrice governed her husband; that she loved the city, its lake and mountains; that everything delighted her in this '*buena posada*.' The ladies who had danced at her balls, and found her all condescension, went on Sunday morning to the ducal residence, and, with tears in their eyes, said to her: 'Appease his Highness's wrath, Madam, and save this good man.' But the Portuguese princess, faithful to her policy as to her pride, refused her mediation. She had hardly done so, when her conscience reproached her; after that refusal, Beatrice found no pleasure in Geneva; and before long, leaving the duke behind her, she went all alone 'beyond the mountains.'†

Moreover it would have been too late. On Sunday morning, the 11th of March, three men were in consultation at the castle of Bonne, and preparing to despatch Lévrier. They were Bellegarde, sufficiently recovered from his fall to discharge his commission and simulate a trial; a confessor intrusted to set the accused at peace with the Church; and the executioner commissioned to cut off his head. His Highness's steward, who had received instructions to have it over 'in a few hours,' ordered the prisoner to suffer the cord—'nine stripes,' says Michel Roset: 'not so much from the necessity of questioning him,' adds Bonivard, 'as from revenge.' This ducal groom (we mean Bellegarde) felt a certain pleasure in treating unworthily a magistrate the very representative of justice. 'Have you no accomplices who conspired with you against my lord's authority?' said he to Lévrier, after the scourging. 'There are no accomplices where there is no crime,' replied the noble citizen with simplicity. Thereupon the Savoyard provost condemned him to be beheaded, 'not because he had committed any offence,'

* Bonivard, *Police de Genève. Mém. d'Archéol.* v. p. 382. Spon, *Hist. de Genève*, i. p. 367. Savyon, *Annales*, p. 118.

say the judicial documents, but because he was 'a lettered and learned man, able to prevent the success of the enterprise of Savoy.'* After delivering the sentence, Bellegarde left Lévrier alone.

He had long been looking death in the face. He did not despise life, like Berthelier; he would have liked to consecrate his strength to the defence of right in Geneva; but he was ready to seal with his blood the cause he had defended. 'Death will do me no evil,' he said. He called Berthelier to mind, and the lines written on that martyr of liberty being engraved in his memory, Lévrier repeated them aloud in his gloomy dungeon, and then approaching the wall, he wrote with a firm hand:

> Quid mihi mors nocuit? . . . .

'Yes,' said he, 'death will kill my body and stretch it lifeless on the ground; but I shall live again; and the life that awaits me beyond the grave cannot be taken from me by the sword of the cruellest tyrant.' He finished the inscription he had begun, and wrote on the prison wall:

> . . . Virtus post fata virescit;
> Nec cruce nec sævi gladio perit illa tyranni.

But he thought not of himself alone; he thought upon Geneva; he reflected that the death of the defenders of liberty secured its victory, and that it was by this means the holiest causes triumphed,

> Et qu'un sang précieux, par martyre espandu,
> A la cause de Dieu servira de semence.

Shortly after Bellegarde's departure the confessor entered, discharged his duty mechanically, uttered the sentence: *Ego te absolvo*—and withdrew, showing no more sympathy for his victim than the provost had done. Then appeared a man with a cord: it was the executioner. It was then ten o'clock at night. The inhabitants of the little town and of the adjacent country were sleeping soundly, and no one dreamt of the cruel deed that was about to cut short the life of a man who might have shone in the first rank in a

* Galiffe, *Matériaux pour l'Histoire de Genève*, ii. p. 243.

great monarchy. Bellegarde had no cause to fear that he would be disturbed in the accomplishment of his crime; still he dreaded the light; there was in his hardened conscience a certain uneasiness which alarmed him. The headsman bound the noble Lévrier, armed men surrounded him, and the martyr of law was conducted slowly to the castle yard. All nature was dumb, nothing broke the silence of that funereal procession; Charles's agents moved like shadows beneath the ancient walls of the castle. The moon, which had not reached its first quarter, was near setting, and shed only a feeble gleam. It was too dark to distinguish the beautiful mountains in the midst of which stood the towers whence they had dragged their victim: the trees and houses of Bonne were scarcely visible; one or two torches, carried by the provost's men, alone threw light upon this cruel scene. On reaching the middle of the castle yard, the headsman stopped and the victim also. The ducal satellites silently formed a circle round them, and the executioner prepared to discharge his office. Lévrier was calm: the peace of a good conscience supported him in this dread hour. He thought of God, of law, of duty, of Geneva, of liberty, and of the legitimate authority of St. Peter, whom in the simplicity of his heart, he regarded as the sovereign of the city. It was really the prince-bishop whom he thus designated, but not wishing to utter the name of a prelate whom he despised, he substituted that of the apostle. Alone in the night, in those sublime regions of the Alps, surrounded by the barbarous figures of the Savoyard mercenaries, standing in that feudal court-yard, which the torches illumined with a sinister glare, the heroic champion of the law raised his eyes to heaven and said: 'By God's grace I die without anxiety, for the liberty of my country and the authority of St. Peter.' The grace of God, liberty, authority—these main principles of the greatness of nations were his last confession. The words had hardly been uttered when the executioner swung round his sword, and the head of the citizen rolled in the castle yard. Immediately, as if struck with fear, the murderers respectfully gathered up his remains and placed them in a coffin. 'And his body was laid in earth in the parish church of Bonne, with the head separate.' At that moment the moon set, and black darkness hid the stains of blood which Lévrier had left on the pavement of the court-yard.* 'Calamitous death,' exclaims the old *Citadin de Genève*, 'which cost upwards of a million of Savoyard lives in the cruel wars that followed, in which no one received quarter, because the unjust death of Lévrier was always brought forward.'† There is considerable exaggeration in the number of Savoyards who, according to this writer, expiated Lévrier's murder by their death. The crime had other consequences—and nobler ones.

Moral victories secure success more than material victories. Over the corpses of Berthelier and Levrier we might give a christian turn to the celebrated saying: 'It is the defeated cause that is pleasing to God.' The triumph of brute force in the castle of Bonne and in front of Cæsar's tower agitated, scandalised, and terrified men's minds. Tears were everywhere shed over these two murders. . . . . But patience! These bloody 'stations' will be found glorious 'stations' leading to the summit of right and liberty. A book has been written telling the history of the founders of religious liberty. I may be deceived, but it appears to me that the narrative of the struggles of the first huguenots might be entitled: *History of the founders of modern liberty*. My consolation when I find myself called upon to describe events hitherto unknown, relating to persons unnoticed until this hour, and taking place in a little city or obscure castle, is, that these facts have, in my opinion, a European, a universal interest, and belong to the fundamental principles of existing civilisation. Berthelier, Lévrier, and others have hitherto been only Genevese heroes; they are worthy of being placed on a loftier pedestal, and of being hailed by society as heroes of the human race.

* The castle of Bonne is only an hour and a half's drive from Geneva. To enter the ruins you must pass through the rooms of a peasant who lives within the walls.

† Bonivard, *Chroniq.* ii. pp. 408–412. Michel Roset, *Chron.* MS. liv. ii. ch. ii. Spon, *Hist. de Genève*, ii. p. 368. *Le Citadin de Genève*, pp. 313, 314. Gautier MS.

The haste with which the victim had been sacrificed, the remote theatre of the crime, the hour of night that had been chosen, all show that Charles had an uneasy conscience. He soon discovered that he had not been mistaken in his fears. The indignation was general. The men of independence took advantage of the crime that had been committed to magnify the price of liberty. 'A fine return,' they said, 'for the honors we have paid Monsieur of Savoy and his wife!' Though their anger broke out against the duke, the bishop had his share of their contempt. The reflection that he had permitted his friends to be sacrificed on one side of the Alps while he was amusing himself on the other, shocked these upright souls. 'A pretty shepherd,' they said, 'who not only abandons his flock to the wolves, but the faithful dogs also that watch over it!' They were disgusted with priestly government; some citizens even went so far as to say: 'We had better grant Monsieur of Savoy his request, than let ourselves be murdered for a prelate who gives us no credit for it. If the duke takes away certain things, he will at least guarantee the rest; while the bishop devours us on one side and lets us be devoured on the other.'* They concluded that ecclesiastical principalities only served to ruin their subjects—at Geneva as well as at Rome. Liberals and ducals held almost the same language. The temporal power of the bishop was a worm-eaten building that would tumble down at the first shock.

When the news of the murder at Bonne was heard among the young worldlings who frequented the court, they were aghast, and a change came over them. All that the duke had done to win them, the splendid entertainments, the graces of the duchess, the charms of her ladies were forgotten. In the ball-room they could see nothing but Death leaning on his scythe and with hollow eyes looking round for some new victim. Their past pleasures seemed a mockery to them. A brilliant representation had taken place: on a sudden the curtain fell, the lights were extin-

* Bonivard, *Chroniq.* ii. p. 410. Savyon, *Annales*, p. 119.

guished, and the most enthusiastic spectators, seized with terror, hastened to escape far from a place which appeared to run with blood. That murder, 'in the night by torchlight, put all the city in great alarm,' says a chronicler.

Amid all these cries of indignation, of contempt, of terror, there was a small group of firm men who saw the dawn of liberty piercing through the darkness of crime. The generous spirits who had received the Divine Word from France—Porral, Maison-Neuve, Vandel, Bernard, even Bonivard—took courage in their tears. 'One single obstacle will check the duke,' they said, 'and that obstacle is God! God desires by means of the duke to chastise Geneva, not destroy it. The stripes that he inflicts are not for its death but for its improvement. Yes! God, after punishing us with the rod of a father, will rise with the sword in his hand against those whose crimes he appears to permit.'*

Charles, perceiving the effect produced by the outrage he had committed, felt ill at ease at Geneva. Nor was that all; for, learning that a numerous French army was entering his states on one side, while the imperial army was advancing on the other, and that a terrible meeting might ensue, he alleged this motive for returning to Turin. Wishing, however, to secure his authority in Geneva, he sent for Hugues, whose patriotism he feared, reminded him of the scene just enacted at Bonne, and required him to promise, upon oath, that he would not take part in the affairs of the city. Hugues entered into the required engagement.† Then Charles hastened to depart, and Bonivard said, with a meaning smile, 'The duchess having crossed the Alps, the duke hastens after her—like a good little canary.'‡

The Genevans breathed at last: the city was without either duke or bishop. Lévrier's martyrdom, which had at first crushed them, now inflamed their courage. As a steel blade long bent returns back with a spring, so Geneva, suf-

* Roset MS. *Chroniq.* liv. ii. ch. ii. Gautier MS. Bonivard, *Chroniq.* ii. p. 411.

† Registres du Conseil des 7, 8 et 12 février.

‡ 'Un bon tarin (serin).' Bonivard, *Police de Genève. Mém. d'Archéol.* v. p. 393.

fering under a blow that seemed as if it would destroy her, rose up with energy. More than this; the empty place was soon filled. Help would come from heaven. The ancient imperial and episcopal city, not content with having set aside bishops and dukes, would within a few years place on the throne Him who exalteth nations. Then, 'dwelling in the shadow of the Almighty,' and sitting tranquilly at the foot of her beautiful mountains, Geneva will raise her head, crowned with a twofold liberty.*

CHAPTER XXIV.

INDIGNATION AGAINST THE MAMELUKES; THE DUKE APPROACHES WITH AN ARMY; FLIGHT OF THE PATRIOTS.

(1524—1525.)

THE duke had no sooner departed than there was a general burst of indignation against him, and against the mamelukes who had delivered up the greatest of the citizens to his sword. Bernard Boulet, the city treasurer, was one of the proudest of these ducal partisans. He had built a fine house, where he gave splendid entertainments to his party and kept a good table, by which means he soon squandered away all his property. But unwilling to renounce his gay life, he clandestinely appropriated the property of the State, and still continued to entertain magnificently. 'Boulet,' said the hugenots, 'thinks only of indulging with his friends in all kinds of pleasure, drunkenness, and in voluptuousness. Foppish in dress, dainty at table, he has no thought for the hunger and nakedness of the poor. Dissipation, bad management, fraud, robbery make up his whole life.' Boulet, who furnished no accounts, owed the city 'at least 6,400

* Berenger, *Hist. de Genève.* Lévrier, *Chron. des Comtes de Savoie,* ii. p. 214.

florins'*—a very large sum for those days. But they feared his influence and malice; and nobody was willing 'to bell the cat.' Syndic Richardet, a good patriot, courageous but hot-headed, entered the council one day determined to put an end to these manifest peculations. 'I call upon the treasurer,' he said, 'to produce the accounts of his office.' The embarrassed Boulet attempted to evade the question; but, being determined to make him give an account of his conduct, the syndic persisted. The mameluke, driven into a corner, exclaimed: 'Are we to be governed by these *huguenots?*'—'He spoke thus from contempt,' says Bonivard. The fiery Richardet could not restrain himself; exasperated because the treasurer insulted him at the very moment he was discharging the duties of his office, he acted after the style of Homer's heroes, and raising his syndic staff above the dishonest mameluke, dealt him such a blow that the staff flew to pieces. It must be remembered that in the middle ages deeds of violence were sometimes reckoned lawful. For instance, an old charter bore that if a respectable man or woman were insulted, every prud'homme who came up was permitted to punish such misconduct by one, two, or three blows; only the prud'homme was required to make oath afterwards that he had given the blows for the sake of peace.† There was instantly a great commotion in the hall; the mameluke councillors uttered cries of anger; the huguenots protested that Richardet had acted without their approval; and the syndic, who was sincere and good at heart, frankly apologised. Throughout all the disturbance Boulet did not utter a word; he was secretly calculating the advantages he could derive from this assault, and was delighted to have suffered it. 'He swallowed it as mild as milk,' says Bonivard.‡ Chance, he thought, favored him, and had opportunely extricated him from a desperate position. What a providence in this violent act of the syndic! The greedy dishonest treasurer would put on the airs of a martyr; his fidelity to the duke, he would say, had drawn upon him this

* Registres du Conseil du 5 février.

† Guizot, *Hist. de la Civilisation.*

‡ Bonivard, *Chroniq.* ii. p. 414. Gautier MS. Spon, *Hist. de Genève.*

savage assault. He would excite Charles III. against Geneva; he would urge him to take the city by storm; and in the midst of all these agitations his accounts would be forgotten—which was the essentlal thing for him.

Boulet did not rejoice alone. His friends the mamelukes having met, agreed to work this assault in snch a way as to make the blow which had severed Lévrier's head be forgotten. 'Good!' said they; 'we have now an opportunity of beginning the old dance again;* that is, to surrender Geneva to Savoy. Go to Chambéry,' they continued; 'make your complaint; say that you are not safe in this huguenot city, and entreat his Highness's council to summon the syndic who offended you to appear before them—even at Chambéry.'

Boulet did all he could to exaggerate his injury. He bandaged his head, he carried his arm in a sling. In vain the surgeon assured him that his left arm was but slightly bruised, and that he had no other wound; no matter: 'I will make my complaint to the bishop,' he said; 'I will make it to the duke!' † He would have gone even to the emperor. The wrath of Achilles, after he had been robbed of Briseis, hardly equalled the wrath of this wretch, and in his opinion, Geneva deserved to receive a punishment as severe as that under which Troy fell. He had retired across the Arve, like Pelides to his tent. Some of his friends, his father-in-law and the judge of Gex in particular, called upon him and sought to pacify him; but he remembered the affront that had been done him, and was implacable. 'Geneva shall pay dearly for it,' he repeated to his friends.

He set out for Chambéry, asked an audience of the ducal council, and reported the syndic's violence. People were very uneasy at Geneva. 'These Savoyards,' said the prior of St. Victor, 'would like nothing better than to plunder the huguenots.' The Savoy baliffs soon appeared; they set up posts at the bridge of Arve, at Les Grottes, and at the Mint—all round the city—and fastened letters of citation to them. The council of Geneva was summoned to appear be-

* Bonivard, *Chroniq.* ii. p. 414.

† Registres du Conseil du 28 octobre 1524.

fore the council of Savoy. That was not all: the macers (massarii) of the Savoyard council declared the possessions of the Genevans in Savoy confiscated, and consequently forbade the farmers and vinedressers to till the land or to grind at the mill. Meadows, fields, vineyards, all were to remain uncultivated. Hitherto it had pertained to God alone to send years of famine; now Messieurs of Chambéry claimed to have the same privilege; and some Genevese farmers, who had begun to till the earth with the permission of the local magistrates, were put in prison by the superior authority. Almost at the same time other citizens were arrested on frivolous pretexts and thrown into one of the dungeons of Château Gaillard. These poor creatures climbed by turns to the loophole, by means of a beam placed against the wall, in order to breathe the fresh air and speak to their wives and children. One day when they were indulging in this consolation, the beam was taken away by the duke's orders, and the unhappy wretches were compelled to crouch at the bottom of their filthy prison.

Boulet wished, however, to enjoy his triumph; he longed to set the magistrates at defiance and ask them whether a blow might not cost them too dear. A bailiff of Chambéry arrived at Geneva, just as if that city had been within his jurisdiction, and posted a 'protection' on the door of Boulet's house. This was a daring usurpation, an insult; but if the treasurer suffered the least harm, the duke would consider it as if done to himself. Boulet reappeared, and had the audacity to show himself at a general council. This was a little too much; the wretch who had brought so many calamities upon the citizens, dared appear among them! Did he hope to receive another blow? Who can say? The Genevans restrained themselves; no one raised a hand against him; but he overheard some persons speaking of his peculations: 'I will produce my books and accounts,' he said. He met with looks that alarmed him. Suppose they were to put him in prison, as they had the right, for he was accused of malversation towards the State. Fearing some mischance, he disappeared again, and went to beseech the ducal council to 'vex' the Genevans. All this was threatening. The syndics gave orders that prayers should be offered up and masses sung for the safety of the city.*

During this time, the bishop was beginning one of his frequent evolutions; his rule being to go with the wind, he turned his prow more to the southward, that is, towards Savoy. He feared lest the Genevans should offend the duke, and wrote to them from Piedmont: 'So conduct yourselves that *God and the world* may have reason to be satisfied.'† He returned to Geneva, but did not stay there. He ought to have intervened between the duke and his own subjects, exposed the serious crimes of the dishonest treasurer, and prevailed upon the council of Chambéry to withdraw their violent threats; but though he was both bishop and prince of the Genevans, he took care not to do them justice. He escaped to St. Claude, more sensible to the charms of a worldly life and of the wine of Arbois, than to the misfortunes of the city. In his eyes the epitome of wisdom was to satisfy *God and the world*, but the seductions of the world were so attractive that he forgot to be the friend of God. Some Genevans even asserted that 'he cared no more for the life to come than a brute beast.' Pierre de la Baume had noticed that since the accession of Clement VII. the house of Savoy had been in greater favor than ever at the court of Rome; it was his policy to keep on good terms with it, to flatter it, in order to obtain a cardinal's hat through its influence, as he did a little later. For a red hat it was worth while abandoning his sheep to the wolves.

But if the bishop turned to every wind, the duke did not. The council of Savoy increased its severity towards Geneva. Richardet had raised his staff against one man; Charles raised his against a whole people. All Geneva was agitated. The citizens besieged the syndics with their complaints; the syndics assembled in council. They described the scenes that were taking place in the country, and all the violence of Savoy. Two of the noblest magistrates, Syndic Dumont

* Registres du Conseil des 2 et 8 décembre 1524; 8, 15, 18, 27, 29 janvier et 5 février 1525. *Journal du Syndic Balard* (*Mém. d'Archéol.* v. p. 2). *Besançon Hugues*, par M. Galiffe fils, p. 268.

† Archives de Genève, lettre de Turin, 1 avril 1525.

and Aimé Girard, hastened to St. Claude to inform the bishop of the oppression of the Savoyards. Girard possessed a lofty soul and impetuous disposition; he described with such spirit the outrages heaped upon Geneva, that De la Baume seemed touched, and promised the Genevans his support. 'If needs be,' he exclaimed, 'I will go to the pope myself . . I will go to the emperor . . . I will beseech them to protect my good right and the franchises of your city.' The deputation was delighted. But the bishop hastened to restrain himself: the duke, the duke's power, and the red hat recurred to his mind. 'Do not let us be in a hurry,' he said more coldly; 'I shall first send the noble Albalesta to the duke.' A month having elapsed, while Albalesta had obtained nothing, the Genevese resolved to take their cause into their own hands. This was what the bishop desired to avoid at any cost. He swore that he would cite the officers of Savoy before the pope, under a penalty of 10,000 ducats.* But Geneva which placed little trust in the bishop, resolved to maintain its independence, and to resist that foreign Pharaoh who had dared to punish with barrenness that earth which God waters with the rain from heaven.

The new campaign required a new leader. Berthelier, Lévrier, those noble-hearted men, were no more. . . . But there was a third, and he the very man they required. Besançon Hugues had neither the impulsiveness of Berthelier nor the firmness of Lévrier; but, mild and tender, he felt a love for his country, the fire of which never ceased to animate him. Moderate, friendly, and of insinuating manners, he was able to win over even his enemies, and often exercised great influence over Pierre de la Baume. Possessing great physical strength, bold, devoted, never sparing himself, he braved the most inclement seasons, and rushed, sword in hand, into the midst of the most furious enemies. Gifted with a rare discernment, which permitted him to see clearly into the most complicated questions, a keen diplomatist, a wise politician, a warm patriot, he was able by his consum-

* Registres du Conseil des 2 et 3 février 1525. *Journal de Balard,* p. 2. Lettre de la Baume, dans les Archives de Genève, sous le n° 930.

mate wisdom to remove obstacles, by his powerful eloquence to convince the most obstinate, even the senators of Berne, and to draw tears from those iron hearts. He bore in his person a *prestige* that secured him an irresistible influence in the councils, and with a few lines, a few words, he could still the popular waves ere they came into collision. He has been called the Nestor, the Sully, the Washington, of Geneva. This is perhaps saying too much: this Nestor was only twenty-five when he began his struggles with the duke, thirty-four at this period of our narrative, and when he died, two or three years before the final Reformation of Geneva, he was under forty. Yet Hugues was, on a small scale and on a small stage, what these great men were on a large one.

The period for electing the syndics having arrived, it was determined to raise to the chief magistracy citizens fitted to maintain the rights of the country; and the name of Hugues was in every mouth. He was returned, as well as Montyon, Pensabin, and Balard. With Hugues for their chief, Geneva feared nothing. But the honest citizen refused the office to which he had been elected. His friends came round him and entreated him to accept: he seemed the only pilot able to steer the ship of the State through the numerous shoals. 'The bishop is your friend; he will protect you,' they said.—'Yes,' he answered, 'as he protected Lévrier.'—'If you refuse,' said Balard, 'we shall refuse also.'—'The duke,' replied Hugues, 'has forbidden me personally to meddle in city affairs; I have given him my promise. Lévrier's death has taught us what the duke's wrath can do. I would rather be a confessor than a martyr.' Did Hugues give way to a momentary weakness? We may be allowed to doubt it. He desired to keep the promise he had made, and had other motives besides. Thinking that he would be of little use in the council, and that Geneva must be saved by other means, he wished to remain free in his movements. But many could not understand him, and their anger broke through all restraint. 'Hugues is wanting in his most sacred duties,' they said. These proud republicans spared nobody. His friend and brother-in-law, the ex-syndic Baud, captain of the artillery, proposed to the council-general to deprive him of his citizenship for one year. Strange contradiction! almost at the same moment this man was raised to the head of the republic and in danger of being expelled from it. But the people seemed to have an instinctive sentiment that Hugues would not be wanting at last: 'He gives way now,' they said, 'only to succeed better hereafter.' Baud's proposition was rejected.*

Geneva began by a singular measure. The general council having assembled in the church of St. Pierre on the 10th of January, 1525, it was resolved to appeal to the pope against the attacks of Savoy, and delegates were despatched to lay the appeal before him. The Genevans were men of precedent: they desired to have recourse to a tribunal recognised for ages. 'The popes,' observed some of them, 'are the defenders of the liberties of the people.' But others, like Bonivard, well read in history, shook their heads, and argued that if princes had been excommunicated by popes, it was not for having violated the liberties of their people, but for resisting the ambition of pontiffs. They mentioned Philip Augustus and Philip the Fair. The appeal to the pope would serve to show that he took part with oppressors only. However, the deputies of Geneva started on their journey. It was ten years before the day when the Reformation was proclaimed within its walls. This measure is a remarkable indication of the peaceful and loyal sentiments by which the magistrates were animated.

At the same time the syndics waited upon the bishop's official; they would have liked for the bishop himself to plead their cause before the pope. 'If my lord consents to pass the mountains and support us at Rome,' said they, 'we will give him a hundred gold crowns, and will add five-and-twenty for you.' The official smiled: 'A hundred crowns!' he said, 'that will not be enough to shoe his horses.'—'We will give him two hundred, then,' answered the syndics. The bishop, who was always short of money, put this sum into his purse, and then endeavored to arrange the matter

* Registres du Conseil du 2 janvier, 3 février, 1525. *Besançon Hugues*, par M. Galiffe fils, p. 219.

without disturbing himself, by merely sending a deputy to Chambéry.

Never was deputy worse received. The president of the ducal council, annoyed that so small a city should dare resist a prince so mighty as his master, looked contemptuously at the deputy and exclaimed : 'The duke is sovereign prince of Geneva. What was Geneva a hundred years ago? a paltry town. Who is it that made this town into a city? The duke's subjects who owe him toll and service.* The Genevans desire us to cancel the penalties pronounced against them. . . . Ha, ha! Messieurs of Geneva, we will increase them. If within a month from this you do not make your submission, we will send you so many soldiers, that you must e'en take the trouble to obey his Highness.' The destruction of the liberties of Geneva seemed to be at hand.

The Genevans now had recourse to the bishop a second time, and conjured him to pass the Alps. Between this second demand and the first, many events had occurred in the political world. Pierre de la Baume was a zealous agent of the imperialist party, and the emperor had informed him that he wanted him for certain matters. Flattered that Charles V. should send for him, he appeared to grant the Genevese their prayer. 'I will go,' he said, and immediately quitted Geneva. Bonivard, who knew La Baume well, smiled as he saw the simple burgesses giving their prince-bishop two hundred crowns to defend them. 'He is a great spendthrift,' said the prior, 'and in his eyes the sovereign virtue of a prelate consists in keeping a good table and good wine; he indulges beyond measure. Besides, he is very liberal to women, and strives to show the nobility of his descent by great pomp and not by virtue. . . . You have given him two hundred crowns . . . what will he do with the money? He will gamble or squander it away in some other manner.'† And in fact he had hardly arrived at Turin, when, without pleading the cause of Geneva, without

* 'Unum villagium . . . qui tenentur ei ad angaria et porangaria.'—Registres du Conseil des 25 mars et 10 mai 1525.

† Bonivard, *Mém. d'Archéol.* v. p. 382.

visiting Rome to defend it before the pope, he set off instantly for Milan, where, as agent of Charles V., he plotted against Francis I. But of the pope and of Geneva, not a word.

Such was the episcopal tenderness of Pierre de la Baume. To deliver from foreign and tyrannical oppression the country of which he was both prince and bishop was not in his opinion worth the trouble of taking a single step; but if it were required to go and intrigue in Lombardy for the potentate whom he looked upon as the arbiter of the world, a nod was sufficient to make him hasten thither.

As for the Genevese delegates, Rome saw no more of them than of their bishop: the court of Turin had found the means of stopping them on the road. Besides, had they reached the banks of the Tiber, there was no danger that Clement VII. would have taken up their cause; he would have laughed at such strange ambassadors. All was going on well for the duke; he had succeeded in completely isolating the weak and proud city.*

This prince resolved to bring matters to an end with a restless people who gave him more trouble than his own states. He quitted Turin, crossed the mountains, and 'lodged at Annecy,' says Bonivard. In order to succeed, he resolved to employ a smiling lip and a strong hand; the use of such contrary means was natural as it was politic in him: Charles was always blowing hot and cold. If Geneva sent him deputies, he said: 'Upon the honor of a gentleman, I desire that the letters I have granted in your favor should be observed.' But another day, the same man who had appeared as gentle as a lamb became as fierce as a wolf; he had the deputies seized and thrown into dungeons, as well as any Genevans who ventured into his territories. The soldiers ransacked the country-houses lying round Geneva, carried away the furniture, and drank the wine; they also cut off the supplies of the city, which was a scandalous violation of the most positive treaties.†

* Letters de La Baume, Archives de Genève, n° 930. *Journal du Syndic Balard*, p. 3.

† Registres du Conseil des 4, 25 mai; 29 juin; 10 juillet; 7, 16, 17 et 20 septembre, 1525. Manuscrit Roset, liv. ii. ch. iii.

Still the appeal to Rome made the duke uneasy. The prince of Rome was a priest, the prince of Geneva was a priest also: Charles feared that the two priests would play him some ugly trick behind his back. He determined, therefore, to employ intrigue rather than force, to induce the people to confer on him the superior jurisdiction, which would put him in a position to monopolise the other rights of sovereignty; he resolved to ask for it as if he were doing the Genevese a great favor. Accordingly on the 8th of September the vidame appeared before the council as if he had come to make the most generous proposition on behalf of his Highness. 'On the one hand,' he said, 'you will withdraw the appeal from Rome; and on the other the duke will put an end to all the annoyances of which you complain.' And then he demanded the superior jurisdiction in Geneva for the duke, as if it were mere surplusage. Charles expected this time to attain his end. Indeed, his numerous partisans in the city, seeing that the decisive moment had arrived, everywhere took up the matter warmly. 'Let us accept,' said the mameluke Nergaz. 'If we refuse these generous proposals, our property and our fellow-citizens will never be restored, and none of us will be able to leave our narrow territory without being shut up in his Highness's prisons.'—'Let us accept,' answered all the ducal partisans. Geneva was about to become Savoyard; and the humble but real part reserved for her in history would never have existed. Then the most courageous patriots—Besançon Hugues, Jean Philippe, the two Bauds, Michael Sept, Syndic Bouvier, who had been named in place of Hugues, Ami Bandière, the two Rosets, John Pécolat, and John Lullin—exclaimed: 'If we love the good things of this life so much, our only gain will be to lose them and our liberty with them. The duke entices us to-day, only to enslave us to-morrow. Let us fear neither exile, nor imprisonment, nor the axe. Let us secure the independence of Geneva, though it be at the price of our blood.' Even Bouvier, a weak and wavering character, was electrified by these noble words, and added: 'Rather than consent to this demand, I will leave the city and go to Turkey!' . . . 'No compromise with the duke!' repeated all the independents. The mamelukes persisted: they pointed to the fields lying fallow, to the Genevans in prison . . . and without touching upon the question of the superior jurisdiction (for that was inadmissible) they demanded that the appeal of Geneva against the duke should be withdrawn. There was a majority of eleven in favor of this proposition; forty-two votes were given against it, and fifty-three for it. It was strange that the huguenots supported the appeal to the pope. The pope (very innocently, it must be confessed) seemed to be on the side of liberty. . . . The party of independence was vanquished.*

Charles was not satisfied, however. He hated these majorities and minorities, and all these republican votes; he wanted a passive and unanimous obedience; he attended only to the votes of the minority, and meditated setting every engine to work to get rid of the forty-two huguenots who opposed his designs. At court they were delighted with the result; they made a jest of the forty-two independents who had had the simplicity to give their names, and thus point themselves out to the court of Turin as persons to be despatched first of all. The list was read over and over again; they picked it to pieces—a sarcasm against this man, an insult against that. All necessary measures were taken for the great act of purification which was to be accomplished. The duke gave orders to move up the army that was to enter the city and free it from the rebels.

The enemies of Geneva were not less active within than without. The vidame, a servile agent of Charles, assembled the chiefs of the mamelukes in his house. As all the citizens whose deaths they desired were not included among the forty-two, they occupied themselves at these meetings in drawing up proscription lists. Vidame, mamelukes, Savoyards, congratulated each other on 'cutting off the heads of their adversaries,' and wrote down the names of many of the best citizens.† The disease, according to these conspirators, had spread widely; it was necessary to get rid of

* Registres du Conseil des 7 et 8 septembre. Savyon, *Annales*, p. 122.

† Bonivard, *Police de Genève.* *Mem. d'Archéol.* v. p. 384.

the friends of independence at one blow and not singly. They prepared to seize the patriots in the city, and to slay them outside the city; the parts were distributed; this man will arrest, that man will try, and the other will put to death. At the same time, to prevent the free Genevans from escaping, the duke stationed soldiers on every road. Geneva will be very fortunate if it escapes the plot this time, and if it does not see its old liberties and its hopes of the Gospel and of reformation perish under the sword of Savoy.

Charles III., leading the way to Charles IX., began his persecution of the huguenots. He commenced with his own territories, where he could do as he pleased; Pierre de Malbuisson was seized at Seyssel; Beffant at Annecy; Bullon was arrested on Sunday (frightful sacrilege in the eyes of the catholics!) in the church of Our Lady of Grace, during high mass. 'That matters not,' said the ducal party; 'there are cases where the privileges of the Church must give way to the interests of the State.' During this time, the patriots remaining at Geneva went up and down the city, showing themselves brave even to imprudence, and boldly demanded the convocation of a general council of the people to annul the division which by a majority of eleven had given such satisfaction to the duke. This inflamed Charles's anger to the highest degree; he swore to be avenged of such an insult, and everything was prepared to crush these audacious citizens. The sky grew dark; a dull murmur was heard in the city; there was a general uneasiness; every man asked his neighbor what was going to happen . . . alarm was everywhere.

At last the storm burst. It was the 15th of September. One, two, three—several persons not known in Geneva, peasants, or tradespeople, and men of little importance, appeared at the gates; they were messengers sent to the patriots by their friends and relations settled in Savoy. One message succeeded another. The ducal army is in motion, they were told; it is preparing to quit the villages where it was stationed. Leaders and soldiers declare loudly that they are going to Geneva to put the duke's enemies to death.

Nothing else can be heard but threats, boasts, and shouts of joy. . . A few minutes later the people of the neighborhood ran up and announced that the army was only a quarter of a league distant. The people hastened to the higher parts of the city; they saw the arquebusiers, halberdiers, and flags; they heard the drums and fifes, the tramp of the march, and the hurrahs of the soldiers. The Savoyards were in the fields and the mamelukes in the streets. It was not even possible for the citizens to expose themselves to death on the ramparts. The ducal faction would not permit them to approach. 'Make your escape,' said some to the huguenot leaders; 'if you delay an instant, you are lost.' The mamelukes lifted their heads and exclaimed: 'Now is the day of vengeance!'

The noble citizens threatened by the sword of Charles, or rather by the axe of his executioners, wished to come to some understanding with each other, but they had not the time to confer together. They knew the fate that awaited them, and the alarm of their friends and wives, of those who had nothing to fear, drove them out like a blast of wind. Some would have sold their lives dearly; others said that their task was not yet completed, that if the duke attacked them perfidiously, if the bishop basely abandoned them, they must retire elsewhere, pray for the hour of justice, and procure powerful defenders for Geneva. Their resolution was hardly formed when the field-sergeants approached the gates. The huguenots pursued by the sword of Savoy could neither carry away what would be necessary during their exile, nor take leave of their friends; people in the streets had hardly time to enter their houses. All departed amid the tears of their wives and the cries of their children.

The exodus began, not the exodus of a whole people, but of the flower of the citizens. Many were seen leaving the gates of the city. There was Jean Baud, captain of the artillery, with his brother Claude, a zealous episcopalian, but a friend of independence; Girard, who had succeeded Boulet as treasurer of the city; Jean Philippe, afterwards first syndic; The intrepid Jean Lullin, Hudriot du Molard, and Ami Bandière, who were syndics in the year of the Reformation;

Jean d'Arloz, afterwards one of the Council of Two Hundred; Michael Sept, a frequent deputy to Switzerland; G. Peter, Claude Roset, father of the celebrated syndic and chronicler; J. L. Ramel, Pierre de la Thoy, Chabod, and Pécolat. Others quitted Geneva secretly; some by day, some by night, in disguise, on foot or on horseback, 'in great haste, by different roads, without consulting one another.' Some crept along the edge of the lake, others hastened towards the mountains. Melancholy dispersion, sad calamity.* And yet as they departed, these generous men kept up the hope of seeing liberty victorious. In this dread and critical hour, they cast their eyes over the walls of the old city, and swore that they left it not to escape death, but to save it from oppression. They were going in search of help—not towards the enslaved banks of the Tiber, as they did once in their folly; but towards those noble mountains of Switzerland, which had thrown off the yoke of foreign tyrants. The sword of Savoy pursues them; but, wonderful providence of God! it drives them towards those countries where a new light has dawned, and where they will meet at nearly every step the friends of Zwingle and of the Reformation. It is a prince, a friend of the pope, that is sending them to the school of the Gospel.

The most threatened of all was Besançon Hugues; if he had been taken, his head would have been the first to fall. At that time, he happened to be at a farm he possesssd at Chatelaine, a short distance from Geneva, in the direction of Gex. He was serious, but calm, for he felt the importance of the crisis, and was tranquilly preparing to gather his grapes, for it was vintage time. On the evening of the 15th of September he received a visit from his friend Messire Vuillet, commandant of Gex, who rode up on horseback, and asked him with an air of frankness, to give him a bed for the night. Hugues had no suspicion; the horse was put into the stable; a room was prepared for Vuillet, and the two friends, sitting down at table, talked a long while over their supper. The commandant of Gex, commissioned by

* Registres du Conseil du 23 février 1526. Bonivard, *Chroniq.* ii. p. 416. Savyon, *Annales*, p. 123.

the duke to arrest Hugues, had ordered his officers to be at Chatelaine early in the morning of the 16th; and to make sure of not losing his victim, he had thought the cleverest way was to come and sup as a friend with the man whom he was to deliver up to the death of Berthelier and of Lévrier, to sleep under his roof, to arrest him next morning, and hand him over to the executioners. Hugues as yet knew nothing of what was going on at Geneva.

The flight had already become general; the huguenots hurried away, some in the direction of Friburg by way of Lausanne; others to St. Claude, by the Jura. The bishop, as we have said, had gone into Italy, probably in March, six months before; but he had devoted partisans at St. Claude. Accordingly the fugitives, who still hoped something from the episcopal power, took the latter road. Let us follow the first of these two companies.

At the head of those who had taken the road to Switzerland were De la Thoy and Chabod. They galloped their horses full speed along the Lausanne road; on reaching Versoix, they fell unexpectedly into the midst of the soldiers posted there with orders to stop the Genevans in their flight. De la Thoy, who was well mounted, gave his horse the spur, and escaped; but Chabod was taken and carried to Gex. The news of this arrest spread immediately, and caused great trouble among the fugitives who followed them. They threw themselves into the by-roads, they skirted the foot of the mountains, and in vain did Charles's men-at-arms follow in their track: many of them arrived at Lausanne. Yet it was Friburg they wished to reach, and to do that they had to cross difficult passes where the duke had stationed his soldiers in order to seize them. The Sieur d'Englisberg, avoyer of Friburg, possessed vineyards on the shores of the Lake of Geneva, and was gathering his grapes at La Vaux. While busy with his vats and presses, he learnt what was going on, and, full of compassion for the unhappy men, he sent off a courier to his colleagues. The Friburg council immediately despatched an officer with thirty horsemen, with orders to protect the fugitive huguenots.

During this time, those who had taken the road to Franche-Comté (the bishop's followers) crossed the Jura mountains and 'made a thousand windings to escape,' says Bonivard. They walked but little during the day, much during the night; they flung themselves into the woods and scaled the rocks. These worthy episcopalians fancied that it would be sufficient to see their pastor's face and be saved. And even if he had not returned to St. Claude, that city would afford them a secure asylum. But, cruel disappointment! not only was there no bishop, but his officers repulsed his persecuted subjects. Nobody in the city would give shelter even to the most catholic of the fugitives.

The Genevans, disappointed in their expectations and disconcerted in their plans, determined to continue their flight. It was indeed time: just as they were leaving St. Claude by one gate, the Savoyard soldiers entered by another. Terror added wings to their feet; they hurried along, the rain beating upon them, the horsemen following them hard, at every moment on the brink of falling into the hands of their enemies, and the dangers of their country adding to the wretchedness of their flight. At last they arrived at Besançon, then at Neufchatel, and finally at Friburg, where they met their friends who had come by way of Lausanne. They embraced and grasped each other's hands. But Besançon Hugues . . . they sought him everywhere . . . he could not be found. The anxiety was general. It was known what zeal the ducal archers would have employed to seize him; it was besides so easy to surprise him in his quiet retreat at Chatelaine. Alas! the murderers of Cæsar's tower and of the castle of Bonne might perhaps already have shed the blood of a third martyr!

Hugues and the governor of Gex had passed the evening together; and as the Genevan had, says a manuscript, 'a keener scent than his treacherous friend,' he had led on Vuillet to speak of the circumstances of the times, and had guessed the object of his visit. He had learnt that the only means of saving Geneva was to claim the support of the Swiss. The hour for retiring had come; Hugues with a cheerful look conducted the commandant to the room prepared for him, and bade him good night. The latter had hardly fallen asleep when, saddling his guest's horse, Hugues gallopped off with one or two companions; they took the direction of St. Claude, intending to go from thence to Friburg. At daybreak he found himself on the summit of the mountain of Gex, and at the pass of La Faucille bade farewell to the beautiful valley of the Leman, on which the rays of the rising sun were beginning to fall.

At this moment Messire Vuillet awoke, got up noiselessly, and, seeing from the window that his soldiers were posted round the house, stealthily advanced to seize his prey. . . . The bed was empty, the bird had flown. The commandant of Gex immediately ordered the door to be opened, summoned the provost-marshal, and directed him to pursue the fugitive with the duke's cavalry. The squadron set off at a gallop. Some hours earlier, the archers of Gex had started in pursuit of the other fugitives, making sure of catching them. The road across the mountains wound about in consequence of the valleys and precipices, so that pursuers and pursued, being sometimes on opposite slopes, might see and even hear one another, although there was an abyss between them. When the flight of Hugues was made known, the zeal of the soldiers increased; and the former, knowing his danger, threw himself into impassable roads in order to escape his enemies. 'Ah!' said he afterwards, 'it was not pleasant; for the archers of Monsieur of Savoy followed us as far as St. Claude, then from St. Claude to Besançon and beyond. . . . We were forced to journey day and night, through the woods, through the rain, not knowing where to find a place of safety.' At length he reached Friburg, six days after the arrival of his friends who had gone by Lausanne. Friburgers and Genevese, all welcomed him with transport.*

* The account given by Hugues himself is in the Registres de l'Etat. The narrative written by the author of the *Promenades Historiques dans le Canton de Genève* is embellished after the manner of Sir Walter Scott. Bonivard, *Chroniq.* ii. p. 416. Spon, *Hist. de Genève*, ii. p. 374. Gautier MS. Savyon, *Annales*, p. 123.

CHAPTER XXV.

THE FUGITIVES AT FRIBURG AND BERNE. THE DUKE AND THE COUNCIL OF HALBERDS AT GENEVA.

(SEPTEMBER TO DECEMBER, 1525.)

A STRIKING sight was that presented by the city founded by the Zœhringens. Strange men were wandering round the old cathedral and on the steep and picturesque banks of the Sarine. The people of Friburg looked at them with respect, for they knew that these citizens, the victims of the tyranny of a foreign power, had come to seek an asylum within their walls. They went to the windows to see them pass, and approached them with cordial affection. The Friburgers wished to hear them, and Besançon Hugues, accompanied by a number of the fugitives, was introduced into the council-hall. They gave him a seat on the right of the avoyer, which was the place of honor, and the sitting being opened, the Genevan rose and said: 'Most honored lords, there is a town situated at the natural limits of Switzerland —a town entirely devoted to you, where you can come and go just as at home, where you can bargain, sell, and buy whatever you require, and which would be able to stop your enemies, if ever the League should be attacked from the south. This town, the complement of Helvetia, ought to be allied to the cantons. Did not the Swiss in the time of Cæsar extend as far as L'Ecluse ?* . . . If Geneva should fall into the hands of Savoy, the cannon that ought to defend you will be turned against you . . . Gentlemen, time presses, the fatal moment is at hand . . . Long, unjust, and violent persecutions have placed our liberties on the brink of the abyss. The heroic Berthelier murdered at the foot of Cæsar's tower; the wise Lévrier beheaded in the castle

* Fort de l'Ecluse, between Geneva and Bourg (Ain).

yard of Bonne; Malbuisson, Chabod, and many others recently flung into gloomy dungeons; all our friends remaining at Geneva in danger of losing their lives . . . and we, most honored lords, who are before you, obliged to abandon our property, our business, our families, our country, that we may not fall into the hands of a prince who has sworn our death: to such a state is our free and ancient city reduced. . . . One thing alone can save it . . . the strong hand of the Swiss League . . . Most honored lords, hear our cries, behold our tears, and have compassion on our misery. For God's honor, give us aid and counsel.'

The fugitives who stood around Hugues—Lullin, Girard, the two Bauds, Bandière, Sept, Pécolat, and about twelve other citizens—were deeply moved. These men, men of great energy, appeared as suppliants before the senate of Friburg. Their countenance, their words, entreated this powerful city, and yet a noble pride was visible in their looks. They felt at once their independence and their misery; they had the air of dethroned kings. Some wrung their hands, others shed tears; all prayed with tones of sorrow that the Swiss would come to their assistance. The Friburgers, touched with pity for Geneva and its exiles, and filled with indignation against Charles and his partisans, replied: 'No, we will not desert you.' Words full of kindness, which consoled men overwhelmed with sorrows, and shed a ray of light upon their gloomy path!

The moment was favorable for gaining the Swiss: they were exasperated at seeing Savoy, after the battle of Pavia, basely embrace the cause of the conqueror. In going to the support of Geneva, Switzerland the faithful would give a wholesome lesson to that power which always took the strongest side. Friburg immediately despatched deputies to Berne and Soleure, and some of the fugitives accompanied them. In these two cities the unfortunate Genevans renewed their touching supplications. At Berne, says a chronicler, 'they found a bad beginning but a good end;' at Soleure, the contrary, 'a good beginning but a bad end.' Soleure, however, joined the two other cities in notifying to the duke, that if he valued their friendship he must cease injuring

Geneva. But Berne in particular showed great zeal. There were already in that city a number of devoted friends of Zwingle and the Reformation; among others one of the chief magistrates, Thomas ab Hofen, an intelligent and moderate man, of a temper inclined to melancholy, much employed in the public business of his country, and who for two years had been corresponding with the Reformer of Zurich. These evangelical Bernese soon perceived that there was a hidden but real relationship between the reformation of Zurich and the emancipation of Geneva; and they influenced their countrymen in favor of the Genevans. At the same time they spoke of the Gospel to the fugitives, and some of those men who had come to Switzerland in search of liberty only, found the truth. This movement of the powerful republic towards Geneva preluded new times. Savoy had desired to crush that liberty which was of such old standing in Geneva, and the Reformation which was soon to begin; but, by the wonderful providence of God, the blow intended to kill both secured their existence and gave them a wider development. The word of the reformers, well received by the Bernese people, was to arrive even at Geneva, and that city would thus, by God's counsel, receive from Switzerland not only national independence, but blessings that extend far beyond the destinies of nations.*

Meanwhile the duke had been told of the departure of the fugitives: just as he was going to lay his hand upon the nest, the birds disappeared. Charles and his counsellors were staggered. These energetic citizens would in truth be no longer in Geneva to combat his designs; but it would have been surer, he thought, to put them out of the way either by the sword of the executioner or by a long imprisonment. Charles the Good had often practised both these means with success. In vain did his partisans say, to comfort him, that at least the patriots would not offend him by their presence. Yes, but if they should return—if they should not return alone—if the Swiss . . . There were in the Helvetic League confused noises, distant sounds of Refor-

* Gautier MS. La Corbière MS. Bonivard, *Chroniq.* ii. p. 417.

mation and of liberty, which alarmed the Savoyards. Yet they said, if we profit skilfully by the absence of the huguenots, if we properly muzzle the other Genevans, if we establish ourselves firmly in the city, nobody will be able to turn us out.

And now, as there was no need to hurry, the duke resolved to put off his entrance for a while. The appeal to Rome had wounded him deeply. To see himself, a sovereign prince, head of the most glorious house in Europe, uncle of the king of France, brother-in-law of the emperor, summoned before the pope by a band of nobodies, greatly incensed the vain and haughty Charles III. Before he enters Geneva, the appeal must be withdrawn. The duke sent orders on this subject to M. de Balleyson, his representative in the city. Then, as if to pass away the time, he urged on the persecution of all the Genevans around him. The Sieur of Bonebouges, brother to the Sieur of Montrotier, at the head of the troops of Faucigny, good soldiers but violent men, plundered the country, seized many respectable people in the environs of the city, and shut them up in the castles of Savoy, where they were grossly maltreated.

De Balleyson lost no time in executing his master's orders. He represented to the principal friends of Savoy at Geneva of what an offence the city had been guilty towards the duke by daring to accuse him before the pope. On the 20th of September the general council was convoked. Alas! those energetic men who had so often been its glory, Hugues and his companions in misfortune, were absent, and nearly all the friends they still possessed in Geneva refused to attend. M. de Balleyson appeared before this shadow of a general council and said: 'Our lord the duke wishes to learn from the people of this city of Geneva whether they intend to prosecute a certain appeal before the court of Rome.'* The mamelukes, who were almost alone in the council, shouted out as if with one voice: 'It is not our wish to prosecute the said appeal.'†

* 'Noster dux . . . vult scire et intelligere a populo hujus civitatis Gebennensis . . . si velit et intendat persequi quamdam appellationem . . . in curia Romana.'

† 'Responderunt . . . una voce . . . quod non erat ipsorum voluntas . . . dictas appellationes prosequi.'

This matter being ended, the duke prepared to make his entrance into the city, which he did in the last days of September with a part of the troops which he had 'beyond the Arve.' He found Geneva very different from what he had desired. He had hoped to seize the rebels there, and he found none but slaves. The servile mamelukes cared little for liberty, and were proud to have a master. They called him their 'most dread lord,' approached him with base adulation, and, kissing the chains he brought them, assured him that his coming filled them with joy and comfort.

The duke, who set little store by such cringing men, thought only how he could become prince of the city, and intrigued to get the sovereign authority handed over to him. His ministers had conceived a plan which promised fairly, and the necessary manœuvres were immediately resorted to. The syndics having appeared before his Highness on the 29th of September (1525), the duke said to them rather abruptly: 'The expenses and fines imposed on Geneva by my council of Chambéry amount to twenty thousand gold crowns.' He desired to frighten the Genevans, and induce them to sacrifice their independence in exchange for this debt. But the syndics contented themselves with answering: 'Monseigneur, the city is poor, and we can only offer you . . . our hearts.' This was not what Charles wanted. The duke's chancellor, taking the syndics aside, said to them: 'Come, gentlemen, put yourselves straight, do *something* to satisfy his Highness.' The syndics reflected for two or three days, and unable or unwilling to guess what that 'something' could be, they said to the vidame, the lawful channel between them and the prince: 'What does the duke mean?' The vidame conferred with his master, and appearing before the council on the 10th of October, he said: 'The duke is vicar-imperial and sovereign of the cities included within his states; Geneva is so included. Why do you not then acknowledge him as your master? Do not be afraid; he is a kind prince; he will respect the authority of the bishop and the franchises of the city, and you will enjoy a prosperity hitherto unknown.' This was clearer: the Savoyard prince said plainly that he wanted Geneva. The vidame, observing that his hint had been received without enthusiasm, added: 'If you do not accept the duke willingly, you will be made to accept him by force.' The servile mamelukes, magnifying the advantages of annexation to so powerful a state, would have granted everything on the spot. The moment was critical: the syndics were uneasy and wavering. On the one hand was the ancient independence of their country; on the other, superior and brute force, which none of them could resist. They referred his Highness's demand to the episcopal council, which in turn referred it to the prince-bishop in person. Such a reply was already a concession; the politicians of Savoy fancied themselves near their object. . . . Geneva consents, they will say to the bishop; you cannot answer us by a refusal. The city was on the verge of ruin when an unexpected and noble succor preserved it.*

What Charles had so much dreaded came to pass. Towards the end of October, several stout men of warlike mien and proud look were seen entering by the Swiss gate; they were ambassadors from Berne, Friburg, and Soleure, with Gaspard de Mullinen of Berne at their head. This energetic man was a good catholic; in 1517 he had made a pilgrimage to Jerusalem, and had been created knight of the Holy Sepulchre. A blind conservative, he was conscientiously and stedfastly opposed to every change, religious or political. 'Confederates,' said he continually in the diets, 'resist the doctrine of Luther, or we shall soon be overrun by it.'† It would seem as if Mullinen ought to have supported the prince's pretensions with his iron hand; but in his sight the attempt of Savoy was contrary to treaty, and consequently a revolutionary work. Seeing, therefore, that the Genevese council were wavering, the indignant Bernese went to their place of meeting, and said: 'Stand firm and fear nothing; our lords will support you in all your rights.'‡

* Registres du Conseil des 22, 23, 25, 28 septembre; 3, 6, 8, 10 octobre. Manuscrit de Gautier. *Journal du Syndic Balard*, pp. 14–17. Manuscrit de Roset, liv. ii. ch. v.

† 'Wehret bei Zeiten dass die lutherische Sache nicht die Oberhand gewinne.'—H. Hottinger, *Kirchengesch.* v. p. 103.

‡ Registres du Conseil du 27 octobre. *Journal de Balard*, pp. 18, 19. Manuscrit de Gautier.

This intervention on the part of the Swiss disconcerted the duke. He must change his plan, and have recourse to stratagem in order to free himself from this knight of the Holy Sepulchre. Never were diplomatists more successful in deceiving rude warriors and honest citizens. First, Charles's ministers put the mamelukes forward, who began telling the ambassadors: 'We desire to live under the protection of the duke and the bishop.' Next, Charles declared to the Swiss that he was full of love for all the citizens of Geneva, and ready to grant everything the cantons required. 'The fugitives may return,' he added. 'Here is a safe-conduct for them: take it to them.' The document was placed in Mullinen's hands. He was astonished at the rapid success of his embassy. He turned the paper over and over, without reading it however, and for a good reason. The safe-conduct was in Latin, and the knight of Mullinen with his noble colleagues did not pretend to any knowledge of that language; but how could they suppose that the duke had not given them, as he assured them, complete satisfaction? They imagined that the document, while it secured life and liberty to the fugitives, would open to them the gates of Geneva; and doubting not that Besançon Hugues, Lullin, Girard, and their friends, on their return to the city, would be able to preserve its independence, they thanked the duke and departed satisfied for their homes.

But Hugues was a better Latin scholar and knew his man better than Mullinen. As soon as the ambassador returned, he handed to the Genevese, with an air of triumph, the important paper that was the reward of his journey, and Hugues read it eagerly. On coming to the last phrase he smiled bitterly: *Dummodo non intrent civitatem, nec suburbia ejus*, said the safe-conduct; 'which means,' said Hugues to the deputies, 'that we can return to Geneva provided we do not enter the city or the suburbs . . . The duke will be within and we without . . . What services can we render the city? You know the smallness of our territory. If we are neither in the city nor in the suburbs, we

* Bonivard, *Chroniq.* ii. p. 418–421. Gautier MS.

are on the lands of Savoy . . . Now if Berthelier was arrested close under the walls (at La Treille), if Lévrier was seized at the very gate of St. Pierre, what would befall us on the ducal territory? . . The duke is laying a snare: it is a condition which nullifies the act.—The bird which the duke has sent us,' he added, 'has a fine head and beautiful plumage; but there is a tail at the end which spoils all the rest.'—'This grace is a mere trap,' said the indignant exiles. The knight of Mullinen was offended and annoyed at the manner in which the Duke of Savoy had befooled him, and perhaps began to imagine that a knowledge of Latin might be of use. 'My lords,' said the fugitives to the councils of Berne and Friburg, 'the duke is a great traitor. He fears not God, but he fears men the more. For this reason, make us free of your cities; for if he knows that we are your allies, then only will he leave us in peace.'* At the same time the Genevans, wishing to show the duke what confidence they placed in his safe-conduct, sent for their wives and children. This was making an energetic answer to Savoy.

The poor Genevese women with hearts full of bitterness began their journey. Women did not travel much at the beginning of the sixteenth century; and these, who had hardly been out of Geneva, thought, as they went to Friburg and Berne, that they were going almost to the end of the world. What a sad journey was theirs! Frightened at the real or supposed dangers of the road, surprised at the strange language whose unintelligible sounds began to echo in their ears, bathed in tears, and broken-hearted, they folded the poor children in their arms; for they were terrified at the strange scenes and new faces, and clung with their weak hands round their mothers' necks. At length this troop of afflicted women entered Friburg; but their arrival at first only increased the distress, and when these loving wives embraced their husbands, their tears of joy were mingled abundantly with tears of sorrow. The 'foreigners,' as they were called, although of respectable families, were at that time

* Bonivard, *Chroniq.* ii. pp. 418, 421. Gautier MS.

destitute of everything, and were almost like beggars at the doors of their friends. At the first moment they were compelled to leave their families in the street, not knowing where to shelter them. It was a heart-rending time. What! not a room, not even a stable where these exhausted women and children could lie upon the straw! The afflicted mothers pressed the little creatures to their bosom—kissed their pale lips . . . and then regretted Geneva.

At length the foreigners took courage and went before the council. 'We sent for our families,' they said, 'but we can neither lodge them nor feed them . . . Permit them to enter the hospital.' The prayer was granted, and these well-born women who not long ago were robed in silk and dancing with Beatrice of Portugal, were seen exchanging the palace for a hospital. 'The people were moved to pity,' says Bonivard. It must be remembered, however, that in those times staying in a hospital was not degrading: travellers often lodged in such places.*

The arrival of the women and children at first increased the distress of the citizens; they were discouraged and seemed to have reached the depths of misery. The sight of these beloved beings reminded them of Geneva and softened their hearts. But on a sudden they roused themselves; they went from Friburg to Berne; they spoke in private houses, in the halls of the tribes, in the public places, and appealed to the sympathy of the Swiss. They represented that the duke had put their leaders to death; that he had forced them to forsake their homes and their business, and to fly to a foreign land; that, being reduced to the greatest poverty, they had been compelled to place their wives in a position which they would once have rejected with contempt, and that, to put a climax to this misery, the city which they loved, and for whose independence they were ready to sacrifice everything, was invaded and enslaved . . . These great souls were troubled; these proud citizens, so resolute before the face of a cruel prince, were depressed in the presence of their afflicted families, of their exile, of the

* Bonivard, *Chroniq.* ii. p. 421.

ruin of Geneva, and tears betrayed their weakness. The Bernese looked with admiration on these noble citizens, whose tattered garments bore witness to their wretched condition. Many of the tribes of the city of Berne and the majority of the Council of Two Hundred declared for the vanquished cause, and the conclusion of an alliance with Geneva seemed near at hand.

The bishop, already alarmed by Charles's intrigues, was startled when he heard of this. If Berne accepted the reformed doctrine like Zurich, if Geneva should follow the example of Berne, the prelate seated in the chair of the bishops and on the throne of princes, would see them both taken from under him. Pierre de la Baume, like many ecclesiastical sovereigns, cared nothing for the welfare of those whom he called his subjects ; but he cared a great deal for the title of prince, and would not suffer either the duke or the Swiss to deprive him of it. In order to preserve it, he would have convoked the whole world, had that been possible. Accordingly, even when at table, he felt uneasy and would pause frequently, musing with himself and saying: 'The duke is at Geneva ; the fox in the poultry-yard. . . . Let the fowls look out ! . . . And then, on the other hand, they are playing tricks in the cantons. . . . The bears look as if they wished to descend from the mountains. . . . Unhappy shepherd ! . . . I will do anything,' he said, 'to preserve the jurisdiction of the Church.' He began at once, and endeavored first to coax his flock :* 'We are very glad to hear of your good disposition,' he wrote to them ; 'and you will do us great pleasure by informing us of all that is necessary for the welfare of our dear city. . . . Do you, on your part, so conduct yourselves that God and the world may have cause to be satisfied.'† In 1525, as in 1523, the prelate's device was still *God and the world.*

These efforts came to nothing. The government of

* 'Il s'efforça d'abord d'*apigeonner* ses ouailles.' *Apigeonner*, to entice pigeons by offering them corn.

† Lettre de La Baume, Archives de Genève sous le nº 934. *Mém. d'Archéol.* ii. pp. 8, 9.

bishops and princes, established in different parts of christendom, was at first mild and paternal, compared with the government of certain lay lords; but long ago, the bishops had lost the superiority which could legitimatise their authority, and the lay power had, on the contrary, gained great influence in the world. In France, especially since the thirteenth century, royalty, by displaying a character of kindness, had favored the progress of the people in things material, intellectual, and even moral; and if Francis I., notwithstanding a personal character by no means estimable, holds a brilliant place in history, it must be ascribed to this quality in French royalty. But almost all the bishop-princes of Geneva who preceded the Reformation, cared little for the development of the nation, except it were to thwart it. John of Savoy and Pierre de la Baume were nothing but selfish dissolute priests. No halo was seen on their brows; and thus they found one day that there was no firm ground under their feet. Ecclesiastical authorities, even when honest, are apt to despise the temporal interests of their subjects; and as unhappily spiritual interests do not much affect ambitious prelates, the immortal souls and the earthly liberties of their flocks are equally oppressed by them.

The duke, who knew better than anybody the weakness of the episcopal power (which he had mainly caused), felt his ambition increase, and resolved to put an end to it. With this intent he would take a step which, by giving him what Savoy had coveted for centuries, would fortify him with a title calculated to impose silence on the complaints of the prelate, the accusations of the fugitives, and the demands of the Swiss. He determined to convene a general council, composed almost exclusively of his creatures, from which he would obtain, either by persuasion or by a great display of force, the homage due to a sovereign. To attain his object he began by toning down his insolent conduct and his unjust pretensions. Treasurer Boulet, first cause of all these disturbances, being obliged to furnish his accounts at the hôtel-de-ville, was condemned. The citizens imprisoned or fined received the promise of an early amnesty;

and imagining he had thus gained every heart, Charles desired the people to be called together, that all the community might know of the good-will he entertained towards them. The syndics and the bishop's vicar, perceiving that the fatal hour had arrived, refused his demand. They were not strong, but fear came upon them in that solemn moment when they saw Geneva suspended over the abyss. Gruet, the vicar, stammered out some excuses: 'Nobody would come to the council,' he said, 'but rabble and ruffians.' It was precisely what the duke wanted. Being already master of Geneva and claiming to make everything bend under his absolute will, he would not allow Gruet to finish his speech: 'It is my council's advice,' he said, 'that the people should assemble to-morrow, Sunday at eight in the forenoon, in the cloister of St. Pierre. Have this published by sound of trumpet, and let the heads of families be informed by sending from door to door.' Then turning to the vicar, he added: 'You will be present with all the episcopal council.' He informed them that he would visit the assembly on his way to mass, and would then tell them his pleasure; so that the council might prepare their answer during service-time, and he would receive it on his way back. The ducal partisans ran from street to street and from house to house in order to muster all their forces at an assembly called in the name of a prince whose subjects lived at Chambéry and Turin.* The liberals, who were still numerous in Geneva, pretty generally kept away: they did not consider a council assembled by the duke to be legitimate.

The next day, Sunday, December 10, the great bell of the cathedral having summoned the citizens, men whose names are for the most part unknown appeared to form a council. The most important portion in this *popular* assembly was not the people, but the duke, who appeared between nine and ten o'clock, accompanied by the bishop of Maurienne, the episcopal council, the chancellor of Savoy, and his cham-

* Registres du Conseil du 9 novembre 1525. *Journal de Balard*, p. 28. Savyon, *Annales*, p. 127. *Besançon Hugues*, par Galiffe fils, p. 276.

berlains, esquires, officers, and many gentlemen from his states; before and behind came the archers of Savoy. Carrying their halberds with a threatening air, and impatient to reduce this herd of shopkeepers under their prince, these mercenaries gave the meeting the appearance of a battle-field rather than of a council. Nothing like it had ever been witnessed in the city. Resolved that day to make the conquest of Geneva, Charles proudly mounted to the place reserved for the sovereign; his courtiers drew up to the right and left, and his soldiers formed in a circle round the assembly, while above their heads flashed the broad-pointed bills at the ends of the long staves, as if to frighten the citizens. The duke reclining upon the throne, which was covered with rich tapestry, ordered his chancellor to explain his sovereign intentions. The latter, making a low bow, read: 'About three months ago, as the duke was preparing to cross the mountains on Italian business, he learnt that certain seditious people, who have fled to the country of the League, were sowing dissensions between him and the bishop, between Geneva and the Swiss. . . . Whereupon his Highness, who has always been a mild and gentle prince to this city, seeing it threatened by a frightful calamity, neglected his own interests, hastened to you, and has spared neither money nor pains to restore peace among you. In return for so many benefits, this magnanimous prince asks but one thing . . . that you should recognise him as your sovereign protector.' The protection was evidently a mere veil to hide dominion and despotism; accordingly the few honest citizens there present were dispirited and silent. It was necessary to make haste, for the duke wished to avert all opposition. Having read the paper, the chancellor stepped forward, and cried as loud as he could, for his voice was weak: 'Are you willing to live in obedience to your bishop and prince, and under the protection of my lord duke? . . . The question should now have been put to the vote; but the impatient mamelukes carried it by acclamation, shouting out with all their might: 'Yes, yes!' The chancellor resumed: 'My lord, seeing the great love this city feels towards him, cancels all the penalties it has incurred, takes off all sequestrations, remits all fines, which amount to twenty-two thousand crowns, and pardons all rebels—those excepted who have fled to Switzerland.' Such are usually the amnesties of tyrants; those are excepted who ought to be included, and those included who do not need it. 'Thanks, thanks!' replied the mamelukes. 'As my chancellor may not have been distinctly heard,' said Charles to Syndic Montyon, 'have the goodness to repeat what he has said in my name.' After this, his Highness, with his chancellor, courtiers, gentlemen, and halberdiers, left the assembly and went to mass. It looked like a triumphal procession. As for those left behind, if there were venal citizens who dared to raise their heads, there were others whose uneasy consciences bowed them down.*

As soon as the Genevese were left to themselves, Montyon, a fanatical partisan of Savoy, got on a bench and repeated, not without embarrassment, the chancellor's address. The halberdiers being away, the assent was no longer unanimous. There were still many honest men in Geneva who clung to the ancient institutions of the State and held a Savoyard usurpation in horror. Some, at the very moment when the liberty of their country was about to be thrown into the abyss, were smitten with a last love for her. 'The address is full of guile,' they said. Many, however, acceded to the 'protection,' but added, 'saving the authority of the prince-bishop and the liberties of the city,' which nullified the vote.†

Such was the *Council of Halberds*. It had given Geneva the Duke of Savoy for her *protector*, and had imposed on the citizens *obedience* towards that prince. An encroaching, powerful, able court, like that of Turin, could easily make an hereditary sovereignty out of such a concession. But a course of violence and stratagem provokes the resistance

* Bonivard, *Chroniq.* ii. pp. 424–427. Galiffe, *Matériaux pour l'Histoire de Genève*, ii. pp. 318–323. *Journal de Balard*, pp. 28–30. Gautier MS. The conclusion of this council is wanting in the Registers; it was probably suppressed as an infringement of the liberties of Geneva.

† See preceding note. Roset MS. liv. ii. ch. vi.

of noble minds. After the action of despotism, the reaction of liberty was to begin; the bow too violently bent by the duke was to break in his hand.

The next day, in fact, Charles, who fancied himself already prince of the city, wishing to enter upon his new career, requested the city to hand over to him the jurisdiction in criminal matters, which was refused. Nor was this the only check; the procurator-fiscal having, by his Highness's orders, sent from house to house to collect votes against the alliance with the Swiss, many flatly refused to give them. At this moment the duke appeared as if he were stunned. He had matters on his mind which troubled and disturbed him; they made him mistrustful and anxious. The assembled people had just taken the oath of obedience to him . . . and to his first two requests (such legitimate requests as he thought them) they had replied by a No! After having given an example of his extreme violence, Charles gave another of his extreme weakness. He thought Geneva crushed; but Geneva, even when crushed, alarmed him. He pressed his foot upon her neck, but he felt the corpse moving under him. Even the mamelukes he began to consider as obstinate republicans, secretly defending their independence. His head began to reel, his heart to fail him. The essential trait of his character, it will be remembered, was to begin everything and finish nothing. This union of violence and folly, of which several Roman emperors have furnished examples, was found also in Charles. At the moment he had gained an important victory, and just as it was necessary for him to remain on the field of battle to profit by it, he turned his back and fled precipitately into Piedmont. It was asserted that Beatrice had recalled him. 'Venus overcame Pallas,' says Bonivard. The prior of St. Victor is always inclined to be sarcastic. But if (as is possible) it was the desire to join the duchess which induced Charles III. to let that city of Geneva slip from his hands, which the house of Savoy had coveted for ages, it is a proof that if he was violent enough to take it, he was too weak to keep it. However that may be, on the 12th of December, 1525, the duke quitted the city, and from that day neither he nor his successors entered it again. If Charles had remained, and followed the advice of his ministers, he would probably have established his authority, and bound Geneva to Rome. The triumph of the power of Savoy at the extremity of Lake Leman would have had serious consequences. But the victory he was about to win—which he had even gained . . . was lost by his cowardly desertion, and lost for ever.*

So did not think the syndic Montyon and fifty of the most servile mamelukes. Proud of the decision of the Council of Halberds, they resolved to make it known to the Swiss. The horseman intrusted with the message departed, and, on his arrival at Friburg, delivered the letters to the avoyer. 'The fugitives are deceiving you,' said the writers; 'the entire community desires to live under the protection of our most dread lord the Duke of Savoy.' This accusation revived all the energy of the huguenots. The mamelukes charged them with lying. . . . From that hour they feared neither the dungeon nor the sword. Imprison them in Cæsar's tower, in the castle of Bonne, or elsewhere, it matters not: they are ready to expose themselves to the violence of the enemy. 'Appoint a commissioner,' said some of them; 'let him come with us to Geneva, and he will tell you which of the two has lied, we or the mamelukes.' John Lullin and two or three of his friends departed without a safe-conduct, accompanied by De Sergine, a Friburg notary, resolved to prove that Geneva desired to be free. The unexpected news of Lullin's arrival spread through the city; numbers of citizens immediately crowded round the bold and imprudent huguenot, gazed upon him with tenderness, and anxiously asked for news of the exiles. Fathers, brothers, sons, friends came in great anxiety of mind to hear the tidings of those they loved dearest. 'Alas!' said Lullin, 'how can I tell of their misery and sorrow?' . . . He described them as exiled, oppressed with fears for their country, despised by some, ill-treated by others, destitute, 'reduced to Job's dunghill,' obliged in order to support their families to receive alms from such strangers as had compassion on their wretched-

* Registres du Conseil, décembre 1525. *Journal de Balard*, p. 33. Gautier MS.

ness. But here the generous huguenot, whose wounded heart was bursting with tears and full of bitterness, could contain himself no longer: 'It is you,' he exclaimed, 'it is you that increases our sorrow—yes, you!' He indignantly complained that the Genevans remaining in Geneva disavowed those who had left it to save her independence, and made them pass for liars. He asked them how it was that, as the foreign prince had fled beyond the Alps, Geneva did not reclaim the liberty which he had taken away. 'Is it thus that citizens defend the ancient rights handed down by their fathers?' This touching language, the presence of him who uttered it and of the two or three fugitives at his side, the sight of their poverty, their distress, their patriotism, and their heroic courage, stirred the citizens. The Savoyard agents, Balleyson, Saleneuve, and their soldiers, remained in the city to no purpose: Geneva awoke from her slumbers. 'Friburg desires to know the real state of this city?' said a few patriots to Sergine; 'come, then, with us to the council—come and see for yourself.' The most energetic men were still in Switzerland; but by degrees all in Geneva who loved liberty were seen to shake off the silence to which they had been reduced. They encouraged one another to make an imposing demonstration. Erelong the justification of the *foreigners* took place, and it was conducted with all the solemnity that a simple people could give it.*

* Gautier MS. Galiffe, *Matériaux*, ii. p. 333. Spon, *Hist. de Genève*, ii. p. 385.

CHAPTER XXVI.

THE PEOPLE AND THE BISHOP DEFEND THE CAUSE OF THE FUGITIVES.

(DECEMBER 1525 TO FEBRUARY 1526.)

ON the 22nd of December, ten days after Charles's departure, crowds of citizens poured from every quarter towards the hôtel-de-ville. The syndics and the council, who were then sitting, were informed that certain persons desired to be admitted; the doors were opened, and the petitioners entered. At their head walked John Bandière, a man about sixty years old, whose son Ami (syndic in the Reformation year) was among the fugitives. This venerable man advanced, surrounded by the children of his son and of other exiles.* With him came several citizens who, though they had remained in the background during recent events, might yet with good right appear in the front line. There was the amiable Ami Porral, afterwards syndic, who zealously embraced the evangelical faith; Pierre de Joye, cousin of that De Joye whom Bishop John had desired to put to death; the bold Robert Vandel, syndic in 1529, his brother Peter, Sept, De Chapeaurouge, Falquet, Lect, Delapalud, Malbuisson, Favre, Lullin, Denis Hugues, son of the estimable Besançon: in short, says a document of the time, about 100 citizens, the flower of Geneva. These men desired not only

* The official Registers of the Council (Dec. 22) say: 'Bandière leading three or four boys.' Syndic Balard, an eye-witness, says: 'Bandière, accompanied by the children of some of those who have retired to Germany.' (*Journal*, p. 34.) Bonivard says the same. *Chroniq.* ii. p. 435. It is therefore a mistake in a writer, otherwise very learned in the history of Geneva, to say that: 'There was not a single little child with him.' (Galiffe, *Matériaux*, &c. ii. p. 334.) His son did not fall into the same error. (Galiffe fils, *Besançon Hugues*, p. 277.)

to bear testimony in favor of men unjustly accused; but observing that those to whom the reins of the State had been confided were slumbering, that the chariot was leaving the track and about to fall into the ditch, they thought it their duty to set the drivers on the right road. Bandière, his face wet with tears, (says a manuscript), spoke first: 'Most honorable lords,' he said, 'you see these children; do you not know their fathers? Are not these poor little ones orphans already, though their fathers are still alive?'*—'Yes,' exclaimed the councillors.—'Those citizens,' continued Bandière,' 'who, for having defended the liberties of Geneva, were compelled, through a thousand dangers, to seek refuge in Germany yonder,†—are not they good men?' . . . 'They are,' was the answer. 'Are they not citizens of this city—the good men whose fathers, sons, and connexions you have before you?'—It was cheerfully acknowledged.

Having thus the testimony of the council in favor of the refugees—a testimony of which the Friburg deputy made a note—the venerable Bandière continued: 'These refugees, whom you acknowledge to be good men, are surprised that you should have disavowed them in letters sent to the League. For this reason, we who are here present declare boldly that we approve them, both in their words and in their acts, and count them to be faithful and devoted citizens. At the same time, most honorable lords, we protest against every encroachment attempted by a foreign power on the rights of our prince and the liberties of the city.'

Thus the slumbering Geneva, whom Charles had thought dead, cast off the bonds with which that prince had bound her, and, rejecting the duke with one hand, called the fugitives back with the other. Bandière handed in his declaration in writing, and demanded letters-testimonial. Syndic Montyon, in great embarrassment, said that it was necessary to deliberate before answering. 'Where is the necessity?' exclaimed the energetic Robert Vandel.—'It is not the custom to give testimonials here,' was the reply. The huguenot, astonished at this refusal of a simple receipt, grew im-

* Bonivard, *Chroniq.* ii. p. 435.

† By 'Germany' they meant German Switzerland.

patient, and, turning towards De Sergine, desired him to draw up the act himself.

The syndics and councillors had not yet remarked this person. 'Not imagining they had such a visitor in their house,' says Bonivard, 'they looked at him with astonishment.' Their astonishment increased when they saw the Friburger rise and say, addressing the whole assembly: 'Sirs, do you acknowledge those who are in the country of the Helvetians to be men worthy of all honor; and do you ratify all that may be done by them for the welfare of this illustrious city?' The syndics and councillors, surprised at this extraordinary question, kept silent; but all the other citizens present, voting as if in general council, answered 'Yes!' De Sergine, calling the council to witness the complete approval that had been given the fugitives, withdrew, followed by the hundred citizens, proud of having made the voice of the people heard in the very bosom of an enslaved senate.*

De Sergine, unwilling to lose a moment, sat down without ceremony on the steps of the hôtel-de-ville, as might have been done, perhaps, in the simple republics of antiquity, and prepared to draw up the letters-testimonial that were required of him. A certain number of patriots stood around him; others went through the city reporting what had just taken place. Men rejoiced everywhere; they directed their steps towards the hôtel-de-ville remembering that God never forsakes a people that does not forsake itself. Every minute fresh citizens came and increased the strange assembly gathered round the notary, and every new-comer was eager to have his name at the foot of the declaration. All were speaking and arguing at once; some wept, others laughed; they felt that a new breath was passing over the city, and that its ancient liberties were recovering their vitality. All voices united in proclaiming the praises of the fugitives. 'Yes, certainly they are better than us,' said the crowd, 'for they have forsaken everything that our liberties might be

* Registres du Conseil du 22 décembre 1522. Galiffe, *Matériaux*, ii. pp. 324–330, where the speeches are given at length. Gautier MS. Spon, *Hist. de Genève*, &c.

preserved.' For a long time no such enthusiasm and joy had been witnessed in Geneva; and comparisons were drawn between this noble assembly, where every one gave his name at the peril of his life, and that gloomy Council of the Halberds, held in the duke's presence: on one side pomp and tyranny; on the other, simplicity and liberty. Forsaken by the bishop, threatened by the duke, watched by the Count of Genevois, surrounded by the armed soldiers of Saleneuve and Balleyson, ever prompt to acts of violence, the citizens followed each other, from noon until five o'clock, to sign the document which was to secure their alliance with Switzerland and the triumph of their liberties.

The mamelukes, however, wishing to stop a movement which threatened to rob the duke of all his recent advantages, had recourse to secret practices. Creeping up to some of the patriots of their acquaintance whom they saw approaching, they would say: 'Beware! when the duke returns with his army, he will lay his hand on these testimonials, he will count the names, he will mark the most guilty with a cross, and send them to rejoin the shades of Berthelier and Lévrier.' The duke had, in truth, his revenge in reserve; but the citizens heeded it not, and replied to this manœuvre by giving in their names with greater enthusiasm. The approach of the festivals of Christmas and of the New Year compelled many to stay in their shops, who were thus prevented from signing; to provide against which, men went from house to house, asking who would vote for the alliance with Switzerland. There were not a hundred persons in Geneva who refused. The protest of the hôtel-de-ville decided the fate of the city. Many of the first subscribers were in the number of those who received the Gospel most gladly. The dawn of the emancipation which was then beginning to appear, was to be followed by the full light of the Reformation. But before that glorious day arrived, what struggles, what wars, what dangers, Geneva would still have to go through!*

* Registres du Conseil du 22 décembre 1526. *Journal de Balard*, pp. 34, 35. Galiffe, *Matériaux*, ii. pp. 330–333. Pictet, *Hist. de Genève*, ii. pp. 401–408. Gautier MS. Spon, *Hist. de Genève*.

Ere long the movement descended, spreading from the hôtel-de-ville through all the streets of the city ; and to the noble protest of the principal citizens were added the rejoicings of the young folks and of the people. The holidays of Christmas and of the New Year had arrived. The 'children of Geneva,' masked or with blackened faces, paraded the streets to the sound of the drum, singing and shouting all over the city : 'Long live the huguenots!' During this time the citizens held frequent meetings both by day and by night, at which they boldly called for the return of the patriots, though they saw the dangers that would accompany them. Some of the independents visited Switzerland by stealth, to report all that had taken place and bring back the fugitives in triumph.

The Savoyard party, who still had the power in their hands, were firmly resolved not to give it up. The episcopal council sat all night. The syndics, the vicar, and the vidame in particular, were losing their heads. To prevent the movement from succeeding, they took useless and contradictory steps, calculated rather to increase the irritation in men's minds : nothing prospered with them. 'Fancy how surprised they are,' wrote the worthy Porral to Hugues. 'They will go mad, please God. The vidame is always indoors with the gout ; may God keep him there! They have forbidden the boatmen to ferry any body over the water at night . . . They are afraid that God will give them what they deserve.' The procurator-fiscal issued writs against all who had signed the protest. 'If you will not answer according to my pleasure,' he said to them, 'I will force you to speak.—'Really,' said Porral, who already felt the need of another liberty than political liberty, 'really, I think that after they have compelled us to deny our parents, neighbors, and friends, they will constrain us next to deny God himself.'

Yet, if the party of Savoy appeared 'sick,' that of liberty was still very weak. Both portions of the community turned at the same time towards the bishop. 'His authority is in question,' said certain patriots ; 'he will side with us against Savoy. Let us summon him.'—'The bishop cannot side with the rebels,' said the episcopal council and the mamelukes; 'let us hasten his return.' As the prelate was still beyond the Alps, the two parties wrote to him, each for itself: 'Return speedily; without you we can do nothing.'*

This was embarrassing to Pierre de la Baume. On the one hand, he clung to his principality, and at certain moments he would have withstood the duke; but on the other hand, he felt himself unable to resist that prince, and thus he fluctuated perpetually between duty and fear. He started for Geneva, not knowing what he would do there.

On Thursday, February 1, 1526, one hundred and sixty mounted citizens rode out of the city to meet the prelate: 'Why, they are all huguenots,' said Biolley, an ardent mameluke and secretary to the council, as he saw them pass. There was however something else. On each side of the bishop rode Saleneuve and Balleyson, both devoted servants of the duke, and Charles, distrusting La Baume, expected that he would obey them as if they were his guardians. The prelate loved neither his Highness nor the citizens of Geneva, 'but only to fill his purse, that he might empty it afterwards in playing *gaudeamus*,' says a contemporary. The two chamberlains, however, kept so close to him that he could not speak freely to anybody. He behaved politely towards them, and seemed to be their very humble servant; but as soon as he arrived at the bridge of Arve, where Savoy ended and the Genevese territory began, the bishop spurred his horse, and rode in front of his 'guardians,' as a sign that he was lord and master. Then assuming his right position, he obliged them from that moment to speak to him uncovered.†

The Savoyard nobles were determined, however, not to lose their prey. The next day (February 2), after dinner, as the two guardians were keeping the bishop 'at a gaming-table,' it was whispered him that Robert Vandel wanted him. Vandel, one of the Genevese liberals, possessed all his confidence, and the bishop desired much to see him; but

* Registres du Conseil du 22, 29 décembre 1525. Bonivard, *Chroniq.* ii. p. 425. Galiffe, *Matériaux*, ii. pp. 339, 340.

† Bonivard, *Chroniq.* ii. pp. 430, 431.

Saleneuve and Balleyson continued their game, and Pierre de la Baume knew not what to do to escape them. Unable to hold out any longer, he rose, alleging some very natural pretext, and hastened to a little room at the back of the house, where Vandel was. 'Well, Robert,' said the prelate rather sharply, 'they tell me that you have made a declaration in the city contrary to my authority.'—'You have been deceived,' replied Vandel, who read him the protest of the hôtel-de-ville. 'Well, well,' said the prelate, 'there is no great harm in that.' Vandel then represented to him that if Geneva owed a double obedience, one to the duke, another to the bishop, as the Council of Halberds had determined, the first would certainly swallow up the second. Pierre de la Baume had no doubt of it.—'There is somebody,' he said, lowering his voice, 'very glad of my coming, but he will be vexed afterwards. . . . I will not lose an inch of my jurisdiction, were I to spend all my property in defending it. I will have no alliance with the Swiss, however; this I promised the duke.' Vandel represented to him that the Genevans sought this alliance only to protect the episcopal sovereignty against the usurpations of Savoy; and then, knowing the prelate's avarice, he added shrewdly: 'When the alliance with the Swiss is concluded, we will proceed against the duke's creatures, we will confiscate their property, and, my lord . . . that will do you no harm.'—'What are you saying, Robert?' Vandal explained his meaning more fully. Such language moved the bishop to turn round.—'Really,' he answered. 'Well, we will talk more fully about it another time; for the moment, farewell.' The converted prelate went back to his two keepers.*

The bishop, won over by Vandel, made many reflections during the night, and the next day he desired to see the syndics and the council, who had greatly irritated him by their concessions to the duke. 'Tell me how you have been going on since my departure,' he said mildly, and then continued sharply: 'You asked me to join in your appeal to Rome, and then you withdrew from it without my con-

* Letter of Ami Porral. Galiffe, *Matériaux*, ii. pp. 341, 342. Boni vard, *Chroniq.* ii. p. 432.

sent. . . . This is bad; you should have done your duty without fear, whatever wrong might be done you. . . . I will not give up the appeal; I would rather convene the people. . . . God and the world shall be satisfied with me.' La Baume had seen the duke in Piedmont. 'His Highness,' said he, turning towards his episcopal council, 'told me that he meant to have the sovereignty of Geneva, and asked me for a day to come to an understanding about it; but I answered immediately that although Pierre de la Baume is his humble subject, his Highness has no business in my city. . . . I am determined to maintain the rights of my church and the liberties of my city—until death.' Then turning again to the syndics: 'As for those who have retired into Switzerland,' he said, 'I hold them to be honest people, and, saving the alliance, I approve of all they may do.'

On a sudden the bishop asked himself what he should say to the duke if such language was reported to him. . . . Startled at his own courage, he became confused, hesitated, and, speaking low to the first syndic, he said: 'I wish you did as they do at Venice. Your council is not secret; it ought to be so. Understand clearly that I embrace the city party; but the benefices I possess in his Highness's states compel me to do so secretly. . . . If in any circumstances I seem opposed to your interests, remember that it is in appearance only.' At the same time, the bishop wrote and told the fugitives of his intention to pay all the expenses which the independence of the city necessitated; but he added: 'If I write you the contrary, pay no attention to it; I shall do so only through fear of the duke, and not to make him angry.' The spirit of his policy was deception. Such was the last bishop of Geneva.*

The annual nomination of the syndics was about to take place, and the city was in great commotion. Both parties counted on this election: the mamelukes to establish the duke in Geneva, and the huguenots to expel him. The great patriots were in exile; victory seemed assured to the ducals.

* *Journal de Balard*, pp. 41–43. Bonivard, *Chroniq.* ii. p. 433. Gautier MS. Savyon, *Annales*, p. 130.

Yet the timidest even of the huguenots took courage, and swore to elect 'honest men who would secure the liberty of the city.' The general council having assembled on the 4th of February, 1526, the mameluke syndic Montyon proposed eight candidates, from whom, according to the order prescribed by the duke, they must elect four syndics. Then Robert Vandel stood up: 'I am authorized by the citizens,' he said to Montyon, 'to inform you that they will not be muzzled (*brigidari*).' Then, turning to the people, he asked: 'Is it not true?' All replied: 'Yes, yes!' many at the same time calling out 'Jean Philippe.' Philippe was not only not one of the eight, but he was one of the exiles. 'We will make Jean Philippe syndic,' repeated the huguenots, 'and thus show that he and the others in Switzerland are good citizens.' If Besançon Hugues was not the popular choice, it was probably because the people were still angry with that noble exile for his refusal in the preceding year.

At this moment the bishop's procurator-fiscal Mandalla appeared. La Baume's courage was not heroic; he trembled at the idea of a purely huguenot election, and desired to get a moderate list—half servile, half liberal—passed. In his name, Mandalla proposed four candidates, among whom was the traitor Cartelier. 'That will quiet all angry feelings,' said the procurator. It was not a clever manœuvre, for Cartelier's name was sufficient to discredit the others.

The polling began. Each man went up to the secretary and gave in his vote. The most energetic of the two parties counted the votes received. The procurator-fiscal watched the election with anxiety. Soon, vexed and dispirited, he ran and told the bishop that the people took no account of his message. . . . Pierre de la Baume was frightened. The zealous fiscal ran again to the polling-place: 'My lord conjures you,' he said, 'at least not to elect Jean Philippe, considering that he is not in the city.'—'We will make no choice that will be disagreeable to the bishop,' they answered politely, and at the same time continued giving their votes to the exile. The people of Geneva were determined to show, in a striking manner, that they were breaking with Savoy and uniting with Switzerland, and treading boldly in the path of liberty. The bishop, still more alarmed, finding that his procurator obtained nothing, sent his vicar to protest, in his name, against so dangerous an election. 'It shall be done as our prince pleases,' said they courteously; and then, 'without noise or murmur, were elected four huguenots. Sire Jean Philippe (they said in the city) received more votes than any of the others.' The citizens cared no more for the bishop than for the duke, when the reëstablishment of their liberties was concerned. The people had never been more united; the opposition counted only eleven, and after the election everybody declared that they sided with the majority. They said one to another that a free and courageous people, if God comes to their aid, can never perish.

Confusion was in the bishop's palace. As soon as opposition is made to the duke, said some, revolution breaks its bounds . . . this election must be annulled. The bishop ordered that another general council should be held on the morrow, and, calculating on his personal influence, he appeared at it, attended by his councillors and officers; but the people were deaf, and confirmed Philippe's election; only they appointed his brother-in-law (D. France) to take his place during his absence. Not satisfied with this, the people repealed all statutes contrary to the liberties of Geneva passed under fear of Charles of Savoy. The bishop, alarmed at these republican proceedings, exclaimed: 'Is there nobody that wishes to maintain these ordinances?' No one answered. Everything fell, and the ancient constitution was restored. After having changed the laws, they set about changing the persons. They would have no partisans of Savoy to preserve the liberties of Geneva. Huguenot councillors were elected in the place of mamelukes. The restoration of Genevese liberties had been so promptly accomplished that the ducal faction could not believe their eyes. 'Our *brewers* were never more astonished,' said the huguenots. (The *brewers* were the men who *brewed* or plotted treason.) There were men in the ducal party who changed their opinions as the wind changes; they were now seen accosting the patriots and shaking hands with them. . .

'See,' said the huguenots, 'how well they counterfeit the air of good fellowship!' . . . Then all true friends of their country exclaimed: 'Let us praise God! *Laus Deo!*'*

Thus did liberty triumph. The Genevese people had restored their franchises, dismissed the mamelukes, rejected the cruel protectorate of Charles III., sought the alliance of Switzerland; and after all that, they gave God the glory.†

As the cause of Savoy was lost, the bishop, so long wavering, made a show of placing himself on the side of the free and the bold. He sent Pierre Bertholo to carry this important news to Jean Philippe and all those exiles of whom he was so afraid. The latter had not lost their time; they endeavored to enlighten the Swiss, and Hugues continually argued and repeated that Geneva was not under subjection to the duke. At this time Bertholo arrived. 'The ordinances of Savoy are repealed,' he told the refugees; 'patriots replaced the serviles everywhere, and one of you has been elected syndic—Jean Philippe!' They could hardly believe this news. What! one of these wretched fugitives, of these *mendicants* (as their enemies called them), raised by the people of Geneva to the head of the State! . . . What a refutation of the ducal calumnies! But the 'foreigners' did not forget themselves in the joy which this message caused them. Taking Bertholo with them, they proceeded to the Bernese council, and reported the unexpected intelligence brought by the messenger. 'Up to the present time,' said the avoyer, 'I have invited Besançon Hugues alone, as your chief, to sit down at my side; now, Messire Jean Philippe, take your seat above Besançon, as syndic of Geneva.' The alliance would no longer meet with obstacles. 'We accept you as fellow-freemen,' continued the avoyer, 'without heed to those growlers and their threats, which do not last long now-a-days.'‡

* Registres du Conseil des 4, 5, 10, 12 février. *Journal de Balard*, pp. 41–45. Galiffe, *Matériaux*, ii. p. 347. Bonivard, *Chroniq.* ii. pp. 436–439.

† Gautier MS. Registres du Conseil des 11 et 13 février 1526. *Balard's Journal*, p. 48.

‡ Registres du Conseil du 24 février. Bonivard, *Chroniq.* ii. p. 439.

The people of Geneva were about to rise, if we may so speak, from the grave. They had acted with decision, with energy, with unwavering firmness. They desired to have for their magistrates none but men able to maintain their laws and independence, and had boldly erased from the code of the republic all ordinances contrary to the liberties of Geneva. Accordingly, 'a person of mark,' who lived at the beginning of the seventeenth century, exclaimed, after studying these facts: 'This history is a marvellous one, and calls to my mind a tract in the *Philetes* of Plato, touching the moral good comprised in the three ideas: *Reality*, *Proportion*, and *Truth*. It is full of the special marks of the wise and merciful providence of God, who has guided, up to this present hour, this *ship of his miracles* through an infinity of shoals. The more thoroughly we contemplate human action, so much the deeper appear the counsels of God.'* What we are about to see appears to confirm these words.

---

hands; affection and confidence were in every feature. 'In the name of the most holy and most high Trinity,' said the three free states, 'in the name of God the Father, Son, and Holy Ghost, we reciprocally promise mutual friendship and intercourse, in order that we may be able to preserve the good that God has given us in justice, repose, and true peace. . . . And if hereafter one or many should wish to molest the syndics, councils, or freemen of the city of Geneva in their persons, honor, goods, or estate, we, the avoyers, councils, and freemen of the cities of Berne and Friburg—by virtue of our oath made and sworn—are bound to give the said city favor, aid, and succor, and to march out our armies . . at their charge, however.'* The required formalities having been fulfilled: 'Gentlemen,' said Jean Philippe, 'we will depart and carry this good news ourselves to our country.' The councils of Berne and Friburg ordered that a number of deputies from each canton equal to that of the fugitives should accompany them, with power to seal the alliance at Geneva. All the exiles left on the same day; but how different was the return from that breathless flight which had not long ago brought them to Friburg! 'They went, not in fear and dread as they had come, but taking the high road through the Pays de Vaud, where all strove to do them honor; for,' says Bonivard, 'they still smelt the reek of the roast meat of Morat.'

On the 23rd of February the news of the speedy arrival of the exiles and delegates of the cantons spread through Geneva; citizen told it to citizen, great was the joy, and arrangements were made for their reception. The syndics on horseback, carrying their batons, followed by all who had horses, went out to meet them, and the people collected near the Swiss gate to receive them. A salute of guns announced their approach. They walked three abreast: in the middle was a Genevan fugitive, on his right and left a deputy of Berne and of Friburg; this order, continued through the whole line, announced more clearly than all the rest the close union of the three cities. Geneva, allied to the Swiss, might

* *Hist. Helvétique*, v. p. 10. We have followed the original document, which is still to be seen in the public library at Berne.

be able to preserve its independence ; Geneva was saved. A conversion had been wrought in its people. Hitherto they had turned to the south ; now they turned towards the north : they began to cast off Rome and to catch a glimpse of Wittemberg. There are certain movements in nations that transform their destinies. The citizens could not take their eyes off those unhappy men who had had such difficulty in escaping the archers of Savoy, and who, strange to say, were returning holding Berne and Friburg by the hand. They had gone away, still disposed to appeal to Rome ; but having heard much talk in Switzerland of the Reformation, they were to be the first to welcome Farel and the Gospel to Geneva. . . . Relations and friends pressed in their arms these fugitives, whom they had thought they should never see again. 'They were sumptuously entertained at the hôtel-de-ville. A *morality on the said alliance* was performed; and a bonfire was lighted on the Place Molard.'* The Council of Two Hundred was convened.

This important council assembled, but instead of two hundred citizens, three hundred and twenty met together. This sitting was to be a festival ; everybody desired to be present. It was known that Hugues would speak : the respect they felt for the great citizen and his companions in misfortune, the adventures he had to relate, mixed up (it was reported) with strange facts, excited interest and curiosity. Hugues rose to speak : there was deep silence : 'You know, sirs,' he began, 'that five or six months ago, on the morrow of Holy Cross (September 15, 1525), we left here in great haste by different roads ; without communicating with one another, not knowing where to go to escape the rage of the most illustrious duke, Monseigneur of Savoy. We were warned by friends that, on the demand of certain persons in this city, the prince was resolved to take us and put us ignominiously to death, because we had resisted innovations opposed to our liberties. Ah ! sirs, that was no child's play, believe me. The archers and agents of my lord of Savoy

* Berne MS. *Histoire de Genève*, usually ascribed to Bonivard. See also Gautier MS. Registres du Conseil du 24 février. Bonivard, *Chroniq.* ii. pp. 439, 440.

pursued us as far as St. Claude, from St. Claude to Besançon, and beyond. . . . We had to travel day and night in the woods, through wind and rain, not knowing where to go in quest of safety. . . . At last we considered that we had friends at Friburg, and thither we went.'

The citizens, rivetting their eyes on Hugues, did not lose a word of his narrative and of the details which he added. They seemed to bear him company through those woods and mountains, among the ravines and snow; they fancied they heard behind them the tramp of the armed men in pursuit of them. . . . What struck them was not only the epic element in the flight and return of these free men, of which ancient Greece would doubtless have made one of the finest myths in her history; it was in an especial manner the sovereign importance which these acts had for them. During those sacred days, Geneva and her destinies had turned on their axis; her gates were opened on the side of light and liberty; the flight, the residence at Berne and Friburg, and the return of Hugues and his companions, are one of the most important pages in the annals of the city.

Hugues continued: he told them how Friburg and Berne had seen no other means of securing their liberties than by receiving them into their alliance. . . . 'Here are the letters duly sealed with their great seals,' said the noble orator, presenting a parchment. 'They are written in German; but I will tell you their substance, article by article, without deceiving you in any—on my life.' He read the act of alliance, and added: 'Sirs, my comrades and I here present promise you, on our lives and goods, that the said citizenship is such. Consider, sirs, if you will ratify and accept it.' The assembly testified its approbation with thanks to God, and resolved to convoke a general council for the next day.*

The catholic party and the ducal party were aroused. The Swiss alliance, an immense innovation, threatened all the conquests they had made with so much trouble in Geneva during so many generations. The bishop, full of un-

* Registres du Conseil du 24 février 1526.

easiness, consulted with the canons and some others on whom he thought he could rely. All told him that if Berne had its way in Geneva, there would be no more bishop, no more prince. To work then! All the powers of feudalism and the papacy conspired against an alliance which first gave Geneva liberty and afterwards the Gospel. At first they wished to prevent the general council from meeting. It was customary to summon it by tolling the great bell; now Canon Lutry had the key of the tower where this bell hung. In the evening the reverend father, followed by some armed men, climbed step by step up the narrow stairs which led to the bell-loft, and placed the men in garrison there. 'You are here,' he said, 'to defend the bell and not to give it up;' he then went down, double-locked the door, and carried away the key. In the morning the door was found to be locked, and Lutry refused to open it. 'The canons,' it was said in the city, 'are opposed to the assembling of the people.' The irritated citizens ran together. 'Whereupon there was a great uproar and alarm in the church of St. Pierre, so that De Lutry was constrained to open the door and give up the bell.'*

It was all over; they resolved still to fight a last battle, even with the certainty of being defeated. The general council met; the bishop went thither in person, attended by his episcopal followers, in the hope that his presence might intimidate the huguenots. 'I am head, pastor, and prince of the community,' he said. 'It concerns my affairs, and I wish to know what will be laid before you.'—'It is not the custom for my lord to be present,' said Hugues; 'the citizens transact none but political matters here† which concern them wholly. His presence, however, is always pleasing to us, provided nothing be deduced from it prejudicial to our liberties.' Thereupon Hugues proposed the alliance. Then Stephen de la Mare got up. In 1519 he had shone in the foremost rank of the patriots; but, an ardent Roman Catholic, he had since then placed liberty in the second rank and the Church in the first. It was he who had undertaken

* *Journal de Balard*, p. 51. Savyon, *Annales*, p. 131.

† 'De politia.'—Registers of the Council, Feb. 25, 1526.

to oppose the proposition. 'It is sufficient for us to live under the protection of God, St. Peter, and the bishop. . . . I oppose the alliance.' De la Mare could not proceed, so great was the confusion that broke out in the assembly; the indignation was general, yet order and quiet were restored at last, and the treaty was read. 'Will you ratify this alliance?' said first syndic G. Bergeron. 'Yes, yes!' they shouted on every side. The syndic continued: 'Let those who approve of it hold up their hands!' There was a forest of hands, every man holding up both at once. 'We desire it, we approve of it,' they shouted again. 'Those of the contrary opinion?' added the syndic. Six hands only were raised in opposition. Pierre de la Baume from his episcopal throne looked down upon this spectacle with anxiety. Even to the last he had reckoned upon success. By selecting De la Mare, the old leader of the patriots, and placing him at the head of the movement against the alliance with the Swiss, he fancied that he had hit upon an admirable combination; but his hopes were disappointed. Alarmed and irritated, seeing what this vote would lead to, and determined to keep his principality at any cost, the bishop-prince exclaimed: 'I do not consent to this alliance; I appeal to our holy father the pope and to his majesty the emperor.' But to no purpose did the Bishop of Geneva, on the eve of losing his states, appeal to powers the most dreaded—no one paid any attention to his protest. Joy beamed on every face, and the words 'pope, emperor,' were drowned by enthusiastic shouts of 'the Swiss. . . . the Swiss and liberty!' Besançon Hugues, who, although on the side of independence, was attached to the bishop, exerted all his influence with him. 'Very well, then,' said the versatile prelate, 'if your franchises permit you to contract an alliance without your prince, do so.'—'I take note of this declaration,' said Hugues; and then he added: 'More than once the citizens have concluded such alliances without their prince—with Venice, Cologne, and other cities.' The Register mentions that after this the prince went away satisfied. We rather doubt it; but however that may be, the bishop by his presence had helped to sanction the measure which he had so much at heart to prevent.*

What comforted Pierre de la Baume was the sight of Besançon Hugues at the head of the movement. That great citizen assured the bishop that the alliance with Switzerland was not opposed to his authority; and he did so with perfect honesty.† Hugues was simply a conservative. He desired an alliance with Switzerland in order to preserve Geneva in her present position. He desired to maintain the prelate not only as bishop, but also as prince: all his opposition was aimed at the usurpations of Savoy. But there were minds in Geneva already wishing for more. Certain citizens, in whom the new aspirations of modern times were beginning to show themselves, said that the municipal liberties of the city were continually fettered, and often crushed, by the princely authority of the bishop. Had he not been seen to favor the cruel murders which the Savoyard power had committed in Geneva? 'The liberties of the people and the temporal lordship of the bishop cannot exist together; one or other of the two powers must succumb,' they said. The history of succeeding ages has shown but too plainly the reasonableness of these fears. Wherever the bishop has remained king, he has trampled the liberties of the people under foot. There we find no representative government, no liberty of the press, no religious liberty. In the eyes of the bishop-prince these great blessings of modern society are monsters to be promptly stifled. Some Genevans comprehended the danger that threatened them, and, wishing to preserve the liberties they had received from their ancestors, saw no other means than by withdrawing from the ministers of religion a worldly power which Jesus Christ had refused them beforehand. Some—but their number was very small then—went further, and began to ask whether the authority of a bishop in religious matters was not still more contrary to the precepts of the Gospel, which acknowledged no other authority than that of the

* Council Registers, Feb. 25. *Balard's Journal*, p. 51. Galiffe, *Matériaux*, ii. p. 362. Savyon, *Annales*, p. 131.

† Galiffe, *Matériaux*, ii. p. 364.

word of God; and whether liberty could ever exist in the State so long as there was a despot in the Church. Such were the great questions beginning to be discussed in Geneva more than three hundred years ago: the present time seems destined to solve them.

In spite of the loyal assurances of Besançon Hugues, the bishop was disturbed. Sitting with liberty at his side, he felt ill at ease; and the terror spreading through the ranks of the clergy could not fail to reach him. If the bishop of Geneva should be deprived of his principality, who can tell if men will not one day deprive the pope of his kingship? The alarm of the canons, priests, and friends of the papacy continued to increase. Did they not know that the Reformation was daily gaining ground in many of the confederated states? Friburg, indeed, was still catholic; but Zurich was no longer so, and everything announced that Berne would soon secede. The great light was to come from another country, from a country that spoke the language of Geneva; but Geneva was then receiving from Switzerland the first gleams that precede the day. Some Genevans were already beginning to profess, rather undisguisedly, their new religious tendencies; Robert Vandel, the bishop's friend, openly defended the Reformation. 'Sire Robert is not very good for Friburg,' said some; 'but he is good for Berne, *very good!*' which meant that he preferred Holy Scripture to the pope. The priests said that if Geneva was united to Switzerland, there was an end of the privileges of the clergy; that simple christians would begin to occupy themselves with religion; and that in Geneva, as in Basle, Scaffhausen, and Berne, laymen would talk about the faith of the Church. Now there was nothing of which the clergy were more afraid. The ministers of the Romish religion, instead of examining the Scriptures, of finding in them doctrines capable of satisfying the wants of man, and of propagating them by mild persuasion, were occupied with very different matters, and would not suffer any one but themselves to think even of the Bible and its contents. Never was a calling made a more thorough fiction. It was said of them: *They have taken away the key of knowledge;*

they enter not in themselves, and them that were entering in they hindered.

These ideas became stronger every day, and the attachment of the priests to their old customs was more stubborn than ever. It was difficult to avoid an outbreak; but it should be observed that it was provoked by the canons. These rich and powerful clerics, who were determined to oppose the alliance with all their power, and, if necessary, to defend their clerical privileges with swords and arquebuses, got together a quantity of arms in the house of De Lutry, the most fanatical of their number, in order to make use of them 'against the city.' On the night of the 26th of February, these reverend seigniors, as well as the principal mamelukes, crept one after another into this house, and held a consultation. A rumor spread through the city, and the citizens told one another 'that M. de Lutry and M. de Vausier had brought together a number of people secretly to get up a riot.' The patriots, prompt and resolute in character, were determined not to give the mamelukes the least chance of recovering their power. 'The people rose in arms,' the house was surrounded; it would appear that some of the chiefs of the ducal party came out, and that swords were crossed. 'A few were wounded,' says the chronicler. However, 'proclamation was made to the sound of the trumpet through the city,' and order was restored.*

The conspiracy of the canons having thus failed, the members of the feudal and papal party thought everything lost. They fancied they saw an irrevocable fatality dragging them violently to their destruction. The principal supporters of the old order of things, engrossed by the care of their compromised security, thought only of escaping, like birds of night, before the first beams of day. They disguised themselves and slipped out unobserved, some by one gate, some by another. It was almost a universal panic. The impetuous Lutry escaped first, with one of his colleagues; the bishop-prince's turn came next. Bitterly upbraided by the Count of Genevois for not having prevented the alliance, Pierre de la Baume took alarm both at the huguenots and

* Bonivard, *Chroniq.* ii. p. 444. *Journal de Balard*, pp. 52, 53.

the duke, and escaped to St. Claude. The agents of his Highness of Savoy trembled in their castles; the vidame hastened to depart on the one side, and the goaler of the Château de l'Ile, who was nicknamed the *sultan*, did the same on the other.

The most terrified were the clerics and the mamelukes who had been present at the meeting at Canon de Lutry's. They had taken good care not to stop after the alarm that had been given them, and when the order was made by sound of trumpet for every man to retire to his own house, they had hastened to escape in disguise, trembling and hopeless. The next morning the city watch, followed by the sergeants, forcibly entered De Lutry's house, and seized the arms, which had been carefully hidden; but they found the nest empty, for all the birds had flown. 'If they had not escaped,' said Syndic Balard, 'they would have been in danger of death.' The canons who had not taken flight sent two of their number to the hôtel-de-ville to say to the syndics: 'Will you keep us safe and sure in the city? if not, will you give us safe-conduct, that we may leave it?' They thought only of following their colleagues.

The flight of the 26th of February was the counterpart of the 15th of September. In September the new times had disappeared in Geneva for a few weeks only; in February the old times were departing for ever. The Genevese rejoiced as they saw these leeches disappear, who had bled them so long, even to the very marrow. 'The priests and the Savoyards,' they said, 'are like wolves driven from the woods by hunger: there is nothing left for them to take, and they are compelled to go elsewhere for their prey.' Nothing could be more favorable to the Swiss alliance and to liberty than this general flight. The partisans of the duke and of the bishop having evacuated the city, the senate and the people remained masters. The grateful citizens ascribed all the glory to God, and exclaimed: 'The sovereignty is now in the hands of the council, without the interference of either magistrates or people. *Everything was done by the grace of God.*'*

* *Journal de Balard*, pp. 52, 53. Galiffe, *Matériaux*, ii. p. 368. Bonivard, *Police de Genève*, pp. 392, 393; *Chroniq.* ii. pp. 440, 444.

At the very time when the men of feudalism were quitting Geneva, those of liberty were arriving, and the great transition was effected. On the 11th of March eight Swiss ambassadors entered the city in the midst of a numerous crowd and under a salute of artillery: they were the envoys from the cantons who had come to receive the oaths of Geneva and give theirs in return. The next day these freemen, sons of the conquerors of Charles the Bold, all glowing with desire to protect Geneva from the attacks of Charles the Good, appeared before the general council. At their head was Sebastian de Diesbach, an energetic man, devout catholic, great captain, and skilful diplomatist. 'Magnificent lords and very dear fellow-freemen,' he said, 'Friburg and Berne acquaint you that they are willing to live and die with you. . . . Will you swear to observe the alliance that has been drawn up?'—'Yes,' exclaimed all the Genevans, without one dissentient voice. Then the Swiss ambassadors stood up and raised their hands towards heaven to make the oath. Every one looked with emotion on those eight Helvetians of lofty stature and martial bearing, the representatives of the energetic populations whose military glory at this time surpassed that of all other nations. The noble Sebastian having pronounced the oath of alliance, his companions raised their hands also, and repeated his words aloud. The citizens exclaimed with transport: 'We desire it, we desire it!' Then with deep emotion said some: 'Those men were born in a happy hour, who have brought about so good a business.' Eight deputies of Geneva, among whom were Francis Favre, and G. Hugues, brother of Besançon, proceeded to Berne and Friburg to make the same oath on the part of their fellow-citizens.*

The men of the old times were not discouraged: if they had been beaten at Geneva, might they not conquer at Friburg and Berne? Indefatigable in their exertions, they resolved to set every engine to work in order to succeed. Stephen de la Mare, three other deputies of the duke,

* Registers of March 12, 1526. *Balard's Journal*, p. 54. Spon, *Hist. de Genève*, ii. p. 392. Gautier MS. Galiffe, *Matériaux*, ii. pp. 369–392. Savyon, *Annales*, p. 132.

Michael Nergaz, and forty-two mamelukes went into Switzerland to break off the alliance. But Friburg and Berne replied: 'For nothing in the world will we depart from what we have sworn.' The hand of God was manifest, and accordingly when Hugues heard of this answer, he exclaimed: 'God himself is conducting our affairs.'

Then was Geneva intoxicated with joy. On the morrow after the taking of the oath in the general council, the delight of the people broke out all over the city. Bonfires were lighted in the public places; there was much dancing, masquerading, and shouting; patriotic and satirical songs reëchoed through the streets; there was an outburst of happiness and liberty. 'When a people have been kept so long in the leash,' said Bonivard, 'as soon as they are let loose, they are apt to indulge in dangerous gambols.'*

While the people were rejoicing after their fashion, the wise men of the council resolved to show their gratitude to God in another manner. The councils issued a general pardon. Then an indulgence and concord were proclaimed, and all bound themselves to live in harmony. They went further: they desired to repair the injustice of the old régime. 'Bonivard,' said some, 'has been unjustly deprived of his priory of St. Victor because of his patriotism.'—'What would you have us do?' they answered; 'the pope has given the benefice to another.'—'I should not make it a serious matter of conscience to disobey the pope,' said Bonivard slily.—'And as for us,' said the syndics, 'we do not care much about him.' In later years the magistrates of Geneva gave the most palpable proofs of this declaration; for the moment they confined themselves to resettling the ex-prior in the house of which the pope had robbed him. Another more important reparation had still to be effected.

In this solemn hour, when the cause of liberty was triumphing, amid the joyful shouts of a whole people, two names were pronounced with sighs and even with tears: 'Berthelier! Lévrier!' said the noblest of the citizens. 'We have reached the goal, but it was they who traced out

* *Balard's Journal*, pp. 54, 55. Bonivard, *Chroniq.* ii. p. 447. Roset MS. *Chroniq.* liv. ii. ch. x.

the road with their blood.' An enfranchised people ought not to be ungrateful to their liberators. By a singular coincidence the anniversary of Berthelier's death revived more keenly the memory of that disastrous event. On the 23d of August a hundred citizens appeared before the council: 'Seven years ago this very day,' they said, 'Philibert Berthelier was beheaded in the cause of the republic; we pray that his memory be honored, and that, for such end, a solemn procession shall march to the ringing of bells from the church of St. Pierre to that of Our Lady of Grace, where the hero's head was buried.' That was not without danger: Our Lady's was on the Savoy frontier, and his Highness's soldiers might easily have disturbed the ceremony. The council preferred ordering a solemn service in memory of Berthelier, Lévrier, and others who died for the republic. The Genevans, acknowledging the great blessings with which the hand of God had enriched them, wished to repair all wrongs, honor all self-sacrifice, and walk with a firm step in the paths of justice and of liberty. It was by such sacrifices that they meant to celebrate their deliverance.*

Geneva did not stand alone in feeling these aspirations towards modern times. It was doubtless in the sixteenth century a great example of liberty; but the movement tending towards new things was felt among all those nations whom the Bible compares to a troubled sea: the tide was rising over the whole surface. During the first half of the sixteenth century Europe was awaking; the love of ancient learning enlightened the mind, and the brilliant rays of christian truth, so long intercepted, were beginning to pierce the clouds. A world till then unknown was opening before man's astonished eyes, and everything seemed to announce a civilisation, independence, and life as yet unknown to the human race. The mind of Europe awoke, and moving forward took its station in the light, insatiable of life, of knowledge, and of liberty.

The great question was to know whether the new world,

* Registers of the Council, Aug. 23, 1526. Gautier MS.

which seemed to be issuing from the abyss, would repose on a solid foundation. More than once already awakened society had appeared to break its bonds, to throw off its shroud, and uplift the stone from the sepulchre. It had happened thus in the ninth, eleventh, and twelfth centuries, when the most eminent minds began to ask the reason of things;* but each time humanity had wanted the necessary strength, the new birth was not completed, the tomb closed over it again, and it fell once more into a heavy slumber.

Would it be the same now? Would this awakening of the sixteenth century be also like a watch in the night?

Certain men, elect of God, were to give this new movement the strength it needed. Let us turn towards that country whence Geneva would receive those heroes baptised with the Holy Spirit and with fire.

The scene of our history is about to change. 'A man of mark' whom we have already quoted, said, when speaking of Geneva: 'On this platform appear actors who do not speak so loud as great kings and emperors on the spacious theatre of their states; but what matters how the speaker is dressed, if he says what he ought?'† We are leaving for a time this modest platform. We shall no longer have to speak of a little nation whose greatest heroes are obscure citizens. We are entering a mighty empire where we shall be in the company of kings and queens, of great personages and famous courtiers. Yet the dissimilarity between the two theatres is not so wide as one might expect. In that vast country of France, where historians usually describe nothing but the great stream formed by the numerous combinations of policy, a few springs are seen welling forth, at first unnoticed, but they swell by degrees, and their waters will one day have more influence on the destiny of the world than the floods of that mighty river. One of these springs appeared at Etaples, close upon the shores of the Channel; another at Gap in Dauphiny; and others in other places. But the most important, that which was to unite them all and spread a new life even to the most distant

* 'Quærere rationem quomodo sit.'—Anselm.

† 'Lettre d'un personnage de marque,' Berne MS. *Hist. Helvét.* 125.

countries, welled up at Noyon, an ancient and once illustrious town of Picardy. It was France who gave Lefèvre and Farel—France, too, gave Calvin. That French people, who (as some say) cared for nothing but war and diplomacy; that home of a philosophy often sceptical and sometimes incredulous and mocking; that nation which proclaimed and still proclaims itself the eldest daughter of Rome, gave to the world the Reformation of Calvin and of Geneva—the great Reformation, that which is the strength of the most influential nations, and which reaches even to the ends of the world. France has no nobler title of renown: we do not forget it. Perhaps she will not always disdain it, and after having enriched others she will enrich herself. It will be a great epoch for her future development, when her dearest children drink at those living fountains that burst from her bosom in the sixteenth century, or rather at that eternal fountain of the Word of God, whose waters are for the healing of nations.

BOOK II.

FRANCE. FAVORABLE TIMES.

CHAPTER I.

A MAN OF THE PEOPLE AND A QUEEN.

(1522–1526.)

THE Reformation was concerned both with God and man: its aim was to restore the paths by which God and man unite, by which the Creator enters again into the creature. This path, opened by Jesus Christ with power, had been blocked up in ages of superstition. The Reformation cleared the road, and reopened the door.

We willingly acknowledge that the middle ages had not ignored the wonderful work of redemption: truth was then covered with a veil rather than destroyed, and if the noxious weeds be plucked up with which the field had gradually been filled, the primitive soil is laid bare. Take away the worship paid to the Virgin, the saints, and the host; take away meritorious, magical, and supererogatory works, and other errors besides, and we arrive at simple faith in the Father, Son, and Holy Ghost. It is not the same when we come to the manner in which God enters again into man. Roman catholicism had gone astray in this respect; there were a few mystics in her fold who pretended to tread this mysterious way; but their heated imaginations misled them, while in the place of this inward worship the Roman doctors substituted certain ecclesiastical formalities mechanically executed. The only means of recovering this royal road was to return to the apostolical times and seek for it in the Gospel. Three acts are necessary to unite man again with God. Religion penetrates into man by the depths of his conscience; thence it rises to the height of his knowledge, and finally pervades the activity of his whole life.

The conscience of man had been seared not only by the sin which clings to our nature, but also by the indulgences and mortifications imposed by the Church. It required to be vivified by faith in the atoning blood of Christ.

Tradition, scholasticism, papal infallibility, mingling their confused questions and numerous superstitions with the natural darkness of the heart, man's understanding had been completely obscured. It needed to be enlightened by the torch of God's word.

A society of priests, exercising absolute dominion, had enslaved christendom. For this theocratic and clerical society it was necessary to substitute a living society of the children of God.

With Luther began the awakening of the human conscience. Terrified at the sin he discovered in himself, he found no other means of peace but faith in the grace of Christ Jesus. This starting-point of the German reformer was also that of every Reformation.

To Zwingle belongs in an especial manner the work of the understanding. The first want of the Swiss reformer was to know God. He inquired into *the false and the true, the reason of faith.* Formed by the study of the Greek classics, he had the gift of understanding and interpreting Scripture, and as soon as he reached Zurich he began his career as a reformer by explaining the New Testament.

Calvin perfected the third work necessary for the Reformation. His characteristic is not, as the world imagines, the teaching of the doctrines to which he has given his name; his great idea was to unite all believers into one body, having the same life, and acting under the same Chief. The Reform was essentially, in his eyes, the renovation of the individual, of the human mind, of christendom. To the Church of Rome, powerful as a government, but otherwise enslaved and dead, he wished to oppose a regenerated Church whose members had found through faith the liberty of the children of God, and which should be not only a pillar of truth, but a principle of moral purification for all the human race. He conceived the bold design of forming for these modern times a society in which the individual liberty and equality of its members should be combined with adhesion to an immutable truth, because it came from God, and to a holy and strict, but freely accepted law. An energetic effort towards moral perfection was one of the devices written on his standard. Not only did he conceive the grand idea we have pointed out; he realised it. He gave movement and life to that enlightened and sanctified society which was the object of his noble desires. And now wherever churches are founded on the twofold basis of truth and morality—even should they be at the antipodes—we may affirm that Calvin's sublime idea is extended and carried out.

It resulted from the very nature of this society that the democratic element would be introduced into the nations where it was established. By the very act of giving truth and morality to the members of this body, he gave them liberty. All were called to search for light in the Bible; all were to be taught immediately of God, and not by priests only; all were called to give to others the truth they had found. 'Each one of you,' said Calvin, 'is consecrated to Christ, in order that you may be associated with him in his kingdom, and be partakers of his priesthood.'* How could the citizens of this spiritual republic be thought otherwise than worthy to have a share in its government? The fifteenth chapter of the Acts shows us the *brethren* united with the apostles and elders in the proceedings of the Church, and such is the order that Calvin desired to reëstablish. We have already pointed out some of the reasons by virtue of which constitutional liberty was introduced into the bosom of the nations who received the Reform of Geneva. To these must be added the reason just mentioned.

Disunited from each other, the three great principles of Luther, Zwingle, and Calvin would have been insufficient.

* Calvin on St. Peter, ch. ii. v. 9.

Faith, if it had not possessed for its foundation the knowledge of the Word of Ged, would have easily degenerated into a mystical enthusiasm. The abstract authority of Scripture, separated from a living faith, would have ended in a dead orthodoxy ; and the social principle, deprived of these two foundations, would have succeeded only in raising one of those artificial edifices in the air which fall down as soon as built.

God, by giving in the sixteenth century a man who to the lively faith of Luther and the scriptural understanding of Zwingle joined an organising faculty and a creative mind, gave the complete reformer. If Luther laid the foundations, if Zwingle and others built the walls, Calvin completed the temple of God.

We shall have to see how this doctor arrived at a knowledge of the truth ; we shall have to study his labors and his struggles until the moment when, quitting for ever a country whose soil trembled under his feet and threatened to swallow him up, he went to plant upon a lowly Alpine hill that standard around which he meditated rallying the scattered members of Jesus Christ. But we must first see what was the state of France at the time when the reformer was brought to the Gospel.

The history of the Reformation in France, prior to the establishment of Calvin at Geneva, is divided into two parts: the first includes the favorable times, the second the unfavorable. We confess that the favorable times were occasionally the reverse, and that the unfavorable times were often favorable; and yet we believe that, generally speaking, this distinction may be justified. This subject has been frequently treated of; we shall, however, have to describe some phases of the French Reformation which have not always been set forth by those who have written its history.

Two persons, a man and a woman, whose social position and character present the most striking contrasts, labored with particular zeal to propagate the Gospel in France at the epoch of the Reformation.

The woman appears first. She is the most beautiful and intelligent, the wittiest, most amiable and influential, and, with the exception of her daughter, the greatest of her age. Sister, mother of kings, herself a queen, grandmother of the monarch whom France (right or wrong) has extolled the most, namely, Henry IV., she lived much in the great world, in great ceremonials, with great personages, among the magnificence of the Louvre, St. Germain, and Fontainebleau. This woman is Margaret of Angoulême, Duchess of Alençon, Queen of Navarre, and sister of Francis I.

The man who appears next (he was younger than her by seventeen years) contrasts with all these grandeurs by the lowness of his origin. He is a man of the people, a Picardin; his grandfather was a cooper at Pont l'Evêque; his father was secretary to the bishop, and, in the day of his greatest influence in the world, he apprenticed his own brother Anthony to a bookbinder. Simple, frugal, poor, of a disposition 'rather morose and bashful'*—such is the humble veil that hides the greatness of his genius and the strength of his will. This man is Calvin.

This man and this woman, so opposite as regards their condition in the world, resemble each other in their principal features. They both possess faith in the great truths of the Gospel; they love Jesus Christ; they have the same zeal for spreading with unwearied activity the truths so dear to them; they have the same compassion for the miserable, and especially for the victims of religious persecution. But while the man sometimes presumes upon his manly strength, the woman truly belongs to the weaker sex. She possesses indeed a moral virtue which resists the seductions of the age; she keeps herself pure in the midst of a depraved court; but she has also that weakness which disposes one to be too indulgent, and permits herself to be led away by certain peculiarities of contemporary society. We see her writing tales whose origin may be explained and even justified, since their object was to unveil the immorality of priests and monks, but they are nevertheless a lamentable tribute paid to the spirit of her age. While Calvin sets up against the papacy *a forehead harder than adamant*, Margaret, even in

* Calvin, *Preface to the Psalms.*

the days of her greatest zeal, is careful not to break with Rome. At last she yields, outwardly at least, to the sovereign commands of her brother, the persevering hostility of the court, clergy, and parliament, and though cherishing in her heart faith in the Saviour who has redeemed her, conceals that faith under the cloak of Romish devotion; while Calvin propagates the Gospel, in opposition to the powers of the world, saying: 'Such as the warfare is, such are the arms. If our warfare is spiritual, we ought to be furnished with spiritual armor.'* Margaret doubtless says the same thing; but she is the king's sister, summoned to his council, accustomed to diplomacy, respected by foreign princes; she hopes that a union with the evangelical rulers of Germany may hasten on the Reformation of France. Finally, while Calvin desires *truth* in the Church above all things, Margaret clings to the preservation of its *unity*, and thus becomes the noble representative of a system still lauded by some protestants—*to reform the Church without breaking it up:* a specious system, impossible to be realised. And yet this illustrious lady, in spite of her errors, plays a great part in the history of the Reformation: she was respected by the most pious reformers. An impartial historian should brave hostile prejudices, and assign her the place which is her due.

Let us enter upon the French Reformation, at the moment when, after great but isolated preparations, it is beginning to occupy a place in the affairs of the nation.†

The defeat at Pavia had plunged France into mourning. There was not a house where they did not weep for a son, a husband, or a father; and the whole kingdom was plunged in sorrow at seeing its king a prisoner. The recoil of this great disaster had not long to be waited for. 'The gods chastise us: let us fall upon the Christians,' said the Romans of the first centuries; the persecuting spirit of Rome woke up in France. 'It is our tenderness towards the Lutherans that has drawn upon us the vengeance of heaven,' said the

* Calvin on 2 Cor. x. 4.

† For an account of preceding times, see the *History of the Reformation of the Sixteenth Century,* vol. iii. bk. xii.

zealous catholics, who conceived the idea of appeasing heaven by hecatombs.

The great news of Pavia which saddened all France was received in Spain with transports of joy. At the time when the battle was fought, the young emperor was in Castile, anxiously expecting news from Italy. On the 10th of March, 1525, he was discussing, in one of the halls of the palace at Madrid, the advantages of Francis I. and the critical situation of the imperial army.* 'We shall conquer,' Pescara had written to him, 'or else we shall die.' At this moment a courier from Lombardy appeared at the gate of the palace: he was introduced immediately. 'Sire,' said he, bending the knee before the emperor in the midst of his court, 'the French army is annihilated, and the King of France in your Majesty's hands.' Charles, startled by the unexpected news, stood pale and motionless; it seemed as if the blood stagnated in his veins. For some moments he did not utter a word, and all around him, affected like himself, looked at him in silence. At last the ambitious prince said slowly, as if speaking to himself: 'The King of France is my prisoner. . . . I have won the battle.' Then, without a word to any one, he entered his bed-room and fell on his knees before an image of the Virgin, to whom he gave thanks for the victory. He meditated before this image on the great exploits to which he now thought himself called. To become the master of Europe, to reëstablish everywhere the tottering catholicism, to take Constantinople, and even to recover Jerusalem—such was the task which Charles prayed the Virgin to put him in a condition to carry through. If these ambitious projects had been realized, the revival of learning would have been compromised, the Reformation ruined, the new ideas rooted out, and the whole world would have bowed helplessly beneath two swords—that of the emperor first, and then that of the pope. At length Charles rose from his knees; he read the humble letters of the King of France, gave orders for processions to be made, and attended mass next day with every mark of the greatest devotion.†

* Guicciardini, *History of the Wars of Italy*, ii. bk. xvi. p. 500.

† Guicciardini, *Wars of Italy* (Despatch of Suardin, ambassador of Mantua, March 15, 1525). Sanuto, Ranke, *Deutsche Geschichte*, ii. p. 315.

All christendom thought as this potentate did: a shudder ran through Europe, and every man said to himself as he bent his head: 'Behold the master whom the fates assign us!' At Naples a devout voice was heard to exclaim: 'Thou hast laid the world at his feet!'

It has been said that if in our day a king should be made prisoner, the heir to the throne or a regent would succeed to all his rights; but in the sixteenth century, omnipotence dwelt in the monarch's person, and from the depths of his dungeon he could bind his country by the most disastrous treaties.* Charles V. determined to profit by this state of things. He assembled his council. The cruel Duke of Alva eloquently conjured him not to release his rival until he had deprived him of all power to injure him. 'In whom is insolence more natural,' he said, 'in whom is fickleness more instinctive than in the French? What can we expect from a king of France? . . . Invincible emperor, do not miss the opportunity of increasing the authority of the empire, not for your own glory, but for the service of God.'† Charles V. appeared to yield to the duke's advice, but it was advice according to his own heart; and while repeating that a christian prince ought not to triumph in his victory over another, he resolved to crush his rival. M. de Beaurain, viceroy of Naples, Lannoy, and the Constable of Bourbon, so detested by Francis I., waited all three upon the royal captive.

Francis had overplayed the part of a suppliant, a character so new for him. 'Instead of a useless prisoner,' he had written to Charles, 'set at liberty a king who will be your slave for ever.' Charles proposed to him a dismemberment of France on three sides. The Constable of Bourbon was to have Provence and Dauphiny, and these provinces, united with the Bourbonnais which he possessed already, were to be raised into an independent kingdom. The king of England was to have Normandy and Guienne; and the emperor would be satisfied with French Flanders, Picardy, and Burgundy. . . . When he heard these monstrous

* M. Rosseeuw Saint-Hilaire, *Hist. d'Espagne*, vi. p. 436.

† Guicciardini, *Wars of Italy*, ii. bk. xvi. pp. 510, 511.

propositions, Francis uttered a cry and caught up his sword, which his attendants took from his hands. Turning towards the envoys he said: 'I would rather die in prison than consent to such demands.' Thinking that he could make better terms with the emperor, he soon after embarked at Genoa and sailed to Spain. The delighted Charles gave up to him the palace of Madrid, and employed every means to constrain him to accept his disastrous conditions.* Who will succeed in baffling the emperor's pernicious designs? A woman, Margaret of Valois, undertook the task.† The statesmen of her age considered her the best head in Europe; the friends of the Reformation respected her as their mother. Her dearest wish was to substitute a living christianity for the dead forms of popery, and she hoped to prevail upon her brother, 'the father of letters,' to labor with her in this admirable work. It was not in France only that she desired the triumph of the Gospel, but in Germany, England, Italy, and even Spain. As Charles's projects would ruin all that she loved—the king, France, and the Gospel—she feared not to go and beard the lion even in his den.

The duchess as she entered Spain felt her heart deeply agitated. The very day she had heard of the battle of Pavia, she had courageously taken this heavy cross upon her shoulders; but at times she fainted under the burden. Impatient to reach her brother, burning with desire to save him, fearing lest she should find him dying, trembling lest the persecutors should take advantage of her absence to crush the Gospel and religious liberty in France, she found no rest but at the feet of the Saviour. Many evangelical men wept and prayed with her; they sought to raise her drooping courage under the great trial which threatened to weigh her down, and bore a noble testimony to her piety. 'There are various *stations* in the christian life,' said one of these reformers, Capito. 'You have now entered upon that

* *Mémoires de Du Bellay*, p. 121. Guicciardini, *Wars of Italy*, ii. bk. xvi. pp. 511, 512.

† See *History of the Reformation of the Sixteenth Century*, vol. iii. bk. xii. ch. xv.

commonly called *the Way of the Cross.** . . . Despising the theology of men, you desire to know only Jesus Christ and Him crucified.'†

Margaret crossing in her litter (September, 1525) the plains of Catalonia, Arragon, and Castile, exclaimed:

I cast my eyes around,
  I look and look in vain . . .
The loved one cometh not;
  And on my knees again
I pray unceasing to my God
To heal the king—to spare the rod.

The loved one cometh not . . .
  Tears on my eyelids sit:
Then to this virgin page
  My sorrows I commit:—
Such is to wretched me
Each day of misery.‡

She sometimes fancied that she could see in the distance a messenger riding hastily from Madrid and bringing her news of her brother. . . . But alas! her imagination had deceived her, no one appeared. She then wrote:

O Lord, awake, arise!
  And let thine eyes in mercy fall
  Upon the king—upon us all.

Once or twice a day she halted at some inn on the road to Madrid, but it was not to eat. 'I have supped only once since my departure from Aigues-Mortes,' she said.§ As soon as she entered the wretched chamber, she began to write to her brother at the table or on her knees. 'Nothing to do you service,' she wrote: 'nothing, even to casting the ashes of my bones to the wind, will be strange or painful to me; but rather consolation, repose, and honor.'‖

* 'In istum pietatis gradum evasisti, qui vulgo dicitur *via crucis*.'—Capito, Dedicatory Epistle to the *Comm. sur Osée*.

† 'Christumque Jesum et hunc crucifixum tibi solum reservas.'—Ibid.

‡ *Les Marguerites de la Marguerite des Princesses*, i. pp. 467, 473.

§ Ibid, ii. p. 41.

‖ *Lettres de la Reine de Navarre, sur la route de Madrid*, ii. p. 42.

The defeat of Pavia and the excessive demands of Charles V. had given the king such shocks that he had fallen seriously ill; the emperor had therefore gone to Madrid to be near him. On Wednesday, September 19, 1525, Margaret arrived in that capital. Charles received her surrounded by a numerous court, and respectfully approaching her, this politic and phlegmatic prince kissed her on the forehead and offered her his hand. Margaret, followed by the noble dames and lords of France who had accompanied her, and wearing a plain dress of black velvet without any ornament, passed between two lines of admiring courtiers. The emperor conducted her as far as the door of her brother's apartments, and then withdrew.

Margaret rushed in; but alas! what did she find? a dying man, pale, worn, helpless. Francis was on the brink of the grave, and his attendants seemed to be waiting for his last breath. The duchess approached the bed softly, so as not to be heard by the sick man; unobserved she fixed on him a look of the tenderest solicitude, and her soul, strengthened by an unwavering faith, did not hesitate; she believed in her brother's cure, she had prayed so fervently. She seemed to hear in the depths of her heart an answer from God to her prayers; and while all around the prince, who was almost a corpse, bowed their heads in dark despair, Margaret raised hers with hope towards heaven.

Prudent, skilful, decided, active, a Martha as well as a Mary, she established herself at once in the king's chamber, and took the supreme direction. 'If she had not come he would have died,' said Brantôme.* 'I know my brother's temperament,' she said, 'better than the doctors.' In spite of their resistance, she had the treatment changed; then she sat down at the patient's bedside, and left him no more. While the king slept, she prayed; when he awoke, she spoke to him in encouraging language. The faith of the sister gradually dispelled the brother's dejection. She spoke to him of the love of Christ; she proposed to him to commemorate his atoning death by celebrating the holy euchar-

* Brantôme, *Mémoires des Dames illustres*, p. 113.

ist. Francis consented. He had hardly communicated when he appeared to wake up as if from a deep sleep: he sat up in his bed, fixed his eyes on his sister, and said: 'God will heal me body and soul.' Margaret in great emotion answered: 'Yes, God will raise you up again and make you free.' From that hour the king gradually recovered his strength, and he would often say: 'But for her, I was a dead man.'*

Margaret, seeing her brother restored to life, thought only of restoring him to liberty. She departed for Toledo, where Charles V. was staying; the seneschal and seneschaless of Poitou, the Bishop of Senlis, the Archbishop of Embrun, the president De Selves, and several other nobles, accompanied her. What a journey! Will she succeed in touching her brother's gaolor, or will she fail? This question was continually before her mind. Hope, fear, indignation moved her by turns; at every step her agitation increased. The emperor went out courteously to meet her; he helped her to descend from her litter, and had his first conversation with her in the Alcazar, that old and magnificent palace of the Moorish kings. Charles V. was determined to take advantage of his victory. Notwithstanding the outward marks of politeness, exacted by the etiquette of courts, he wrapped himself up in imperturbable dignity, and was cold, nay almost harsh. Margaret, seeing that her brother's conqueror kept the foot upon his neck, and was determined not to remove it, could no longer contain herself. 'She broke out into great anger:'† like a lioness robbed of her cubs, full of majesty and fury, she startled the cold and formal Charles, says Brantôme. Yet he restrained himself, preserved his icy mien, made no answer to the duchess, and busying himself with showing her the honors due to her rank, he conducted her, accompanied by the Archbishop of Toledo and several Spanish noblemen, to the palace of Don Diego de Mendoza, which had been prepared for her.

Alone in her chamber the princess gave free vent to her tears; she wrote to Francis: 'I found him very cold.'‡ She

* Brantôme, *Dames illustres.*

† Ibid, p. 113.

‡ *Lettres de la Reine de Navarre,* i. p. 188.

reminded him that the King of heaven 'has placed on his throne *an ensign of grace;* that we have no reason to fear the majesty of heaven will reject us; and that he stretches out his hand to us, even before we seek for it.' And being thus strengthened, she prepared for the solemn sitting at which she was to plead her brother's cause. She quitted the palace with emotion to appear before the council extraordinary, at which the emperor and his ministers sat with all the grandeur and pride of Castile. Margaret was not intimidated, and though she could not perceive the least mark of interest on the severe and motionless faces of her judges, 'she was triumphant in speaking and pleading.' But she returned bowed down with sorrow: the immovable severity of the emperor and of his councillors dismayed her. 'The thing is worsened,' she said, 'far more than I had imagined.'*

The Duchess of Alençon, firmer than her brother, would not agree to the cession of Burgundy. The emperor replied with irritation: 'It is my patrimonial estate—I still bear the name and the arms.' The duchess, confounded by Charles's harshness, threw herself into the arms of God. 'When men fail, God does not forget,' she said. She clung to the rock; 'she leant,' says Erasmus, 'upon the unchangeable rock which is called Christ.'†

She soon regained her courage, asked for another audience, returned to the attack, and her agitated soul spoke with new eloquence to the emperor and his ministers. Never had the Escurial or the Alcazar seen a petitioner so ardent and so persevering. She returned to her apartments in alternations of sorrow and joy. 'Sometimes I get a kind word,' she wrote, 'and then suddenly all is changed. I have to deal with the greatest of dissemblers.'‡ This beautiful and eloquent ambassadress filled the Spaniards with admiration. They talked at court of nothing but the sister of Francis I. Letters received in France and Germany from Madrid and

* *Lettres de la Reine*, i. p. 192.

† 'Vere innitentem saxo illi immobili, quod est Christus Jesus.'—Erasmi *Epp.* p. 970.

‡ *Lettres de la Reine*, i. pp. 1–207.

Toledo extolled her sweetness, energy, and virtues. The scholars of Europe felt their love and respect for her increase, and were proud of a princess whom they looked upon as their Mæcenas. What charmed them was something more than that inquiring spirit which had led Margaret in her earliest years towards literature and divinity, and had made her learn Latin and Hebrew;* Erasmus enthusiastically exclaimed when he heard of the wonders she was doing in Spain: 'How can we help loving, in God, such a heroine, such an amazon?'† The courage with which the Duchess of Alençon had gone to Spain to save her brother led some christians to imagine that she would display the same heroism in delivering the Church from her long captivity.

CHAPTER II.

MARGARET SAVES THE EVANGELICALS AND THE KING.

(1525–1526.)

The captive Francis was not Margaret's only sorrow. If her brother was a prisoner to the emperor, her brethren in the faith were prisoners to her mother. The parliament of Paris having issued a decree against the Lutherans, and the pope having on the 17th of March invested with apostolical authority the councillors authorised to proceed against them,‡ the persecutors set vigorously to work. The regent Louisa of Savoy, mother of Francis I. and of Margaret, inquired of the Sorbonne: 'By what means the *damnable*

* La Ferrière-Percy, *Marguerite d'Angoulême*, p. 18.

† 'Talem heroïnam, talem viraginem, non possum non amare in Deo.'—Ibid. One writer has *virginem*, but this is wrong, for Margaret was at this time a widow.

‡ 'Auctoritate apostolica.'—Bull of May 17, 1525. Drion, *Hist. Chron.* p. 14.

doctrine of Luther could be extirpated?' The fanatic Beda, syndic of that corporation, enchanted with such a demand, replied without hesitation on the part of the Faculties: 'It must be punished with the utmost severity.' Accordingly Louisa published letters-patent, '*to extinguish the damnable heresy of Luther*.'*

France began to seek in persecution an atonement for the faults which had led to the defeat of Pavia. Many evangelical christians were either seized or banished. Marot, valet-de-chambre to the Duchess of Alençon, the best poet of his age, who never spared the priests, and translated the Psalms of David into verse, was arrested; Lefèvre, Roussel, and others had to flee; Caroli and Mazurier recanted the faith they had professed.† 'Alas!' said Roussel, 'no one can confess Jesus any longer except at the risk of his life.'‡—'It is the hour of triumph,'§ proudly said Beda and the men of the Roman party. A blow more grievous still was about to reach Margaret.

A gentleman, a friend of Erasmus, of letters, and especially of Scripture, who had free access to the court of the duchess, and with whom that princess loved to converse about the Gospel and the new times—Berquin had been arrested on a charge of heresy; then set at liberty in 1523 by the intercession of Margaret and the king's orders. Leaving Paris, he had gone to his native province of Artois. A man of upright heart, generous soul, and intrepid zeal, 'in whom you could see depicted the marks of a great mind,' says the chronicler, he worthily represented by his character that nobility of France, and especially of Artois, so distinguished at all times by its devotedness and valor. Happy in the liberty which God had given him, Berquin had sworn to consecrate it to him, and was zealously propagating in the cottages on his estate the doctrine of salvation

* Letters-patent of June 10, 1525, for the execution of the bull of May 17.—Drion, *Hist. Chron.* p. 14.

† 'Ad canendam palinodiam adactis.'—Schmidt, Roussel to Farel.

‡ 'Vix citra vitæ periculum audet quis Christum pure confiteri.'—Ibid.

§ 'Ut jam sibi persuadeant triumphum.'—Ibid.

by *Christ alone.** The ancient country of the Atrebates, wonderfully fertile as regards the fruits of the earth, was equally fertile as regards the seed from heaven. Berquin attacked the priesthood such as Rome had made it. He said: 'You will often meet with these words in Holy Scripture: '*honorable marriage, undefiled bed,* but of *celibacy* you will not find a syllable.' Another time he said: 'I have not yet known a monastery which was not infected with hatred and dissension.' Such language, repeated in the refectories and long galleries of the convents, filled the monks with anger against this noble friend of learning. But he did not stop there: 'We must teach the Lord's flock,' he said, 'to pray with understanding, that they may no longer be content to gabble with their lips like ducks with their bills, without comprehending what they say.'—'He is attacking us,' said the chaplains. Berquin did not, however, always indulge in this caustic humor; he was a pious christian, and desired to see a holy and living unity succeed the parties that divided the Roman Church. He said: 'We ought not to hear these words among christians; I am of the Sorbonne, I am of Luther; or, I am a Grey-friar, or Dominican, or Bernardite. . . . Would it be too much then to say: *I am a christian?* . . . Jesus who came for us all ought not to be divided by us.'†

But this language aroused still greater hatred. The priests and nobles, who were firmly attached to ancient usages, rose up against him; they attacked him in the parishes and châteaux, and even went to him and strove to detach him from the new ideas which alarmed them. 'Stop!' they said with a sincerity which we cannot doubt, 'stop, or it is all over with the Roman hierarchy.' Berquin smiled, but moderated his language; he sought to make men understand that God loves those whom he calls to believe in Jesus Christ, and applied himself 'to scattering the divine seed' with unwearied courage. With the Testament

* 'Lutheranæ impietatis acerrimus propugnator.'—Chevillier, *Imprimerie de Paris,* p. 136.

† *Encomium matrimonii—Quærimonia pacis—Admonitio de modo orandi:* writings of Erasmus, translated by Berquin.

in his hand, he perambulated the neighborhood of Abbeville, the banks of the Somme, the towns, manors, and fields of Artois and Picardy, filling them with the Word of God.

These districts were in the see of Amiens, and every day some noble, priest, or peasant went to the palace and reported some evangelical speech or act of this christian gentleman. The bishop, his vicars and canons met and consulted together. On a sudden the bishop started for Paris, eager to get rid of the evangelist who was creating a disturbance throughout the north of France. He waited upon the archbishop and the doctors of the Sorbonne; he described to them the heretical exertions of the gentleman, the irritation of the priests, and the scandal of the faithful. The Sorbonne assembled and went to work: unable to seize Berquin, they seized his books, examined them, and 'after the *manner of spiders* sucked from them certain articles,' says Crespin, 'to make poison and bring about the death of a person who, with integrity and simplicity of mind was endeavoring to advance the doctrine of God.'* Beda especially took a violent part against the evangelist. This suspicious and arbitrary doctor, a thorough inquisitor, who possessed a remarkable talent for discovering in a book everything that could ruin a man by the help of forced interpretations, was seen poring night and day over Berquin's volumes. He read in them: 'The Virgin Mary is improperly invoked instead of the Holy Ghost.'—'Point against the accused,' said Beda.—He continued: 'There are no grounds for calling her a treasury of grace, our hope, our life: qualities which belong essentially to our Saviour alone.'—Confirmation!—'Faith alone justifies.'—Deadly heresy!—'Neither the gates of hell, nor Satan, nor sin can do anything against him who has faith in God.'—What insolence!† Beda made his report: 'Of a truth,' said his colleagues, 'that is enough to bring any man to the stake.'

Berquin's death being decided upon, the Sorbonne applied to the parliament, who raised no objections in the matter. A man was put to death in those times for an offensive pas-

* Crespin, *Martyrologue*, fol. pp. 102, 103.

† Ibid.

sage in his writings; it was the censorship of a period just emerging from the barbarism of the middle ages. Demailly, an officer of the court, started for Abbeville, proceeded to the gentleman's estate, and arrested him in the name of the law. His vassals, who were devoted to him, murmured and would have risen to defend him; but Berquin thought himself strong in his right; he remembered besides these words of the Son of God: '*Whosoever shall compel thee to go a mile, go with him twain;*' he entreated his friends to let him depart, and was taken to the prison of the Conciergerie, which he entered with a firm countenance and unbending head.*

This sad news which reached the Duchess of Alençon in Spain moved her deeply, and while she was hurrying from Madrid to Toledo, Alcala, and Guadalaxara, soliciting everybody, 'plotting' her brother's marriage with the sister of Charles V., and thus paving the way to the reconciliation of the two potentates, she resolved to save her brethren exiled or imprisoned for the Gospel. She applied to the king, attacking him on his better side. Francis I., Brantôme tells us, was called the father of letters. He had sought for learned men all over Europe and collected a fine library at Fontainebleau.† 'What!' said his sister to him, 'you are founding a college at Paris intended to receive the enlightened men of foreign countries; and at this very time illustrious French scholars, Lefèvre of Etaples and others, are compelled to seek an asylum out of the kingdom. . . . You wish to be a propagator of learning, while musty hypocrites, black, white, and grey, are endeavoring to stifle it at home.'‡ Margaret was not content to love with word and tongue; she showed her love by her works. The thought of the poor starving exiles, who knew not where to lay their heads, haunted her in the magnificent palaces of Spain; she distributed four thousand gold pieces among them, says one of the enemies of the Reformation.§

* *Journal d'un Bourgeois de Paris sous François I.* (printed from a MS. by the Société de l'Histoire de France), pp. 377, 378.

† *Mémoires de Brantôme*, i. p. 241.

‡ *Collection de Mémoires pour l'Histoire de France*, p. 23.

§ 'Quatuor aureorum millia inter doctos distribuenda.'—Flor. Rémond, *Hist. de l'Hérésie*, ii. p. 223.

She did more: she undertook to win over her brother to the Gospel, and endeavored, she tells us, to rekindle *the true fire* in his heart; but alas! that fire had never burnt there. Touched, however, by an affection so lively and so pure, by a devotedness so complete, which would have gone, if necessary, even to the sacrifice of her life, Francis, desirous of giving Margaret a token of his gratitude, commanded the parliament to adjourn until his return all proceedings against the evangelicals. 'I intend,' he added, 'to give the men of letters special marks of my favor.' These words greatly astonished the Sorbonne and the parliament, the city and the court. They looked at each other with an uneasy air; grief, they said, had affected the king's judgment. 'Accordingly they paid no great attention to his letter, and on the 24th of November, 1525, twelve days after its receipt, orders were given to the bishop to supply the money necessary for the prosecution of the heretics.'*

Margaret had no time to sympathise any longer with the fate of her friends. Charles V., who spoke with admiration of this princess, thought, not without reason, that she encouraged the king to resist him; he proposed, therefore, to make her a prisoner, as soon as her safe-conduct had expired. It appears that it was Montmorency who, being warned of the emperor's intention by the secret agents of the regent, gave information to the duchess. Her task in Spain seemed finished; it was from France now that the emperor must be worked upon. Indeed, Francis, disgusted with the claims of that prince, had signed his abdication and given it to his sister. The French Government with this document in their hands might give a new force to their demands. Margaret quitted Madrid, and on the 19th of November she was at Alcala.† But as she fled, she looked behind and asked herself continually how she could save Francis from the 'purgatory of Spain.' Yet the safe-conduct was about

* *Preuves des Libertés de l'Eglise Gallicane*, by Pierre Pithou, ii. p. 1092. *Bulletin de la Société de l'Histoire du Protestantisme François*, p. 210.

† *Lettres de la Reine de Navarre*, ii. p. 47. See also the first volume of these letters, p. 207, et seq.

to expire, the fatal moment had arrived; the alguazils of Charles were close at hand. Getting on horseback at six in the morning, the duchess made a four days' journey in one, and reëntered France just one hour before the termination of the truce.

Everything changed at Madrid. Charles, alarmed at the abdication of Francis, softened by the approaching marriage of this monarch with his sister, obtaining in fine the main part of his demands, consented to restore the King of France to liberty. It was Burgundy that had delayed the arrangement. The king was not more inclined than the duchess to detach this important province from France; the only difference between the brother and the sister was, that the religion of the one looked upon oaths as sacred, while the religion of the other made no account of breaking them; and this Francis soon showed. On the 14th of January, 1526, some of his courtiers, officers, and domestics gathered round their master for an act which in their simplicity they called sacred. The king swore in their presence that he would not keep one of the articles which Charles wished to force upon him. When that was done Francis bound himself an hour after by an oath, with his hand upon the Scriptures, to do what Charles demanded. According to the tenor of the treaty, he renounced all claim to Italy; surrendered Burgundy to the emperor, to whom it was stated to belong; restored Provence, which Charles ceded to the Constable of Bourbon; and thus France was laid prostrate.* The treaty was communicated to the pope: 'Excellent,' he said, after reading it; 'provided the king does not observe it.' That was a point on which Clement and Francis were in perfect accord.†

Margaret had no hand in this disgraceful trick; her only thought had been to save the king and the evangelicals.

* Buchon, ii. p. 280.

† Raumer, *Gesch. Europeas*, ii. p. 313.

CHAPTER III.

WILL THE REFORMATION CROSS THE RHINE?

(1525–1526.)

MARGARET, who returned from Spain full of hope in her brother's deliverance, was determined to do all in her power for the triumph of the Gospel. While the men of the ultramontane party, calling to mind the defeat of Pavia, demanded that heaven should be appeased by persecutions, Margaret thought, on the contrary, that humiliated France ought to turn towards Jesus Christ, in order to obtain from him a glorious deliverance.

But would Francis tread in his sister's steps? History presents few characters more inconsistent than the character of this prince. He yielded at one time to Margaret, at another to the Sorbonne. He imprisoned and set free, he riveted the chains and broke them. All his actions were contradictory; all his projects seem to exclude each other: on his bright side, he was the father of letters; on his dark side, the enemy of all liberty, especially of that which the Gospel gives; and he passed with ease from one of these characters to the other. Yet the influence which Margaret exercised over him in favor of the reformed seemed strongest during the eight or nine years that followed his captivity; Francis showed himself not unfavorable to the evangelicals during this period, except at times when irritated by certain excesses. Like a capricious and fiery steed, he sometimes felt a fly stinging him, when he would rear and throw his rider; but he soon grew calm and resumed his quiet pace. Accordingly many persons thought during the years 1525–1534 that the country of St. Bernard and Waldo would not remain behind Germany, Switzerland, and England. If the Reform had been completed, France would have been saved from the abominations of the Valois, the despotism of the Bourbons, and the enslaving superstitions of the popes.

Nine years before, the Reformation had begun in Germany: would it not cross the Rhine? . . . Strasburg is the main bridge by which German ideas enter France, and French ideas make their way into Germany. Many have already passed, both good and bad, from the right bank to the left and from the left to the right; and will still pass as long as the Rhine continues to flow. In 1521 the movement had been very active. There had been an invasion at Strasburg of the doctrines and writings of Luther: his name was in every mouth. His noble conduct at the diet of Worms had enraptured Germany, and the news spread in every direction. Men repeated his words, they devoured his writings. Zell, priest of St. Lawrence and episcopal penitentiary, was one of the first awakened. He began to seek truth in the Scriptures, to preach that man is saved by grace; and his sermons made an immense impression.

A nobleman of this city, Count Sigismond of Haute-Flamme (in German Hohenlohe) a friend and ally of the duchess, who called him her *good cousin*, was touched with Luther's heroism and the preaching of Zell. His conscience was aroused; he endeavored to live according to the will of God; and feeling within him the sin that prevented it, he experienced the need of a Saviour, and found one in Jesus Christ. Sigismond was not one of those nobles, rather numerous then, who spoke in secret of the Saviour, but, before the world, seemed not to know him; Lambert of Avignon* admired his frankness and his courage.† Although a dignitary of the Church and dean of the great chapter, the count labored to spread evangelical truth around him, and conceived at the same time a great idea. Finding himself placed between the two countries and speaking both languages, he resolved to set himself the task of bringing into

* For Lambert of Avignon, see the *History of the Reformation of the Sixteenth Century*, vol. iv. bk. xiii. ch. iii.

† 'Videmus quosdam tui ordinis, qui abscondite Christo adserunt, publice autem negant.'—Lambert to Hohenlohe.

France the great principles of the Reformation. As soon as he received any new work of Luther's, he had it translated into French and printed, and forwarded it to the king's sister.* He did more than that; he wrote to Luther, begging him to send a letter to the duchess, or even compose some work calculated to encourage her in her holy undertakings.† The count, who knew Margaret's spirit and piety, and her influence over the king, doubted not that she was the door by which the new ideas which were to renovate the world, would penetrate into France. He composed and published himself a work entitled the *Book of the Cross*, in which he set forth the death of Christ as the essence of the Gospel.

Sigismond's labors with the priests and nobles around him were not crowned with success. The monks especially looked at him with astonishment, and replied that they would take good care not to change the easy life they were leading. Lambert, who had a keen eye, perceived this, and said to the count with a smile: 'You will not succeed; these folks are afraid of damaging their wallets, their kitchens, their stables, and their bellies.'‡

But he succeeded better with Margaret. He had no sooner heard of the defeat at Pavia than he wrote her a letter full of sympathy. 'May God reward you,' she answered, 'for the kindness you have done us in visiting with such tender love the mother and the daughter, both poor afflicted widows! You show that you are not only a cousin according to flesh and blood, but also according to the spirit. We have resolved to follow your advice so far as the Father of all men is propitious to us.'§ Sigismond wrote again to the duchess while she was in Spain; and when he heard of her return to France, manifested a desire to go to Paris to advance the work of the Reformation. He was at the same

* 'Neque cessat libellos tuos in gallicam linguam versos mittere Gallorum regis sorori.'—Epist. Gerbilii ad Lutherum. Rœhrich, *Reform in Elsass*, p. 457.

† 'Libello aliquo per te in tam sancto instituto ut perseveraret adhortari.'—Ibid.

‡ 'Timent miseri et cæci suis peris, culinis, stabulis, et ventribus.'—Lambert *in Joel.*

§ *Lettres de la Reine de Navarre*, i. p. 180.

time full of confidence in Margaret's zeal. 'You think me more advanced than I am,' she replied; 'but I hope that He who, in despite of my unworthiness, inspires you with this opinion of me, will deign also to perfect his work in me.'*

The Duchess of Alençon did not however desire, as we have said, a reformation like that of Luther or Calvin. She wished to see in the Church a sincere and living piety, preserving at the same time the bishops and the hierarchy. To change the inside, but to leave the outside standing—such was her system. If they left the Church, two evils would in her opinion result which she wished to avoid; first, it would excite an insurmountable opposition; and second, it would create divisions, and lead to the rupture of unity. She hoped to attain her ends by a union between France and Germany. If Germany excited France, if France moderated Germany, would they not attain to a universal Reformation of the Church? She had not drawn up her plan beforehand, but circumstances gradually led her to this idea, which was not her own only, but that of her brother's most influential advisers, and which was sometimes that of her brother himself. Would she succeed? . . . Truth is proud and will not walk in concert with error. Besides, Rome is proud also, and, if this system had prevailed, she would no doubt have profited by the moderation of the reformers to maintain all her abuses.

The great event which Margaret was waiting for magnified her hopes. Whenever Francis I. passed the Pyrenees, it would be in her eyes like the sun rising in the gates of the east to inundate our hemisphere with its light. Margaret doubted not that her brother would immediately gather round him all the friends of the Gospel, like planets round the orb of day. 'Come in the middle of April,' she wrote to Hohenlohe, who was in her eyes a star of the first magnitude; 'you will find all your friends assembled. . . . The spirit, which by a living faith unites you to your only Chief (Jesus Christ), will make you diligently communicate your assistance to all who need it, especially to those who are

* *Lettres de la Reine de Navarre*, i. p. 211.

united to you in spirit and in faith. As soon as the king returns to France, he will send to them and seek them in his turn.' Margaret imagined herself already at the court of France, with the count at her side, and around her the exiles, the prisoners, the doctors. . . What an effect this mass of light would have upon the French! All the ice of scholastic catholicism would melt before the rays of the sun. 'There will indeed be some trouble at first,' she said; 'but the Word of truth will be heard. . . *God is God.* He is what he is, not less invisible than incomprehensible. His glory and his victory are spiritual. He is conqueror when the world thinks him conquered.'*

The king was still a prisoner; the regent and Duprat, who were opposed to the Reformation, wielded supreme power; the priests, seeing the importance of the moment, united all their efforts to combat the evangelical influences, and obtained a brilliant triumph. On Monday, the 5th of February, 1526, a month before the return of Francis I., the sound of the trumpet was heard in all the public places of Paris, and a little later in those of Sens, Orleans, Auxerre, Meaux, Tours, Bourges, Angers, Poitiers, Troyes, Lyons, and Macon, and 'in all the bailiwicks, seneschallies, provostries, viscounties, and estates of the realm.' When the trumpet ceased, the herald cried by order of parliament: 'All persons are forbidden to put up to sale or translate from Latin into French the epistles of St. Paul, the Apocalypse, and *other books.* Henceforward no printer shall print any of the books of Luther. No one shall speak of the ordinances of the Church or of images, otherwise than holy Church ordains. All books of the Holy Bible, translated into French, shall be given up by those who possess them, and carried within a week to the clerks of the court. All prelates, priests, and their curates shall forbid their parishioners to have *the least doubt* of the Catholic faith.'† Translations, books, explanations, and even doubts were prohibited.

This proclamation afflicted Margaret very seriously. Will

* *Lettres de la Reine de Navarre,* i. p. 212. M. Genin has translated this letter back from the German: these retranslations need correction.

† *Journal d'un Bourgeois de Paris sous François I.,* p. 276.

her brother ratify these fierce monastic prohibitions, or will he coöperate in the victory of truth? Will he permit the Reformation to pass from Germany into France? One circumstance filled the Duchess of Alençon with hope: the king declared in favor of Berquin. It will be recollected that this gentleman had been imprisoned in the Conciergerie. Three monks, his judges, entered his prison, and reproached him with having said that 'the gates of hell can do nothing against him who has faith.' This notion of a salvation entirely independent of priests exasperated the clergy.—'Yes,' answered Berquin, 'when the eternal Son of God receives the sinner who believes in his death and makes him a child of God, this divine adoption cannot be forfeited.' The monks, however, could see nothing but a culpable enthusiasm in this joyful confidence. Berquin sent Erasmus the propositions censured by his judges. 'I find nothing impious in them,' replied the prince of the schools.

The Sorbonne did not think the same. The prior of the Carthusians, the prior of the Celestines, monks of all colors, 'imps of antichrist,' says the chronicler, 'gave help to the band of the Sorbonne in order to destroy by numbers the firmness of Berquin.'—'Your books will be burnt,' said the pope's delegates to the accused, 'you will make an apology, and then only will you escape. But if you refuse what is demanded of you, you will be led to the stake.'—'I will not yield a single point,' he answered. Whereupon the Sorbonnists, the Carthusians, and the Celestines exclaimed: 'Then it is all over with you!' Berquin waited calmly for the fulfilment of these threats.

When the Duchess of Alençon heard of all this, she immediately wrote to her brother, and fell at her mother's knees. Louisa of Savoy was not inaccessible to compassion, in the solemn hour that was to decide her son's liberty. That princess was one of those profane characters who think little of God in ordinary times, but cry to him when the sea in its rage is about to swallow them up. Shut in her closet with Margaret, she prayed with her that God would restore the king to France. The duchess, full of charity and a woman of great tact, took advantage of one of these moments to attempt to soften her mother in favor of Berquin. She succeeded: the regent was seized with a sudden zeal, and ordered the pope's delegates to suspend matters until after the king's return.*

The delegates, in great surprise, read the letter over and over again: it seemed very strange to them. They deliberated upon it, and, thinking themselves of more consequence than this woman, quietly pursued their work. The haughty and resolute Louisa of Savoy, having heard of their insolence, was exasperated beyond measure, and ordered a second letter to be written to the pontiff's agents,† who contented themselves with saying, '*Non possumus*,' and made the more haste, for fear their victim should escape them. The king's mother, still more irritated, applied to the parliament, who held Berquin in respect, and who said boldly that the whole thing was nothing but a monkish conspiracy. At this the members of the Roman party made a still greater disturbance. Many of them (we must acknowledge) thought they were doing the public a service. 'Erasmus is an apostate,' they said, 'and Berquin is his follower.‡ . . . Their opinions are heretical, schismatic, scandalous. . . . We must burn Erasmus's books . . . and Berquin with them.'§

But Margaret did not lose courage. She recollected that the widow in the Gospel had obtained her request by her importunity. She entreated her mother, she wrote to her brother: 'If you do not interfere, Berquin is a dead man.'‖ Francis I. yielded to her prayer, and wrote to the first president that he, the king, would make him answerable for Berquin's life if he dared to condemn him. The president stopped all proceedings; the monks hung their heads, and

* 'Jussi fuerunt supersedere ad regium usque adventum.'—Berquinus Erasmo, April 17, 1526.

† 'Binis litteris regiæ matris.'—Ibid.

‡ 'Erasmum hæreticum et apostatum subinde clamantes, et Berquinum illius fautorem.'—Ibid.

§ 'Ut libri Erasmi velut hæretici cremerentur et una cum iis Berquinus.'—Ibid.

‖ 'Perierat nisi mater regis sublevasset eum.'—Erasmi *Epp.* p. 1522.

Beda and his friends, says the chronicler, 'were nigh bursting with vexation.'*

Yet Margaret did not hide from herself that she had still a hard struggle before her, which would require strength and perseverance. She felt the need of support to bring to a successful end in France a transformation similar to that which was then renewing Germany. The Count of Hohenlohe, at Strasburg, was not enough: she wanted at her side a staff that would enable her to bear with her brother's rebukes. God appeared willing to give her what she wished.

There was at court a prince, young, lively, witty, handsome, brave and gay, though somewhat harsh at times: he had already gone through surprising adventures, and, what was no small recommendation in Margaret's eyes, had been the companion of Francis in the field and in prison. He was Henry d'Albret, King of Navarre—king by right if not in fact—and at that time twenty-four years old. Community of misfortune had united Francis and Henry in close friendship, and young d'Albret soon conceived a deep affection for his friend's sister. Henry loved learning, possessed great vivacity of temper, and spoke with facility and even with eloquence. It was a pleasant thing to hear him gracefully narrating to the court circles the manner in which he had escaped from the fort of Pizzighitone, where he had been confined after the battle of Pavia. 'In vain,' he said, 'did I offer the emperor a large ransom; he was deaf. Determined to escape from my goalers, I bribed two of my guards; I procured a rope-ladder, and Vivis and I—(Vivis was his page)—let ourselves down from the window during the night. My room was at a great height, situated in the main tower above the moat. But, resolved to sacrifice my life rather than the states of my fathers, I put on the clothes of one of my attendants, who took my place in my bed. I opened the window; it was a dark night; I glided slowly down the high walls; I reached the ground, crossed the ditches, quitted the castle of Pavia, and, by God's help,

* Crespin, *Martyrologue*, f° 113.

managed so well that I got to St. Just on Christmas Eve' (1525).*

Henry d'Albret, having thus escaped from his enemies, hastened to Lyons, where he found Madame, and where Margaret arrived soon after, on her return from Spain. Smitten with her beauty, wit, and grace, the King of Navarre courted her hand. Everything about him charmed all who saw him; but Margaret's hand was not easy to be obtained. She had been first asked in marriage for the youthful Charles, King of Spain; and such a union, if it had been carried out, might not perhaps have been without influence upon the destinies of Europe. But the age of the monarch (he was then but eight years old) had caused the negotiation to fail, and the sister of the King of France married the Duke of Alençon, a prince of the blood, but a man without understanding, amiability, or courage. Chief cause of the disasters of Pavia, he had fled from the field of battle and died of shame.

Margaret at first did not accept the homage of the young King of Navarre. She was not to find in him all the support she needed; but that was not the only motive of her refusal; she could not think of marriage so long as her brother was a prisoner. Henry was not discouraged; he did all he could to please the duchess, and, knowing her attachment for the Gospel, he never failed, when present in the council, to take up the defence of the pious men whom Cardinal Duprat wished to put to death. This intervention was not a mere idle task. The persecution became such, that Margaret withdrawing from the attentions of the prince, thought only of the dangers to which the humble christians were exposed whose faith she shared.

We shall see that the pope and the Sorbonne had more influence in France than the regent and the king.

* Lettre de Henri de Navarre au conseiller du comté de Périgord, 27 décembre 1525.

CHAPTER IV.

DEATH OF THE MARTYRS; RETURN OF THE KING.

(1526.)

At the very moment when the duchess, the Count of Hohenlohe, and others were indulging in the sweetest hopes, the darkest future opened before their eyes. Margaret had dreamt of a new day, illumined by the brightest sunshine, but all of a sudden the clouds gathered, the light was obscured, the winds rose, and the tempest burst forth.

There was a young man about twenty-eight years of age, a licentiate of laws, William Joubert by name, whom his father, king's advocate at La Rochelle, had sent to Paris to study the practice of the courts. Notwithstanding the prohibition of the parliament, William, who was of a serious disposition, ventured to inquire into the catholic faith. Conceiving doubts about it, he said in the presence of some friends, that 'neither Genevieve nor even Mary could save him, but the Son of God alone.' Shortly after the issuing of the proclamation, the licentiate was thrown into prison. The alarmed father immediately hurried to Paris: his son, his hope . . . a heretic! and on the point of being burnt! He gave himself no rest: he went from one judge to another: 'Ask what you please,' said the unhappy father: 'I am ready to give any money to save his life.'* Vainly did he repeat his entreaties day after day; on Saturday, February 17, 1526, the executioner came to fetch William; he helped him to get into the tumbrel, and led him to the front of Notre Dame: 'Beg Our Lady's pardon,' he said. He next took him to the front of St. Genevieve's church: 'Ask pardon of St. Genevieve.' The Rocheller was firm in his faith,

* *Journal d'un Bourgeois*, p. 251.

and would ask pardon of none but God. He was then taken to the Place Maubert, where the people, seeing his youth and handsome appearance, deeply commiserated his fate; but the tender souls received but rough treatment from the guards. 'Do not pity him,' they said: 'he has spoken evil of Our Lady and the saints in paradise, and holds to the doctrine of Luther.' The hangman then took up his instruments, approached William, made him open his mouth, and pierced his tongue. He then strangled him and afterwards burnt his body. The poor father returned alone to Rochelle. But the parliament was not satisfied with one victim; erelong it made an assault upon the inhabitants of a city which the enemies of the Gospel detested in an especial manner.

A well-educated young man of Meaux had come to Paris; he had translated 'certain books' from Latin into French: he took Luther's part and spoke out boldly: 'We need not take holy water to wash away our sins,' he said; 'the blood of Christ alone can cleanse us from them. We need not pray for the dead, for immediately after death their souls are either in paradise or in hell; there is no purgatory; I do not believe in it.'* 'Ah!' said the angry monks, 'we see how it is; Meaux is thoroughly infected with false doctrines; one *Falry*,† a priest, with some others, is the cause of these perversions.' The young man was denounced to the parliament. 'If you do not recant, you will be burned,' they said. The poor youth was terrified; he was afraid of death. They led him to the front of the cathedral of Notre Dame; there he mounted a ladder, bareheaded, with lighted taper in his hand, and cried out for: 'Pardon of God and of Our Lady!' Then the priests put in his hands the books he had translated; he read them 'every word' (the titles doubtless), and afterwards pronounced them to be false and damnable. The books were burnt before his face; and as for him, 'he was taken to the Celestines' prison and put upon bread and water.'

He was not the only man of his native city who had to make expiation for the zeal with which he had received the Reform. A fuller, also a native of Meaux, who followed like

* Ibid. p. 277.

† *Journal d'un Bourgeois.* Either Farel or Lefèvre (Fabry).

him the 'sect of Luther,' suffered a similar punishment about the same time.* 'This Luthereau,' said the burghers of Paris, 'has the presumption to say that the Virgin and the saints have no power, and such like nonsense.'

Picardy next furnished its tribute. Picardy in the north and Dauphiny in the south were the two provinces of France best prepared to receive the Gospel. During the fifteenth century many Picardins, as the story ran, went to *Vaudery.* Seated round the fire during the long nights, simple catholics used to tell one another how these *Vaudois* (Waldenses) met in horrible assembly in solitary places, where they found tables spread with numerous and dainty viands. These poor christians loved indeed to meet together from districts often very remote. They went to the rendezvous by night and along by-roads. The most learned of them used to recite some passages of Scripture, after which they conversed together and prayed. But such humble conventicles were ridiculously travestied. 'Do you know what they do to get there,' said the people, 'so that the officers may not stop them? The devil has given them a certain ointment, and when they want to go to *Vaudery*, they smear a little stick with it. As soon as they get astride it, they are carried up through the air, and arrive at their *sabbath* without meeting anybody. In the midst of them sits a goat with a monkey's tail: this is Satan, who receives their adoration!' . . . These stupid stories were not peculiar to the people: they were circulated particularly by the monks. It was thus that the inquisitor Jean de Broussart spoke in 1460 from a pulpit erected in the great square at Arras. An immense multitude surrounded him; a scaffold was erected in front of the pulpit, and a number of men and women, kneeling and wearing caps with the figure of the devil painted on them, awaited their punishment. Perhaps the faith of these poor people was mingled with error. But be that as it may, they were all burnt alive after the sermon.†

A young student, who already held a living, though not yet in priest's orders, had believed in the Gospel, and had

* Ibid. p. 281.

† *Histoire des Protestants de Picardie*, by L. Rossier, p. 2.

boldly declared that there was no other saviour but Jesus Christ, and that the Virgin Mary had no more power than other saints.* This youthful cleric of Thérouanne in Picardy had been imprisoned in 1525, and terrified by the punishment. On Christmas-eve, with a lighted torch in his hand and stripped to his shirt, he had 'asked pardon of God and of Mary before the church of Notre Dame.' In consideration of his 'very great penitence,' it was thought sufficient to confine him for seven years on bread and water in the prison of St. Martin des Champs. Alone in his dungeon, the scholar heard the voice of God in the depths of his heart; he began to weep hot tears, and 'forthwith,' says the chronicler, 'he returned to his folly.' Whenever a monk entered his prison, the young cleric proclaimed the Gospel to him; the monks were astonished at such raving; all the convent was in a ferment and confusion. Dr. Merlin, the grand penitentiary, went to the prisoner in person, preached to him, advised and entreated him, but all to no effect. By order of the court, the young evangelist 'was burnt at the Grève in Paris,' and others underwent the same punishment. Such was the method employed in that cruel age to force the doctrine of the Church back into the hearts of those who rejected it: they made use of scourges to beat them, and cords to strangle them.

It was not only in Paris that severity was used against the Lutherans: the same was done in the provinces. Young Pierre Toussaint, prebendary of Metz, who had taken refuge at Basle after the death of Leclerc,† having regained his courage, returned to France and proclaimed the Gospel. His enemies seized him, and gave him up to the Abbot of St. Antoine. This abbot, a well-known character, was a violent, cruel, and merciless man.‡ Neither Toussaint's youth, nor his candor, nor his weak health could touch him; he threw his victim into a horrible dungeon full of stagnant

* *Journal d'un Bourgeois*, p. 291.

† See the *History of the Reformation of the Sixteenth Century*, vol. iii. bk. iv. ch. viii. to xiv.

‡ 'S. Antonii abbati crudelissimo Evangelii hosti prodiderunt me.'—Herzog, *Œcolampade*, *Pièces Justificatives*, p. 280.

water and other filth,* where the young evangelist could hardly stand. With his back against the wall, and his feet on the only spot in the dungeon which the water did not reach, stifled by the poisonous vapors emitted around him, the young man remembered the cheerful house of his uncle the Dean of Metz and the magnificent palace of the Cardinal of Lorraine, where he had been received so kindly while he still believed in the pope. What a contrast now! Toussaint's health declined, his cheeks grew pale and his trembling legs could hardly support him. Alas! where were those days when still a child he ran joyously round the room riding on a stick,† and when his mother seriously uttered this prophecy: 'Antichrist will soon come and destroy all who are converted.' The wretched Toussaint thought the moment had arrived. . . . His imagination became excited, he fancied he saw the terrible antichrist foretold by his mother, seizing him and dragging him to punishment; he screamed aloud, and was near dying of fright.‡ He interested every one who saw him; he was so mild; harmless as a new-born child, they said, so that the cruel abbot knew not how to justify his death. He thought that if he had Toussaint's books and papers, he could find an excuse for burning him. One day the monks came to the wretched young man, took him out of the unwholesome pit, and led him into the abbot's room. 'Write to your host at Basle,' said the latter; 'tell him that you want your books to amuse your leisure, and beg him to send them to you.' Toussaint, who understood the meaning of this order, hesitated. The abbot gave utterance to terrible threats. The affrighted Toussaint wrote the letter, and was sent back to his pestilential den.

Thus the very moment when the evangelical christians were hoping to have some relief was marked by an in-

* 'In carcere pleno aqua et sordibus.'—Herzog, *Œcolampade, Pièces Justificatives.*

† 'Cum equitabam in arundine longa.'—Tossanus Farello, Neufchatel MS.

‡ 'Pro tormento quibus me affecerunt, ut sæpe desperarem de vita.—Herzog, *Œcolampade*, p. 280.

crease of severity. The Reform—Margaret was its representative at that time in the eyes of many—the afflicted Reform saw her children around her, some put to death, others in chains, all threatened with the fatal blow. The sister of Francis I., heart-broken and despairing, would have shielded with her body those whom the sword appeared ready to strike; but her exertions seemed useless.

Suddenly a cry of joy was heard, which, uttered in the Pyrenees, was reëchoed even to Calais. The *Sun* (for thus, it will be remembered, Margaret called her brother) appeared in the south to reanimate the kingdom of France. On the 21st of March Francis quitted Spain, crossed the Bidassoa, and once more set his foot on French ground. He had recovered his spirits; an overflowing current of life had returned to every part of his existence. It seemed that, delivered from a prison, he was the master of the world. He mounted an Arab horse, and, waving his cap and plume in the air, exclaimed as he galloped along the road to St. Jean de Luz: 'Once more I am a king!' Thence he proceeded to Bayonne, where his court awaited him, with a great number of his subjects who had not been permitted to approach nearer to the frontier.

Nowhere was the joy so great as with Margaret and the friends of the Gospel. Some of them determined to go and meet the king and petition him on behalf of the exiles and the prisoners, feeling persuaded that he would put himself at the head of the party which the detested Charles V. was persecuting. These *most pious Gauls*, as Zwingle calls them,* petitioned the monarch; Margaret uttered a cry in favor of the miserable;† but Francis, though full of regard for his sister, could not hide a secret irritation against Luther and the Lutherans. His profane character, his sensual temperament, made him hate the evangelicals, and policy demanded great reserve.

Margaret had never ceased to entertain in her heart a

* 'Galli piissimi ad iter se accingunt obviam ituri regi, nomine ejectorum christianorum.'—Zwingl. *Epp.* i. p. 480—March 7, 1526.

† 'Sæpius rejem adiit . . . ut commiseratione erga Lutheranos animum mitigaret.'—Flor. Rémond, *Hist. Hæresis*, ii. p. 223.

hope of seeing the Count of Hohenlohe come to Paris and labor at spreading the Gospel in France. Sigismond, a man of the world and at the same time a man of God, an evangelical christian and yet a church dignitary, knowing Germany well, and considered at the court of France as belonging to it, appeared to the Duchess of Alençon the fittest instrument to work among the French that transformation equally demanded by the wants of the age and the Word of God. One day she took courage and presented her request to her brother: Francis did not receive her petition favorably. He knew Hohenlohe well, and thought his evangelical principles exaggerated; besides, if any change were to be made in France, the king meant to carry it out alone. He did not, however, open his heart entirely to his sister: he simply gave her to understand that the time was not yet come. If the count came to Paris; if he gathered round him all the friends of the Gospel; if he preached at court, in the churches, in the open air perhaps, what would the emperor say, and what the pope?—'Not yet,' said the king.

The Duchess of Alençon, bitterly disappointed, could hardly make up her mind to communicate this sad news to the count. Yet it must be done. 'The desire I have to see you is increased by what I hear of your virtue and of the perseverance of the divine grace in you. But . . . my dear cousin, all your friends have arrived at the conclusion that, *for certain reasons*, it is not yet time for you to come here. As soon as we have *done something*, with God's grace, I will let you know.'

Hohenlohe was distressed at this delay, and Margaret endeavored to comfort him. 'Ere long,' she said, 'the Almighty will do us the grace to perfect what he has done us the grace to *begin*. You will then be consoled in this company, where you are *present* though *absent* in body. May the peace of our Lord, which passeth all understanding, and which the world knoweth not, be given to your heart so abundantly that no cross can afflict it!'*

At the same time she increased her importunity with her

* *Lettres de la Reine de Navarre*, i. p. 212.

brother; she conjured the king to inaugurate a new era; she once more urged the propriety of inviting the count. 'I do not care for that man,' answered Francis sharply. He cared for him, however, when he wanted him. There is a letter from the king 'to his very dear and beloved cousin of Hohenlohe,' in which he tells him that, desiring to raise a large army, and knowing 'his loyalty and valor, his nearness of lineage, love, and charity,' he begs him most affectionately to raise three thousand foot-soldiers.* But where the Gospel was concerned, it was quite another matter. To put an end to his sister's solicitation, Francis replied to her one day: 'Do you wish, then, for my sons to remain in Spain?' He had given them as hostages to the emperor. Margaret was silent: she had not a word to say where the fate of her nephews was concerned. She wrote to the count: 'I cannot tell you, my friend, all the vexation I suffer: *the king would not see you willingly;* the reason is the liberation of his children, which he cares for quite as much as for his own.' She added: 'I am of good courage towards you, rather on account of our fraternal affection than by the perishable ties of flesh and blood. For the *other* birth, the *second* delivery—there lies true and perfect union.' The Count of Hohenlohe, Luther's disciple, did not come to France.

This refusal was not the only grief which Francis caused his sister. The love of the King of Navarre had grown stronger, and she began to return it. But the king opposed her following the inclination of her heart. Margaret, thwarted in all her wishes, drinking of the bitter cup, revolting sometimes against the despotic will to which she was forced to bend, and feeling the wounds of sin in her heart, retired to her closet and laid bare her sorrows to Christ.

> O thou, my priest, my advocate, my king,
> On whom depends my life—my everything;
> O Lord, who first didst drain the bitter cup of woe
> And know'st its poison (if man e'er did know),
> These thorns how sharp, these wounds of sin how deep—

* *Lettres de la Reine de Navarre*, i. p. 466—March 21, 1528.

Saviour, friend, king, oh! plead my cause, I pray:
Speak, help, and save me, lest I fall away.*

The religious poems of Margaret, which are deficient neither in grace, sensibility, nor affection, belong (it must not be forgotten) to the early productions of the French muse; and what particularly leads us to quote them is that they express the christian sentiments of this princess. This is the period at which it seems to us that Margaret's christianity was purest. At an earlier date, at the time of her connection with Briçonnet, her faith was clouded with the vapors of mysticism. At a later date, when the fierce will of Francis I. alarmed her tender and shrinking soul, a veil of catholicism appeared to cover the purity of her faith. But from 1526 to 1532 Margaret was herself. The evidences of the piety of the evangelical christians of this period are so few, that we could not permit ourselves to suppress those we find in the writings of the king's sister.

The Duchess of Alençon resorted to poetry to divert her thoughts; and it was now, I think, that she wrote her poem of the *Prisoner*. She loved to recall the time when the King of Navarre had been captured along with Francis I.; she transported herself to the days immediately following the battle of Pavia; she imagined she could hear young Henry d'Albret expressing his confidence in God, and exclaiming from the lofty tower of Pizzighitone:

Vainly the winds o'er the ocean blow,
Scattering the ships as they proudly go;
But not a leaf of the wood can they shake,
Until at the sound of thy voice they awake.

The captive, after describing in a mournful strain the sorrows of his prison, laid before Christ the sorrow which sprang from a feeling of his sins:

Not *one* hell but many million
I've deserved for my rebellion.
. . . .

* *Marguerites de la Marguerite*, i. p. 144.

But my sin in thee was scourged,
And my guilt in thee was purged.*

The noble prisoner does not seek the salvation of God for himself alone; he earnestly desires that the Gospel may be brought to that Italy where he is a captive—one of the earliest aspirations for Italian reformation.

Can you tell why from your home—
Home so peaceful—you were torn?
'T was that over stream and mountain
The precious treasure should be borne
By thee, in thy vessel frail,
To God's elect† . . .

On a sudden the prisoner remembers his friend; he believes in his tender commiseration and thus invokes him:

O Francis, my king, of my soul the best part,
Thou model of friendship, so dear to my heart,
A Jonathan, Orestes, and Pollux in one,
As thou seest me in sorrow and anguish cast down,
My Achates, my brother, oh! what sayest thou?‡

But Henry d'Albret called Francis I. his Jonathan to no purpose; Jonathan would not give him his sister. The king had other thoughts. During his captivity the emperor had demanded Margaret's hand of the regent.§ But Francis, whom they were going to unite, contrary to his wishes, to Charles's sister, thought that one marriage with the house of Austria was enough, and hoping that Henry VIII. might aid him in taking vengeance on Charles, was seized with a strong liking for him. 'If my body is the emperor's prisoner,' he said, 'my heart is a prisoner to the King of England!'‖ He gained over Cardinal Wolsey, who told his master that there was not in all Europe a woman worthier of the crown of England than Margaret of France.¶ But the christian heart of the Duchess of Alençon revolted at

* *Marguerites* (*Complainte du Prisonnier*), p. 448.
† Ibid, p. 456.
‡ Ibid, p. 460.
§ Manuscrits Béthune, nº 8496, fº 13.
‖ *Lettres de la Reine de Navarre*, i. p. 31.
¶ *Hist. du Divorce de Henri VIII.* i. p. 47. Polydore Virgil, p. 686.

the idea of taking the place of Catharine of Arragon, whose virtues she honored ;* and Henry VIII. himself soon entered on a different course. It was necessary to give up the design of placing Margaret on the throne of England by the side of Henry Tudor . . . a fortunate thing for the princess, but a misfortune perhaps for the kingdom over which she would have reigned.

Yet the Duchess of Alençon did not see all her prayers refused. On leaving his prison, the sight of Francis I. was confused. By degrees he saw more clearly into the state of things in Europe, and took a few steps towards that religious liberty which Margaret had so ardently desired of him. It would even seem that, guided by his sister, he rose to considerations of a loftier range.

CHAPTER V.

DELIVERY OF THE CAPTIVES AND RETURN OF THE EXILES.

(1526.)

THERE was an instinctive feeling in christendom that up to this time its society had been but fragmentary, a great disorder, an immense chaos.† It felt an earnest want of that social unity, of that supreme order, and of that all-ruling idea which the papacy had not been able to give. By proclaiming a new creation, the Reformation was about to accomplish this task. The isolation of nations was to cease ; all would touch each other ; reciprocal influences would multiply from generation to generation. . . The Reformation prepared the way for the great unity in the midst of the world.

* *History of the Reformation of the Sixteenth Century*, vol. v. bk. xix. ch. v.

† Guizot, *Histoire de la Civilisation en Europe.*

Evangelical christians felt a consciousness, indistinct perhaps, though deep, of this new movement in human affairs, and many would have wished that France should not yield to Germany or England the privilege of marching in the van of the new order of things. They said that since the emperor had put himself at the head of the enemies of the Reformation, the king ought to place himself in the front rank of its defenders. The Duchess of Alençon in particular was constantly soliciting the king, and praying him to recall to France the men who would bring into it the true light. But Francis received her proposals coldly, sometimes rudely, and cut short every attempt to answer; still the duchess was indefatigable, and when the king shut the door against her, 'she got in through the keyhole.' At last Francis, who loved his sister, esteemed learning, and despised the monks, yielded to her pressing entreaties, and above all to the new ideas and the exigencies of his political plans. The gates of the prisons were opened.

Berquin was still a prisoner, sorrowful but comforted by his faith, unable to see clearly into the future, but immovable in his loyalty to the Gospel. The king determined to save him from 'the claws of Beda's faction.' 'I will not suffer the person or the goods of this gentleman to be injured,' he said to the parliament on the 1st of April; 'I will inquire into the matter myself.' The officers sent by the king took the christian captive from his prison, and, though still keeping watch over him, placed him in a commodious chamber. Berquin immediately set about forming plans for the triumph of truth.

Clement Marot had paid dearly for the privilege of being Margaret's secretary; he was in prison, and consoled himself by composing his little poems. Margaret obtained his full release, and Marot hastened to his friends, exclaiming in a transport of joy:

In narrow cell without a cause,
Shut up in foul despite of laws
By wicked men, the king's decree
In this New Year has set me free.*

* The year began at Easter; its commencement on the 1st of January was not definitively settled until much later.

Michael of Aranda, who, in 1524, had preached the Gospel with such power at Lyons, had been removed from Margaret, whose almoner he was. She sent for him and imparted to him her plan for introducing the Gospel into the Catholic Church of France, by renewing without destroying it. 'I have procured your nomination to the bishopric of Trois-Châteaux in Dauphiny,'* she said. 'Go, and evangelise your diocese.' He accepted; the truth had already been scattered in Dauphiny by Farel and others. Did Aranda share Margaret's views, or had ambition anything to do with his acceptance? It is hard to say.

A fourth victim of the persecution was soon saved. The young prebendary of Metz, the amiable Pierre Toussaint, was still in the frightful den into which the abbot of St. Antoine had thrust him. His host at Basle had not sent the books which the treacherous priest had constrained him to write for; no doubt the worthy citizen, knowing in whose hands his friend was lying, had foreseen the danger to which their receipt would expose him. Several evangelical christians of France, Switzerland, and Lorraine, particularly the merchant Vaugris, had successively interceded in his favor, but to no purpose. Finding all their exertions useless, they applied at last to Margaret, who warmly pleaded the cause of the young evangelist before the king. In July, 1526, the order for his release arrived. The officers charged with this pleasing task descended to the gloomy dungeon selected by the abbot of St. Antoine, and rescued the lamb from the fangs of that wild beast. Toussaint, thin, weak, pale as a faded flower, came out slowly from his fearful den. His weakened eyes could hardly support the light of day, and he knew not where to go. At first he went to some old acquaintances; but they were all afraid of harboring a heretic escaped from the scaffold. The young prebendary did not possess Berquin's energy; he was one of those sensitive and delicate natures that need a support, and he found himself in the world, in the free air, almost as much alone as in his dungeon. 'Ah!' he said, 'God our heavenly Father, who

* 'Suo Michaeli de Arando *Episcopo Sancti Pauli* in Delphinatu.'—Cornel. Agrippa, *Epp.* p. 385.

has fixed bounds to the wrath of man which it cannot pass, has delivered me in a wonderful manner from the hands of the tyrants; but alas! what will become of me? The world is mad and spurns the rising Gospel of Jesus Christ.'* A few timid but well-meaning friends said to him: 'the Duchess of Alençon alone can protect you; there is no asylum for you but at her court. Make application to a princess who welcomes with so much generosity all the friends of learning and of the Gospel, and profit by your residence to investigate closely the wind that blows in those elevated regions.' Toussaint did what they told him; he began his journey, and, despite his natural timidity, arrived at Paris, where we shall meet with him again.

More important deliverances still were in preparation. Strasburg was to rejoice. There was no city out of France where the king's return had been hailed with so much enthusiasm. Many evangelical christians had sought refuge there from the cruelties of Duprat, and were sighing for the moment that would restore them to their country. Among the number of the refugees was the famous Cornelius Agrippa. His reputation was not unblemished; a book on the 'Vanity of Science' does him little credit; but he seems at this time to have been occupied with the Gospel. Having received a letter from the excellent Papillon, who told him how favorable the king appeared to the new light, Agrippa, who, surrounded by pious men, took their tone and tuned his voice in harmony with theirs, exclaimed: 'All the Church of the saints with us, hearing of the triumphs of the Word at the court and in the most part of France, rejoiced with exceeding great joy.† I bless the Lord for the glory with which the Word is crowned among you. Would to God that we were permitted, as well as you, to return to France!' Another country was equally attractive to this scholar: 'Write to

* 'Insaniat mundus, et insultet adversus renascens Christi Evangelium.'—Tossanus Œcolampadio, July 26, 1526. Herzog, *Œcolampade*, ii. p. 286.

† 'Gavisa est vehementissme tota Ecclesia sanctorum qui apud nos sunt, audientes fructum Verbi apud aulicos, itidem apud Galliam fere omnem.'—Cornel. Agripp. *Epp.* p. 829.

me what they are doing at Geneva . . . tell me if the Word is loved there, and if they care for learning.'*

Men more decided than Cornelius Agrippa were to be found at Strasburg. During all the winter the hospitable house of Capito had often witnessed the meetings of those christians who had raised highest the standard of the Gospel in France. There assembled the aged Lefèvre, the first translator of the Bible, who had escaped the stake only by flight; the pious Roussel, Vedastes, Simon, and Farel who had arrived from Montbéliard. These friends of the Reformation concealed themselves under assumed names: Lefèvre passed as Anthony Peregrin; Roussel as Tolnin; but they were known by everybody, even by the children in the streets.† They often met Bucer, Zell, and the Count of Hohenlohe, and edified one another. Margaret undertook to bring them all back to France. The court was then in the south; the king was at Cognac, his birthplace, where he often resided; the duchess (his mother and sister) at Angoulême. One day when they met, Margaret entreated her brother to put an end to the cruel exile of her friends: Francis granted everything.

What joy! the aged Lefèvre, the fervent Roussel, are recalled *with honor*, says Erasmus.‡ The Strasburgers embraced them with tears; the old man felt happy that he was going to die in the country where he was born. He immediately took the road to France in company with Roussel; others followed them; all believed that the new times were come. In their meetings the evangelicals called to mind these words of the prophet: *The ransomed of the Lord shall return and come to Zion with songs and everlasting joy upon their heads: they shall obtain joy and gladness, and sorrow and sighing shall flee away.*§ Lefèvre and Roussel

* 'Scribe quid Gebennis agatur, aut scilicet Verbum ament?' The authenticity of this letter is doubted by Bayle, but it appears to me to be established by arguments which are too long to be admitted here.

† 'Omnes Galli, contubernales ac hospites mei. . . Latere cupiunt, et tamen pueris noti sunt.'—Capito to Zwingle, Nov. 20, 1521. Zwingl. *Epp.* i. p. 439.

‡ 'Faber honorifice in Galliam revocatur.'—Erasmi *Epp.* p. 829.

§ Isaiah xxxv. 10.

hastened to their protectress. Margaret received them kindly, lodged them in the castle of Angoulême, where she was born, on that smiling hill which she loved so much, near that 'softly flowing' Charente, as she describes it. Lefèvre and Roussel had many precious conversations with her. They loved to speak of their life at Strasburg, of the new views they had found there, and of the brotherly communion they had enjoyed. 'We were there,' they said, 'with William Farel, Michael of Aranda, Francis Lambert, John Vedastes, the Chevalier d'Esch, and many other evangelicals . . . scattered members of a torn body, but one in Christ Jesus. We carefully put out of sight all that might interrupt the harmony between brethren; the peace that we tasted, far from being without savor, like that of the world, was perfumed with the sweet odor of God's service.'

This meeting at Strasburg had borne fruit. The energetic Farel, the learned Lefèvre, the spiritual Roussel, gifted with such opposite natures, had reacted upon each other. Farel had become more gentle, Roussel more strong; contact with iron had given an unusual hardness to a metal by nature inclined to be soft. The sermons they heard, their frequent conversations, the trials of exile, and the consolation of the Spirit of God, had tempered the souls which had been not a little discouraged by persecution. Roussel had taken advantage of his leisure to study Hebrew, and the Word of God had acquired a sovereign importance in his eyes. Struck by the virtues of which the early christians had given an example, he had found that we must seek for the secret of their lives in the history of the primitive Church, in the inspired Scripture of God. 'The purity of religion will never be restored,' he used to say, 'unless we drink at the springs which the Holy Ghost has given us.'*

It was not enough for the refugees to have returned; their christian activity must be employed to the advantage of France. At the beginning of June, Roussel went to Blois. Margaret wished to make this city—the favorite residence of the Valois, and notorious for the crimes perpetrated there

* 'Nisi adsint qui fontes porrigant, quos reliquit nobis Spiritus sanctus.'—MS. in the Library of Geneva. Schmidt, *Roussel*, p. 188.

in after years—a refuge for the persecuted, a caravanserai for the saints, a stronghold of the Gospel. On the 29th of June Lefèvre also went there.* The king intrusted him with the education of his third son and the care of the castle library. Chapelain, physician to the Duchess of Angoulême, and Cop, another doctor, of whom we shall see more hereafter, were also in that city; and all of them, filled with gratitude towards Francis I., were contriving the means of imparting 'something of christianity to the Most Christian King'†—which was, in truth, very necessary.

Thus things were advancing. It seemed as if learning and the Gospel had returned with the king from banishment. Macrin, whose name Zwingle placed side by side with that of Berquin, was set at liberty.‡ Cornelius Agrippa returned to Lyons. Sprung from an ancient family of Cologne, he had served seven years in the imperial army; he then became a great *savant* (and not a great magician, as was supposed), doctor of theology, law, and medicine. He published a book on Marriage and against celibacy, which excited much clamor. Agrippa was astonished at this, and not without reason. 'What!' he exclaimed, 'the tales of Boccaccio, the jests of Poggio, the adulteries of Euryalus and Lucretia, the loves of Tristan and of Lancelot, are read greedily, even by young girls§ . . . and yet they cry out against my book on Marriage!'—This explains an incident in history; the youthful readers of Boccaccio became the famous 'squadron' of Catherine de' Medici, by whose means that impure woman obtained so many victories over the lords of the court.

When men heard of these deliverances, they thought that Francis I., seeing Charles V. at the head of the Roman party, would certainly put himself at the head of the evan-

* 'Faber Stapulensis hodie hinc discedens, Blesios petiit.'—Cornel. Agripp. *Epp.* p. 4848.

† 'Quod transferas non nihil de christianismo ad christianissimum regem.'—Ibid. p. 859.

‡ 'Berquinus et Macrinus liberabuntur.'—Zwingl. *Epp.* viii. 1.

§ 'Leguntur avide etiam a puellis novellæ Boccatii.'—Cornel. Agripp. *Epp.* p. 833.

gelical cause, and that the two champions would decide on the battle-field the great controversy of the age. 'The king,' wrote the excellent Capito to the energetic Zwingle, 'is favorable to the Word of God.'* Margaret already saw the Holy Ghost reviving in France the *one*, *holy*, and *universal Church*. She resolved to hasten on these happy times, and, leaving Angoulême and Blois in the month of July, arrived in Paris.

Toussaint was waiting for her. Having reached the capital under an assumed name, the young evangelist at first kept himself in concealment. On hearing of the arrival of the sister of Francis, he asked permission to see her in private; and the princess, as was her custom, received him with great kindness. What a contrast for this poor man, just rescued from the cruel talons of the abbot of St. Antoine, to find himself in the palace of St. Germain, where Margaret's person, her urbanity, wit, lively piety, indefatigable zeal, love of letters, and elegance, charmed all who came near her! Toussaint, like the poet, was never tired of admiring

A sweetness living in her beauteous face
Which does the fairest of her sex eclipse,
A lively wit, of learning ample store,
And over all a captivating grace,
Whether she speaks, or silent are her lips.†

One thing, however, charmed Toussaint still more: it was the true piety which he found in Margaret. She treated him with the kindness of a christian woman, and soon put him at his ease. 'The most illustrious Duchess of Alençon,' he wrote, 'has received me with as much kindness as if I had been a prince or the person who was dearest to her.‡ I hope,' he added, 'that the Gospel of Christ will soon reign in France.'§ The duchess, on her part, touched with the faith of the young evangelist, invited him to come again and

* 'Rex Verbo favet.'—Capito Zwinglio.

† Epitre de Marot à la duchesse d'Alençon, 1526.

‡ 'Principem aliquem vel hominem sibi carissimum.'—Tossanus Œcolampadio. Herzog, *Œcolampade*, t. ii. p. 286.

§ 'Brevi regnaturum Christi Evangelium per Galliam.'—Ibid.

see her the next day. He went and he went again; he had long and frequent conversations with Margaret on the means of propagating the Gospel everywhere.* 'God, by the light of his Word,' he said, 'must illumine the world, and by the breath of his Spirit must transform all hearts. The Gospel alone, Madame, will bring into regular order all that is confused.'—'It is the only thing that I desire,' replied Margaret.† She believed in the victory of truth; it seemed to her that the men of light could not be conquered by the men of darkness. The new life was about to rise like the tide, and ere long cover with its wide waves the arid *landes* of France. Margaret espied tongues of fire, she heard eloquent voices, she felt swelling hearts throbbing around her. Everything was stirring in that new and mysterious world which enraptured her imagination. It was to inaugurate this new era, so full of light, of faith, of liberty, that her brother had been delivered from the prisons of Charles V. 'Ah!' she said to Toussaint in their evangelical conversations, 'it is not only myself that desires the triumph of the Gospel; even the king wishes for it.‡ And, believe me, our mother (Louisa of Savoy!) will not oppose our efforts.§ The king,' she protested to the young man, 'is coming to Paris to secure the progress of the Gospel—if, at least, the war does not prevent him.'‖ Noble illusions! Certain ideas on this subject, in accord with his policy, were running, no doubt, in the king's mind; but at that time Francis was thinking of nothing but compensating himself for the privations of captivity by indulging in gallantry.

The young prebendary of Metz was under the spell: he indulged in the greatest hopes, and joyfully hailed the new firmament in which Margaret would shine as one of the brightest stars. He wrote to Œcolampadius: 'This illustrious princess is so taught of God, and so familiar with

* 'Multum sumus confabulati de promovendo Christi Evangelio.'—Tossanus Œcolampadio.

† 'Quod solum est illi in votis.'—Ibid.

‡ 'Nec illi solum, verum etiam regi ipsi.'—Ibid.

§ 'Nec horum conatibus refragatur mater.'—Ibid.

‖ 'Eam ob causam rex contendit Lutetiam.'—Ibid.

Holy Scripture, that no one can ever separate her from Jesus Christ.'* Some have asked whether this prediction was verified. Margaret of Navarre, terrified by her brother's threats, certainly made a lamentable concession in after years, and this is proved by a letter Calvin addressed to her; but she was, nevertheless, a tree planted by the rivers of water. The storm broke off a few branches: still the roots were deep, and the tree did not perish.

Toussaint often found the halls of the palace of St. Germain filled with the most distinguished personages of the kingdom, eager to present their homage to the sister of Francis I. Side by side with ambassadors and nobles dressed in the most costly garments, and soldiers with their glittering arms, were cardinals robed in scarlet and ermine, bishops with their satin copes, ecclesiastics of every order, with long gowns and tonsured heads.† These clerics, all desirous of attaining to the highest offices of the Church, approached the illustrious princess, spoke to her of the Gospel, of Christ, of *inextinguishable love;* and Toussaint listened with astonishment to such strange court language. His former patron, the Cardinal of Lorraine, archbishop of Rheims and of Lyons, whom we must not confound with his infamous nephew, one of the butchers of the St. Bartholomew massacre, gave the young prebendary a most affable reception, never ceasing to repeat that he loved the Gospel extremely. . . Margaret, who permitted herself to be easily persuaded, took the religious prattle of this troop of flatterers for sound piety, and inspired the young christian with her own blind confidence.

Yet the latter sometimes asked himself whether all these fine speeches were not mere court compliments. One day he heard Briçonnet, Bishop of Meaux, in whom the most credulous still placed some hope, rank the Roman Church very high and the Word of God very low: 'Hypocritical priest!' said Toussaint aside, 'you desire more to please men than to please God!' If these sycophant priests chanced to meet

* 'Certe dux Alenconiæ sic est edocta a Domino, sic exercita in litteris sacris, ut a Christo avelli non possit.'—Tossanus Œcolampadio.

† 'Cum suis longis tunicis et capitibus rasis.'—Ibid.

with any noble scoffers or atheists, in some apartment far from that of the princess or on the terrace of St. Germain, they fearlessly threw aside the mask, and turned into ridicule the evangelical faith they had cried up before the sister of Francis I. When they had obtained the benefices they coveted, they changed sides; they were the foremost in attacking the Lutherans;* and if they observed any evangelicals coming, they turned their backs upon them. Then would Toussaint exclaim: 'Alas! they speak well of Jesus Christ with those who speak well of him; but with those who blaspheme, they blaspheme also.'†

Lefèvre and Roussel having come to Paris from Blois, about the end of July, 1526, the young and impetuous Toussaint, full of respect for them, hastened to tell them of his vexations, and demanded that they should unmask these hypocrites and boldly preach the Gospel in the midst of that perverse court. 'Patience,' said the two scholars, both rather temporising in disposition, and whom the air of the court had perhaps already weakened, 'patience! do not let us spoil anything; the time is not yet come.'‡ Then Toussaint, upright, generous, and full of affection, burst into tears. 'I cannot restrain my tears,' he said.§ 'Yes; be wise after your fashion; wait, put off, dissemble as much as you please; you will acknowledge, however, at last, that it is impossible to preach the Gospel without bearing the cross.‖ The banner of divine mercy is now raised, the gate of the kingdom of heaven is open. God does not mean us to receive his summons with supineness. We must make haste, for fear the opportunity should escape us and the door be shut.'

Toussaint, grieved and oppressed by the tone of the court, told all his sorrows to the reformer of Basle: 'Dear Œcolam-

* 'Primi stant in acie adversus eos quos mundus vocat Lutheranos.' —Tossanus Œcolampadio.

† 'Cum bene loquentibus bene loquuntur de Christo, cum blasphemantibus blasphemant'—Ibid.

‡ 'Nondum est tempus, nondum venit hora.'—Tossanus Œcolampadio.

§ 'Certe continere non possum a lacrimis.'—Ibid.

‖ 'Sint sapientes, quantum velint, expectent, differant, et dissimulent . . . non poterit prædicari Evangelium absque cruce.'—Ibid.

padius,' he said, 'when I think that the king and the duchess are as well disposed as possible to promote the Gospel of Christ, and when I see at the same time those who are called to labor the foremost at this excellent work having continual recourse to delay, I cannot restrain my grief. What would not you do in Germany, if the emperor and his brother Ferdinand looked favorably on your efforts?' Toussaint did not hide from Margaret herself how his hopes had been disappointed. 'Lefèvre,' he said, 'is wanting in courage; may God strengthen and support him!' The duchess did all she could to keep the young evangelist at her court; she sought for men who, while having a christian heart and a christian life, would not, however, break with the Church; she accordingly offered the ex-prebendary great advantages, but begging him at the same time to be moderate. Toussaint, a man of susceptible and somewhat hard character, haughtily repelled these advances. He was stifled at the court; the air he breathed there made him sick; admiration had yielded to disgust. 'I despise these magnificent offers,' he said, 'I detest the court more than any one has done.* Farewell to the court . . . it is the most dangerous of harlots.'† Margaret conjured him at least not to quit France, and sent him to one of her friends, Madame de Contraigues, who, abounding in charity for the persecuted evangelists, received them in her château of Malesherbes in the Orléanais. Before leaving, the young Metzer, foreseeing that a terrible struggle was approaching, recommended the friends he left behind him to pray to God that France would show herself worthy of the Word.‡ He then departed, praying the Lord to send to this people the teacher, the apostle, who, being himself a model of truth and devotedness, would lead it in the new paths of life.

* 'Aula, a qua sic abhorreo ut nemo magis.'—Neufchatel MS.

† 'Aula, meretrix periculosissima.'—Tossanus Œcolampadio.

‡ 'Rogate Dominum pro Gallia ut ipsa tandem sit digna Verbo.'—Herzog, *Œcolampade*, p. 288.

CHAPTER VI.

WHO WILL BE THE REFORMER OF FRANCE?

(1526.)

Many evangelical christians thought as Toussaint did. They felt that France had need of a reformer, but could see no one who answered to their ideal. A man of God was wanted, who, possessing the fundamental truths of the Gospel, could set them forth in their living harmony; who, while exalting the divine essence of christianity, could present it in its relations to human nature; who was fitted not only to establish sound doctrine, but also by God's grace to shed abroad a new life in the Church; a servant of God, full of courage, full of activity, as skilful in governing as in leading. A Paul was wanted, but where could he be found?

Would it be Lefèvre? He had taught plainly the doctrine of justification by faith, even before Luther; this we have stated elsewhere,* and many have repeated it since. It is a truth gained to history. But Lefèvre was old and courted repose; pious but timid, a scholar of the closet rather than the reformer of a people.

Would it be Roussel? Possessing an impressionable and wavering heart, he longed for the good, but did not always dare to do it. He preached frequently at the duchess's court before the most distinguished men of the kingdom; but he did not proclaim the whole counsel of God. He knew it, he was angry with himself, and yet he was continually falling into the same error. 'Alas!' he wrote to Farel, 'there are many evangelical truths one half of which I am obliged to conceal. If the Lord does not rekindle my zeal by his presence, I shall be very inferior to what I ought to

* *History of the Reformation*, &c. vol. iii. bk. xii. ch. ii.

be.'* The pious but weak Roussel was just the man the duchess required—fitted to advance christian life without touching the institutions of the Church. Sometimes, however, dissatisfied with his position, and longing to preach the Gospel without any respect to persons, he wished to go to Italy . . . and then he fell again into temporising.†

The most decided christians saw his incompetence. In their eyes the men around the Duchess of Alençon who stopped halfway were incapable of reforming France. It needed, they thought, a man of simple soul, intrepid heart, and powerful eloquence, who, walking with a firm foot, would give a new impulse to the work too feebly commenced by Lefèvre and his friends; and then these christians, going to the other extreme, thought of Farel. At that time this reformer was the greatest light of France. What love he had for Jesus Christ! What eloquence in preaching! What boldness in pressing onwards and surmounting obstacles! What perseverance in the midst of dangers! But neither Francis nor Margaret would have anything to do with him: they were afraid of him. When the king recalled the other exiles, Farel was left behind. He was then at Strasburg with one foot on the frontier, waiting the order for his return, but the order did not come. The court had no taste for his aggressive preaching and his heroic firmness; they wished for a softened and a perfumed Gospel in France. The noble Dauphinese, when he saw all his friends returning to their country while he remained alone in exile, was overwhelmed with sorrow and cried to God in his distress.

Roussel understood Margaret's fears; Farel, he knew, was not a courtier, and would never agree with the duchess. Yet, knowing the value of such a servant of God, the noble and pious Roussel tried whether they could not profit in some other way by his great activity, and if there was not some province that could be opened to his mighty labors. 'I will obtain the means of providing for all your wants,' he wrote to him on the 27th of August from the castle of Am-

* 'Dissimulanda nobis sunt plurima et tot decoquenda.'—Roussel to Farel, Geneva MS. Schmidt, *Roussel*, p. 198.

† 'Petam Venetias.'—Ibid, p. 193.

boise, 'until the Lord gives you at last an entrance and brings you to us.'* That was also Farel's earnest desire; he was not then thinking of Switzerland; his country possessed all his love; his eyes were turned night and day towards those gates of France so obstinately closed against him; he went up to them and knocked. They still remained shut, and returning disheartened he exclaimed: 'Oh! if the Lord would but open a way for me to return and labor in France!' On a sudden the dearest of his wishes seemed about to be realized.

One day, when there was a grand reception at court, the two sons of Prince Robert de la Marche came to pay their respects to the king's sister. Since the eighth century La Marche had formed a principality, which afterwards became an appanage of the Armagnacs and Bourbons.† The Gospel had found its way there. Margaret, who possessed in a high degree the spirit of proselytism, said to Roussel, indicating with her eyes those whose conversion she desired: 'Speak to those two young princes; seize, I pray, this opportunity of advancing the cause of Jesus Christ.'—'I will do so,' replied the chaplain eagerly. Approaching the young noblemen, Roussel began to converse about the Gospel. De Saucy and De Giminetz (for such were their names) showed no signs of astonishment, but listened with the liveliest interest. The evangelist grew bolder, and explained his wishes to them freely.‡ 'It is not for yourselves alone,' he said, 'that God has given you life, but for the good of the members of Jesus Christ. It is not enough for you to embrace Christ as your Saviour; you must communicate the same grace to your subjects.'§ Roussel warmed at the idea of seeing the Gospel preached among the green pastures which the Vienne, the Creuse, and the Cher bathe with

* 'Quousque Dominus ingressum aperuerit.'—Roussel to Farel, Geneva MS. Schmidt, *Roussel*, p. 198.

† Now the departments of Creuse and Haute Vienne.

‡ 'Cum hos reperirem ex animo favere, cœpi libere animum explicare meum, et quid in illis desiderem.'—Roussel to Farel, Dec. 7, 1526, Geneva MS. Schmidt, *Roussel*, p. 200.

§ 'Non satis quod Christum amplectuntur.'—Ibid.

their waters; through Guéret, Bellac, and the ancient territory of the Lemovices and Bituriges. The two young princes on their part listened attentively to the reformer, and gave the fullest assent to his words.* Margaret's chaplain made another step; he thought he had found what he was seeking for the zealous Farel; and when the sons of Robert de la Marche told him they felt too weak for the task set before them, he said: 'I know but one man fitted for such a great work; it is William Farel; Christ has given him an extraordinary talent for making known the riches of his glory. Invite him.' The proposition delighted the young princes. 'We desire it still more than you,' they said; 'our father, and we will open our arms to him. He shall be to us as a son, a brother, and a father.† Let him fear nothing: he shall live with us. Yes, in our own palace. All whom he will meet there are friends of Jesus Christ. Our physician, Master Henry, a truly christian man; the son of the late Count Francis; the lord of Château-Rouge, and his children, and many others, will rejoice at his arrival. We ourselves,' they added, 'will be there to receive him. Only bid him make haste; let him come before next Lent.'—I promise you he shall,' replied Roussel. The two princes undertook to set up a printing establishment in order that Farel might by means of the press circulate evangelical truth, not only in La Marche, but throughout the kingdom. Roussel wrote immediately to his friend; Toussaint added his entreaties to those of the chaplain. 'Never has any news caused me more joy,' he said: 'hasten thither as fast as you can.'‡

The young princes of La Marche were not the only nobles of the court whom the Duchess of Alençon's influence attracted into the paths of the Gospel. Margaret was not one of 'those who cry aloud,' says a christian of her time, 'but of those whose every word is accompanied with teach-

* 'Audiunt, assentiuntur.'—Roussel to Farel, Dec. 7, 1526.

† 'Te perinde ac filium et fratrem, imo si vis patrem habituri.'—Ibid.

‡ 'Quæ res sic animum meum exhilaravit, ut nulla magis. . . . Perinde advola.'—Tossanus Farello, Neufchatel MSS.

ing and imbued with gentleness.' Her eye was always on the watch to discover souls whom she could attract to her Master. Lords, ladies, and damsels of distinction, men of letters, of the robe, of the sword, and even of the Church, heard, either from her lips, or from those of Roussel or of some other of her friends, the Word of life. The nobility entertained a secret but very old dislike to the priests, who had so often infringed their privileges; and they would have liked nothing better than to be emancipated from their yoke. Margaret feared that the young nobles would be only half converted—that there would be no renewal of the heart and life in them; and the history of the wars of religion shows but too plainly how well her fears were founded. Knowing how difficult it is 'to tread the path to heaven,' she insisted on the necessity of a real and moral christianity, and said to the gay youths attracted by the charms of her person and the splendor of her rank:

Who would be a christian true
  Must his Lord's example follow;
Every worldly good resign
  And earthly glory count but hollow;
Honor, wealth, and friends so sweet
He must trample under feet;—
But, alas! to few 't is given
Thus to tread the path to heaven!

With a willing joyful heart
  His goods among the poor divide;
Others' trespasses forgive;
  Revenge and anger lay aside.
Be good to those who work you ill;
If any hate you, love them still:—
But, alas! to few 't is given
Thus to tread the path to heaven!

He must hold death beautiful,
  And over it in triumph sing;
Love it with a warmer heart
  Than he loveth mortal thing.
In the pain that wrings the flesh
  Find a pleasure, and in sadness;
Love death as he loveth life,
  With a more than mortal gladness:—

But, alas! to few 't is given
Thus to tread the path to heaven!*

Would Margaret succeed? A queen with all the splendors of her station is not a good reformer; the work needs poor and humble men. There is always danger when princes turn missionaries; some of the persons around them easily become hypocrites. Margaret attracted men to the Gospel; but the greater part of those who were called by her did not go far; their christianity remained superficial. There were, indeed, many enlightened understandings in the upper ranks of French society, but there were few consciences smitten by the Word of God. Many—and this is a common error in every age—could see nothing but intellectual truths in the doctrine of Jesus Christ: a fatal error that may decompose the religious life of a Church and destroy the national life of a people. No tendency is more opposed to evangelical protestantism, which depends not upon the intellectual, but upon the moral faculty. When Luther experienced those terrible struggles in the convent at Erfurth, it was because his troubled conscience sought for peace; and we may say of the Reformation, that it always began with the awakening of the conscience. Conscience is the palladium of protestantism, far more than the statue of Pallas was the pledge of the preservation of Troy. If the nobility compromised the Reformation in France, it was because their consciences had not been powerfully awakened.

Farel would have been the man fitted for this work. He was one of those whose simple, serious, earnest tones carry away the masses. His voice of thunder made his hearers tremble. The strength of his convictions created faith in their souls, the fervor of his prayers raised them to heaven. When they listened to him, 'they felt,' as Calvin says, 'not merely a few light pricks and stings, but were wounded and pierced to the heart; and hypocrisy was dragged from those wonderful and *more than tortuous* hiding-places which lie deep in the heart of man.' He pulled down and built up with equal energy. Even his life—an apostleship full of

* *Marguerites de la Marguerite*, i. p. 333.

self-sacrifice, danger, and triumph—was as effectual as his sermons. He was not only a minister of the Word; he was a bishop also. He was able to discern the young men fitted to wield the weapons of the Gospel, and to direct them in the great war of the age. Farel never attacked a place, however difficult of access, which he did not take. Such was the man then called into France, and who seemed destined to be its reformer. The letters of Roussel and Toussaint inviting Farel were conveyed to Strasburg, and arrived there in the month of December, 1526.

Farel, who had remained alone in that city after the departure of his friends, kept, as we have already mentioned, his eyes turned towards France. He waited and waited still, hesitating to go to Switzerland, whither he was invited; but those gates of France, from which he could not turn away his eyes, still remained closed. He reflected; he asked himself what place God had reserved for him. His piercing glance would have desired to penetrate the future. . . Should he not return into Dauphiny? At Gap and Manosque he had relatives favorable to the Gospel: his brother Walter, clerk of the episcopal court; his brother Jean-Jacques, who expounded the Bible with as much boldness as himself; Antoine Aloat, the notary, who had married one of his nieces; his brother-in-law, the noble Honorat Riquetti, 'one of the ancestors of Mirabeau,' as the record-keeper of the Hautes Alpes informs us.* There are certainly few names we might be more surprised at seeing brought together than those of Farel and Mirabeau; and yet between these two Frenchmen there are at least two points of contact: the power of their eloquence, and the boldness of their reforms.

Farel did not return to Gap; had he done so, we may suppose how he would have been received, from the reception given to him some years later, the particulars of which an archæologist has discovered in the 'Annals of the Capu-

* *Les Guerres de la Religion dans les Hautes Alpes*, par M. Charronnet, archiviste de la préfecture: Gap, 1861, p. 17. M. Charronnet discovered this 'unexpected fact,' as he calls it, in the municipal archives of Manosque (procès d'Aloat). The family name of Mirabeau was Riquetti.

chins' of Gap. Farel, already an old man, wishing to preach the Gospel in his native country before God summoned him from the world, went and took up his quarters in a corn-mill at the gates of his native town, where he 'dogmatised' the peasants from a French Bible, which he explained 'in his fashion'—to use the words of the Roman catholic author. Ere long he began to preach in the very heart of the town, in a chapel dedicated to St. Colomba. The magistrate forbade his speaking, and the parliament of Grenoble desired 'to have him burnt,' say the Capuchins. Farel replied by a formal refusal of obedience; upon which the vice-bailiff, Benedict Olier, a zealous catholic, escorted by several sergeants and police officers, proceeded to the chapel where Farel was preaching. The door was shut; they knocked, but nobody answered; they broke in, and found a considerable throng; no one turned his head, all were listening greedily to the reformer's words. The officers of justice went straight to the pulpit; Farel was seized, and with 'the crime' (the Bible) in his hand, according to the forcible expression of the Capuchins, was led through the crowd and shut up in prison. But the followers of the new doctrine were already to be found in every class—in the workman's garret, in the tradesman's shop, in the fortified mansion of the noble, and sometimes even in the bishop's palace. During the night the reformers, either by force or stratagem, took the brave old man out of prison, carried him to the ramparts, and let him down into the fields in a basket. 'Accomplices' were waiting for him, and the preacher escaped along with them.* Now let us return to the year 1526.

Berthold Haller, the reformer of Berne, invited Farel to Switzerland. The Bernese possessed certain districts in Roman Switzerland where a missionary speaking the French language was necessary. The invitations of the pious Haller were repeated. If France is shut, Switzerland is opening; Farel can hesitate no longer; God removes him from one of these countries and calls him to the other; he will obey.

* *Les Guerres de la Religion dans les Hautes Alpes*, par M. Charronnet, pp. 19–22.

Farel, sadly grieved at the thought that his native country rejected him, modestly departed from Strasburg, on foot, one day in the month of December, 1526; and, journeying up the Rhine, directed his steps towards those Alpine districts of which he became one of the greatest reformers.* He was on the road when the messenger of Toussaint and Roussel arrived at Strasburg. . . It was too late. His friends, knowing that he was going to Berne, sent the letters after him, and it was at Aigle, where Farel had set up as a schoolmaster, that he received the invitation of the lords of La Marche. What shall he do? He might return. Shall he put aside the call of God and of the lords of Berne to follow that which the princes have sent him? There was a fierce struggle in his soul. Was not France his birthplace? It was; but . . . it is too late! God has spoken, he said to himself; and though invited by princes, Farel remained at the humble desk in his little school in the small town of Aigle, situated between the majestic Dent du Midi and the rugged glaciers of the Diablerets. Thus the reformer whom many christians thought of for France was lost to her.

France was not, however, without resources; she still possessed Berquin, whom some called her *Luther;* but while the exiles and the prisoners had heard the hour of their deliverance strike, Berquin, though treated with more consideration, was still deprived of his liberty. Margaret was unwearied in her petitions to the king. She even attempted to soften Montmorency; but the Romish theologians made every attempt to counteract her influence. Friends and enemies were equally of opinion that if Berquin were free, he would deal many a hard blow at the hierarchy. At length, after an eight months' struggle, Margaret triumphed; Berquin left his prison in November, 1526, just at the time when Farel was leaving France.

The Duchess of Alençon's gratitude immediately burst forth. Calling Montmorency by a tenderer name than usual, she said: 'I thank you, my son, for the pleasure you have done me in the cause of poor Berquin. You may say that

* *Hist. of the Ref. of the Sixteenth Century,* vol. iv. bk. xv. ch. i.

you have taken me from prison, for I value it as a favor done to myself.'* . . . 'My lord,' she wrote to the king, 'my desire to obey your commands was already very great, but you have doubled it by the charity you have been pleased to show towards poor Berquin. He for whom he suffered will take pleasure in the mercy you have shown his servant and yours for your honor; and the confusion of those who have forgotten God will not be less than the perpetual glory which God will give you.'†

As soon as Berquin was free he began to meditate on his great work, which was to destroy the power of error. His liberation was not in his eyes a simple deliverance from prison—it was a call. He cared little (as Erasmus entreated him) to indulge in sweet repose on the banks of the Somme; his earnest desire was to fight. He held that the life of a christian man should be a continual warfare. No truce with Satan! Now, to him, Satan was the Sorbonne, and he had no more doubts about the victory than if the war were ended already. Berquin was universally known, loved, and respected. To Farel's decision and zeal he added a knowledge of the world, which was then most necessary. Margaret clung to him at least as much as to Roussel. It was generally thought among christians that God had brought him forth from prison in order to set him at the head of the Reform in France: Berquin himself thought so. The friends of the Reformation rejoiced, and an important circumstance increased their hopes.

Another joy was in store for Margaret. Francis perceived at last that Henry VIII. preferred Anne Boleyn to his illustrious sister, whose maid of honor she had formerly been. From that hour he no longer opposed the wishes of the King of Navarre, and in November consented to his union with Madame of Alençon.

On the 24th of January, 1527, a brilliant throng filled the chapel of the palace of St. Germain, where the marriage of the king's sister was to be solemnised, and every mouth

* *Lettres de la Reine de Navarre*, i. p. 219.

† *Lettres de la Reine de Navarre*, ii. p. 77. The editor thinks that this letter was sent to Madrid; but in my opinion it is an error.

extolled the genius, grace, and virtues of the princess. Margaret of France and Henry d'Albret were united, and for a week there were magnificent tournaments. Francis made very fine promises to the married pair. 'Make your mind easy,' he said to Henry; 'I will summon the Emperor to restore your kingdom of Navarre, and if he refuses, I will give you an army to recover it.'* But not long after, this prince, when drawing up a diplomatic paper by which he bound Charles V. to restore his two sons, then hostages at Madrid, inserted this clause: '*Item*, the said king promises not to assist or favor the King of Navarre in recovering his kingdom, although he has married his beloved and only sister.'†

At that time Margaret was thinking of other things than earthly kingdoms. At this solemn moment she turned her eyes towards eternity, and poured out her heart on the bosom of a friend. 'A thousand chances may separate us from this world,' she said to Madame de la Rochefoucauld. 'Whether we be near or far, in peace or in war, on horseback or in our bed . . . God takes and leaves whom he pleases.'‡ The queen soon found that her lot was not all sunshine, and that Henry d'Albret's humor was not always the same. Her husband's weakness urged her to seek more earnestly 'the heavenly lover,' as she said to Madame de la Rochefoucauld; and the splendid wedding, which was long talked of, made her desire the better marriage. It was then she wrote:

Would that the day were come, O Lord,
  So much desired by me,
When by the cords of heavenly love
  I shall be drawn to thee!
United in eternal life,
The husband thou, and I the wife.

That wedding-day, O Lord,
  My heart so longs to see,
That neither weaith, nor, fame, nor rank
  Can pleasure give to me.

---

* *Dames Illustres*, by H. de Coste, ii. p. 271.
† Béthune MSS. n° 8546, f° 107.
‡ *Lettres de la Reine de Navarre*, i. p. 222.

To me the world no more
Can yield delight.
Unless thou, Lord, be with me there . . .
Lo! all is dark as night.*

Prayer did not constitute the sole happiness of the new queen: activity, charity, an eagerness to help others, did not bring her less pleasure. By her marriage she acquired more liberty to protect the Reform. 'All eyes are fixed on you,' Capito wrote to her.† She thought that Roussel her confessor, and Michael of Aranda her bishop, were about to advance notably the kingdom of God, and rejoiced at seeing these men of learning and morality pronounce daily more strongly in favor of the truth.‡

The world was at one of the great turning-points of its history; and the friends of letters and of the Gospel said to themselves that France, which had always been in the van of society during the middle ages, would not now fall to the rear. Pure faith, they thought, would penetrate every class, would renew the fountains of moral life, and teach the people at once obedience and liberty. Placed between the middle and the modern age, Francis I. would make the new times replace the old in everything. All, in fact, was changing. Gothic architecture gave way to the creations of the Renaissance; the study of the classic authors took the place of the scholasticism of the universities; and in the halls of the palace, mingled with nobles and priests, was seen a crowd of new persons—philologers, archæologists, poets, painters, and doctors of the Roman law. When the light was thus making its way everywhere, would the Church alone remained closed against it? The Renaissance had opened the gates to a new era; and the Reformation would give the new generation the strength necessary to enter them.

But where was the man who could give to the world,

* *Marguerites*, i. p. 513.

† 'Sunt in te omnium oculi defixi.'—Capito, *Comment. in Oseam.*

‡ 'Apud bonos et doctos, quorum non pauci sunt Parisiis, bene audis.'—Zwingle, *Epp.* i. p. 548.

and especially wherever the French language was spoken, that strong and salutary impulse? It was not Lefèvre, Roussel, Farel, or Berquin. . . . Who was it then?

It is time that we should learn to know him.

CHAPTER VII.

CALVIN'S EARLY STUDIES AND EARLY STRUGGLES.

(1523–1527.)

The tendencies of an epoch are generally personified in some man whom it produces, but who soon overrules these tendencies and leads them to the goal which they could not otherwise have reached. To the category of these eminent personages, of these great men, at once the children and the masters of their age, the reformers have belonged. But whilst the heroes of the world make the forces of their epoch the pedestal of their own greatness, the men of God think only how they may be made to subserve the greatness of their Master. The Reformation existed in France, but the reformer was still unknown. Farel would have been a powerful evangelist; but his country had rejected him, and being besides a man of battle, he was neither the doctor nor the guide which the work of the sixteenth century required. A greater than Farel was about to appear, and we shall proceed to watch his first steps in the path along which he was afterwards to be the guide of many nations.

In the classes of the college of La Marche in Paris there were, in the year 1526, a professor of about fifty, and a scholar of seventeen; they were often seen together. The scholar, instead of playing with his class-fellows, attached himself to his master during the hours of recreation, and listened eagerly to his conversation. They were united as a distinguished teacher and a pupil destined to become a great man sometimes are. Their names were Mathurin Cordier and John Calvin.* Mathurin was one of those men of ancient mould, who always prefer the public good to their own interests and glory; and accordingly, neglecting the brilliant career which lay before him, he devoted his whole life to the education of children. Prior to Calvin's arrival at Paris, he had the head class in the college and taught it with credit; but he was not satisfied; he would often pause in the middle of his lessons, finding that his pupils possessed a mere superficial knowledge of what they should have known thoroughly. Teaching, instead of yielding him the pleasure for which he thirsted, caused him only sorrow and disgust. 'Alas!' he said, 'the other masters teach the children from ambition and vain-glory, and that is why they are not well grounded in their studies.' He complained to the director of the college. 'The scholars who join the first class,' he said, 'bring up nothing solid: they are puffed out only to make a show, so that I have to begin teaching them all over again.'† Cordier therefore desired to resign the first class and descend to the fourth, in order to lay the foundations well.

He had just taken this humble department upon himself, when one day, in the year 1523, he saw a boy entering his school, thin, pale, diffident but serious, and with a look of great intelligence. This was John Calvin, then only fourteen years old. At first he was shy and timid in the presence of the learned professor; but the latter discovering in him a scholar of a new kind, immediately became attached to him, and took delight in developing his young and comprehensive intellect. Gradually the apprehensions of the Noyon boy were dissipated, and during the whole time he spent at college he enjoyed the instructions of the master, 'as a singular blessing from God.' Accordingly, when both of them, in after years, had been driven from France, and had taken up their abode among the mountains of Switzerland, Calvin, then one of the great doctors of Europe, loved

* *History of the Reformation*, vol. iii. bk. xii. ch. xv.

† A Mathurin Cordier, Dédicace du *Commentaire de la* 1re *Ep. aux Thess.* par Calvin: Genève, 17 février 1550.

to turn back with humility to these days of his boyhood, and publicly displaying his gratitude, he said to Cordier: 'O Master Mathurin, O man gifted with learning and great fear of God! when my father sent me to Paris, while still a child, and possessing only a few rudiments of the Latin language, it was God's will that I should have you for my teacher, in order that I might be directed in the true path and right mode of learning; and having first commenced the course of study under your guidance, I advanced so far that I can now in some degree profit the Church of God.'*

At the time of Calvin's admission to college, both master and pupil, equally strangers to evangelical doctrine, devoutly followed the exercises of the Romish worship. Doubtless Cordier was not satisfied with teaching his favorite pupil Latin and Greek; he initiated him also in that more general culture which characterised the Renaissance; he imparted to him a certain knowledge of antiquity and of ancient civilisation, and inspired him early with the ardor which animated the classical school; but when Calvin says he was directed by Cordier 'in the true path,' he means the path of science, and not that of the Gospel.

Some time after the scholar's arrival, the director of the college, perceiving him to be more advanced than his classmates, determined to remove him to a higher form. When Calvin heard of this, he could not repress his sorrow, and gave way to one of those fits of anger and ill-humor of which he never entirely cured himself. Never did promotion cause such grief to a scholar. 'Dear Master Mathurin,' he said, 'this man, so thoughtless and void of judgment, who arranges my studies at his will, or rather according to his silly fancy, will not permit me to enjoy your instructions any longer; he is putting me too soon into a higher class. . . What a misfortune!'†

It was only a question of removing him, however, from

* A Mathurin Cordier, Dédicace du *Commentaire de la* 1re *Ep. aux Thess.* par Calvin: Genève, 17 février 1550.

† The language of the text is taken from the French; in his Latin Commentary, Calvin says: 'Ab homine stolido, cujus arbitrio vel potius libidine.' &c.—Dédicace du *Comm. de la* 1re *Ep. aux. Thess.*

one class to another, and not, as some have supposed, to another college. Calvin, while pursuing higher studies, still remained under the same roof as Cordier. He ran to him in the intervals of his lessons; he hung upon his lips, and during the whole time of his stay at La Marche, he continued to profit by Cordier's exquisite taste, pure latinity, vast erudition, and admirable gifts in forming youth.

Yet the moment came when it was necessary to part. John Calvin had told his professor that he was intended for a priest, according to the arrangement of his father, who hoped that, thanks to the protection of his powerful friends, his son would attain to high dignity in the Church. The scholar must therefore enter one of the colleges appointed for the training of learned priests. There were two of these in Paris: the Sorbonne and the Montaigu,* and the last was chosen. One day, therefore, in 1526, the moment arrived when the young man had to take leave of the excellent Cordier. He was greatly distressed: he would be separated from him, not only during the hours of study, but for long days together. All through life his affectionate nature clung to those who showed sympathy to him. He left his master with a heart overflowing with gratitude. 'The instruction and the training that you gave me,' he said in after years, 'have served me so well, that I declare with truth, that I owe to you all the advancement which has followed. I wish to render testimony of this to those who come after us, in order that if they derive any profit from my writings, they may know that it proceeds in part from you.'† God has often great masters in reserve for great men. Cordier, the teacher, subsequently became the disciple of his scholar, and in his turn thanked him, but it was for a divine teaching of inestimable value.

When Calvin entered Montaigu College he was distressed, for he could not hope to find there the master he had lost; yet he was eager and happy at having a wider field of studies opening before him.

* Chevillier, *Origine de l'Imprimerie,* p. 89.

† 'Atque hoc posteris testatum, &c.'—Dédicace à Mathurin Cordier du *du Comm. de la* 1re *Ep. aux Thess.*

One of the first professors he noticed was a Spaniard,* who, under a cold exterior, hid a loving heart, and whose grave and silent air concealed deep affections. Calvin felt attracted towards him. The fame of the young scholar had preceded him at Montaigu; and accordingly the doctor from the Iberian peninsula fixed on him an attentive eye. Slow, calm, and deliberate, as Spaniards generally are, he carefully studied young Calvin, had several intimate conversations with him, and soon passed from the greatest coldness to the liveliest affection. 'What a wonderful genius!' he exclaimed.†

The professor had brought from Spain the fervent catholicism, the minute observances, the blind zeal that characterise his nation.

The scholar of Noyon could not, therefore, receive from him any evangelical knowledge; on the contrary, the Spaniard, delighted at seeing his pupil 'obstinately given to the superstitions of popery,'‡ hoped that the young man would be a shining light in the Church.

Calvin, full of admiration for the poets, orators, and philosophers of antiquity, studied them eagerly and enriched his mind with their treasures; in his writings we often meet with quotations from Seneca, Virgil, and Cicero. He soon left all his comrades far behind. The professor, who looked on him with surprise, promoted him to the class of philosophy, although he had not attained the required age.§ Then a new world, the world of thought, opened before his fine understanding; he traversed it with indefatigable ardor. Logic, dialectics, and philosophy possessed for him an indescribable charm.‖

Calvin made many friends among his fellow-collegians; yet he soared high above them all by the morality of his

* 'Hispanum habuit doctorem.'—Bezæ *Vita Calvini.*

† 'Ingenium acerrimum.'—Bezæ *Vita Calvini.*

‡ Calvin, Preface to his *Commentary on the Psalms.*

§ 'Ita profecit ut cæteris sodalibus in grammatices curriculo relictis.' —Calvin, Preface to *Commentary on the Psalms.*

‖ 'Ad dialectices et aliarum quas vocant artium studium promoveretua.'—Ibid.

character. There was no pedantry, no affectation about him; but when he was walking in the courts of the college, or in the halls where the pupils assembled, he could not witness their quarrels, their follies, their levity of manner, and not reprove them faithfully. 'He finds fault with everything,' complained a scholar of equivocal conduct. 'Profit rather by the advice of so young and conscientious a censor,' answered the wiser ones.* 'Roman catholics whose testimony was beyond reproach,' says Theodore Beza, 'told me of this many years after, when his name had become famous.'† 'It is not the act alone,' said Calvin subsequently, 'but the look, and even the secret longing, which make men guilty.'—'No man,' says one of his adversaries, 'ever felt so great a hatred of adultery.'‡ In his opinion chastity was the crown of youth, and the centre of every virtue.

The heads of Montaigu College were enthusiastic supporters of popery. Beda, so notorious for his violent declamations against the Reformation, for his factious intrigues, and for his tyrannical authority, was principal.§ He watched with satisfaction young Calvin, who, a strict observer of the practices of the Church, never missed a fast, a retreat, a mass, or a procession. 'It is a long time,' it was said, 'since Sorbonne or Montaigu had so pious a seminarist.' As long as Luther, Calvin, and Farel were in the Papal Church, they belonged to its strictest sect. The austere exercises of a devotee's life were the schoolmaster that brought them to Christ. 'I was at that time so obstinately given to the superstitions of popery,' said Calvin, 'that it seemed impossible that I should ever be pulled out of the deep mire.

He surprised his tutors no less by his application to study. Absorbed in his books, he often forgot the hours for his meals and even for sleep. The people who lived in the neighborhood used to show each other, as they returned home in the evening, a tiny and solitary gleam, a window lit

* 'In suis sodalibus vitiorum censor.'—Bezæ *Vita Calvini.*

† 'Quod ex nonnullis etiam catholicis idoneis testibus . . . audire memini.'—Ibid.

‡ 'Nemo adulteria acrius odisse videbatur.'—Papyrius Masso.

§ *Dictionnaire de Bayle,* art. *Beda.*

up nearly all the night through: they long talked of it in that quarter. John Calvin outstripped his companions in philosophy, as he had done in grammar. He then applied to the study of theology, and, strange to say, was enraptured with Scotus, Bonaventura, and Thomas Aquinas. The last-mentioned writer had especial charms for him. If Calvin had not been a reformer he would have become a Thomist. Scholastics appeared to him the queen of sciences; but he was the impassioned lover at first, only that he might be afterwards its terrible adversary.

His father, secretary to the diocese of Noyon, always entertained the hope of making his son a dignitary of the Church. With this object he cultivated the favor of the bishop, and spoke humbly to the canons. John had been for some years chaplain at La Gesine, but this did not satisfy the father; and, accordingly, when the living of St. Martin of Marteville became vacant, Gerard Cauvin solicited and, to his great delight, obtained that church for the student of Montaigu, who, as yet, had only received the tonsure. This was in the year 1527. Calvin, taking advantage probably of vacation time, went to see his family and his new parish. It has been supposed that he preached there. 'Although he had not yet taken orders,' says Beda, 'he delivered several sermons before the people.' Did he really go into the pulpits of his native country at the time when his inward struggles were beginning? To have heard him would have been a great satisfaction to his father, and his age was no obstacle to his preaching; some great preachers have begun still earlier. But it seems to us, after examining the passage, that he did not speak in his own church until later, when the Gospel had completely triumphed in his heart. But, however that may be, Calvin had a parish at eighteen: he was not, however, in holy orders.

A new light which had but little resemblance to the false radiance of scholasticism, began to shine around him. At that time there was a breath of the Gospel in the air, and that reviving breeze reached the scholar within the walls of his college, and the monk in the recesses of his convent; no one was protected against its influence. Calvin heard people talking of the Holy Scriptures of Lefèvre, of Luther, of Melancthon, and of what was passing in Germany. When the rays of the sun rise in the Alps, it is the highest peaks that catch them first; in like manner, the most eminent minds were enlightened first. But what some accepted, others rejected. In the colleges there were sharp and frequent altercations, and Calvin was at first in the number of the most inflexible adversaries of the Reformation.

A young man of Noyon, his cousin, and a little older than him, often went to see him at college. Pierre Robert Olivétan, without possessing the transcendant genius of his young relation, was gifted with a solid mind, great perseverance in the discharge of his duties, unshaken fidelity to his convictions, and a holy boldness when it became necessary to combat error. This he showed at Geneva, where his was one of the first voices raised in favor of the Gospel. When Calvin discovered that the friend of his childhood was tainted with heresy, he felt the keenest sorrow. What a pity! he thought; for Olivétan was acquainted not only with Latin, but with Greek and even Hebrew. He read the Old and New Testaments in their original languages, and was familiar with the Septuagint. The study of the Holy Scriptures, of which Picardy seems to have been the birthplace in France (Lefèvre, Olivétan, and Calvin were all three Picardins), had increased considerably since Lefèvre's translation was published. It is true that most of those who engaged in it 'looked at the Scriptures in a cursory manner,' says Calvin; 'but others dug deep for the treasure that lay hidden there.' Of this number was Olivétan, and he it was who one day gave to the people speaking the French tongue a translation of the Scriptures that became famous in the history of the Bible.

The chronology of Calvin's life during the period of his studies is less easily settled than that of Luther. We have been able to point out almost the very days when the most striking transformations of his faith were completed in the reformer of Germany. It is not so with the reformer of Geneva. The exact moment when this struggle, this defeat, or that victory took place in Calvin's soul, cannot be determined. Must we therefore suppress the history of his spiritual combats? To pass them over in silence would be to fail in the first duty of an historian.*

Olivétan, who was then in all the fervor of proselytism, felt great interest in his catholic cousin, while the latter would have wished at any cost to bring back his friend into the bosom of the Church. The two youthful Picardins had many long and animated conversations together, in which each strove to convert the other.† 'There are many false religions,' said Olivétan, 'and only one true.' Calvin assented. 'The false are those which men have invented, according to which we are saved by our own works; the true is that which comes from God, acccording to which salvation is given freely from on high. . . Choose the true.'‡ Calvin made a sign of dissent. 'True religion,' continued Olivétan, 'is not that infinite mass of ceremonies and observances which the Church imposes upon its followers, and which separate souls from Christ. O my dear friend! leave off shouting out with the papists: "The fathers! the doctors! the Church!" and listen instead to the prophets and apostles. Study the Scriptures.'§ 'I will have none of your doctrines,' answered Calvin; 'their novelty offends me. I cannot listen to you. Do you imagine that I have been trained all my life in error? . . . No! I will strenuously resist your attacks.|| In after years Calvin said: 'My heart, hardened by superstition, remained insensible to all these appeals.' The two cousins parted, little satisfied with each other. Calvin, terrified at his friend's innovations, fell on his knees in the chapels, and prayed the saints to intercede

* In the French edition, Calvin's words are quoted literally from the French text of the *Opuscules*, and his Latin only is given in the notes. This will account for any slight differences that may be observed between the English version and the authorities at the foot of the page.

† 'A cognato quodam suo Petro Roberto Olivetano.'—Bezæ *Vita Calvini.*

‡ 'De vera religione admonitus.'—Ibid.

§ 'Legendis sacris libris se tradere.'—Ibid.

|| 'At ego novitate offensus . . . Ægerrime adducebar ut me in ignoratione et errore tota vita versatum esse confiterer, strenue animoseque resistebam.'—Calvini *Opuscula*, p. 125.

for this misguided soul.* Olivétan shut himself up in his chamber and prayed to Christ.

Yet Calvin, whose mind was essentially one of observation, could not be present in the midst of the great movement going on in the world without reflecting on truth, on error, and on himself. Oftentimes when alone, and when the voices of men had ceased to be heard, a more powerful voice spoke to his soul, and his chamber became the theatre of struggles as fierce as those in the cell at Erfurth. Through the same tempests both these great reformers reached the same haven. Calvin arrived at faith by the same practical way which had led Farel and Augustine, Luther and St. Paul.

The student of Montaigu, uneasy and troubled after his controversies with his young relative, shut himself up in his little room and examined himself; he asked himself what he was, and where he was going. . . 'O Lord,' he said, 'thou knowest that I profess the Christian faith such as I learnt it in my youth.† . . . And yet there is something wanting. . . . I have been taught to worship thee as my only God; but I am ignorant of the true worship I ought to give.‡ . . . I have been taught that thy Son has ransomed me by his death; . . . but I have never felt in my heart the virtue of this redemption.§ I have been taught that some day there will be a resurrection; but I dread it as the most terrible of days.‖ . . . Where shall I find the light that I need? . . . Alas! thy Word, which should enlighten thy people like a lamp, has been taken from us.¶ . . . Men talk in its place of a hidden knowledge, and of a small number of initiates whose oracles we must receive. . . O God, illumine me with thy light!'

The superiors of Montaigu College began to feel some uneasiness about their student. The Spanish professor, in-

* 'Ad sanctos primum confugere.'—Calvini *Opuscula*, p. 125.

† 'Ego, Domine, ut a puero fueram educatus.'—Ibid.

‡ 'Sed cum me penitus fugeret vera colendi ratio.'—Ibid.

§ 'Redemptionem, cujus virtus nequaquam ad me perveniret.'—Ib.

‖ 'Cujus diei memoriam, velut rei infaustissimæ abominarer.'—Ibid.

¶ 'Verbum tuum . . . ademptum.'—Ibid.

clined, like his countrymen, to the spirit of intolerance, saw with horror the young man, whose devotion had charmed him at first, discontented with the traditional religion, and ready perhaps to forsake it. Could the best of their pupils fall into heresy? . . . The tutors entered into converation with Calvin, and, as yet full of affection for the young man, sought to strengthen him in the Roman faith. 'The highest wisdom of Christians,' they said, 'is to submit blindly to the Church,* and their highest dignity is the righteousness of their works.'†—'Alas!' replied Calvin, who was conscious of the guilt within him, 'I am a miserable sinner!'—'That is true,' answered the professors, 'but there is a means of obtaining mercy: it is by satisfying the justice of God.‡ . . . Confess your sins to a priest, and ask humbly for absolution. . . . Blot out the memory of your offences by your good works, and, if anything should still be wanting, supply it by the addition of solemn sacrifices and purifications.'

When he heard these words, Calvin reflected that he who listens to a priest listens to Christ himself. Being subdued, he went to church, entered the confessional, fell on his knees, and confessed his sins to God's minister, asking for absolution and humbly accepting every penance imposed upon him. And immediately, with all the energy of his character, he endeavored to acquire the merits demanded by his confessor. 'O God!' he said, 'I desire by my good works to blot out the remembrance of my trespasses.'§ He performed the 'satisfactions' prescribed by the priest; he even went beyond the task imposed upon him, and hoped that after so much labor he would be saved. . . But, alas! his peace was not of long duration. A few days, a few hours perhaps, had not passed, when, having given way to a movement of impatience or anger, his heart was again troubled: he thought he saw God's eye piercing to the depths of his soul and discovering its impurities. 'O God!' he exclaimed in alarm, 'thy

* 'Non altiorem intelligentiam convenire quam ut se ad Ecclesiæ obedientiam subigerent.'—Calvini *Opusc.* p. 125.

† 'Dignitatem porro in operum justitiâ collocabant.'—Ibid.

‡ 'Si pro offensis tibi satisfieret.'—Ibid.

§ 'Ut bonis operibus malorum memoriam apud te deleremus.'—Ibid.

glance freezes me with terror.'* . . . He hurried again to the confessional.—'God is a strict judge,' the priest told him, 'who severely punishes iniquity. Address your prayers to the saints first.'† And Calvin, who, in after years, branded as blasphemers those who invented 'false intercessors,' invoked the saints and prayed them by their intercession to appease a God who appeared to him so inexorable.

Having thus found a few moments of relief, he applied again to his studies; he was absorbed in his books; he grew pale over Scotus and Thomas Aquinas; but in the midst of his labors a sudden trouble took possession of his mind, and pushing away from him the volumes that lay before him, he exclaimed: 'Alas! my conscience is still very far from true tranquillity.'‡ His heart was troubled, his imagination excited, he saw nothing but abysses on every side, and with a cry of alarm he said: 'Every time that I descend into the depths of my heart; every time, O God, that I lift up my soul to thy throne, extreme terror comes over me.§ . . . I see that no purification, no satisfaction can heal my disease.‖ My conscience is pierced with sharp stings.'¶

Thus step by step did Calvin descend to the lowest depths of despair; and quite heartbroken, and looking like one dead, he resolved to take no further pains about his salvation. He lived more with his fellow-pupils, he even shared in their amusements; he visited his friends in the city, sought such conversation as would divert his thoughts, and desired, with the Athenians of old, either to tell or to hear some new thing. Will the work of God, begun in his heart, remain unperfected?

This year an event took place which could not fail to stir the depths of Calvin's soul.

* 'Quam formidolosus tuus conspectus.'—Calvini *Opus.* p. 125.

† 'Quia rigidus esset judex et severus vindex, jubebant ad sanctos primum confugere.'—Ibid.

‡ 'Procul adhuc aberam a certa conscientiæ tranquillitate.'—Ibid.

§ 'Quoties enim vel in me descendebam, vel animum ad te attollebam, extremus horror me incessebat.'—Ibid.

‖ 'Nulla piacula, nullæ satisfactiones mederi possent.'—Ibid

¶ 'Eo acrioribus pungebatur aculeis conscientia.'—Ibid.

CHAPTER VIII.

CALVIN'S CONVERSION AND CHANGE OF CALLING.

(1527.)

The kingdom of Christ is strengthened and established more by the blood of martyrs than by force of arms,' said the doctor of Noyon one day.* At this period he had occasion to experience the truth of the statement.

One day in the year 1527, a man thirty-six years old, of good family—he was related to M. de Lude—of ecclesiastical rank, prothonotary, and holding several benefices, Nicholas Doullon by name, having been accused of heresy, stood in front of the cathedral of Notre Dame, while an immense crowd of citizens, priests, and common people were looking on. The executioner had gone in the morning to the prison, stripped the prothonotary of his official robes, and having passed a rope round his neck and put a taper in his hand, had conducted him in this guise to the front of the church of the Virgin. The poor fellow had seen better days: he had often gone to the palaces of the Louvre, St. Germain, and Fontainebleau, and mingled with the nobles, in the presence of the king, his mother, and his sister; he had also been one of the officers of Clement VII. The good folks of Paris, whom this execution had drawn together, said to one another as they witnessed the sad spectacle: 'He frequented the king's court, and has lived at Rome in the pope's service.†

Doullon was accused of having uttered a great blasphemy against the glorious mother of our Lord and against our Lord himself: he had denied that the host was very Christ.

* Calvin, *Comm. sur S. Jean*, xviii. v. 36.

† *Journal d'un Bourgeois de Paris sous François I.* p. 317.

The clergy had taken advantage of the king's absence, and had used unprecedented haste in the trial. 'He was taken the Thursday before,' and four days later was standing bare-headed and barefooted, with the rope about his neck, in front of the metropolitan church of Paris. Everybody was listening to hear the apology he would make to the Virgin; but they listened in vain; Doullon remained firm in his faith to the last. Accordingly, the hangman again laid hands on him, and the prothonotary, guarded by the sergeants, and preceded and followed by the crowd, was led to the Grève, where he was fastened to the stake and burnt alive.* The execution of a priest of some dignity in the Church made a sensation in Paris, especially in the schools and among the disciples of the Reform. 'Ah,' said Calvin subsequently, 'the torments of the saints whom the hand of the Lord makes invincible, should give us boldness; for thus we have beforehand the pledge of our victory in the persons of our brethren.'

While death was thinning the ranks of the evangelical army, new soldiers were taking the place of those who had disappeared. Calvin had been wandering for some time in darkness, despairing of salvation by the path of the pope, and not knowing that of Jesus Christ. One day (we cannot say when) he saw light breaking through the obscurity, and a consoling thought suddenly entered his heart. 'A new form of doctrine has risen up,' he said.† 'If I have been mistaken . . . if Olivétan, if my other friends, if those who give their lives to preserve their faith are right . . . if they have found in that path the peace which the doctrines of the priests refuse me?' . . . He began to pay attention to the things that were told him; he began to examine into the state of his soul. A ray of light shone into it and exposed his sin. His heart was troubled: it seemed to him that every word of God he found in Scripture tore off the veil and reproached him with his trespasses. He shed floods of tears. 'Of a surety,' he said, 'these new preachers

* *Journal d'un Bourgeois de Paris sous François I.* p. 317.

† 'Interim exercitata est longe diversa doctrinæ forma.'—Calvini *Opusc.* p. 125.

know how to prick the conscience.* Now that I am prepared to be really attentive, I begin to see, thanks to the light that has been brought me, in what a slough of error I have hitherto been wallowing;† with how many stains I am disfigured . . . and above all, what is the eternal death that threatens me.'‡ A great trembling came over him; he paced his room as Luther had once paced his cell at Erfurth. He uttered (he tells us) deep groans and shed floods of tears.§ He was crushed beneath the weight of his sin. Terrified at the divine holiness, like a leaf tossed by the wind, like a man frightened by a violent thunderstorm, he exclaimed: 'O God! thou keepest me bowed down, as if thy bolts were falling on my head.'‖ . . . Then he fell at the feet of the Almighty, exclaiming: 'I condemn with tears my past manner of life, and transfer myself to thine. Poor and wretched, I throw myself on the mercy which thou hast shown us in Jesus Christ: I enter that only harbor of salvation.¶ . . . O God, reckon not up against me that terrible desertion and disgust of thy Word, from which thy marvellous bounty has rescued me.'**

Following Olivétan's advice, Calvin applied to the study of Scripture, and everywhere he found Christ. 'O father!' he said, 'his sacrifice has appeased thy wrath; his blood has washed away my impurities; his cross has borne my curse; his death has atoned for me†† . . . We had devised for ourselves many useless follies‡‡ . . . but thou hadst placed thy

* 'Habebant præterea quo conscientiam meam stringerent.'—Calvini *Opusc.* p. 126.

† 'Animadverti in quo errorum sterquilinio fuissem volutatus.'—Ibid.

‡ 'Quæ mihi imminebat, æternæ mortis agnitione, vehementer consternatus.'—Ibid.

§ 'Non sine gemitu ac lacrymis.'—Ibid.

‖ *Opusc. Franç.* p. 172; *Opusc. Lat.* p. 126; *Institution,* iii. 2.

¶ 'Unicum salutis portum.'—*Opusc. Lat.* p. 114.

** 'Ne horrendam illam a Verbo tuo defectionem ad calculum revoces.—Ibid. p. 126.

†† 'Sacrificio iram Dei placavit, sanguine maculas abstersit, morte pro nobis satisfecit.'—*Opusc. Lat.* p. 114; *Opusc. Franç.* p. 156.

‡‡ 'Multas inutiles nugas.'—*Opusc. Lat.* p. 123.

Word before me like a torch, and thou hast touched my heart, in order that I should hold in abomination all other merits save that of Jesus.'*

Calvin had, however, the final struggle to go through. To him, as to Luther, the great objection was the question of the Church. He had always respected the authority of a Church which he believed to have been founded by the apostles and commissioned to gather mankind round Jesus Christ; and these thoughts often disturbed him. 'There is one thing,' he told the evangelicals, 'which prevents my believing you: that is, the respect due to the Church.† The majesty of the Church must not be diminished.‡ . . . I cannot separate from it.'

Calvin's friends at Paris, and afterwards perhaps Wolmar and others at Orleans and Bourges, did not hesitate to reply to him.§ 'There is a great difference between separating from the Church and trying to correct the vices with which it is stained.‖ . . . How many antichrists have held the place in its bosom which belongs to the pastors only!'

Calvin understood at last that the unity of the Church cannot and ought not to exist except in the truth. His friends, perceiving this, spoke openly to him against the Pope of Rome.—'Men take him for Christ's vicar, Peter's successor, and the head of the Church. . . But these titles are empty scarecrows.¶ Far from permitting themselves to be dazzled by these big words, the faithful ought to discriminate the matter truly. If the pope has risen to such height and magnificence, it is because the world was plunged in ignorance and smitten with blindness.** Neither by the

* 'Ut pro merito abominarer, animum meum pupugisti.'—Ibid.

† 'Una præsertim res animum ab illis meum avertebat, ecclesiæ reverentia.'—*Opusc. Lat.* p. 125.

‡ 'Ne quid Ecclesiæ majestati decederet.'—Ibid. p. 126.

§ Calvin always uses the plural number, when speaking of those who raised objections against him: *admonebant, loquebantur*, &c.

‖ 'Multum enim interesse an secessionem quis ab ecclesia faciat, an vitia corrigere studeat.'—*Opusc. Lat.* p. 126.

¶ 'Ejusmodi titulos inania esse terriculamenta.'—Ibid.

** 'Cum mundus ignorantia et hebetudine velut alto sopore oppressus esset.'—*Opusc. Lat.* p. 126.

voice of God, nor by a lawful call of the Church, has the pope been constituted its prince and head; it is by his own authority and by his own will alone. . . He elected himself.* In order that the kingdom of Christ may stand, the tyranny with which the pope oppresses the nations must come to an end.'† Calvin's friends, as he tells us, 'demolished by the Word of God the princedom of the pope and his exceeding elevation.'‡

Calvin, not content with hearing the arguments of his friends, 'searched the Scriptures thoroughly,' and found numerous evidences corroberating the things that had been told him. He was convinced. 'I see quite clearly,' he said, 'that the true order of the Church has been lost; § that the keys which should preserve discipline have been counterfeited;‖ that christian liberty has been everthrown;¶ and that when the princedom of the pope was set up, the kingdom of Christ was thrown down.'** Thus fell the papacy in the mind of the future reformer; and Christ became to him the only king and almighty head of the church.

What did Calvin then? The converted often believed themselves called to remain in the Church that they might labor at its purification; did he separate himself from Rome? Theodóre Beza, his most intimate friend, says: 'Calvin, having been taught the true religion by one of his relations named Pierre Robert Olivétan, and having carefully read the holy books, began to hold the teachings of the Roman Church in horror, and had the intention of renouncing its communion.'†† This testimony is positive; and yet Beza only says in this extract that he 'had the intention.' The

* 'Sed voluntarium et a seipso lectum.'—Ibid.

† 'Illam tyrannidem, qua in Dei populum grassans est.'—Ibid.

‡ 'Tantam ejus altitudinem, Dei Verbo, demoliebantur.—Ibid.

§ 'Verum ecclesiæ ordinem tunc interiisse.'—Ibid.

‖ 'Claves quibus ecclesiæ disciplina continetur, fuisset pessime adulteratas.'—Ibid.

¶ 'Collapsam christianam libertatem.'—Ibid.

** 'Prostratum fuisse Christi regnum, cum erectus fuisset hic principatus.'—Ibid.

†† Theod. Beza, *Vie de Jean Calvin*, p. 8. The Latin goes farther: 'Ac proinde sese ab illis sacris sejungere cœpisset.

separation was not yet decided and absolute. Calvin felt the immense importance of the step. However, he resolved to break with catholicism, if necessary, in order to possess the truth. 'I desire concord and unity, O Lord,' he said; 'but the unity of the Church I long for is that which has its beginning and its ending in thee.* If, to have peace with those who boast of being the first in the Church, I must purchase it by denying the truth . . . then I would rather submit to everything than condescend to such an abominable compact!' The reformer's character, his faith, his decision, his whole life are found in these words. He will endeavor to remain in the Church, but . . . with the truth.

Calvin's conversion had been long and slowly ripening; and yet, in one sense, the change was instantaneous. 'When I was the obstinate slave of the superstitions of popery,' he says, 'and it seemed impossible to drag me out of the deep mire, God by a sudden conversion subdued me, and made my heart obedient to his Word.'† When a city is taken, it is in one day and by a single assault that the conqueror enters and plants his flag upon the ramparts; and yet for months, for years perhaps, he has been battering at the walls.

Thus was this memorable conversion accomplished, which by saving one soul became for the Church, and we may even say for the human race, the principle of a great transformation. Then, it was only a poor student converted in a college; now, the light which this scholar set on a candlestick has spread to the ends of the world, and elect souls, scattered among every nation, acknowledge in his conversion the origin of their own.

It was in Paris, as we have seen, that Calvin received a new birth; it cannot be placed later, as some have wished to do, without contradicting the most positive testimony. Calvin, according to Theodore Beza, was instructed in the true religion by Olivétan, *before* he went to Orleans;‡ we

* 'Illa ecclesiæ unitas quæ abs te inciperet, ac in te desineret.'—*Opusc. Lat.* p. 124.

† 'Animum meum subita conversione ad docilitatem subegit Deus.'—Calvini *Præf. in Psalm.*

‡ 'A cognato Olivetano de vera religione admonitus . . . *Profectus ergo Aureliam.*'—Bezæ *Viti Calvini.*

know, moreover, that Calvin, either at Bourges or at Orleans, 'wonderfully advanced the kingdom of God.'* How could he have done so if he had not known that kingdom? Calvin at the age of nineteen, gifted with a deep and conscientious soul, surrounded by relations and friends zealous for the Gospel, living at Paris in the midst of a religious movement of great power, was himself touched by the Spirit of God. Most certainly everything was not done then; some of the traits, which we have indicated after the reformer himself, may, as we have already remarked, belong to his residence at Orleans or at Bourges; but the essential work was done in 1527. Such is the conclusion at which we have arrived after careful study.

There are men in our days who look upon conversion as an imaginary act, and say simply that a man has changed his opinion. They freely grant that God can create a moral being once, but do not concede him the liberty of creating it a second time—of transforming it. Conversion is always the work of God. There are forces working in nature which cause the earth to bring forth its fruit; and yet some would maintain that God cannot work in the heart of man to create a new fruit! . . . Human will is not sufficient to explain the changes manifested in man; there, if anywhere, is found something mysterious and divine.

The young man did not immediately make his conversion publicly known; it was only one or two of his superiors that had any knowledge of his struggles, and they endeavored to hide them from the pupils. They fancied it was a mere passing attack of that *fever* under which so many people were suffering, and believed that the son of the episcopal secretary would once more obediently place himself under the crook of the Church. The Spanish professor, who came from a country were fiery passions break out under a burning sky, and where religious fanaticism demands its victims, had doubtless waged an implacable war against the student's new convictions; but information in this respect is wanting. Calvin carefully hid his treasure; he stole away

* Théod. de Béze, *Hist. des Egl. Réf.* pp. 6, 7.

from his companions, retired to some corner, and sought for communion with God alone. 'Being naturally rather wild and shy,' he tells us,* 'I have always loved peace and tranquillity; accordingly I began then to seek for a hiding-place and the means of withdrawing from notice into some out-of-the-way spot.' This reserve on Calvin's part may have led to the belief that his conversion did not take place until later.

The news of what was passing in Paris reached the little town in Picardy where Calvin was born. It would be invaluable to possess the letters which he wrote to his father during this time of struggle, and even those of Olivétan; but we have neither. John's relations with Olivétan were known at Noyon; there was no longer any doubt about the heretical opinions of the young curé of St. Martin of Motteville . . . What trouble for his family, and especially for the episcopal notary! To renounce the hope of one day seeing his son vicar-general, bishop, and perhaps cardinal, was distressing to the ambitious father. Yet he decided promptly, and as it was all important for him that Calvin should be something, he gave another direction to his immoderate thirst for honors. He said to himself that by making his son study the law, he would perhaps be helping him to shake off these new ideas; and that in any case, the pursuit of the law was quite as sure a road, and even surer, to attain to wealth and high station.† Duprat, at first a plain lawyer, and afterwards president of the parliament, is now (he thought) high chancellor of France, and the first personage in the realm after the king. Gerard, whose mind was fertile in schemes of success for himself and for others, continued to build his castles in the air in honor of his son; only he changed his sphere, and instead of placing them in the domain of the Church, he erected them in the domain of the State.

Thus, while the son had a new faith and a new life, the father had a new plan. Theodore Beza has pointed out this coincidence. After speaking of Calvin's vocation to the

* Preface to the *Commentary on the Psalms.*

† 'Quod jurisprudentiam certius iter esse ad opes et honores videret.' —Bezæ *Vita Calvini.*

ecclesiastical profession, he adds that a double change, which took place at that time in the minds of both father and son, led to the setting aside of this resolution in favor of another.* The coincidence struck Calvin himself, and it was he no doubt who pointed it out to his friend at Geneva. It was not therefore the resolution of Gerard Cauvin that decided his son's calling, as some have supposed. At the first glance the two decisions seem independent of each other; but it appears probable to me that it was the change in the son which led to that of the father, and not the change in the father which led to that of the son. The young man submitted with joy to the order he received. Gerard, by taking his son from his theological studies, wished to withdraw him from heresy; but he was mistaken. Had not Luther first studied the law at Erfurth? Did not Calvin by this same study prepare himself better for the career of a reformer, than by the priesthood?

Conversion is the fundamental act of the Gospel and of the Reformation. From the transformation effected in the individual the transformation of the world is destined to result. This act, which in some is of very short duration and leads readily to faith, is a long operation in others; the power of sin is continually renewed in them, neither the new man nor the old man being able, for a time, to obtain a decisive victory. We have here an image of christianity. It is a struggle of the new man against the old man—a struggle that has lasted more than eighteen hundred years. The new man is continually gaining ground; the old man grows weaker and retires; but the hour of triumph has not yet come. Yet that hour is certain. The Reformation of the sixteenth century, like the Gospel of the first (to employ the words of Christ), 'is like unto leaven, which a woman took and hid in three measures of meal, *until the whole was leavened*.'† The three great nations on earth have already tasted of this heavenly leaven. It is fermenting, and soon all the 'lump' will be leavened.

* 'Sed hoc consilium interrupit utriusque mutatus animus.'—Bezæ *Vita Calvini.*

† Matthew xiii. 33.

CHAPTER IX.

BERQUIN DECLARES WAR AGAINST POPERY.

(1527.)

Will the reformer whom God is now preparing for France find in Francis I. the support which Luther found in Frederick the Wise? Since his return from captivity in Spain, the king, as we have seen, appeared to yield to the influence of his sister and to the movement of the age. Slightly touched by the new breath, he sometimes listened to the sermons of the evangelicals, and read fragments of the Holy Scriptures with Margaret. One day, when the beauty of the Gospel had spoken to his heart, he exclaimed: 'It is infamous that the monks should dare to call that *heresy* which is the very doctrine of God!' But the Reformation could not please him; liberty, which was one of its elements, clashed with the despotism of the prince; and holiness, another principle, condemned his irregularities.

Opposition to popery had, however, a certain charm for Francis, whose supreme rule it was to lower everything that encroached upon his greatness. He well remembered that the popes had more than once humbled the kings of France, and that Clement VII. was habitually in the interest of the emperor. But political motives will never cause a real Reformation; and hence there are few princes who have contributed so much as Francis I. to propagate superstition instead of truth, servility instead of liberty, licentiousness instead of morality. If the Word of God does not exercise its invisible power on the nations, they are by that very defect deprived of the conditions necessary to the maintenance of order and liberty. They may shine forth with great brilliancy, but they pass easily from disorder to tyranny.

They are like a stately ship, decorated with the most glorious banners, and armed with the heaviest artillery; but as it wants the necessary ballast, it drives between two extreme dangers, now dashing against Scylla, and now tossed upon Charybdis.

While Francis I. was trifling with the Reform, other powers in France remained its irreconcilable enemies. The members of the parliament, honorable men for the most part, but lawyers still, unable to recognise the truth (and few could in those days) that spiritual matters were not within their jurisdiction, did not confine themselves to judging temporal offences, but made themselves the champions of the law of the realm against the law of God. The doctors of the Sorbonne, on their part, seeing that the twofold authority of Holy Scripture and of conscience would ruin theirs, opposed with all their strength the substitution of the religious for the clerical element. 'They inveighed against the reformers,' says Roussel, 'and endeavored to stir up the whole world against them.'* The more the king inclined to peace, the more the Sorbonne called for war, counting its battalions and preparing for the fight. The general placed at its head was, Erasmus tells us, 'a many-headed monster, breathing poison from every mouth.'† Beda—for he was the monster—taking note of the age of Lefèvre, the weakness of Roussel, the absence of Farel, and not knowing Calvin's power, said to himself that Berquin would be the Luther of France, and against him he directed all his attacks.

Louis de Berquin, who was liberated by the king, in November, 1526, from the prison into which the Bedists had thrown him, had formed the daring plan of rescuing France from the hands of the pope. He was then thirty years of age, and possessed a charm in his character, a purity in his life, which even his enemies admired, unwearied application in study, indomitable energy, obstinate zeal, and firm perseverance for the accomplishment of his work. Yet there was one fault in him. Calvin, like Luther, proceeded by the

* 'Inde adversarii ansam sumpsere debacchandi in nos et commovendi universos.'—Rufus Farello, Genev. MSS. Schmidt, p. 198.

† 'Quotque capitibus afflaret venenum.'—Erasmi *Epp.* p. 1280.

positive method, putting the truth in front, and in this way seeking to effect the conversion of souls; but Berquin inclined too much at times to the negative method. Yet he was full of love, and having found in God a father, and in Jesus a saviour, he never contended with theologians, except to impart to souls that peace and joy which constituted his own happiness.

Berquin did not move forward at hazard; he had calculated everything. He had said to himself that in a country like France the Reformation could not be carried through against the king's will; but he thought that Francis would allow the work to be done, if he did not do it himself. When he had been thrust into prison in 1523, had not the king, then on his way to Italy, sent the captain of the guards to fetch him in order to save his life?* When in 1526 he had been transferred as a heretic by the clerical judges to lay judges, had not Francis once more set him at liberty?†

But Berquin's noble soul did not suffer the triumph of truth to depend upon the support of princes. A new era was then beginning. God was reanimating society which had lain torpid during the night of the middle ages, and Berquin thought that God would not be wanting to the work. It is a saying of Calvin's 'that the brightness of the divine power alone scatters all silly enchantments and vain imaginations.' Berquin did not distinguish this truth so clearly, but he was not ignorant of it. At the same time, knowing that an army never gains a victory unless it is bought with the deaths of many of its soldiers, he was ready to lay down his life.

At the moment when he was advancing almost alone to attack the colossus, he thought it his duty to inform his friends: 'Under the cloak of religion,' he wrote to Erasmus, 'the priests hide the vilest passions, the most corrupt manners, the most scandalous unbelief. We must tear off the veil that conceals this hideous mystery, and boldly brand the Sorbonne, Rome, and all their hirelings with impiety.'

At these words his friends were troubled and alarmed;

* *Journal d'un Bourgeois de Paris*, p. 170.

† Ibid, p. 277.

they endeavored to check his impetuosity. 'The greater the success you promise yourself,' wrote Erasmus, 'the more afraid I am. . . O my friend! live in retirement; taste the sweets of study, and let the priests rage at their leisure. Or, if you think they are plotting your ruin, employ stratagem. Let your friends at court obtain some embassy for you from the king, and under that pretext leave France.* Think, dear Berquin, think constantly what a hydra you are attacking, and by how many mouths it spits its venom. Your enemy is immortal, for a faculty never dies. You will begin by attacking three monks only; but you will raise up against you numerous legions, rich, mighty, and perverse. Just now the princes are for you; but backbiters will contrive to alienate their affection. As for me, I declare I will have nothing to do with the Sorbonne and its armies of monks.'

This letter disturbed Berquin. He read it again and again, and each time his trouble increased. He an ambassador . . . he the representative of the king at foreign courts! Ah! when Satan tempted Christ he offered him the kingdoms of this world. Better be a martyr on the Grève for the love of the Saviour! Berquin separated from Erasmus. 'His spirit, said his friends, 'resembles a palm-tree; the more you desire to bend it, the straighter it grows.' A trifling circumstance contributed to strengthen his decision.

One day Beda, syndic of the Sorbonne, went to court where he had some business to transact with the king on behalf of that body. Some time before, he had published a refutation of the 'Paraphrases and Annotations' of Erasmus, and Francis I., who boasted of being a pupil of this king of letters, having heard of Beda's attack, had given way to a fit of passion. As soon, therefore, as he heard that Beda was in the palace, he gave orders that he should be arrested and kept prisoner. Accordingly the syndic was seized, shut up in a chamber, and closely watched. Beda was exasperated, and the hatred he felt against the Reformation was turned against the king. Some of his friends,

* 'Curarent amici ut prætextu regiæ legationis longius proficisceretur.'—Erasmi *Epp.* p. 1280.

on hearing of this strange adventure, conjured Francis to set him at liberty. He consented on the following day, but on condition that the syndic should appear when called for.*

The Sorbonne, said Berquin to himself, represents the papacy. It must be overthrown in order that Christ may triumph. He began first to study the writings of Beda, who had so bitterly censured those of his adversaries, and extracted from them twelve propositions 'manifestly impious and blasphemous' in the opinion of Erasmus. Then, taking his manuscript, he proceeded to court and presented it to the king, who said: 'I will interdict Beda's polemical writings.' As Francis smiled upon him, Berquin resolved to go further, namely, to attack the Sorbonne and popery, as equally dangerous to the State and to the Church, and to make public certain doctrines of theirs which struck at the power of the throne. He approached the king, and said to him in a lower tone: 'Sire, I have discovered in the acts and papers of the Sorbonne certain secrets of importance to the State . . . some mysteries of iniquity.'† Nothing was better calculated to exasperate Francis I. 'Show me those passages,' he exclaimed. Meantime he told the reformer that the twelve propositions of the syndic of the Sorbonne should be examined. Berquin left the palace full of hope. 'I will follow these redoubtable hornets into their holes,' he said to his friends. 'I will fall upon these insensate babblers, and scourge them on their own dunghill.' Some people who heard him thought him out of his mind. 'This gentleman will certainly get himself put to death,' they said, 'and he will richly deserve it.'‡

Everything seemed to favor Berquin's design. Francis I. was acting the part of Frederick the Wise: he seemed even more ardent than that moderate protector of Luther. On the 12th of July, 1527, the Bishop of Bazas appeared at court, whither he had been summoned by the king. Francis gave him the twelve famous propositions he had received

* Chevillier, *Origine de l'Imprimerie de Paris.*

† 'Deprehenderat quædam arcana in illorum actis.'—Erasmi *Epp.* p. 110.

‡ *Journal d'un Bourgeois de Paris*, p. 170.

from Berquin, and commanded him to take them to the rector of the university, with orders to have them examined, not only by doctors of divinity, of whom he had suspicions in such a matter,* but by the four assembled faculties. Berquin hastened to report this to Erasmus, still hoping to gain him over by the good news.

Erasmus had never before felt so alarmed; he tried to stop Berquin in his 'mad' undertaking. The eulogies which this faithful christian lavished upon him particularly filled him with terror: he would a thousand times rather they had been insults. 'The love which you show for me,' he wrote to Berquin, 'stirs up unspeakable hatred against me everywhere. The step you have taken with the king will only serve to irritate the hornets. You wish for a striking victory rather than a sure one; your expectations will be disappointed; the Bedists are contriving some atrocious plot.† . . . Beware! . . . Even should your cause be holier than that of Christ himself, your enemies have resolved to put you to death. You say that the king protects you . . . do not trust to that; the favor of princes is short-lived. You do not care for your life, you add; good! but think at least of learning, and of our friends who, alas! will perish with you.'

Berquin was grieved at this letter. In his opinion the moment was unparalleled. If Erasmus, Francis I., and Berquin act in harmony, no one can resist them; France, and perhaps Europe, will be reformed. And it is just when the King of France is stretching out his hand that the scholar of Rotterdam draws his back! . . . What can be done without Erasmus? . . . A circumstance occurred, however, which gave some hope to the evangelist.

The Sorbonne, little heeding the king's opposition, persevered in their attacks upon learning. They forbade the professors in the colleges to read the 'Colloquies' of Erasmus with their pupils, and excommunicated the king of the

* 'Quos in hac materia suspectos habebat.'—Registers of the Faculty.

† 'Satia odoror, ex amicorum literis, Beddaicos aliquid strox moliri.' —Erasmi *Epp.* p. 1052.

schools in the schools themselves. . . Erasmus, who was a vain, susceptible, choleric man, will now unite with Berquin: the latter had no doubt of it. 'The time is come,' wrote Berquin to the illustrious scholar; 'let us pull off the mask behind which these theologians hide themselves.' But the more Berquin urged Erasmus, the more Erasmus shrank back; he wished for peace at any cost. It was of no use to point to the blows which the Sorbonne were aiming at him; it pleased him to be beaten, not from meekness, but from fear of the world. The wary man, who was now growing old, became impatient, not against his slanderers, but against his friend. His 'son' wanted to lead him as if he were his master. He replied with sadness, almost with bitterness: 'Truly I admire you, my dear Berquin. You imagine, then, that I have nothing else to do than spend my days in battling with theologians. . . I would rather see all my books condemned to the flames than go fighting at my age.' Unhappily, Erasmus did not abandon his books only, he abandoned truth; and there he was wrong. Berquin did not despair of victory, and undertook to win it unaided. He thought to himself: 'Erasmus admires in the Gospel a certain harmony with the wisdom of antiquity, but he does not adore in it the foolishness of the cross: he is a theorist, not a reformer.' From that hour Berquin wrote more rarely and more coldly to his illustrious master, and employed all his strength to carry by main force the place he was attacking. If Erasmus, like Achilles, had retired to his tent, were not Margaret and Francis, and Truth especially, fighting by his side?

The catholic party grew alarmed, and resolved to oppose a vigorous resistance to these attacks. The watchword was given. Many libels were circulated; men were threatened with the gaol and the stake; even ghosts were conjured up; all means were lawful. One sister Alice quitted the fires of purgatory and appeared on the banks of the Rhone and Saone to confound 'the damnable sect of heretics.' Any one might read of this prodigy in the 'Marvellous History of the Ghost of Lyons,' written by one of the king's almoners. The Sorbonne knew, however, that phantoms were not sufficient; but they had on their side something more than phantoms. They could oppose Berquin with adversaries who had flesh and blood like himself, and whose power seemed irresistible. These adversaries were a princess and a statesman.

CHAPTER X.

EFFORTS OF DUPRAT TO BRING ABOUT A PERSECUTION: RESISTANCE OF FRANCIS I.

(1527–1528.)

A WOMAN reigned in the councils of the king. Inclined at first to ridicule the monks, she had after the defeat of Pavia gone over to the side of the priests. At the moment when the kingly authority received such a blow, she had seen that their power remained, and had made them her auxiliaries. This woman was Louisa of Savoy, Duchess of Angoulême, mother of Francis I., worthy predecessor of Catherine de' Medici. A clever woman, 'an absolute lady in her wishes both good and bad,' says Pasquier; a free-thinker, who could study the new doctrine as a curiosity, but who despised it; a dissolute woman, of whom Beaucaire, Brantôme, and others relate many scandalous anecdotes; a fond and absolute mother, who all her life preserved an almost sovereign authority over her son,—Louisa held in her hand two armies which she managed at will. One of these was composed of her maids of honor, by whose means she introduced into the court of France gallantry, scandal, and even indecency of language; the other was formed of intelligent, crafty men, who had no religion, no morality, no scruples; and at their head was Duprat.

The latter was the patron upon whom the Sorbonne thought they could rely. Enterprising and systematic, at once supple and firm, slavish and tyrannical, an intriguer and debauchee, often exasperated, never discouraged, 'very clever, knowing, and subtle,' says the *Bourgeois de Paris*; 'one of the most pernicious men that ever lived,' says another historian:* Duprat sold offices, ground the people down, and if any of them remonstrated against his disorders, he sent the remonstrants to the Bastile.† This man, who was archbishop of Sens and cardinal, and who aspired to be made legate *a latere*, having become a prince of the Roman Church, placed at its service his influence, his iron will, and even his cruelty.

But nothing could be done without the king. Louisa of Savoy and the cardinal, knowing his fickleness and his love of pleasure, and knowing also that in religious matters he cared only for pomp and ceremony, hoped to induce him easily to oppose the Reformation. Yet Francis hesitated and even resisted. He pretended to have a great taste for letters, of which the Gospel, in his eyes, formed part. He yielded willingly to his sister, who pleaded warmly the cause of the friends of the Gospel. He detested the arrogance of the priests. The boldness with which they put forward ultramontane ideas; set another power (the power of the pope) above his; attacked his ideas in conversations, pamphlets, and even in the pulpit; their restless character, their presumptuous confidence in the triumph of their cause,—all this irritated one of the most susceptible monarchs that ever reigned; and he was pleased at seeing a man like Berquin take down the boasting of the clergy.

Yet it may well be that the king was influenced by higher motives. He saw the human mind displaying a fresh activity in every direction. The literary, the philosophical, the political, the religious world were all undergoing important transformations in the first half of the sixteenth century. In the midst of all these different movements, Francis I. may have sometimes had a confused feeling that there was one which was the mainspring, the dominant fact, the generating principle, and, if I may use the words, the *fiat lux* of the new creation. He saw that the Reformation was the great

* Reynier de la Planche, *Hist. de l'Etat de France*, p. 5.

† *Journal d'un Bourgeois de Paris*, p. 160.

force then acting in the world: that all others were subordinate to it; that to it belonged, according to an ancient prophecy, *the gathering of the people*;* and in these moments, when his sight was clear, he wished to join himself to that invisible power which was effecting more than all the other powers. Unfortunately his passions soon disturbed his sight, and after having caught a glimpse of the day, he plunged back again into night.

As for Duprat he felt no hesitation; he resolutely put himself on the side of darkness, impelled by ambition and covetousness: he was always with the ultramontanists. The struggle was about to begin between the better aspirations of the king and the plots of the court of Rome. It was hard to say with which of these two powers the victory would ultimately remain. The chancellor-cardinal had, however, no doubt about it: he arranged the attack with skill, and thought he had hit upon a way, as vile as it was sure, of checking the Reform.

The king had to provide for the heavy charges which the treaty of Madrid imposed upon him, and he had no money. He applied to the clergy. 'Good!' said they; 'let us take advantage of the opportunity given us.' They furnished 1,300,000 livres, but demanded in return, according to Duprat's suggestion, that his Majesty 'should extirpate the damnable and insupportable Lutheran sect which some time since had secretly crept into the kingdom.'† The king, who wanted money, would be ready to grant everything in order to fill his coffers; it seemed, then, that all was over not only with Berquin, but with the Reformation.

Margaret, who was then at Fontainebleau with the King of Navarre, heard of the demand the clergy had made to the king, and trembled lest Francis should deliver up her friends to the persecutions of the cardinal. She immediately endeavored to exercise over her brother that influence to which in those days he yielded readily. She succeeded: the king, although putting the contribution of the clergy

* Genesis xlix. 10.

† Isambert, *Revue des anciennes Lois Françaises*, xii. p. 258.

into his treasury, did not order 'the extirpation of the Lutheran heresy.'

Yet Margaret did not feel secure. She experienced the keenest anguish at the thought of the danger which threatened the Gospel.

True God of heaven, give comfort to my soul!

she said in one of her poems. Her soul was comforted. The aged Lefèvre, who was at that time translating the Bible and the homilies of St. Chrysostom on the Acts of the Apostles, and teaching his young pupil, the Duke of Angoulême, to learn the Psalms of David by heart, rekindled her fire, and with his failing voice strengthened her in the faith. 'Do not be afraid,' he said; 'the election of God is very mighty.'*—'Let us pray in faith,' said Roussel; 'the main thing is that faith should accompany our prayers.' The friends at Strasburg entreated Luther to strengthen her by some good letter. As soon as Erasmus heard of the danger which the Gospel ran, he was moved, and, with the very pen with which he had discouraged Berquin, he wrote:

'O queen, still more illustrious by the purity of your life than by the splendor of your race and of your crown, do not fear! He who works everything for the good of those whom he loves, knows what is good for us, and, when he shall judge fit, will suddenly give a happy issue to our affairs.† It is when human reason despairs of everything that the impenetrable wisdom of God is made manifest in all its glory. Nothing but what is happy can befall the man who has fixed the anchor of his hopes on God. Let us place ourselves wholly in his hands. But what am I doing? . . . I know, Madame, that it is not necessary to excite you by powerful incentives, and that we ought rather to thank you for having protected from the malice of wicked men sound learning and all those who sincerely love Jesus Christ.'‡

* 'Dei autem electio efficacissima et potentissima.'—Fabri *Comment.*

† 'Omnia repente vertet in lætum exitum.'—Erasmus Reginæ Navarræ, Aug. 1527.

‡ 'Bonas litteras ac viros sincere Christum amantes tueri.'—Ibid.

The queen's condition tended ere long to give a new direction to her thoughts. She hoped for a daughter, and often spoke about it in her letters. This daughter was indeed given her, and she became the most remarkable woman of her age. Calm and somewhat dejected, Margaret, who was then living alone in the magnificent palace of Fontainebleau, sought diversion in the enjoyment of the beauties of nature, during her daily walks in the park and the forest. 'My condition,' she wrote on the 27th of September, 1527, 'does not prevent my visiting the gardens twice a day, where I am wonderfully at my ease.' She walked slowly, thinking of the child about to be given her, and rejoicing in the light of the sun. Then reverting to him who held the chief place in her heart, she called to mind the true sun (Jesus Christ), and, grieving that his rays did not enlighten the whole of France, exclaimed :

O truth, unknown save to a few,
No longer hide thyself from view
Behind the cloud, but bursting forth
Show to the nations all thy worth.
Good men thy coming long to see,
And sigh in sad expectancy.
Descend, Lord Jesus, quickly come,
And brighten up this darkling gloom;
Show us how vile and poor we are,
And take us, Saviour, to thy care.*

It seems that Margaret's presence near the king checked the persecutors; but she was soon compelled to leave the field open. The time of her confinement drew near. Henry d'Albret had not visited Bearn since his marriage; perhaps he desired that his child should be born in the castle of Pau. In October, 1527, the King and Queen of Navarre set out for their possessions in the Pyrenees.† On the 7th of January, two months later, Jeanne d'Albret was born; the statement that she was born at Fontainebleau or at Blois is a mistake.

The Queen of Navarre had hardly left for Bearn, when

* *Marguerites de la Marguerite des Princesses,* p. 90.

† *Lettres de la Reine de Navarre,* i. p. 224; ii. p. 87.

Duprat and the Sorbonne endeavored to carry their cruel plans into execution. Among the number of the gentlemen of John Stuart, Duke of Albany, was a nobleman of Poitou named De la Tour. The Duke of Albany, a member of the royal family of Scotland, had been regent of that kingdom, and De la Tour had lived with him in Edinburgh, where he had made the most of his time. 'When the lord duke was regent of Scotland,' people said, 'the Sieur de la Tour sowed many Lutheran errors there.'* This French gentleman must therefore have been one of the earliest reformers in Scotland. He showed no less zeal at Paris than at Edinburgh, which greatly displeased the priests. Moreover, the Duke of Albany, who was in high favor with the king, was much disliked by the ambitious chancellor. An indictment was drawn up; Francis I., whose good genius was no longer by his side, shut his eyes; De la Tour and his servant, an evangelical like himself, were condemned by the parliament for heresy. On the 27th of October these two pious christians were bound in the same cart and led slowly to the pig-market to be burnt alive. When the cart stopped, the executioners ordered the servant to get down. He did so and stood at the cart's tail. They stripped off his clothes, and flogged him so long and so severely that the poor wretch declared that he 'repented.' Some little mercy was consequently shown him, and they were content to cut out his tongue. They hoped by this means to shake De la Tour's firmness; but though deeply moved, he raised his eyes to heaven, vowed to God that he would remain true to him, and immediately an ineffable joy replaced the anguish by which he had been racked. He was burnt alive.

Margaret must have heard at Pau of the death of the pious De la Tour; but however that may be, she left for Paris immediately after her delivery, giving her people orders to make haste. What was it that recalled her so promptly to the capital? Was it the news of some danger threatening the Gospel? A council was about to assemble at Paris; did she desire to be at hand to ward off the

* *Journal d'un Bourgeois de Paris*, p. 327.

blows aimed at her friends? That is the reason given by one historian.* 'She had determined to make haste,' and, her confinement scarcely over, this weak and delicate princess, urging her courier to press on, crossed the sands and marshes of the Landes. In a letter from Barbezieux, she complains of the bad roads by which her carriage was so roughly jolted. 'I can find nothing difficult, nor any stage wearisome. I hope to be at Blois in ten days.'†

It was time. De la Tour's death had satisfied neither the chancellor nor the Sorbonne. They desired 'the extirpation of heresy,' and not merely the death of a single heretic. Not having succeeded by means of the clergy tax, they were determined to strive for it in another manner. Duprat listened to the reports, and took note of what he observed in the streets. Nothing annoyed him so much as hearing of laymen, and even women, who turned away their heads as they passed the churches, slipped into lonely streets, met in cellars or in garrets, where persons who had not received holy orders prayed aloud and read the Holy Scriptures. Had he not in 1516 abrogated the pragmatic sanction and stripped the Gallican Church of its liberties? Would he not, therefore succeed with far less trouble in sacrificing this new and free Church, a poor and contemptible flock? As a provincial council was to be held at Paris, Duprat resolved to take advantage of it to strike a decisive blow.

On the 28th of February, 1528, the council was opened. The cardinal-archbishop having gone thither in great pomp, rose and spoke amid dead silence: 'Sirs, a terrible pestilence, stirred up by Martin Luther, has destroyed the orthodox faith. A tempest has burst upon the bark of St. Peter, which, tossed by the winds, is threatened with dreadful shipwreck.‡ . . . There is no difference between Luther and Manichæus. . . . And yet, reverend fathers, his adherents multiply in our province; they hold secret conventicles in many places; they unite with laymen in the most private

* A. Favin, *Histoire de Navarre*, 1612.

† *Lettres de la Reine de Navarre*, i. p. 236.

‡ 'Dirum concussæ Petri naviculæ naufragium intentari.'—Labbæi *Concilia*, xiv. p. 432.

chambers of the houses;* they discuss the catholic faith with women and fools.' . . .

It will be seen that it was not heresy, properly so called, that the chancellor condemned in the Reformation, but liberty. A religion which was not exclusively in the hands of priests was, in his eyes, more alarming than heresy. If such practices were tolerated, would they not one day see gentlemen, shopkeepers, and even men sprung from the ranks of the people, presuming to have something to say in matters of state? The germ of the constitutional liberties of modern times lay hid in the bosom of the Reformation. The chancellor was not mistaken. He wished at one blow to destroy both religious and political liberty. He found enthusiastic accomplices in the priests assembled at Paris. The council drew up a decree ordering the bishops and even the inhabitants of the dioceses to denounce all the Lutherans of their acquaintance.

Would the king sanction this decree? Duprat was uneasy. He collected his thoughts, arranged his arguments, and proceeded to the palace with the hope of gaining his master. 'Sire,' he said to Francis, 'God is able without your help to exterminate all this heretical band;† but, in his great goodness, he condescends to call men to his aid. Who can tell of the glory and happiness of the many princes who, in past ages, have treated heretics as the greatest enemies of their crowns, and have given them over to death? If you wish to obtain salvation; if you wish to preserve your sovereign rights intact; if you wish to keep the nations submitted to you in tranquillity: manfully defend the catholic faith, and subdue all its enemies by your arms.'‡ Thus spoke Duprat; but the king thought to himself that if his 'sovereign rights' were menaced at all, it might well be by the power of Rome. He remained deaf as before.

* 'Cum laicis sese in penetralibus domorum recipere.'—Labbæi *Concilia*, xiv. p. 442.

† Posset sine dubio Deus, absque principibus, universam hæreticorum cohortem conterere ac exterminare.'—Ibid. p. 432.

‡ 'Ejus hostes viriliter debellare.'—Ibid. p. 462.

'Let us go further,' said the chancellor to his creatures; 'let the whole Church call for the extirpation of heresy.' Councils were held at Lyons, Rouen, Tours, Rheims, and Bourges, and the priests restrained themselves less in the provinces than in the capital. 'These heretics,' said the fiery orators, 'worship the devil, whom they raise by means of certain herbs and sacrilegious forms.'* But all was useless; Francis took pleasure in resisting the priests, and Duprat soon encountered an obstacle not less formidable.

If it was the duty of the priests to denounce the 'enchanters,' it was the business of the parliament to condemn them; but parliament and the chancellor were at variance. On the death of his wife, Duprat, then a layman and first president of parliament, had calculated that this loss might be a gain, and he entered the Church in order to get possession of one of the richest benefices in the kingdom. First, he laid his hands on the archbishopric of Sens, although at the election there were twenty-two votes against him and only one for him.† Shortly after that, he seized the rich abbey of St. Benedict. 'To us alone,' said the monks, 'belongs the choice of our abbot; and they boldly refused to recognise the chancellor. Duprat's only answer was to lock them all up. The indignant parliament sent an apparitor to the archbishop's officers, and ordered them to appear before it; but the officers fell upon the messenger, and beat him so cruelly that he died. The king decided in favor of his first minister, and the difference between the parliament and the chancellor grew wider.

Duprat who desired to become reconciled with this court, whose influence was often necessary to him, fancied he could gain it over by means of the Lutherean heresy, which they both detested equally. On their side the parliament desired nothing better than to recover the first minister's favor. These intrigues succeeded. 'The chancellor and the counsellors mutually gave up the truth, which they looked upon as a mere nothing, like a crust of bread which one throws

* 'Usu herbarum et sacrilego ritu characterum.'—Labbæi *Concilia*, xiv. p. 426.

† *Journal d'un Bourgeois*, p. 229.

to a dog,' to use the words of a reformer. Great was the exultation then in sacristy and in convent.

As chancellor, Sorbonne, and parliament were agreed, it seemed impossible that the Reformation should not succumb under their combined attacks. They said to one another: 'We must pluck up all these *ill weeds*;' but they did not require, however, that it should be done in one day. 'If the king will only grant us some little isolated persecution,' said the enemies of the Reform, 'we will so work the matter that all the grist shall come to the mill at last.'

But even that they could not obtain from the king; the terrible mill remained idle and useless. The agitation of the clergy was, in the opinion of Francis, mere monkish clamor; he desired to protect learning against the attacks of the ultramontanists. Besides, he felt that the greatest danger which threatened his authority was the theocratic power, and he feared still more these restless and noisy priests. The Reformation appeared to be saved, when an unexpected circumstance delivered it over to its enemies.

CHAPTER XI.

REJOICINGS AT FONTAINEBLEAU AND THE VIRGIN OF THE RUE DES ROSIERS.

(1528.)

EVERYTHING appeared in France to incline towards peace and joy. The court was at Fontainebleau, where Francis I. and the Duchess of Angoulême, the King and Queen of Navarre, and all the most illustrious of the nobility, had assembled to receive the young Duke of Ferrara, who had just arrived (20th of May, 1528) to marry Madame Renée, daughter of Louis XII. and Anne of Brittany. It was a time of rejoicing. Francis I., whose favorite residence was Fontainebleau, had erected a splendid palace there, and laid out 'beautiful gardens, shrubberies, fountains, and all things pleasant and recreative.'—'Really,' said the courtiers, 'the king has turned a wilderness into the most beautiful residence in christendom—so spacious that you might lodge a little world in it.'* Foreigners were struck with the magnificence of the palace and the brilliancy of the court. The marriage of the daughter of Louis XII. was approaching: there was nothing but concerts and amusements. There were excursions in the forest, and sumptuous banquets in the palace, and learned men (says Brantôme) discoursed at table on 'the higher and the lower sciences.' But nothing attracted the attention of the foreign visitors so much as the Queen of Navarre. 'I observed her,' says a bishop, a papal legate, 'while she was speaking to Cardinal d'Este, and I admired in her features, her expression, and in every movement, an harmonious union of majesty, modesty, and kindness.'† Such was Margaret in the midst of the court; the goodness of her heart, the purity of her life, and the abundance of her works spoke eloquently to those about her of the beauty of the Gospel.

The princess, who was compelled to take part in every court entertainment, never let an opportunity pass of calling a soul to Jesus Christ. In the sixteenth century there was no evangelist, among women at least, more active than she; this is a trait too important in the French Reformation to be passed by unnoticed. The maids of honor of the Duchess of Angoulême were no longer the virtuous damsels of Queen Claude. Margaret feeling the tenderest compassion for these young women, called now one and now another to Christ; she conjured her 'dears,' (as she styled them) not to be 'caught by pleasure,' which would render them hateful to God.

> Farewell, my dear!
> The court I flee
> To seek for life
> Beneath the tree.

---

* Brantôme, *Mémoires*, i. p. 277.

† Letter of Pierre-Paul Vergerio, Bishop of Capo d'Istria, to Victoria Colonna, Marchioness of Pescara. *Life and Times of Paleario*, by M. Young, ii. p. 356.

If that my prayer
Could influence thee,
Thou shouldst not linger,
After me.

Stay not, my dear,
But come with me,
And seek for life
Beneath the tree.*

Francis I., who loved the chase, would often go into the forest, attended by his young lords, and hunt the boar and deer for days together. These youths took great pleasure in talking of their skill to the ladies of the court, or in challenging one another who could kill the finest stag. . . . The Queen of Navarre sometimes joined good-naturedly in these conversations; she would smilingly call these gay young lords 'bad sportsmen,' and exhort them 'to go a-hunting after better game.'

Here is one of these conversations of Fontainebleau, which she herself relates:

As a youth was riding one day to the wood,
He asked of a lady so wise and good
If the game he sought for could be found
In the forest that spread so thickly round;
For the young man's heart with desire beat high
To kill the deer. The dame, with a sigh,
Replied: 'It 's the season for hunters, 't is true,
But alas! no hunter true are you.

'In the wood where none but believers go
Is the game you seek, but do not know;
It is in that bitter wood of the cross
Which by the wicked is counted dross;
But to huntsmen good its taste is sweet,
And the pain it costs is the best of meat.
If that your mind were firmly set
Every honor but this to forget,
No other game would be sought by you. . .
But . . . you are not a hunter true.'

---

* The *tree* is the cross. *Les Marguerites de la Marguerite*, i. p. 479.

As he heard these words, the hunter blushed,
And with anger his countenance flushed:
'You speak at random, dame,' he cried;
'The stag will I have, and nought beside.'

MARGARET.

'The stag you seek is close in view,
But . . . you are not a hunter true.

'Sit you down by the fountain's brim,
And in patience wait for him;
There, with soul and body at rest,
Drink of that spring so pure and blest:
All other means but this are nought.
For eager in the toils of your heart to be caught,
The stag will come running up to you;
But . . . you are not a hunter true.'

THE YOUNG HUNTER.

'Dame, 't is an idle tale you tell;
Wealth and glory, I know full well,
Are not to be won without toil and care,
Of your water so pure not a drop will I share.'

MARGARET.

'Then the stag will never be caught by you,
For . . . you are not a hunter true.'

The young hunter understands at last what is wanted of him, and, after some further conversation with the lady, he exclaims :

With earnest faith my heart is filled;
All my worldly thoughts I yield
At the voice of my Saviour Christ Jesu!'

MARGARET.

'Yes, now you are a hunter true!'*

This narrative, and others of a like nature contained in the *Marguerites*, were in all probability facts before they became poems. The little ballads were circulated at court;

* *Les Marguerites de la Marguerite*, i. p. 483.

everybody wished to read the queen's 'tracts,' and many of the nobility of France, who afterwards embraced the cause of the Reform, owed their first religious sentiments to Margaret.

For the moment, the great thought that occupied every mind at Fontainebleau was the marriage of the 'very prudent and magnificent Madame Renée.' The gentlemen of France and of Ferrara appeared at court in sumptuous costumes; the princes and princesses glittered with jewels; the halls and galleries were hung with rich tapestry.

> Dance and rejoice, make holiday
> For her whose love fills every heart.*

All of a sudden, on the morrow of. Pentecost, a message fell into the midst of this brilliant and joyous company which excited the deepest emotion. A letter was handed to the king, and the effect it produced was like that occasioned by a clap of thunder in a cloudless sky. Francis, who held the letter in his hand, was pale, agitated, almost quivering, as if he had just received a mortal insult. His anger exploded in an instant, like a mountain pouring out torrents of lava. He gave way to the most violent passion, and swore to take a cruel revenge. Margaret, terrified by her brother's anger, did not say a word, but withdrew, in alarm, to silence and prayer: she scarcely ventured an attempt to calm her brother's emotion. 'The incensed king,' says the chronicler, 'wept hard with vexation and anger.'† The court fêtes were interrupted: the courtiers, joining in unison with their master, called loudly for violent measures, and Francis departed suddenly for Paris. What had caused all this commotion?

The festival of Pentecost (Whitsunday) had been celebrated with great pomp on the 30th of May, 1528; but the devotionists, neglecting the Father, the Son, and above all the Holy Ghost, had thought of nothing all the day long but of worshipping the Virgin and her images. In the

* Nuptial song of Madame Renée. *Chronique de François I.* p. 72.

† *Journal d'un Bourgeois*, p. 347.

quarter of St. Antoine, and at the angle still formed by the streets Des Rosiers and Des Juifs, at the corner of the house belonging to the Sire Loys de Harlay, stood an image of the Virgin holding the infant Jesus in her arms. Numbers of devout persons of both sexes went every day to kneel before this figure. During the festival the crowd was more numerous than ever, and, bowing before the image, they lavished on it the loftiest of titles: 'O holy Virgin! O mediatress of mankind! O pardon of sinners! Author of the righteousness which cleanses away our sins! Refuge of all who return unto God!'* These observances had bitterly grieved those who remembered the old commandment: *Thou shalt worship the Lord thy God, and him only shalt thou serve.*

On the Monday morning, the morrow after the festival, some passers-by fancied they observed something wrong in the place where the image stood: they could not see either the head of the Virgin or of the child. The men approached, and found that both the heads had been cut off; they looked about for them, and discovered them hidden behind a heap of stones close by; they picked up in the gutter the Virgin's robe, which was torn and appeared to have been trampled under foot. These persons who were devout catholics, felt alarmed; they respectfully took up the two heads and carried them to the magistrate. The news of the strange event quickly spread through the quarter. Monks and priests mingled with the crowd, and described the injury done to the image. Men, women, and children surrounded the mutilated figure—some weeping, others groaning, all cursing the sacrilege. A 'complaint' of the times has handed down to us the groans of the people:

Alas! how great the woe,
  And crime that cannot pardoned be! . .
To have hurt Our Lady so,
  Lady full of charity,
And to sinners ever kind!†

---

* 'Mediatrix hominum, ablatrix criminum, peccatorum venia.'

† *Chronique du Roi François I.* p. 67: for the 'complaintes,' see pp. 446–464. *Journal d'un Bourgeois de Paris*, p. 347.

Such were the sentiments of the good catholics who, with tearful eyes and troubled hearts, looked upon the mutilated image.

Who were the authors of this mutilation? It was never known. It has been said that the priests, alarmed at the progress of the Reformation and the disposition of the king, had perpetrated the act in order to use it as a weapon against the Lutherans. That is possible, for such things have been done. I am, however, more inclined to believe that some hot-headed member of the evangelical party, exasperated at hearing that attributed to the Virgin which belongs only to Christ, had broken the idol. Be that as it may, the fanatical party resolved to profit by the sacrilege, and they succeeded.

Francis I., the most susceptible and most irritable of princes, considered this act of violence as an outrage upon his dignity and authority. As soon as he reached Paris, he did everything in his power to discover the guilty party. For two whole days heralds paraded the streets, and stopping at the crossways summoned the people by sound of trumpet and proclaimed: 'If any one knows who has done this, let him declare it to the magistrates and the king; the provost of Paris will pay him a thousand gold crowns, and if the informer has committed any crime, the king will pardon him.' The crowd listened and then dispersed; but all was of no use. Nothing could be learnt about it. 'Very well, then,' said the king, 'I will order commissioners to go and make inquiry at every house.' The commissioners went and knocked at every door, examining one after another all the inhabitants of the quarter; but the result was still the same: 'No one knew anything about it.'

The priests were not satisfied with these proclamations. On Tuesday, the 2nd of June, and during the rest of the week, the clergy of Paris set themselves in motion, and constant processions from all the churches in the city marched to the scene of the outrage. A week after, on Tuesday the 9th of June, five hundred students, each carrying a lighted taper, with all the doctors, licentiates, and bachelors of the university, proceeded from the Sorbonne. In front of them marched the four mendicant orders.

Beautiful it was to see
Such a goodly company;
Monks grey, black, of every hue,
Walking for an hour or two.

The reaction was complete. Learning and the Gospel were forgotten; men thought only of honoring the holy Virgin. The king, the Dukes of Ferrara, Longueville, and Vendôme, and even the King of Navarre, desired to pay the greatest honor to Mary; and accordingly on Thursday the 11th of June, being Corpus Christi Day, a long procession left the palace of the Tournelles.

In the front, with lighted tapers,
  There walked a goodly show;
Then followed next the children,
  Sweetly singing, in a row.

A crowd of priests came chanting,
  And next marched him who bore*
The body of our Jesus . . .

The canopy was carried
  By the good King of Navarre,
And by Vendôme, and by Longueville,
  And the proud Duke of Ferrare.

Then last of all there followed
  The king with head all bare;
The taper in his hand was wrapped
  In velvet rich and rare.

The different guilds, supreme courts, bishops, ambassadors, high officers of the crown, and princes of the blood, were all present. They walked to the sound of hautboys, clarions, and trumpets, playing with great state. When the procession arrived at the ill-omened spot, the king devoutly went up to it, and fell on his knees and prayed. On rising, he received from the hands of his grand almoner a small silver-gilt statue of the Virgin, which he piously set up in the room of the former one, and placed his taper before the image as a testimony of his faith. All the members of the procession did the same, as they marched past to the sound

* The Bishop of Lisieux.

of the trumpets. The people manifested their joy by acclamations:

Long live the king of fleur-de-lys
And all his noble family!

Ere long the mutilated image, removed to the church of St. Germain, began to work miracles. Four days afterwards, a child having been brought into the world still-born,

The mother writhed and wept,
And bitterly groaned she;
And loudly prayed that death
Would take her suddenly.

She tossed and tumbled so,
That all the gossips there
Shed floods of bitter tears
And wildly tore their hair.

Then one who counselled wisely,
Said: 'Take the child that's dead,
And bear him to the Queen of Heaven!' . . .
Which they devoutly did.

The infant changed color, adds the chronicle; it was baptised, and, after it had returned its soul to God, was buried. The miracle, it is clear, did not last long.

Notwithstanding all these tapers, miracles, and trumpet-sounds, the king was still excited. Neither he nor the fanatics were satisfied. The flush which some fancied they saw on the cheeks of the poor little still-born child, was not sufficient; they wanted a deeper red—red blood. Duprat, the Sorbonne, and the parliament said that their master had at last come to his senses, and that they must take advantage of the change. Francis, who held the reins firmly, had hitherto restrained the coursers bound to his chariot. But now, irritated and inflamed, he leant forward, slackened the bit, and even urged them on with his voice. These fiery wild horses were about to trample under foot all who came in their way, and the wheels of his chariot, crushing the unhappy victims, would sprinkle their blood even upon the garments of the prince.

The persecution began.

CHAPTER XII.

PRISONERS AND MARTYRS AT PARIS AND IN THE PROVINCES.

(1528.)

There lived in Paris one of those poor christians of Meaux known as *christaudins*, or disciples of Christ. This man, full of admiration for the Son of God and of horror for images, had been driven from his native city by persecution, and had become a waterman on the Seine. One day a stranger entered his boat, and as the Virgin was everywhere the subject of conversation, since the affair of the Rue des Rosiers, the passenger began to extol the power of the 'mother of God,' and pulling out a picture of Mary, offered it to his conductor. The boatman, who was rowing vigorously, stopped; he could not contain himself, and, taking the picture, said sharply: 'The Virgin Mary has no more power than this bit of paper,' which he tore in pieces and threw into the river. The exasperated catholic did not say a word; but as soon as he landed, he ran off to denounce the heretic. This time at least they knew the author of the sacrilege. Who could tell but it was he who committed the outrage in the Rue des Rosiers? The poor *christaudin* was burnt on the Grève at Paris.*

All the evangelical christians of Meaux had not, like him, quitted La Brie. In the fields around that city might often be seen a pious man named Denis, a native of Rieux. He had heard the divine summons one day, and filled with desire to know God, he had come to Jesus. Deeply impressed with the pangs which the Saviour had endured in order to save sinners, he had from that hour turned his eyes unceas-

* *Journal d'un Bourgeois de Paris*, pp. 321, 375.

ingly upon the Crucified One. Denis was filled with astonishment when he saw christians putting their trust in ceremonies, instead of placing it wholly in Christ. When, in the course of his many journeys, he passed near a church at the time they were saying mass, it seemed to him that he was witnessing a theatrical representation* and not a religious act. His tortured soul uttered a cry of anguish. 'To desire to be reconciled with God by means of a mass,' he said one day, 'is to deny my Saviour's passion.'† The parliament gave orders to confine Denis in the prison at Meaux.

As Briçonnet was still at the head of the diocese, the judges requested him to do all in his power to bring back Denis to the fold. One day the doors of the prison opened, and the bishop, at the summit of honor but a backslider from the faith, stood in the presence of the christian under the cross, but still faithful. Embarrassed at the part he had to play, Briçonnet hung his head, hesitated, and blushed; this visit was a punishment imposed upon his cowardice. 'If you retract,' he said to Denis at last, 'we will set you at liberty, and you shall receive a yearly pension.' But Denis had marvellously engraven in his heart, says the chronicler, that sentence delivered by Jesus Christ: 'Whosoever shall deny me before men, him will I also deny before my Father which is in heaven.' Turning therefore an indignant look upon Briçonnet, he exclaimed: 'Would you be so base as to urge me to deny my God?' The unhappy prelate, terrified at this address, fancied he heard his own condemnation, and without saying a word fled hastily from the dungeon. Denis was condemned to be burnt alive.

On the 3rd of July, the town sergeants came to the prison; they took Denis from his cell and bound him to the hurdle they had brought with them. Then, as if to add insult to torture, they pinioned his arms and placed a wooden cross in his hands. Drawing up on each side of him, they said: 'See now how he worships the wood of the cross!' and dragged the poor sufferer on his hurdle through the streets. Some of the spectators, when they saw him holding the

* 'Histrionica representatio.'

† Crespin, *Martyrologue*, p. 102.

piece of wood, exclaimed: 'Truly, he is converted!' but the humble believer replied: 'O my friends! . . . be converted to the true cross!' The procession advanced slowly on account of the crowd, and as they were passing near a pond from which the water, swollen by the rains, was rushing rapidly, Denis gave a struggle, the cross fell, and 'went sailing down the stream.' When the bigots (as the chronicler terms them) saw the cross dancing and floating upon the water, they rushed forward to pull it out, but could not reach it. They came back and avenged themselves 'by insulting the poor sufferer lying on the hurdle.' The stake was reached at last. 'Gently,' said the priests, 'kindle only a small fire, a very small fire, in order that it may last the longer.' They bound Denis to a balanced pole and placed him on the fire, and when the heat had almost killed him, they hoisted him into the air. As soon as he had recovered his senses, they let him down again. Three times was he thus lifted up and lowered, the flames each time beginning their work anew. 'Yet all the time,' says the chronicler, 'he called upon the name of God.'* At last he died.

Not at Paris only did the Roman party show itself without mercy. The wishes of Duprat, of the Sorbonne, and of the parliament, were carried out in the provinces; and wherever truth raised her head, persecution appeared. In the principal church of the small town of Annonay, there hung from the arched roof a precious shrine, which the devout used to contemplate every day with pious looks. 'It contains *the holy virtues*,' said the priests. 'The shrine is full of mysterious relics which no one is allowed to see.' On Ascension Day, however, the *holy virtues* were borne in great ceremony through the city. Men, women, and children were eager to walk in the procession, with their heads and feet bare, and in their shirts. Some of them approached the shrine, and kissed it, passing backwards and forwards beneath it, almost as the Hindoos do when the idol of Juggernaut is dragged through the midst of its worshippers. At the moment when the *holy virtues* passed through the

* Crespin, *Martyrologue*, p. 102.

castle, the gates turned of themselves on their hinges, and all the prisoners were set at liberty, with the exception of the Lutherans.

These silly superstitions were about to be disturbed. A battle began around this mysterious shrine, and as soon as one combatant fell, another sprang up in his place.

The first was a grey friar, a doctor of divinity, whom Crespin calls Stephen Machopolis: the latter appears to be one of those names which the reformers sometimes assumed. Stephen, attracted by the rumors of the Reformation, had gone to Saxony and heard Luther.* Having profited by his teaching, the grey friar determined to go back to France, and Luther recommended him to the counts of Mansfeld, who supplied him with the means of returning to his native country.†

Stephen had scarcely arrived at Annonay before he began to proclaim warmly the virtues of the Saviour and of the Holy Ghost, and to inveigh against the *holy virtues* hanging in the church. The priests tried to seize him, but he escaped. In the meanwhile he had talked much about the Gospel with one of his friends, a cordelier like himself, Stephen Rénier by name. The latter undertook, with still more courage than his predecessor, to convert all these ignorant people from their faith in 'dead men's bones' to the living and true God. The priests surprised the poor man, cast him into prison, and conveyed him to Vienne in Dauphiny, where the archbishop resided. Rénier preferred being burnt alive to making any concession.‡

A pious and learned schoolmaster, named Jonas, had already taken his place in Annonay, and spoke still more boldly than the two Franciscans. He was sent to prison in his turn, and made before the magistrates 'a good and complete' profession of faith. As the priests and the archbishop now had Jonas locked up, they hoped to be quiet at last.

But very different was the result: the two friars and the schoolmaster having disappeared, all those who had received

* Crespin, *Martyrologue*, p. 102.

† Lutherus ad Agricolam, May, 1527. Lutheri *Epp.* iii. p. 173.

‡ Crespin, *Actes des Martyrs*, p. 102, verso.

the Word of life rose up and proclaimed it. The Archbishop of Vienne could contain himself no longer; it seemed to him as if evangelicals sprang ready-armed from the soil, like the followers of Cadmus in days of yore.—'They are headstrong and furious,' said the good folks of Vienne.—'Bring them all before me,' cried the archbishop. Twenty-five evangelical christians were taken from Annonay to the archiepiscopal city, and many of them, being left indefinitely in prison, died of weakness and bad treatment.

The death of a few obscure men did not satisfy the ultramontanes: they desired a more illustrious victim, the most learned among the nobles. Wherever Berquin or other evangelicals turned their steps, they encountered fierce glances and heard cries of indignation. 'What tyrannical madness! what plutonic rage!' called out the mob as they passed. 'Rascally youths! imps of Satan! brands of hell! *vilenaille* brimful of Leviathans! venomous serpents! servants of Lucifer!'* This was the usual vocabulary.

Berquin, as he heard this torrent of insult, answered not a word: he thought it his duty to let the storm blow over, and kept himself tranquil and solitary before God. Sometimes, however, his zeal caught fire; there were sudden movements in his heart, as of a wind tossing up the waves with their foamy heads; but he struggled against these 'gusts' of the flesh; he ordered his soul to be still, and ere long nothing was left but some little 'fluttering.'

While Berquin was silent before the tempest, Beda and his party did all in their power to bring down the bolt upon that haughty head which refused to bend before them. 'See!' they said, as they described the mutilation of Our Lady, 'see to what our toleration of heresy leads! . . . Unless we root it up entirely, it will soon multiply and cover the whole country.'

The doctors of the Sorbonne and other priests went out of their houses in crowds; they spread right and left, buzzing in the streets, buzzing in the houses, buzzing in the palaces. 'These hornets,' says a chronicler, 'make their tedious

* Complaintes et poésies diverses du temps. *Appendice de la Chronique de François I.* pp. 446–464.

noise heard by all they meet, and urge them on with repeated stings.' 'Away with Berquin!' was their cry.

His friends grew alarmed. 'Make your escape!' wrote Erasmus to him. 'Make your escape!' repeated the friends of learning and of the Gospel around him.* But Berquin thought that by keeping quiet he did all that he ought to do. Flight he would have considered a disgrace, a crime. 'With God's help,' he said, 'I shall conquer the monks, the university, and the parliament itself.'†

Such confidence exasperated the Sorbonne. Beda and his followers stirred university and parliament, city, court, and Church, heaven and earth. . . Francis I. was puzzled, staggered, and annoyed. At last, being beset on every side, and hearing it continually repeated that Berquin's doctrines were the cause of the outrage in the Rue des Rosiers, the king yielded, believing, however, that he yielded but little: he consented only that an inquiry should be opened against Berquin. The wild beast leapt with joy. His prey was not yet given to him; but he already foresaw the hour when he would quench his thirst in blood.

A strange blindness is that of popery! The lessons of history are lost upon it. So long as events are in progress, men mistake both their causes and consequences. The smoke that covers the battle-field, during the struggle, does not permit us to distinguish and appreciate the movements of the different armies. But once the battle ended, the events accomplished, intelligent minds discover the principles of the movements and order of battle. Now, if there is any truth which history proclaims, it is that Christianity was established in the world by pouring out the blood of its martyrs. One of the greatest fathers of the West has enunciated this mysterious law.‡ But the Rome of the popes—and in this respect she paid her tribute to human weakness—overlooked this great law. She took no heed of the facts that ought to have enlightened her. She did not understand that the blood of these friends of the Gospel, which she

* 'Semper illi canebant eandem cautionem.'—Erasmi *Epp.* p. 1522.

† 'Ille sibi promittebat certam et speciosam victoriam.'—Ibid.

‡ 'The blood of christians is the seed of the Church.'—Tertullian.

was so eager to spill, would be for modern times, as it had been for ancient times, a seed of transformation. Imprudently resuming the part played by the Rome of the emperors, she put to death, one after another, those who professed the everlasting Truth. But at the very moment when the enemies of the Reform imagined they had crushed it by getting rid of Berquin; at the moment when the irritation of the king allowed the servants of Christ to be dragged on hurdles, and when he authorised torture, imprisonment, and the stake; at the moment when all seemed destined to remain mute and trembling—the true Reformer of France issued unnoticed from a college of priests, and was about to begin, in an important city of the kingdom, that work which we have undertaken to narrate—a work which for three centuries has not ceased, and never will cease, to grow.

We shall attempt to describe the small beginnings of this great work in the next volume.

www.ingramcontent.com/pod-product-compliance
Lightning Source LLC
LaVergne TN
LVHW020932110826
845150LV00004B/840

* 9 7 8 1 4 2 5 5 5 2 9 4 7 *